The Originary Hypothesis

Critical Studies in the Humanities
Victor E. Taylor, Series Editor

This open-ended series provides a unique publishing venue by combining single volumes issuing from landmark scholarship with pedagogy-related interdisciplinary collections of readings. This principle of cross-publishing, placing scholarship and pedagogy side by side within a single series, creates a wider horizon for specialized research and more general intellectual discovery. In the broad field of the humanities, the Critical Studies in the Humanities Series is committed to preserving key monographs, encouraging new perspectives, and developing important connections to pedagogical issues.

Proposals for submission should be directed to the Series Editor,
Victor E. Taylor, Department of English and Humanities
York College of Pennsylvania, York, PA 17405-7199.

The Originary Hypothesis
A Minimal Proposal for Humanistic Inquiry

Adam Katz, Editor

A volume in the series
Critical Studies in the Humanities

General Editor, Victor E. Taylor

The Davies Group, Publishers
Aurora, Colorado USA

Address all requests to:
> The Davies Group, Publishers
> PO Box 440140
> Aurora, CO 80044-0140
> USA

Library of Congress Cataloging-in-Publication Data

The originary hypothesis : a minimal proposal for humanistic inquiry / Adam Katz,
editor.
   p. cm. -- (Critical studies in the humanities)
   Includes bibliographical references.
   ISBN-13: 978-1-888570-36-6 (alk. paper)
   ISBN-10: 1-888570-36-9 (alk. paper)
   1. Anthropology--Philosophy. 2. Anthropology--Methodology. 3. Aesthetics.
   4. Anthropological ethics. I. Katz, Adam.
   GN33.O75 2007
   301.01--dc22
                              2007011775

Printed in the United States of America
0123456789

Contents

The Contributors

Andrew Bartlett teaches analytical writing and literature in the English Department at Kwantlen University College in Surrey, British Columbia. He has published critical articles on Joseph Conrad, Cormac McCarthy, and nuclear war movies, along with book reviews on Canadian fiction. He participates in the annual meetings of the Colloquium on Violence and Religion and a Vancouver reading club, Sparagmos, devoted to the study of Generative Anthropology.

Thomas Bertonneau is the author of over fifty articles on literature, religion, anthropology, and other topics. He serves on the editorial board of *Anthropoetics*, of which he was one of the originators, of *Praesidium*, and of Modern Age, to all of which he also regularly contributes. His book, *The Gospel According to Sci-Fi*, cowritten with Kim Paffenroth of Iona College, appears early next year from Brazos Press. He has articles forthcoming on Augustine and Ibsen, Petronius and Apuleius, V. S. Naipaul, and Karen Blixen. He was the first executive director of the Association of Literary Scholars and Critics. He is a longtime affiliate of the Russell Kirk Center for Cultural Renewal and of the Intercollegiate Studies Institute.

Raoul Eshelman, an American Slavist who has lived and worked in Germany since 1979, has a Ph.D. in Slavic Literature from Konstanz University and his *Habilitation* in the same field from the University of Hamburg. At present he is Slavic Department Coordinator for the Honors M.A. Program in East European Studies at the Ludwig Maximilian University in Munich. He has published numerous articles on GA in English as well as German. His book *Performatism, or the End of Postmodernism*, is forthcoming as a publication of the Davies Group.

Chris Fleming is Lecturer in Philosophy in the School of Humanities and Languages at the University of Western Sydney, Australia. Among his publications is the book *Rene Girard: Violence and Mimesis* (Cambridge: Polity, 2004).

Eric Gans attended Columbia College and the Johns Hopkins University, where he received his doctorate in Romance Languages. He has taught French literature, critical theory, and film at UCLA since 1969, and written a number of books and articles on aesthetic theory as well as on Flaubert, Musset, Racine, and other French writers. Beginning with *The Origin of Language* (1981), Gans developed the concept of generative anthropology and has written five other books on the subject, including *Originary Thinking* (1993), *Signs of Paradox*

(1997), and the forthcoming *The Scenic Imagination: Originary Thinking from Hobbes to the Present Day*.

Peter Goldman is a Professor of English at Westminster College in Salt Lake City, Utah, where he teaches classes on Shakespeare and English Renaissance literature. His publications include articles on Shakespeare, John Bunyan, popular culture, literary theory, and Generative Anthropology. In 1997, he attended Eric Gans' seminar on Generative Anthropology at UCLA, and he serves on the editorial board of *Anthropoetics*. Currently, he is working on a book entitled *Shakespeare and the Problem of Iconoclasm*.

Adam Katz teaches writing at Quinnipiac University, is on the Editorial Board of *Anthropoetics* and writes on the originary hypothesis of Eric Gans, the Holocaust, composition and the innovative fiction of Ronald Sukenick.

Christopher Morrissey, a certified member of the Institute for Advanced Physics, teaches Ancient Greek, Latin, and Classical Mythology at Simon Fraser University in Burnaby. He also teaches Medieval Philosophy, Medieval Ecclesiastical Latin, and a course in the Metaphysics of St. Thomas Aquinas at Redeemer Pacific College in Langley.

John O'Carroll is a lecturer at Charles Sturt University in the School of Social Sciences and Liberal Studies. Previouslyl, he taught at the University of Western Sydney, and at the University of the South Pacific in Fiji. He has written on issues of multiculturalism, culture study, and generative anthropology. With Bob Hodge, he is author of *Borderwork in Multicultural Australia* (Allen and Unwin 2006), and with Chris Fleming a number of articles in *Anthropoetics*.

Richard van Oort (Ph.D. University of California, Irvine) has been on the editorial board of *Anthropoetics* since the journal was founded in 1995. He currently teaches in the English Department at the University of British Columbia in Vancouver, where he is a Postdoctoral Fellow with the Canada Research Chair in Literature / Christianity and Culture held by Professor Mark Vessey. He has published widely on topics in generative anthropology, literary theory, and Shakespeare, and has recently finished a manuscript on the anthropological foundations of humanistic research. His next project is called *Shakespearean Anthropology*.

Matthew Schneider, a founding member of the GA seminar, holds a PhD in English from UCLA. He is professor of English at Chapman University in Orange, California, where he has taught since 1991. The author of *Original*

Ambivalence: Violence and Autobiography in Thomas De Quincey (Peter Lang, 1995) and the forthcoming *A Long and Winding Road: From Blake to the Beatles* (Palgrave Macmillan, 2008), Schneider has also published essays on Jane Austen, John Keats, Charles Dickens, William Blake, critical theory, and Biblical exegesis.

Introduction
The Consequences of the Hypothesis

Adam Katz

...no thinker is close enough to the truth to be justified in theorizing away all difference but his own." Eric Gans, "GA and Mimetic Theory I: Violence" (*Chronicle of Love & Resentment* 329)

While the essays in this book, and those collected in *Anthropoetics* over the last ten years indicate the power of Eric Gans' originary hypothesis, we have to admit that it has barely made a ripple across the fields of humanistic inquiry in the quarter century since Gans first substantially revised Rene Girard's originary scene of scapegoating into one in which the convergence of desire on the central object in the proto-human group as a consequence of mimetic rivalry become crisis which overrides animal hierarchies leading to the self-destruction of the group is arrested by the emission of the aborted gesture of appropriation that is the originary sign and constitutes the sacred, the human, and establishes representation as the distinctively human mode of deferring violence.

Why? Following the minimalist standards of originary thought itself, I will suggest that the conditions making the discovery of the hypothesis possible are also those significantly reducing the possibility of its broader dissemination and acceptance. If we look at postmodern society, we see the conquest of the market, for generative anthropology the most advanced mode of reciprocity yet devised, over all areas of social life and routing presumed alternatives. We also see the prevalence of resistance to an explicit endorsement of this result of the conflicts over modernity on the part of most social elites, resistance I will designate the "white guilt/victimary axis." Why?

The victory of the market represents the greatest expansion of not only reciprocity, but of overtly mimetic desire itself: before the market became the universal mode of exchange mimetic desire and rivalry could be contained within collectivities whose sacred center could explicitly prohibit the transgression of certain limits of envious desire and resentment; and the rivalries between those collectivities, however brutal they might be, were themselves contained by certain technological limits on the one hand, but also, paradoxically, by an undeveloped sense of reciprocity across collectivities, which made imposed rule by militarily and culturally superior powers unexceptional in moral terms. Now, not only has individual desire been liberated but all those other modes of rivalry (national, religious, etc.) are still in play, while Gans' more anthropological insight that humanity is defined by the fact that it is the only species that poses the greatest threat to its own survival is, on another level, the common sense of that species, now threatened not only by nuclear and other "weapons of mass destruction" but, in the white guilt imaginary, by advanced industry with its CO_2 emissions, population growth, i.e., modern life itself.[1]

No one could have discovered the originary hypothesis, I would suggest, much before Gans did, because those receptive to the sacrality of the origin already had originary narratives they considered truthful and ethically satisfying. In fact, to search outside the parameters of those narratives for another, human centered, account, would be more subversive than even the most bald-faced atheist challenge to the sacred center. Meanwhile, those ready to question the center, small minorities, of course, until very recently, have tended to define the enlightenment they represented in opposition to any sacred center: for the Enlightenment thinker of any age, the central danger, the most threatening source of violence, is precisely that instigated over the desire to protect the sacred center from challenge, or from competing versions of the sacred, and the rivalries provoked by such attempts. Meanwhile, insofar as an enlightenment movement is willing to recognize the core truth of originary narratives and not just, say, their social usefulness in restraining the "many," it thereby anyway renders itself irrelevant to any but the "few," since it would confirm the albeit cruder truth contained in the prevailing myths.

If the condition of postmodern society is one of expanded, virtually unlimited mimetic activity, where do we stand with regard to the sacred center, the transcendent sign? We might first look a little more carefully at what, precisely, makes market society, or what Hayek called "catallaxy," such an advanced form of reciprocity.[2] First, the formal symmetry of the partners in the exchange, whatever actual asymmetries might constitute the conditions of the exchange. Longstanding critiques of the "hypocrisy" of such voluntary interactions in fact make the point themselves, involuntarily: the more exchange, the more such islands of formal symmetry; the more formal symmetry, the more possibilities exist for rendering the formal substantive. The discipline of the market entails, precisely, this recognition—ultimately derivative of Judaic monotheism—that universal rules must be established and adhered to before reality matches the rules, in large part because reality never quite will. Second, adherence to the rules of the game of the market imposes a willingness to accept results at odds with the very desires that led one into the game in the first place, in the name of the possibility, but never the certainty, that those desires might be recognized and satisfied at some point further down the road, or that other, unanticipated desires, will come along, whose satisfaction will be just as satisfying. Thus, only the power of the market to set in motion complex, spontaneous orderings can enable us to transcend, once and for all, the "big man" form of social hierarchy that has characterized virtually all of human history following the development of larger groups than the original, primitive ones.

But the above description also accounts for the necessity with which the market simultaneously generates far more resentment than any previous system without any guarantee that the resources to defer such resentment will be available. More relevant to the question I am raising here is a specific kind of resentment, endemic to modern market society since its earliest stages, commonly known as the "Left." An originary analysis of the left will lead us to focus on two features. First, the Left, born in Enlightenment, is predicated upon the rejection of the sacred center, under the assumption that the desires and resentments generated by that center are the primary sources of violence. A new mode of sacrality, or a new sacred object, is surreptitiously substituted for the central one: the martyred scientist, the exemplary scapegoat of traditional sacrality. This mode of sacrality would remain confined to a small group of intellectuals and artists, as was always the case in the ancient world, except for a new phenomenon: the existence of new masses of people constituted by, marginalized within, but representable as "outside" the market system, who can then be persuaded to resent the system as such. The Left, then, is this specific combination, as separate from the myriad resentments, more or less justified, incessantly generated by the market system; resentments that are, in fact, integral parts of it, the source of new desires. Of course, a "Right" emerges which itself is not so much interested in sustaining and enlarging the sacred center, but in defending precisely those elements of the center seen to be under attack by the Left. In the process the Right, in its reactiveness, appropriates the total resentment toward the market system since the market can plausibly be represented as the "cause" of the Left as well as the subversion of traditional community. Both political camps, then, ultimately converge on the market as their target of resentment.

The transcendence of this configuration is a precondition of the broader reception of the originary hypothesis this book hopes to promote; and originary thought in turn has much to contribute to this process. But the more immediate antagonist of generative anthropology is White Guilt, the primary form taken by the Left today. With the end of socialism as a plausible alternative, the Left is forced into an essentially parasitic relation with the sacred center, or cultural mainstream. The event of 9/11, and subsequent U.S. interventions globally, have brought the tension between White Guilt and the sacred center of the market order out into the open, making it very likely that some sort of new "settlement" or dispensation is in the works. Indeed, a great deal of Gans' intellectual energy has, since 9/11, been concerned with this new metastasization of victimary discourse.[3]

Guilt, like all human phenomena, has, for originary thinking, its origin on the originary scene: in the sparagmos or consumption of the sacred object, the new human community is eating the sacred object, which has just saved them from (self)destruction. Guilt, in that case, is first of all directed toward the sacred center, rather than toward others wronged on the periphery. The cultural evolutionary process by which relations between center and periphery are acted out between members on the periphery can never erase that originary guilt: indeed, such originary guilt is all that can provide some "measure" to an intuition that would otherwise be incommensurable with all actual acts. White Guilt is a re-articulation of this originary guilt in response to a very specific set of intuitions or revelations regarding the event we know as "Auschwitz."[4]

We must first of all, of course, associate "Auschwitz" with Nazism in particular, and even more particularly, Nazism's accumulation of Western resentment toward Judaism's "firstness" in revealing monotheistic moral precepts to the world.[5] The actual reception of Auschwitz, though, as an event, has been framed by, on one side, World War I; on the other side by "Hiroshima,"; and, in terms of information regarding the genocide of the Jews itself, the war crimes trials and survivor testimony largely shaped by the testimony given in those trials, motivated by the singular determination to, first, have the events known, and, second, to have them properly remembered and commemorated, to achieve some gesture toward justice. The effect of this series of framings is as follows: Auschwitz is disconnected from the specificity of its victims and aligned with the destructive tendencies of modern nationalism and imperialism (which is to say, it happened to have been the Germans who committed the actual crime, but that's a contingent fact); Auschwitz is viewed as mere preview of what those same tendencies, unleashed now with unimaginably more destructive weaponry, would mean today; and, finally, the meticulous testimony, showing individuals trapped by all of the institutions and norms of an advanced modern society and revealing the vulnerabilities inherent in the modes of solidarity prevalent in such society, had the effect of implicating all "normal" institutions in the genocide (the "banality of evil").

All of these elements come into place with the events of the 60s (it is often remarked upon how astonishingly small the Holocaust loomed in the culture of the 50s), in particular Vietnam, in which the United States, the liberator of peoples from the Nazis, became the new Nazis—and, furthermore, engaged in an intrinsically amoral standoff with the other superpower. The other event registering and rearticulating Auschwitz during the same period, the Six Day War in the Middle East, visible as yet another demonstration of the vulnerability and isolation of the Jewish people, was, for easily grasped reasons, never a serious competitor for the representation that emerged through the self-assertion of the entire international Left and Western elites more generally. My central claim here, though, is simply that this prevailing articulation should be understood as a good faith gesture aimed at deferring violence, and hence as an authentic legatee of the originary scene. And, it might be said, there need not be any antagonism between this articulation, focused on mimetic tendencies within civil society ("normalization") and the more Judeocentric one.

White guilt "proper," though, sets in, when the Nazi-Jew, i.e., perpetrator-victim, model becomes the primary way of making sense of all asymmetries, regardless of their origins or possible resolutions. This mimetic contagion leads us to a situation in which one defending traditional marriage and questioning the consequences of same sex marriage, is likely to be attacked in terms no different from those applicable to neo-Nazis and Klansmen. The logical conclusion of white guilt, the "guilt of the unmarked toward the marked," is to stigmatize all action taken by the more powerful, all imperatives that come from the center, all attitudes and values making a claim to be "normal," as preliminary moves toward an infinitely more destructive recrudescence of Nazism. Ultimately, mimesis itself must be stigmatized, along with risk and initiative and all unregulated desires and we end up with a new mode of sacrality: the victimized Other; but not just any victimized Other—it must be the victimized Other most effectively representable as the antipodes of everything Western, powerful and normal; a victimized Other that embraces its irreconcilability with everything "Western," and offers itself as a sacrifice confirming the ultimate, irremediable guilt of the West: and we have the cult of Palestine, providing a very good basis for the emerging alliance of the Western Left with Islamic totalitarianism.

GA cannot really destroy or seriously undermine this configuration (nor could any other mode of thought or politics)—we must simply hope that is burns itself out. But GA can certainly point to ways in which this contagion can be quarantined, and in the process the originary sources of our civilization retrieved and freshly appreciated, precisely in its universalistic dimensions, abandoned by contemporary liberals and Leftists. Drawing upon the structure for understanding the originary scene I propose in my contribution to this volume, and drawing upon Charles Sanders Peirce's tripartite phenomenology, we could hypothesize that any "intervention," i.e., any entrance into a crisis requiring a new mode of deferral requires a "first," a "second" and a "third." The first is the setting forth of the originary gesture itself as an act of aborted appropriation: the gesture, through a modification of the act of appropriation, an imitation that transcends mimesis by deflecting mimesis from its convergence upon the center, opens a new space at the center. The second is the imitation of this gesture, at first by one, a couple, a few; and the emergence of a distinction between the tendency embedded in the gesture and an opposing one embodied in the ongoing grasping for the object. The third is the rapid, accelerating spread of the gesture and the constitution of the scene itself in a new concatenation of imitative acts.

In terms of social theory, we might see the first as the founding gesture; the second as the establishment of islands of symmetry where previously there was sheer "homogeneity": that is, mimetic contagion reduces action to the lowest common denominator while symmetry establishes some minimal rules of the game, even if the game is confrontation—each actor shapes his responses in accord with the other's previous and projected future acts. The third is the construction of a new mode of reciprocity: unlike symmetry, which has a rather low "ceiling," reciprocity is infinitely expandable: from a peace treaty to trade relations, to educational exchanges, to alliance during war, to cooperation in maintaining international institutions and structures, etc. If 9/11, then, revealed the parasitical relation of the victimary upon white guilt, and the entire victimary/white guilt axis on the presumption of an unbridgeable asymmetry between powerful (perpetrator) and powerless (victim) which presumption, in turn, is determined to represent any interference with the mimetic contagion liberated by this parasitism as implicitly genocidal violence, then—the first step must be the establishment of new modes of symmetry, even if (and this is what white guilt most fears) we must do so without first remedying existing actual asymmetries.

At the same time, given the anthropological truth revealed in Holocaust theology, we cannot regress behind that revelation. Indeed, "Auschwitz," as an effect of our response to the double bind victim testimony places us in, is necessarily an extension and modification of our sacred center, following up on Christianity's universalization of the Judaic God as "the declarative sentence,"[6] and democracy and the marketplace's continued sacralization of the individual. But after 9/11's revelation of the bankruptcy of white guilt/victimary discourse, its counsel of cultural suicide, a more minimal analysis of Auschwitz as an attack on that evolving sacrality is required. Rather than a conversion of all asymmetries into perpetrator/victim dichotomies, what "Auschwitz" would teach us is the necessity of sustaining our guilt toward the sacred center and the articulation of this guilt as a series of differentiations aimed at deferring any claim to control what can't be controlled—the very process of cultural evolution itself.

It is precisely those complex differentiations, distinguishing civilian from military, God and humanity, national from international, economic from political, war from peace, even legislative, judicial and executive, and more, all representing the effort at creating symmetries out homogeneities and reciprocities out of symmetries, must be sustained and re-inscribed, insofar as Islamic totalitarianism shares with its Communist and Nazi predecessors the interest in abolishing them in the name of a foregone conclusion on the millennial verdict of history. It is precisely within these distinctions, in establishing and, when necessary, provisionally transgressing these boundaries, that the inexhaustibility of the individual in his and her freedom and uniqueness, is manifested. This leaves us with the paradox, which the victimary reader will quickly point out, that GA, representing the democratic sacred center, in denying all claims to end history, places itself at the end of history, foreordaining the unforeordainability of history. But what makes this paradox bearable, and even productive, is its extreme minimality, its bare abstractness—the more we think of the possibility of market constitutionalism, international alliances between the freest states, and the construction of new articulations of power and accountability, as the vanguard of historical development, and the more can use these possibilities as markers distinguishing between present tendencies, the less capable we will be of actually filling in the details beyond the most immediate defense and elaboration of such habits and institutions.

So, I would first of all propose situating both the discovery and the neglect of the originary hypothesis in the space I have just outlined: a post-Enlightenment world, in which thought acquires a certain distance from sacred centrality bound up in traditional, ritualized forms while seeking to complement and minimalize the sacred; a post-Auschwitz world, in which we are inescapably cognizant of the violent capacities of both the modern world liberated from traditional restraints, especially as coupled with resentment toward the market system; and, an increasingly victimary ethical setting, revealing both the compulsion to erect new modes of sacrality and the need to defend the existing center from nihilistic assault. The major theoretical event of twentieth-century thought, the "linguistic turn," registers and helps clarify these developments, having roots in both the victimary and the effort at retrieving the ostensive.

Perhaps the best way of engaging the entanglements of GA with the linguistic turn is, first, to take a look at a recent *Chronicle of Love and Resentment* on the matter[7]; and, then, to examine Gans' professed reliance upon Derrida for his founding category of "deferral." For Gans, post-structuralism's argument that structuralism was implicated in the metaphysical tradition it sought to replace was correct:

This becomes all the clearer if we understand metaphysics as the mode of thought that takes the declarative sentence or *proposition* as the fundamental form of language. The Saussurean reduction of meaning to pure difference is the *reductio ad absurdum* of Platonic idealism, not its transcendence. Plato's Ideas — the Good, the Beautiful, the True, the Holy — are reified predicates, components of propositions. By bracketing these words' extralinguistic referents, structuralism only makes explicit the failure of metaphysics to situate language — more specifically, the *origin* of language — in human history. Structuralism is wedded to the metaphysics of the declarative sentence, the linguistic form that makes language a "map" of reality.

At the same time, though,

> Post-structuralism rejects this atemporal formalism, but has no thought of putting a human temporality in its place. Because deconstruction remains wholly tributary to the philosophical-metaphysical tradition, its practitioner cannot see that the deconstruction of metaphysics is not simply a moment in a resentful oscillation with the inevitable but untenable proposition, but that it points to a core of language more fundamental than the declarative sentence.

As Gans goes on to note, "[e]very term in Derrida's ever-changing terminology of deconstruction, from *différance* to *pharmakon* and beyond, can be associated with a moment of the originary event. Before *différance* can refer to the deferral inherent in actualizing the paradigm from which an individual element of language is taken, it describes the originary deferral that presides over the birth of the sign: *the deferral of violence through representation*." Even more important for our argument, though, is Gans' situating of the transition from structuralism to post-structuralism in terms of the emergence of victimary discourse:

> As the first postmodern philosophical mode, structuralism undermines the authority of centralized consciousness. Although it would be stretching a point to call structuralism a *victimary* mode of thought, the effect of its devaluation of human will is to deny the applicability of the traditional scenic center-periphery model to human culture. In its refutation of structuralism's confident assertion that formalism can supplant metaphysics, the post-structuralist critique insists that a center is always implicit in the centerless structural grid. It is this implicit, hidden center that is the object of deconstruction. In post-structuralism,

the devaluation of the center gives way to the denunciation of the center, and to victimary thinking proper.

Gans is being very scrupulous here in insisting that structuralism is not quite victimary, and yet the context of the emergence of structuralist anthropology certainly allows us to stretch the point: in terms of cultural politics, the aim of structuralist anthropology, as Gans says, "even go[ing] beyond the Whorfian notion that specific languages inflect perception of the world, that, for example, the members of different cultures who use different color-words may be said to see colors according to these words," is to revalue and/or eliminate the civilized/primitive distinction presupposed by much of the social sciences from the late nineteenth century on. Derrida's deconstruction of Levi-Strauss then takes the next step of demonizing the center, while rendering explicit what Gans calls the "constituent hypocrisy" of Romanticism[8] that attacking the center is the surest way of participating in it. The effect, in ethical terms, is to open this marginal space to those who can literally identify themselves with the margin of the "West," but the gesture is plagued by an especially rapid version of the law of diminishing returns: the margins become increasingly crowded, the center a decreasingly attractive target, and the scene upon which this entire scene is played out increasingly "marginal" to any of the larger processes which might actually modify the center in some way.

For Gans, Derrida's deferral can be read back as contained within the originary scene: "because language operates only through *différance*, the differentiation of signs through the deferral of their individual meaning ... language is more faithfully exemplified by the overtly "deferred" form of writing than by spoken language's illusory immediacy" (*Signs of Paradox* 29–30). The distinction between the sign as "object, a product, a whole imitating another whole" (30), creating a distinction between an "action-object from his blocked action" and the renounced object, "is the real anthropological point of Derrida's distinction between speech and writing." Yet, the denunciation of self-presence as an "illusion" (insofar as, in mimetic terms, it abstracts the self from the "intersubjective triangle of mimesis" [31]), is unpersuasive insofar as it seems to depend upon the very metaphysical assumptions regarding "reality" that are being deconstructed:

> The signing self defers its self-presence through identification with the object as its giver of form; this deferral of self-identity breaks the paralysis caused by mimetic paradox. "Presence" comes into being filled with absence, difference, and differentiation; but it is presence nonetheless,

the only kind possible, whatever more perfect models the imagination can conceive by extrapolating from the positive moment of this para-doxical process. (32)

One could argue against Gans here that part of the effect of Derrida's dis-placement of speech by writing is precisely to challenge the kind of subject-object distinction Gans is establishing here, in which, in the "subjective" act of speech, "performance and the production of the language-object are one and the same," while "[e]ven when we see someone writing, we only want to know the result, not observe his performance" (30–31). But since the real point is that what Derrida is describing is the co-constitution of subject and object, sign and referent, in what is both originary act and sign, an originary act/sign that is only complete once it has circulated through the group, in which case not only is Gans' argument in favor of a kind of deferred but real self-presence ("the speaker as writer" [31]) strengthened, but we can see what is genuinely anti-originary in Derrida's account. For Derrida, the fear is that Plato has not sufficiently deferred reliance upon the sacred center (just as, as Gans points out in his discussion of "Plato and the Birth of Conceptual Thought," Plato had the same fear regard-ing the Sophists[9]) that, in fact, we can never sufficiently defer such reliance: it is the very establishment of a scene constituted by the return of a sign (however modified, however filled with "absence, difference, differentiation") to its sender that, for Derridean deconstruction, is the worst thing that can happen. Decon-struction is dedicated to deferring the originary event itself because victimary thought can recognize in the scene's unanimity nothing more than a violently imposed or undertaken consensus.

The originary hypothesis, this analysis suggests, depends upon the possibil-ity of seeing language as a system of differential signs; and, further, of seeing that system as deferring any "arrival" of the "center"; only then, finally, can the center be restored to its rightful place in generating the system. While the notion that language could only have been invented in one stroke, in an event, was not a new one, it was, paradoxically, the reduction of language to formal differences that makes it possible to see this leap into signification as a matter confined to the proto-human group/community rather than a relation between humans and their physical environment. This latter notion relies upon some Romantic no-tion of the "imagination" to make the leap, but the point, of course, is to account for the possibility of "imagination," for which we need the association of the sign with some kind of intimate danger. The paradox of this situation lies, first, in the fact that structuralist semiotics is the logical conclusion of the attempt to ban origins from the science of language in the first place, in its de-linking of language and culture from "progress," "civilization," "race" or other categories of Western modernity; and, second, that the deconstructive demonization of a yet inescapable centering should facilitate an affirmation of the center. It must also be here, then, that we find the problem of the present obscurity of the hypothesis: it was through victimary thought that the formal understanding of the sign could first be articulated with sustained, fearful and trembling, attention to the sign, just as, we might add, it was through the victimary that democracy, individualism, egalitarianism, the market and even the "dismantling of metaphysics" all entered and shaped the modern world. Meanwhile, the minimal yet decisive break with the victimary which enabled the formulation of the hypothesis reveals its utter radicality once we consider that its full generative potential relies upon a transcendence of the currently metastasizing victimary discourses.

Originary thinking imposes a certain closure: within variable parameters, there will always be some reciprocal relation between immanence (horizontal mimesis) and vertical transcendence; and we must grasp what source of terror postmodern thought would most likely find in even such an open-ended, minimal closure. Here, postmodern thought is more continuous with modern thought than discontinuous. Certainly, one of the most prominent features of modern thinking is the violent rejection of all origins. And by modern thinking I mean from Descartes and Hobbes forward—this tendency merely intensifies with modern*ist* and then postmodern thinking. The origins proposed by social contract theorists like Locke and Hobbes are already, self-consciously, pseudo-origins, aimed more at deflecting attention away from sacred origins than at discerning actual ones. The origins hypothesized by these modern thinkers don't involve events—they represent the way one would, already living in some kind of civil order, provide reasons for oneself and others who have already acquiesced in that order. To use Gans' understanding of metaphysics, modernity accepts only those origins that can be formulated in declarative terms. The assumption, raised to the primary article of faith in postmodernism, that evocations of origins are mythical, unspeakably violent, and yet inevitable—hence a site of unending vigilance—is already there from the beginning. Perhaps, in fact, this minimal break is nothing more than the renunciation of any possession of the privileged victimary stance.

We really must go back to the beginning if we are to construct a dialogue over origins: nothing in modern or postmodern thought prepares us particularly well for it. What would be the ground rules for a properly minimal account of human origins? Begin here: at one moment there were no signs, at another moment there were—something happened. I would suggest, first, that the ascension into language means the capacity to engage signs as formal realities:

their meaning is in their iteration, in no causal or correlative relation to any external reality or internal constitution, to nothing beyond the signs themselves; by anyone, anywhere. Since the linguistic turn, we are acutely aware of language as a system, which is to say as a self-referential world in itself, constituted by a network of reciprocally defining and modifying terms, that simultaneously opens a world of objects similarly irreducible to any causal relations we might attribute to them. However the sign came into being, then, it must have come with whatever constitutes its "signness," its at least potential systematicity, fully intact—some qualitative difference must be assumed between the time before the emergence of the sign and the time after it. It follows that the emergence of the sign must have been in an unprecedented event which is inseparable from because it issues in the sign as the form of that event. So, our question is now also, what are the terms on which we could account for such an event? To meet the terms of such an event, the emergence of the sign must have been absolutely necessarily in the situation of its emergence; and it must have so transformed those who invented it that it became intrinsic to them as a species thereafter (and, in evolutionary terms, it must have provided some significant advantage over groups that didn't possess the sign). It must have already been possible given the structures and capacities inherent in pre-human groups; and yet it must have transcended those structures and capacities, under some extraordinary, but at the same time explicable, non-accidental circumstances. Furthermore, nothing must be projected back into the event/sign which would not have emerged in and through it—we must assume it met certain exigencies (and only those exigencies) in an unprecedented way.[10]

Such an inquiry must be possible because, unless we are to imagine a non-formative, irrelevant origin (which I'll come to in a moment, but, for now, if we were imagining such, why would we be having this discussion?), the emergence of the sign must be experientially accessible to us now: we must iterate that event each time we engage in semiosis, and so our self-reflexive capacities must not only result from the inherent properties of signification but must also provide us with information regarding them. What distinguishes an account of the emergence of language as an event is that it need not have happened: it was utterly contingent, it is overwhelmingly likely that the conditions of possibility for such an event were present for quite a while and could have gone on being unactualized indefinitely. And yet, for us, as language users, the event has an appearance of inevitability that we can't quite shake. Our own capacity to recognize something utterly new and yet be simultaneously incapable of imagining existence without it (to see existence without it as non-existence) is the kind of pre-theoretical experience which testifies to traces of a memory of the origin.

We could try to account for the origin of language in terms of a series of imperceptible gradations from pre-lingual gestures and sound—this would certainly seem to be the path of least resistance. But, what would count as a "step" from pre-semiotic to semiotic activity? When would we have a sign, rather than "some" of a sign? How would we measure the threshold—more important, how would *they* have measured it? We might see the origin of language in terms of the evolution of the kinds of "problem solving" skills we see in animals, and which we see more of in the more advanced animals. Then we would have to imagine what the new, more complex "problem" would have been, that the initial, formal sign would have been a "skill" capable of "solving," not to mention who would recognize it as a "solution" so as to ensure that it is "applied" again to the "same" problem. Take something as simple (and as close to our originary scene) as a greeting or gesture attesting to peaceful intentions—how could we make sense of that as a recognizable "solution" to a recognizable "problem" (that is, a problem that was, already, in some sense being "worked on"), in the same way we can speak of more effective means for extracting food from some protected space? (I can keep getting closer to the food, but how would I be presumed to be obtaining information regarding the relative probability of deadly violence in encounters with a particular, "imperfect" gesture of greeting—what kind of response could have led me to "improve" upon the first gesture I happened to stumble upon?)

Even more, such a rationalistic approach leaves unaddressed the problem of ritual, which is either coeval with language and the human or requires yet another equally difficult to obtain explanation, and which more decisively distinguishes us from other species than "problem solving"—and, even worse, not only doesn't very clearly solve any problem but seems to create more of them. Gans has drawn attention to Durkheim's insight that religion is primarily a mode of social solidarity[11] but this, by itself, simply brings us back to our original question: why this mode of ensuring social solidarity and how was it discovered, as it must have been discovered, when it was desperately needed? We are still left with the question, at one moment there was no sign, a formal object that cannot be appropriated and leads to no appropriation, but can be iterated—and then at another moment there was. What happened?—no serious thinking within the human sciences can avoid an at least implicit answer to this question. And any answer must explain this transition without presupposing any of the human capacities that result from sign activity, that is, from the results of the transition itself, from the new phenomena it generates.

Cautions about the "genetic fallacy," in other words, could only have local value, with regard to objects created within an existing system—not for the origin of the system itself. Try to hypothesize the origin of language under the assumption that language emerged to meet one exigency, and then became appropriate in addressing other absolutely unrelated ones; or that it emerged accidentally and through some serendipitous process came to sustain the various (related? integrated? random?) spaces of semiosis circulating today. If language was first one kind of thing, then another, and then yet another, and so on, we would need several hypotheses; or, more radically, we might not even be able to hypothesize regarding the earlier forms of "language" (we're not talking about a single thing anymore) within the thing "language" has become. But unless "language" has been undergoing incessant and complete transformation each mode of "its" existence has some internal coherence, which means it evolved out of some earlier mode of different, lesser, or non coherence; which further means our ability to hypothesize the process in which it came to cohere includes our ability to hypothesize regarding the process of transition and hence at least some degree regarding what was transitioned from—whatever was accidental and serendipitous in the transition became, at some point, essential and self-reproducing, and in this transformation (this seizing upon or self-reconfiguring around, the accidental and serendipitous) we can glimpse the exigent circumstances in which the transition was effected.

The argument for the originary hypothesis rests upon the assumption that you can multiply as much as you like various accidental and contingent events, capacities and combinations of events and capacities that might have led to what we could recognize as the first sign, but in the end we will be able to reduce the possibility that such accidents and combinations came together in that way to the elements present upon our originary scene: convergence upon the central object with imminently catastrophic results and an aborted gesture of appropriation as a result of which the convergence ceased. But of course I can't prove this without trying out all the possibilities that might be within the range of my reader's ingenuity, so I will simply pose the problem as a way of treating the hypothesis itself as a sign, one which keeps the conversation going. (Just to get started, though, give it a try: take some combination—increasingly intense mimetic dancing by a group of primate hunters over some period of time, a stormy day disrupting and terrifying the hunting party, a fortuitous, improvised regrouping in which some—let's say, some of the prominent, indispensable members—are lost but others saved as a result of a cry reminiscent of the dance rhythms which now coalesce into a pattern... What will make it all "come together" as something new and iterable without all those elements in place in such a way as to improve upon and not merely clutter the originary hypothesis?)

Perhaps you are not tempted to enter this line of inquiry (maybe it's even a bit embarrassing, like young boys trying to decide who was the greatest baseball

player ever, or, even, worse, scholastic debates over "creation" vs. the eternal existence of the universe), but in that case I would suggest that if we can't articulate
our present in terms of our origin, we also can't articulate our present in terms of
yesterday, except insofar as we must, for mysterious reasons, construct myths of
origin in order to keep ourselves going (do our myths of origin have an origin?).
Such a necessity, and such myths, could only be a source of disgust for those who
see (through) them as such (like our skeptic, who is not "tempted"); recoiling
from such pragmatically useful but intellectually dissatisfying narratives would
lead one to posit that, if we shed such illusions and examine things honestly and
openly, we must see each moment in time as a construct with no reality outside
of its own means and process of construction. We could posit a dominant element within that construct—ultimately we must, if we are to account for the
fact that it seems to hold together, regardless of what we think of that holding
together (or, perhaps, simply to account for that illusory sense of holding together)—but that dominant element owes its dominance to nothing more than
its exercise of it, not even to its position within the construction which came a
moment earlier—even if we could assert its identity with some element within
that previous construct, which we can't. In this case, what moves us from one
moment to the next is the sheer force of one newly self-creating element violently
wrenching pre-eminence away from the prevailing form of domination and imposing its force upon all the other newly subordinated elements—with part of, it
makes perfectly good sense to say the major part of, that force being the imposition of precisely that myth of origin.

For the postmodern, victimary thinker, the only possible response to this
nihilistic violence is a kind of gesture, a gesture which indicates that this construct does not, in fact, hold together, a gesture which deforms it; a gesture
which our postmodern thinker, aware of the delusions of extensions of modernity (like Marxism) which seek to consciously guide that process of construction
(which could be nothing more than a will to take the illusion as real and thereby
redouble the violence), wishes only to deconstruct, not destroy and reconstruct.
I would generously read this gesture as aligned to that of the originary event—at
least in the sense that for those committed to the deconstructive gesture the
originary one might at least be visible—and yet that gesture could never give
us a scene (indeed, it would forcefully repudiate the very request) and therefore
could never give us a sign. On the most elementary level, the postmodern gesture could give us no sparagmos, the collective devouring of the object at the
sacred center, other than as a rush to participate in the originary violence. The
originary hypothesis directly embeds the sign in distribution and consumption,
and then in the ritualistic commemoration of the scene, the repetition of the

sign for the entire community, simultaneously. Here, for victimary thought, is the primary repression, our forgetting that the form we are born into is an illusion generating violence. The only ethical response is to be ready to glimpse, out of the corner of one's eye, so to speak, signs of deformation normally hidden from view by the originary violence of the community. For originary thought, there is a kind of forgetting here as well, but simply because the originary scene itself only needs to be retrieved in the course of the very same kind of emergency which made it necessary and possible in the first place.[12]

It follows from what we have seen so far that it is simply impossible to imagine language or a sign emerging, without some minimal consciousness of what it was and what it was for. Of course the participants on the originary scene did not have the linguistic capacities to describe what they were doing—but insofar as they emitted and obeyed the sign, we must attribute to them some sense of what the alternative would be. And, therefore, similarly with all cultural transformations thereafter: in each case, we must not assume that the initial emission of the new version of the sign, designed to meet some new mimetic crisis, contained within it the entire vocabulary that will, ultimately, be a product of the transmission and circulation of the sign itself; but, by the same token, we must assume that a line is drawn between the consequences of the continuation and intensification of the crisis and something, some gesture, that would at the very least slow it down, or provide a way out, or simply share some recognition of those consequences. Once again, postmodern victimary thought here raises an objection: this is teleology, distinguishing between more and less viable, mature, civilized, etc., societies in the name of an end contained in the beginning, in the name of which the unviable, immature and primitive can be ruthlessly sacrificed. Our preliminary answer is that we could not help but distinguish between signs which are more and less effective in deferring violence, since this distinction first of all arises incessantly within each community; nor could we deny that each sign which does so effectively creates conditions under which more complex modes of mimesis will emerge and hence the need for a sign with greater deferral capacities. The objection to a certain sacrificial logic needs to be registered, though.

Evolutionary theory might have been one pathway into moral nihilism but for postmodern nihilism it would likely be the antidote. The constructionist nihilism I have been describing must deny continuity, because continuity appears to require sacrifice—some elements of the construct contribute to sustaining and expanding the structure and those that don't are to be eliminated. What happens blindly in nature is intolerable in the human. Originary thinking has no objection here, but constructionist nihilism would prefer to contemplate a totalizing and constitutive violence as long as it was unjustified and meaningless, and as long as the a priori impossibility of utterly eliminating difference from the system allows for some gesture of dissent, however ineffectual (ineffectual is in fact better, because otherwise one would inevitably be implicated in the constitutive violence of reality)—rather than far less violence, but violence which is justified and even sanctified. And yet we can't simply dismiss this set of priorities: even according to our hypothesis, the sheer quantity of violence may be less important than its quality, with our special concern for violence leading to the cataclysmic implosion of the community.

Rather, we could hypothesize a form of emergence that eschews sacrificial assumptions while accounting for continuity. We just need to assume some relation between relative order and relative randomness in each instant and variable relation between order and randomness within micro-systems that average out to that proportion characteristic of the whole. At some point in the system order must be increasing, and that increase in order must be attributable to an enhanced self-reference among the elements internal to the micro-system along with enhanced reference to the increasingly (relatively) disordered larger system. If greater order appears, as it must, for those who in turn are produced as those capable of construing that order, it must mean that each element is more predictive of the place and motion of other elements—again, to that perceiver. And if all of the elements are increasingly predictive regarding each other, the internal system as a whole must be more sensitized to whatever is orderly in the external system(s). But the extent to which this predictability and sensitivity is enhanced will depend upon the baseline established from the initial conditions introducing order in the first place, which is to say, constant reference to the origin (what else could terms like "increasingly" refer to?).

I offer this extremely abstract formulation of the kind of punctual origin proposed by the originary hypothesis to show that even here, where we don't even need to be speaking about human beings, the assumption of some originary event is inescapable, at least for those elements within any micro-system. Clearly, with this inhuman example, there is no necessary location for the origin, which has the virtue of demonstrating that what we designate as the origin will not only depend upon the question we are asking but will only appear as such after the fact. Any point along the way at which a measurable increase in order along with the measuring capacities to register it emerge might be a candidate; but, depending upon the question one is asking, there must be some point—a point, it should be added, which will be chosen in terms that intensify the articulation of measured effects and instrument of measurement which has coincided with the increased perception of order. In other words, the origin is both irreducible to and inseparable from its appearance in its effects; rather than discrediting originary thinking, I would suggest that this claim affirms it, because those effects are precisely our desire to sharpen, formalize and preserve particularly pertinent appearances, appearances singled out and maintained as a thread providing minimal regularity through the flow of a world of appearances. And asking what might be the origin, or even, simply, meaning, of *that* desire gives us our "question" (what origin?) and leads us back onto the path bringing us to the originary hypothesis.

What this abstract formulation then allows for is a way of theorizing a non-sacrificial mode of continuity. What reduces randomness to self-referentiality?—elements of the (not-yet-quite) system become more proximal to some elements than to others; those elements then begin to refer to the relations between the proximal elements and itself; but they could only refer to those elements for a modified perceiver of those elements; and the first perceiver must be the referring element itself, which refers to itself performing the referencing. The true mode of continuity of the system, then, is the emergence of modes of measurement of a possible modified version of the system. In principle, there is no element of the system which couldn't modify itself so as to participate in the procedures of measurement, which is to say in the constitution of new modes of symmetry. Unlike natural evolution, human evolution could bring everyone along—not just every individual, but every cultural form which has contributed to the deferral of violence (which is every cultural form) and could therefore itself be modified so as to do so again under changed conditions. This never has been the case, of course, nor is it necessarily the highest priority, but we could contend that the purpose of cultural theorizing is to chart paths toward modes of social evolution which approximate what is possible, once we have satisfied ourselves intellectually that it is, indeed, possible. Generative anthropology is the scourge of all utopianisms, and yet it is the only cultural theory which enables us to imagine the cessation of virtually all violence (as was, indeed, the case on the originary scene itself)—it offers no guarantees, of course, and provides more of a sharpening of our originary intuitions than a "plan," but the end of violence would contradict not a single one of GA's founding assumptions. Originary thinking can call upon us to fight, with force if necessary, against a great many things, but always in the name of a defense of the sacred center, whose weakening is ultimately responsible for the threat to it, and whose strengthening always provides, not a promise of a more equal portion, but at the very least of participation in modifying the terms determinative of the apportionment.

I must confess that don't see a persuasive refutation of this line of argumentation vindicating, simultaneously, origins and historical open-endedness.

Which brings me back to my opening question, regarding the lateness of the discovery of the hypothesis and its minimal effect so far, now adding to those questions that of the almost unanimous resistance to such common sense reasoning, even leaving the hypothesis itself aside. To return to my preliminary answer, it seems to me the only explanation is the terror of the sacred center shared, albeit in very different ways, by "progressives" and "revolutionaries" along with "conservatives" and "reactionaries." For the progressive/revolutionary camp, any sacred center to which we must look back can only serve to subordinate us to what we have liberated ourselves from; while for the conservative/reactionary, such hypothetical speculations can only serve to weaken adherence to actually existing sacred chains. But GA has "good news" for those in both camps. The originary hypothesis provides for a beginning which one can honor and wholeheartedly preserve and that genuinely need not reject the input of virtually any of the revelations to which human beings have thus far pledged themselves. And while consequences follow from this beginning (we are mimetic beings, we are capable of transcending the worst dangers of our mimetic nature), they contain no end and set no real limit for how sophisticated, complex and powerful the modes of reciprocity we might construct will be. We are in the identical position I just attributed to those on the scene (indeed, where else could we be?)—we can draw a line, predicated on some glimpse of intuition we have of where the main danger lies, communicate our inevitably partial sense of where that line is, and hope others will join us in strengthening it.

I certainly don't want to blur the radicality of Gans' hypothesis, though. While eschewing the apocalyptic narrative genre in favor of what he calls the "post-millennial"[13]—the insistence that precisely our clarity about the beginning enables us to conclude that there is no end—the ambitions of GA are prodigious. Even a cursory look at the range of Gans' own originary explorations gives a sense of the kinds of revisions in the objects and methods of study in the human sciences we might look towards: he has engaged the history of monotheism and the Athens/Jerusalem debate; reconfigured debates over early humanity and primitive social forms, touching up evolutionary theory and making a genuinely theoretical "sociobiology" conceivable; proposed a reading of religion as "good anthropology, bad cosmology," which would enable us to take the claims of revelation very seriously without surrendering our critical faculties; rethought the status of categories such as the unconscious, irony and paradox in humanistic thought, along with redefining metaphysics and its end; provided a theory of speech forms and/as speech acts along with powerful critiques of competing theories, such as "speech act" theory, structuralism, deconstruction and, of course, René Girard's mimetic theory.

An important test of the viability of the originary hypothesis as a contending model of humanistic inquiry will be the ability of its representatives to retrieve the desire for the ostensive and the sacred that has been apparent, often but by no means exclusively in pathological ways, in the myriad responses in the breakdown of Western metaphysics from the late 19th century on. Perhaps the origin of humanity will provide a site of conversation here, enabling us to speak about anything: just as the Marxist learned to treat any species of discourse as an effect of the contradiction between the forces and relations of production and the psychoanalyst in terms of the dynamic of desire and repression, a more genuinely dialectical generative anthropology would locate certain assumptions regarding human origins in any act of semiosis. Rather than a charge of false consciousness, though, such probings can be presented as symmetrical, as carried out by equal participants in the scene of inquiry itself—others' intuitions regarding our common origin will always add something to the representation of my own. This, in fact, has been precisely the approach recommended by Gans, and it provides, as a powerful heuristic, a commonly adopted double bind: we haven't finished our discussion until we have emitted a sign we could all sign onto. Even the most antagonistic response to our hypothesis must derive from somewhere on and therefore illuminate the scene, and we would want to hear more about it (for the resentful, this "desiring to hear more" is the mark of cooptation, to which our answer is, why not transform rather than destroy what you are being co-opted into, especially since the latter approach is sure to leave you mute, which you can't possibly want if you are now energetically objecting).

Just as every thought is in effect a revelation (if it's a real thought we couldn't have known it was coming before it came and after it has arrived it embeds some preliminary glimpse into something without which the thought cannot now be imagined) which testifies to the originary scene every sign does likewise and provides current information by pointing to, suspending, and providing a leap (or at least a peek) beyond the current equilibrium of mimetic rivalries. I will direct the reader to some of Gans' and others' working with GA observations regarding and proposals for studying popular culture but for our purposes here I will simply note that the originary hypothesis' distinctive contribution to the study of culture will lie in its insistence upon both the transcendence of the sign and its direct embeddedness in the distribution of goods and our everyday habitus. The emission of the sign on the originary scene is followed by the sparagmos, the equal division of the central object, and then the first ritual, commemorating the scene, and ensuring its iterability. In that case, every sign indicates a particular mode of distribution which all of us on the margin are prepared to enforce; and, in a post-ritual culture, a complex of habits which reinforce, disperse and exhaust the prevailing sign. Our own interest in studying such processes, furthermore, is ultimately the same as those participating in it (which is to say our inquiry is a mode of participation), the deferral of violence through representation, which we are interested in enhancing by learning how to make it more visible in the only way we can: immersion in the infinite variety of ordinary semiosis.

Generative anthropology, as I have already indicated, is resolutely and un-ambiguously universalistic: humanity has a single origin, and while there was no pre-determined trajectory leading from the most primitive to the most advanced, there is a logic to such developments that we can understand after the fact and accordingly privilege certain cultural forms over others as having solved the same problem faced by all forms of social organization in one way or another: the deferral of violence. The deferral of violence within a community of two hundred hunter-gathers is a significant accomplishment, one upon which all future accomplishments rest; but it's something qualitatively different from the unplanned and primarily voluntary cooperation of hundreds of millions of people across the world, and the difference can be located rather precisely and objectively, in terms of the loosening of restraints on mimetic activity: the more advanced society is the one capable of moving another region of social life away from ritualized simulations of mimetic activity into unregulated, spontaneous and free activity without a corresponding increase or danger of violence that threatens the community. But having said this we can go on to say that such judgments can never really be settled once and for all—perhaps contemporary American society, obviously privileged in the criteria I have just provided, will turn out to have fatal "rigidities" and "blockages" that will make it impossible to engage challenges just down the road, and in that case we might turn out to be indebted to those probing (with benevolent or other intent) for precisely such weaknesses. Still, the criteria wouldn't have changed, just the way the form of our judgments line up with this or another particular object.

I must close this discussion, but not without insisting that I still haven't to my own satisfaction, accounted for the resistance to the originary hypothesis, much less to the conditions under which it might become a contending mode of self-understanding in the post-millennial world it would then be helping to create—and, without giving it one more try. Here, I turn to Gans' recent discussion of the scapegoat mechanism[14], perhaps the central issue separating Gans' originary hypothesis from Rene Girard's mimetic theory. It is Gans' rejection of the universality of the "emissary mechanism" or scapegoat that marks the opening of a new problematic incompatible with Girardian mimetic theory. Gans originally, in his initial formulation of the hypothesis, accepted Girard's account of an originary scene in which the mimetic crisis is resolved through the arbitrary selection of a single member of the group upon which the accumulated violence is "discharged." Gans only introduced the originary sign as settling a problem raised in the aftermath, which is the means by which the body of the victim was to then be divided and the results of the scene preserved, or made meaningful. Once he introduced the sign, though, he realized that the emissary mechanism was unnecessary: any object would do equally well.

I will leave aside the reasoning supporting the superiority of Gans' hypothesis to focus on its implications. As Christopher Morrissey (one of our contributors) notes, Girardian mimetic theory is essentially victimary, leading to a moral relativism whereby any victim of superior power, whether it is the innocent victim of a lynch mob or a Nazi war criminal, is equally "scapegoated." Regardless of Girard's own intentions, then, his theory takes the path of least resistance through contemporary victimary thought; more important, it provides us with a clue to what is central to contemporary thought, left and right, traditional and radical, Thomist and Nietzschean: an inability or refusal to break with sacrificial logics. Gans limits the emissary mechanism to a particular historical period—that initiated by the "big man" who transcends the egalitarian originary community by seizing possession of the center of ritual and economic distribution. This is no mere "period," though—it covers all of civilized human history, including the history of empires and tyrants, big men writ large. Indeed, the origins of our own culture, the Greek polis and the Hebrew God "as the declarative sentence" represent the riposte to big men, small and large, imposing, on the one hand, a new mode of public equality and, on the other, a spiritual equality predicated upon resentment toward anyone who would unite the ritual and distributive functions of the community. So we are able to "peek" beyond the shadow cast by the advance of human culture through tyranny and empire.

Still, Athens and Jerusalem are haunted by the continued existence of the big man, not only by his presence outside the protected domain, but by the possibility that those islands of freedom carved out will themselves succumb, whether to external invasion or internal corruption (hence the suspicions directed at the outsider in both cases, significantly one of the signs of the scapegoat for Girard[15]). Needless to say, such fears are far from unreasonable, but equally reasonable in that case is the assumption that without incorporating into our semiosis a preparedness for the recrudescence of the tyrant we will, in fact, not be prepared when we need to be. And such preparedness requires not the abolition of sacrifice but its internalization, in the form of guilt: this internalization of sacrifice has been, I would propose, the work of metaphysics, which in turn paradoxically weakens our resistance to tyranny and scapegoating insofar as we have spiritually liberated ourselves from its rule over the mere material world. We might say that the paranoia toward "systems of domination" by modernist and postmodernist thinkers as well as the hostility toward the tentative probes toward post-sacrificial logics such thinkers have attempted by traditionalists are equally motivated by a terror of what might be unloosed if we were indeed released from sacrificial logics. The deliberate inefficacy of the victimary stance of what I have been calling constructionist nihilism is itself a kind of sacrifice to metaphysics, or representation as equivalence, the "two world theory," or the "primacy of the declarative sentence" (for Gans), because, on the one hand even overcoming the sacrificial logic of metaphysics would in the end be a kind of sacrifice and, on the other hand, what would come after this, final, sacrifice? One can never do enough to distance oneself from metaphysics; one can never sufficiently remind oneself that one can never really thus distance oneself. As I pointed out earlier, guilt is part of the originary configuration—the scene is not concluded, after all, until we have devoured the sacred object; I also proposed that a post millennial "cultural politics" would involve "discharging" this guilt through tribute toward the center, rather than toward the illimitable grievances of the exemplary victim (exemplary because she is *our* victim).

I will conclude on a somewhat different note, and offer a complementary thesis. Insofar as guilt derives from the sparagmos, it is secondary: in other words, guilt is not constitutive, but already framed by the emission of the sign. In that case, there is no reason we can't devise a more suitable tribute to the center. In fact, if guilt becomes an autonomous cultural force, it is because it has become subject to the laws of mimetic contagion, even if it has been created to counter a worse contagion. A guilt directed toward the center is preferable precisely because it is so directed insofar as it has been channeled by the framing sign. What is constitutive is the sign which we emit without knowing who will respond and where it will end, even what it will "mean"—to whomever first put forth/withdrew his hand, out of a sudden glimpse of his own movements in the movement of others as a slowing down which could then be enhanced to cessation, we must attribute both absolute knowledge that this is the only possibility and a minimal faith that this knowledge might be as contagious as its prompt; but we must make this attribution in the most minimal form we can, which for us means that we strengthen our own minimal intuitions regarding the next saving sign by prolonging into infinity the conditions of its confirmation. We will have broken from sacrificial logics once we have enacted a new mode of reciprocally interfering freedom manifested as maximal imprint upon the world and minimal predictable return. My focus is no longer on the return of the tyrant once I simply put forward "constitutional" allocations of powers and modes of accountability that address present limitations but that exclude any possibility of situating myself in the distribution that allocation will provide for, much like a constitutional amendment which must be framed in such a way as to imply as yet unanticipated applications. This perhaps can seen as a forward looking version of John Rawls' "original position," with the important addition that such constitutional acts are signs aimed at inspiring other signs (which is precisely why my relation to the outcome is blind) and not attempts at a final settlement or mode of ordering relations. And once we have gotten into the habit of practicing such freedom, no tyrant will ever be able to return.[16]

What is the field of possibilities within GA as a disciplinary formation? Even if the essays in this book do not and could not cover that field or begin to exhaust those possibilities, I believe I can now introduce them in such a way as provide a preliminary map. I will use the concepts of "omnicentric culture" and "diagonal history" to do so. "Omnicentric" is the term Gans uses to describe the "Christian moral community" (61) in *Originary Thinking*, a community describable on the model of Pascal's universe, "whose center is everywhere, and whose circumference is nowhere," but which is only fully realized with the unlimited individual differentiation made possible by the modern market system. We could picture, it seems to me, an omnicentric culture along purely libertarian, Hayekian lines, as nothing more than the millions upon millions of daily exchanges, each a center in itself and a vortex provisionally organizing other centers. At the other end of the spectrum, insofar as provisional hierarchies among centers must emerge, we cannot set an a priori ceiling to how systemic the articulations of the various hierarchies, however provisional, might be, all the way toward the conceptualization of a sacred social center comprised of the historical gains in reciprocity made from the Mosaic revelation right up to the modern, romantic individual—leaving open, further, the possibility, that this center is uniquely represented by Christian civilization or, perhaps, modern constitutional democracy. In this latter case no less than in the previous, the centrality of each individual is irreducible, and this irreducibility in term indispensable to the whole.

The "diagonal," as a way of thinking "post-linear" historicity, derives from Hannah Arendt's *Thinking*, from her analysis of the "parallelogram of forces" resulting from the narrative structure of history Arendt extracts from Kafka's short story "He." The "agent" of thinking is located "between past and future," "has a definite origin," but "is infinite with respect to it ending" (209)—while for Arendt this is a metaphor for the activity of thought, for us it can no less be a metaphor for originary historicity, predicated upon the assumption that "men... transcend their own finiteness" (211), for us, through the sign. The diagonal, in which the never ceasing struggle between someone pushing back from the future and someone else pushing forward from the past, with "He" in the middle, is produced by the inevitable (and impossible to predict) deflection of "Him" from his original directedness in the midst of what is now a scene, provides us with a necessarily minimal insistence upon progressively more successful modes of deferral, without which human existence would become problematic to the point that our present existence would be beyond miraculous—while yet deferring the complacency that would result from assuming knowledge in advance, or in the process, of exactly what will turn out to be "effective."

In this way we can articulate a confidence in our civilizational conquests and our individual intuitions—if each of us is a center, any of us might constitute a new starting point—along with the skepticism needed to maintain the alertness which would allow us to recognize when a new sign emerges, perhaps as a result of the aggregate of decisions whose significance can only be realized after the fact, maybe just as they are fading from memory; perhaps through unrepeatable revelations incommensurable with any available vocabulary. In any case, what thereby stays in clear focus is the perpetual need to retrieve, restore, defend, re-articulate and project forward the center through which violence is presently and imminently deferred.

For Raoul Eshelman, originary thinking enables us to see those social and intellectual processes currently transcending the current, postmodern age; Eshelman articulates these processes under his GA-inspired category of "performatism." Deliberately setting up a confrontational dialogue with postmodern thought, Eshelman invents a concept which is "no less fixated on framing than is postmodernism" (9); as opposed to the "archaic fascination" frames exercise on the postmodern mind "insofar as they can be easily transgressed, shifted, undercut, or surpassed," the "performatist aesthetic… returns the originary charge to both frames in an *artificial* process of double framing." The performatist text "coercively imposes 'inescapable' forms on us…. In effect, we are made to 'believe' in the aesthetic scene created by the work in spite of our better judgment" (10). Eshelman's careful attention to the post-metaphysical assumptions GA might be said to share with post-structuralism and postmodernism serves to clarify exactly where it is irreducibly distinct: "GA's semiotic monism stands in direct opposition to poststructuralist, neo-Saussurean semiotic dualism and cannot be assimilated back to it without an act of violence that would destroy GA entirely" (7).

This imposed belief marks the return, in what Eshelman does not hesitate to designate a new "epoch," to a moral, ideological and political orientation toward the sacred center. Exploring the political consequences of his argument, Eshelman finds as wide a range of political possibility within originary thought as within any other ideological field: "In general, I have the impression that performatist works are no less critical towards society than postmodern ones.... The real major difference between the two is that performatist works use monist devices of centering and unification...whereas postmodernist ones insist on arguing from a peripheral or victimary position that would seem to guarantee a critical attitude towards capitalism.... If anything, the aesthetic ideology of 'left' performatism presents an alternative to victimary discourse by emphasizing a positive of creating unified new identities or centers that compete with and unsettle the existing system" (21). Eshelman's own critique of Gans' analysis of gay marriage from such a "left performatist" position enacts precisely the kind of political dialogue we might hope for in this new epoch, and his turn toward contemporary art as a reminder that those whose political sympathies lie with the Left need not fear "that GA may be a Trojan Horse for neoconservative ideology" (67) is most welcome; as Gans notes as well in his "Generative Anthropology and Bronx Romanticism," no formulation of the hypothesis or its consequences could ever exclude the possibility of the next one.

The legacy of Romanticism for the modern West is marked by an ambivalence which GA shares: one finds in Gans' discussions of Romanticism the origins of twentieth-century totalitarianism and contemporary victimary thought in some of its most vicious forms; and also the origins of the endlessly self-differentiating individual that Gans sees as the most advanced product of the market system. Two of our contributors point to opposite ends of this polarity. In his "Intensity and Ambiguity in Romantic Poetics," Matthew Schneider essentially defines the Romantic as an abiding concern with the originary: "Romantic poetics hovers around the abortive gesture of appropriation" (2). He then examines the role of the ostensive gesture in Wordsworth, Dickens and Hardy, first of all reading one of Wordsworth's "Lucy" poems as generating its effect through an intense ambiguity in which we are led by vague pronouns to "the most primary form of language, the ostensive, [which] merely designates the renounced object on the originary scene" (8). Schneider lets us see Wordsworth's "reprimitiv[ization]" (10) of poetry not as an escape from modern concerns but as a retrieval of what must concern us now as much as it ever concerned humans: the deferral of violence, which accounts for our interest in "the process through which the desire to make inscriptions at all might first have come about" (11).

In his discussion of Dickens' *A Christmas Carol* (leaving aside his reformulation of the relation between Romanticism and Realism) meanwhile, Schneider shows how a more fully moral stance relies upon, while also transcending the "primitive" ostensive: "Dickens also knows that gestural ambiguity offers little possibility for ethical development. For that the more evolved linguistic form of the declarative is necessary, which is what Scrooge employs when he flings his desperate questions at the mute spirit just before he reads his name on the tombstone" (16). Schneider leaves us with a new appreciation of Romanticism's (long since stereotyped) obsessions with graveyards, ghosts, and the like as a much needed and fully self-aware exploration of questions neglected in the neo-classical epoch: "To the degree to which its particular inscription is *indistinct* or *ambiguous*, the blank tombstone becomes an occasion for anthropological speculation on the broader phenomenon of inscription itself, or *representation*, especially the *origin of representation* within the context of death" (21).

Richard van Oort, meanwhile, returns, in his "Hamlet's Theater of Resentment," to the primal figure of Romanticism, the Prince of Denmark. Van Oort's essay accomplishes a great deal, among other things serving as a compact introduction to GA, explaining, for one thing, the difference Gans' *formal* theory of representation makes in distinguishing his from Girard's mimetic theory: rather than revealing the "scapegoat mechanism" more or less clearly, as Girard would ask, GA can engage the originary effect of the esthetic work itself: "[w]hat makes the art work anthropologically "revelatory" is its reproduction within the individual of the aesthetic effect, an effect that can be traced to the originary event" (3). In addition, van Ort returns us to Gans' subtle theorization of the emergence of modernity in terms of esthetic modifications and developments: "[a]esthetic history becomes a history of increasingly developed thematizations of the center-periphery configuration of the originary event" (4).

Somewhat more interesting for my purposes here, though, is the specific form of violence van Oort finds Hamlet to represent. Tracing the all embracing nature of Hamlet's resentment, van Oort (along the way engaging in some long-standing controversies regarding the status of the ghost in the play) notes that "[t]he ghost is an index of the level of resentment in Denmark. Whoever is capable of seeing it is guaranteed a spot in Hamlet's 'theater of resentment'... We [the spectator/reader] alone are fully of Hamlet's party because we alone are willing to see him die for his cause. The contrary position that the ghost does not exist is represented by Gertrude. She cannot see the ghost because she has no reason to invent one. Like all the others in the opening court scene except Hamlet, she is happy with Claudius as her king" (14). This reality-constructing resentment which also serves as an auto-authorizing mode of authenticity situates him with an especially virulent mode of sacrificial desire: attacking straight on the romantic idolization of Hamlet's alienation, van Oort contends that "Hamlet's tragedy is that he has no real possibility for integrating his personally held difference from the center into a publicly marketable personal identity that can circulate freely (and bloodlessly) on the periphery" (19). Implicit in "Hamlet's posture of alienation from the center [which] had become a form of praxis to be carried out in real life" (20) for the Romantics, I take van Oort's analysis to suggest, is a potentially unlimited violence of which we are not rid to this day.

Peter Goldman also presents us with a formulation of the implications of GA for the emergence of the modern world and modern individual in "The Reforming of Reformation Itself: Public vs. Private Scenes of Representation in Shakespeare's *Measure for Measure*." In a subtle and historically grounded reading of the play Goldman argues that "[m]odernity is characterized by…the development of [the] originary potential" for an individual's "personal sacred" to compete with the "public sacred" (4). Shakespeare's play, as Goldman shows, is a sustained representation of the consequences and paradoxes of this shift toward the priority of the personal sacred: working with the frame established by the Reformation, Shakespeare's play argues for the need to enact publicly the private drama of temptation, sin, discipline and self-reformation, while public power is now authorized in terms of its answerability to the newly dominant private scene: "the Duke is endorsed here for the audience not through his public office, but through his actions during the play—a radically different form of authority, one which is earned, not bestowed by birth and rank" (42).

Moving even beyond such considerations, Goldman shows how the self-reflexivity of Shakespeare's dramatic art works to transform the relation between artist and society, dismantling the centrality of the artist as a kind of god in pre-modern Europe. Drawing upon similarities between Duke Vincento and *The Tempest*'s Prospero, Goldman "disagree[s] with Girard that Prospero represents or parodies Shakespeare himself; rather, I would say that *The Tempest* comically questions the power of the dramatic artist and his role in Renaissance society. Both *Measure for Measure* and *The Tempest* are ironic reflections on the demise of the god-like artist" (44–5). This ironic reflection further radicalizes the play's "Protestantism," revealing the emergence of a kind of omnicentrism, countering victimary discourse as a potent possibility at the very opening of the modern world:

> The larger importance of the action of the play is not simply the reform of Isabella and Angelo, but the reconstruction of the private scene as a locus of sacrality, which requires taking the private and making it public. If the conscience can serve as an internal divinity, then, potentially, any and all of us are similarly divine. We take the authority of private scenes for granted as moderns, but for Shakespeare and his audience the authorization of the private scene requires a new and

radical sublimation of mimetic desire. Shakespeare views the private scene here not from a romantic Rousseauvian but rather a realistic Hobbesian perspective. Modern critics like Foucault who see all discipline as sinister and repressive operate on utopian assumptions about human nature that ignore history. (50)

Why is it that the ancient materialism of the Epicureans, eschewing superstition and any kind of anthropomorphic divine agency, arrives at an ethics of measure, moderation and reciprocity; an ethics that it finds, moreover, in the natural order itself, in its fundamental division into equal units? In his "The Dispensations of Moira: Matter, Mind and Culture from Thales of Miletus to Walter Pater," Thomas Bertonneau suggests that "Pater understands what Eric Gans makes explicit in *Originary Thinking*, that 'religion is in reality the first human science, practicing through myths of origin a primitive form of originary analysis" (12). In returning to the earliest Enlightenment movement and critique of sacrificial discourse, and finding in it a retrieval of the originary intuitions of the "first human science," Bertonneau simultaneously points to the perpetual questioning originary thought represents for materialisms which consider themselves exempt from the pull of the sacred: "Pater seems to be making good on a deficiency in the strict scientism of the materialist tradition, whether that be the Cyrenaicism of the Second Century, the Marxism or Darwinism of the Nineteenth, or the Sociobiology of the Twentieth" (12). For the no less daring materialism Bertonneau recovers for us via originary thought, '[a] god is a hypothesis, a necessary one" (12):

A strict materialism gives rise both to a primarily esthetic attitude towards life and to a pronouncedly subjective, if not egoistic, orientation. Matter impinges on mind as sensation; mind makes out of sensations the appearances, arresting the flux of natural process in concepts. Measuring concepts against the flux, mind then doubts their adequacy; the flux is real, but its fixation in concepts is an illusion. Mind works its way out of this impasse by finding in the flux itself an *order* and so intuiting beyond or beneath ever-changing nature an *ordering principle*, the *Logos*, analogous to itself. (226)

Bertonneau goes on to represent such a materialism as strictly regulated by the equable division on the originary scene following the emission of the sign: "[t]he emergence of signification not only gives human beings newly to themselves *as* human beings; it also gives to them the world, grasped as interpenetrated by the *ethos* or indeed by the *Moira*, or principle of justice, of the common scenic situation" (24). The rigorous renunciation of any principle of being other than matter translates into contempt for the excesses of tyrants (indeed, excess and tyranny almost become synonymous) along with sacrificial spectacles (and the gods who demand them).

Finally, to return to some themes already touched on, Bertonneau finds in Pater's materialism a mode of connoisseurship that provides ethical ballast to the self-forming modern individual, who now appears as "the modern, esthetic version of the ancient Moira, a faith in proportion whereby the individual graduates from dependence on the actual or ritual community to independence in the virtual community of his imagination" (35). Bertonneau's essay confirms the originary hypothesis in its basic assumption that the further back we go, the more we "upload" subsequent intellectual and ethical innovations back to the originary scene, the more we look forward, refining and re-articulating those elements of the scene that we need to constitute our future.

Like van Oort, Christopher Morrissey, in his "The Epigenic Evolution of the Immaterial Intellect on the Originary Scene," frames his discussion in terms of the difference between Gans and Girard; like Bertonneau, Morrissey finds that originary thought provides us with a richer materialism, complementary with rather than antagonistic to, intuitions of the sacred, than modern scientism can (or wishes to). As Gans has done on occasion, Morrissey doesn't so much enter the dialogue of the deaf between evolutionary theory and "intelligent design," as use that pseudo-dispute to highlight what evolutionary theory's metaphysical commitments leave it ill-equipped to account for: the "epigenesis," or "clear and sudden transition" (10) from the pre-human to the human. Morrissey calls upon (via the philosopher John Deely) Aristotle's formal causality, and thereby presents Gans' discovery of the originary scene as an "epistemological break" relative to Girard (who remains tied to both a mechanistic epistemology and an idealistic metaphysics). Only in the originary scene is there

> a correlation of form with matter in that the formal causality of the mental act of representation is generated *together with* the material causality of the scene. That is, in Gans' scene there is an epigenesis. The consequence of his modified scenic hypothesis is that a scapegoat need not necessarily be part of the scene, which is fortunate, since it seems to be a needlessly dogmatic empirical claim to demand the material presence of a scapegoat on the originary scene. (85)

The coincidence of "formal significance" (a "repellent, sacral force") with the "correlative material alignment (a symmetry generated by the 'aborted gesture of appropriation')" (17) makes originary thinking not only more scientific than Girard's hypothesis of a universal scapegoating mechanism; not only more scientific than neo-Darwinian evolutionary theory itself; but a mode of thought capable of (indeed, defined by this capability) rendering itself ever more self-critical or "minimal"—Morrissey cites my own "amendment" to the originary scene regarding the necessity for a "first" signifier but the implications go even further: insofar as what Morrissey calls the "Katz amendment" was suggested by our current crisis (as Gans suggests in "On Firstness"), we can further posit that all enrichments of originary thought as a participatory mode of cultural inquiry will suggest further "minimizations" of (or at least provisional amendments to) the scene. And so Morrissey himself adds—through a reading of the story of human origins given in *Genesis*—to the scene an account of original sin which implies a (perhaps "cultural") feminist reading of the originary scene. If Eve, "usually an outsider from this circle of quarrelling males… suddenly saw a new appropriative opportunity" (26) and proceeded to initiate the sparagmos (to be imitated by "Adam" and the others in turn), then we can locate a gender complementarity on the originary scene, where a specifically feminine resentment takes its place as culturally generative.

Andrew Bartlett's "Accusations of 'Playing God' and the Anthropological Idea of God" also shows how GA enters that space where moral deliberations must be open to all regardless of theological (or anti-theological) presuppositions while also spontaneously evoking the idea of or even word "God" (even for avowed secularists). Like the intersection between science and faith so far inadequately engaged by the "intelligent design" vs. evolution debate, the accusation of "playing God" directed at scientific and technological innovators draws upon what seems to be an unavoidable sense of limits that should not be transgressed that can't really be "rationally" defended but the disregard of which nevertheless the leads to the worst irrationalisms. This space is undoubtedly where the originary hypothesis is poised to make the most direct contribution to contemporary cultural discourse and Bartlett takes us through it with thoroughness, sensitivity and that ability to question all views freely without alienating any of them that seems to me characteristic of the originary thinker.

Bartlett begins with an extremely illuminating explication of Gans' "anthropological idea of God" and his goal of minimizing the difference between believers and non-believers—of placing them on the same scene, so to speak. We can, from one side, accept the secularist claim that humans created God, whose existence is therefore in some sense an "illusion"; and yet the otherwise inexplicable presence of such an "illusion" suggests "something in inherent in the use of language that makes us gullible in this way," a "something," furthermore, which does require us to conceive of the *human* use of language as uniquely human (different, for example, from all animal communication systems), as the deferral of violence through representation; it requires thinking of culture as irreducibly scenic, configured as a structure of sacred center and human periphery in the linguistic event; that configuration entails a respectful commemoration, however minimal, for the humanly necessary "God" present in it. Generative anthropology requires that respect (which, granted, is not "worship") as part of the requirement for an explanation of the origin of human language, an origin for which philosophers such as Nielsen bother not to propose any explanatory model, even as they happily use human language itself to such chastely disenchanting, relentlessly demystifying effect. (32-3)

Bartlett moves on from this indispensable articulation of what we might call an originary or minimal faith to an engaged exploration of the contemporary discourse—from philosophers, to Presidential Commissions, and the basic "grammar" of the notion—of "playing God." Through a series of "translations," or, perhaps, "successive approximations," of the phrase, Bartlett arrives at one which includes all and slights none of the relevant actors:

The scientific projector accused in this context is best described as *exercising scientific knowledge and technological skill in such a way that a majority of the human community to which the scientist belongs deeply doubts the pragmatic viability and moral wisdom of the exercise, whereas the scientist (and any minority in the community supporting him) neither feels nor expresses such doubts.* In such a case, the scientist and his party in their utter lack of doubt are *usurping the originary power which ought to belong only to God (the Being of the inaccessible center-as-such).* (65)

No special wisdom is attributed to the "majority" here; rather, Bartlett relocates the question of "playing God" from tampering with "natural" or "divine" laws or prerogatives to the unwarranted generation of resentment within the community and the desire to usurp the centrality of God, or His originary "silence" or "powerful passivity on the originary scene" (67), which is the very guarantee of the scene. To put it a little differently, the accusation represents the response to the unthinkable attempt to double or replicate (which would in actuality be to abolish) the unique human origin. Such a denial of humanity has already caused immense violence in the twentieth century and, if it once again overcomes the resentment of the majority (and, even more, carries that majority away with it), will likely generate such violence as this time we may not survive.

Chris Fleming and John O'Carroll undertake an ambitious project in their "What is the Human? Eric Gans and the Structure of the Hypothesis"—and, one which is sure to pick up fellow inquirers in direct proportion to the development of a sympathetic awareness of the hypothesis within the human sciences. Indeed, Fleming and O'Carroll's essay is precisely the kind that is needed to promote such awareness. They place GA squarely on the terrain of the epistemology of the social sciences. Originary thinking has long shown its power primarily on the "interpretative" side of the human sciences while—notwithstanding Gans' own insistence on and wide ranging demonstrations of the viability, indeed superiority of GA on the "harder" terrain of anthropology, economics, sociology and so on. Fleming and O'Carroll argue directly and effectively for the scientificity of the hypothesis (all the while keeping in mind the specificity of *this* hypothesis), taking us rigorously through each step in Gans' formulation of it: we need only assume the distinguishing mimetic character of the higher animals; we must assume an event, once we speak of an origin; representation must therefore be scenic and narrative (the event at the origin can be retold); the semiotic means through which the hypothesis can be constructed is at the same time the very thing we need to account for, and so on, down to the centrality of this striving for minimality itself:

> For Gans, it seems that minimality has a "truth" of its own. Less is, indeed, more for Gans, and in a number of ways. In one this regard, communicative efficacy has an ethical value of its own, in furnishing the conditions of a universal dialogue for the grounding of the human. It provides also an economy of expression arising from superior expression of the ground and nature of the human. But above and beyond all, it leads to a special kind of accuracy of statement. Now one might imagine that in saying this that Gans risks an enlarged empirical requirement: a date, for instance for the origin of the world. But generative anthropology is not like that; it straddles science and the humanities, but does so in a way that minimizes the risk of empirical falsification. (13)

Fleming and O'Carroll then proceed to "*situate* the Gansian hypothesis in relation to other models of argument and hypothesizing" (14). Moving through a range of positions in the philosophy of science, they settle on the work of Imre Lakatos and his post-positivist theory of the "research program." Drawing upon Lakatos' vocabulary, Fleming and O'Carroll argue that Gans' constitutes a "progressive" rather than "degenerating" program, one which supersedes and incorporates what is of value in its predecessors and competitors:

his work *does* preserve the content of preceding theories (as we saw in the case of poststructuralism, for instance, but also, more importantly, of Girard's work on mimesis and sacrifice). Crucially, it does this in a way adequate to the original theories, and yet also on its own terms (self-corroboration and the probably best explanation). Gans' approach to the human can be assessed not against an empirically irretrievable past, but against what we are continually learning about the human *today*. (19)

Fleming and O'Carroll bring us back to the specific contribution of the originary hypothesis to the human sciences, that which makes it virtually inexhaustible: a precise definition of the distinctly human, irreducible to biological predicates and yet guaranteed and clarified rather than obscured by the infinite generativity, variability and deconstructability of cultural forms.

In this context, I will briefly mention my own attempt to take up the "The Question of Originary Method: The Generative Thought Experiment." I was interested in pursing the implications of what seems to me the necessary assumption that knowledge itself is generated scenically, attached to and iterating a series of scenes leading us back to the originary one. It further follows, it seems to me, that the originary scene is never definitively closed—we are participants in the creation of the human, while that very participation paradoxically renders the origin ever more minimal, resourceful, and *prior*. The originary scene is hence our best model for the construction of knowledge (while knowledge follows the originary scene in producing ever more effective and general signs of deferral), which further means that our understanding of knowledge and the boundary separating it from the "disciplines" of ethics, esthetics, politics and others must be re-constituted in ways that contemporary discourses offer little help with—I draw upon Charles Sanders Peirce's "pragmaticism," and I look forward to seeing which other conceptual vocabularies might find their own "vocation" more fully as they converge with that of the hypothesis, as our own discipline becomes a cultural reality in its own right.

Eric Gans has provided two contributions to this volume. In "On Firstness," Gans gathers together his recent thinking on victimary discourse and White Guilt to bear on what he has come to call today's "Final Conflict" between the bearers of modernity and those of traditionalist, now radicalized, anti-modern, anti-market and increasingly anti-Semitic forces gathered, of course, under the aegis of totalitarian Islam. The concept of "firstness" may, as Gans generously acknowledges, have been introduced into GA by me, but the way in which Gans embeds it in the entire history of economic and cultural exchange—a history sharpened by today's aforementioned antagonism—is wholly his own. Those

familiar with Gans' books and his *Chronicles of Love and Resentment* will recognize here an extraordinarily compressed account of years of anthropological,
cultural and historical reflection, moving from the originary scene and the primitive, egalitarian community it founds, through the "potlatch" and the emergence
of the "Big Man" (kernel of the imperial tyrants of the ancient—and not only
ancient—world) who usurps the sacred center, through the discovery of monotheism via the (paradoxical and still scandalous) Jewish claim to have discovered the universal God, up to the risk taking producer in modern market society
(which—like every cultural advance—produces a more minimal and hence more
faithful—model of the originary scene). Firstness is the most powerful lever of
cultural generativity and simultaneously the primary motive of resentment (or,
at least, the kind of resentment that targets social forms as a whole). This tension
has revealed its greatest intensity today, as the cumulative effects of firstness are
seen by the bearers of White Guilt as unmitigated victimization:

> If modernity is defined by the substitution of market exchange for the
> Maussian system of traditional society, then postmodernism is an aspi-
> ration toward a beyond-modernity. Victimary thinking does not reject
> firstness as such; it aspires to the *originary* firstness of a renunciatory
> gesture that points the way to immediate reciprocity, while rejecting
> the firstness defined by the market as a hypocritical perversion. (6)

But,

> The moral potlatch of the sufferer from White Guilt, addressed more
> to his fellows than his Others, effects no fundamental change in the ex-
> change system. Far from provoking the "subalterns" to offer the hoped-
> for counter-gift of abandoning their resentment, this asymmetrical ges-
> ture is likely to encourage them to express it all the more. Victimary
> behavior implicitly presupposes that its renunciatory gestures will have
> no effect on the system that supports them, that the asymmetry will
> always endure. But today, by dint of repetition, the cumulative mimetic
> effect of these gestures has finally provoked an adversary determined to
> reverse this asymmetry for good. It is now clear that abandoning the
> asymmetrical firstness of the market does not lead to the renewal of
> originary reciprocity, but only to an asymmetry that is far more brutal
> and far less productive. (7)

Indeed, "GA has an important part to play in what is shaping up as a "final conflict" between liberal market society and the remnants of the Maussian

world, which in its oppositional stance acquires traits that accentuate its difference from what it opposes." (7–8).

> The Bronx romantic, like all romantics, wants to be remembered. But
> because the Bronx contains nothing memorable, he devises a theory that
> allows him to be remembered for having reduced memorability to a
> minimum. Minimization is close to Collins' useful concept of *prehu-
> miliation*. But the difference is that whereas prehumiliation reenacts (or
> "preenacts") the primordial passage from victim to divinity, minimiza-
> tion reduces the divinity/victim differential to a minimum. GA is not so
> much prehumiliated as preshrunk. The Bronx romantic seeks recogni-
> tion for providing the least obtrusive mediation between the personal
> imageries of others. (146)

Gans' "Generative Anthropology and Bronx Romanticism" stands out in
this volume. As the autobiography of a minimal concept it would ideally be
referred to in the most indirect way, in the course of constituting another absolutely unique locus of identity, which is in turn to reverberate historically in
unpredictable and yet unmistakable ways. To return to "On Firstness," "One
responds to an innovation not by duplicating it but by innovating in turn" (9).
Back to "Bronx Romanticism": "Some moments of historical space-time are
privileged" (1), but only insofar as they reveal the means and provide the motive
for accentuating and thereby producing the privilege of that track of time and
absenting oneself from it so that it becomes a "mediation between the personal
imageries of others."

This articulation of self-centering and ascesis is a universally accessible
cultural stance, but on the condition, it seems to me, that one takes up the
"amateurism" that Gans here associates with the indefinite deferral of the exit
from adolescence: "[t]he Bronx Romantic is drawn to amateurism because he
preserves the most radical Romantic intuition: that life is adolescence and maturity is death. In order to remain at the originary center, he must remain vigilant
toward the seductions of professional life" (9). My own experience of originary
thought has been one of "growing up," of acknowledging for the first time an
obligation to the center; at the same time, though, GA's recognition of the essential contingency of that center disabuses one of the illusion of the legitimacy
of those who claim to have (or know how to get) things "under control" in favor
of a reliance upon good-faith improvisations, allergic reactions to any resentment that seeks to leave its rightful orbit, free experimentation in "stanceless-
ness" and a belief in the accessibility of something we must ultimately call, in

all its protean nature, "reality." At any rate, I will leave the last words to Gans, his own concluding words, which perhaps help to explain why after a quarter-century the originary hypothesis has met with little success on the marketplace it does more to valorize than any other theory to be found on it; and why we might still legitimately hope for such success, as long as that's not quite what we are hoping for:

> The true amateur never sells his soul to the crowd, above all to his pro-fessional crowd. He theorizes the operations of the collective and the sacrificial with all the generosity of which he is capable, but he forbears to tailor his ideas to the fluctuations of the intellectual marketplace. The more we respect the market as the determiner of value, the more vigilantly we must resist its judgment as to our understanding of it. The truth of the market at any given moment is never what the market at that moment wants to hear.

> The power of the Romantic attitude lies in permitting us to assimilate the contours of our individual life to the originary unity of the human. This is a unity that remains virtual and can never be fully actualized. Darwinians who propose a unitary explanation of the human within the confines of their field, be it sociobiology or evolutionary psycholo-gy, inevitably fail to grasp the paradox inherent in reducing the human invention/discovery of the transcendent realm of the sign to the model of natural adaptation. But the Bronx Romantic remains faithful to the intuition that if one is to understand how humanity and its culture might have come into being, one must not stray far from the central singularity from which all roads diverge. (9)

Notes

1. Gans' discussions of White Guilt have been conducted in his *Chronicles of Love and Resentment* on the *Anthropoetics* website. See White Guilt I (http://www.anthropoetics.ucla.edu/views/vw310.htm); White Guilt II (http://www.anthropoetics.ucla.edu/views/vw311.htm); White Guilt III: Democracy and Firstness (http://www.anthropoetics.ucla.edu/views/vw313.htm); White Guilt IV: Auschwitz and Hiroshima (http://www.anthropoetics.ucla.edu/views/vw316.htm); and White Guilt V: The Vietnam Syndrome (http://www.anthropoetics.ucla.edu/views/vw320.htm) and Ending White Guilt (http://www.anthropoetics.ucla.edu/views/vw337.htm).
2. The best introduction to Gans' understanding of the historical role of the market in terms of the originary hypothesis is perhaps his essay included as Chapter One of this volume.
3. Like his discussions of White Guilt, Gans' analyses of terrorism, Islam and our post-9/11 environment will be found in his Chronicles. To mention just a few: "Antisemitism and Anti-Americanism" (http://www.anthropoetics.ucla.edu/views/vw279.htm); "The New Antisemitism and the Bankruptcy of Victimary Thought" (http://www.anthropoetics.ucla.edu/views/vw290.htm); "Affirmation of Life III: Originary Analysis of Terrorism" (http://www.anthropoetics.ucla.edu/views/vw293.htm); and, most recently, "The Final Conflict" (http://www.anthropoetics.ucla.edu/views/vw338.htm).
4. I am relying here upon a recent *Chronicle*, "Originary Guilt," No. 333, April 15, 2006. (http://www.anthropoetics.ucla.edu/views/vw333.htm)
5. Again, see Chapter One of this Volume.
6. The name of God given in the Mosaic revelation, "ehyeh asher ehyeh," "breaks through the confining symmetry of resentment. It is no longer a matter of replacing the Egyptian gods by another god, even if he be unique, but of substituting for the center closed by the rival Other an open center that is a pure locus of presence." The declarative sentence "neither designates a particular center like the ostensive, nor attempts, like the imperative, to reconstitute it. The declarative does not refer directly to the world; it constructs a model of the world on the internal scene of representation that all men have inherited from the originary event. The God whose 'name' is a declarative sentence makes himself accessible only as spirit" (*Science and Faith* 62-3).
7. "GA and the Linguistic Turn," No. 334, April 22, 2006. (http://www.anthropoetics.ucla.edu/views/vw334.htm)
8. *Originary Thinking*, 166.
9. See *Signs of Paradox*, 75-91.
10. For some of the places where Gans discusses and defends his hypothesis, *Science and Faith*, 3-5; *Originary Thinking*, 7-9; *Signs of Paradox*, 15-29; *The End of Culture*, 19-21; and his very helpful introduction to Generative Anthropology at http://www.anthropoetics.ucla.edu/gaintro.htm. For a discussion of originary analysis, see *Originary Thinking*, 7-9, and the "Introduction" to *Signs of Paradox*. Quite a few of

his *Chronicles of Love & Resentment* are worth looking at in this regard—see, for example, Chronicles 283 "What's New and Old About the Origin of Language (I)" (http://www.anthropoetics.ucla.edu/views/vw283.htm) and 284 "What's New and Old About the Origin of Language (II)" (http://www.anthropoetics.ucla.edu/views/vw284.htm).

11. See Gans' "The Sacred and the Social: Defining Durkheim's Anthropological Legacy."

12. I leave out of consideration various possible "mixtures"—for example, perhaps the most common approach, which is to make peace with provisional, pragmatic myths of origin, in the name of some moral or political intuition (say, the queer historian who considers the Stonewall Revolt such a myth of origin, but accepts this as a site of cultural productivity). I do so because the next question, how do you account for the moral or political intuition leading you to make peace with this "constituent hypocrisy" leads us back into the same alternatives I have been exploring. I also don't address the objection that we can't "prove" any hypothesis, because once we admit the legitimacy of hypothesizing, which we have done once we accept that some event or series of events lies behind our moral and cognitive intuitions, we cannot put a "cap" on that inquiry and can furthermore work on distinguishing stronger from weaker hypotheses.

13. See his Chronicle of Love & Resentment 253 (December 22, 2001), "Post-Millennial Thoughts" (http://www.anthropoetics.ucla.edu/views/vw253.htm).

14. "GA and Mimetic Theory II: The Scapegoat" (No. 332, March 18, 2006), (http://www.anthropoetics.ucla.edu/views/vw332.htm).

15. See Girard's *The Scapegoat*, especially Chapter Two, "Stereotypes of Persecution."

16. I take up these questions in my forthcoming "Originary Political Thinking and Commonsense Sacrality."

Works Cited

Arendt, Hannah. *The Life of the Mind.* San Diego*New York*London: Harcourt Brace & Company. 1978.

Gans, Eric. "The Sacred and the Social: Defining Durkheim's Anthropological Legacy." Anthropoetics VI, no. 1 Spring/Summer 2000. (On-line)

———. *Signs of Paradox: Irony, Resentment, and Other Mimetic Structures.* Stanford, CA: Stanford University Press, 1997.

———. *Originary Thinking. Elements of a Generative Anthropology.* Stanford, CA: Stanford University Press, 1993.

———. *Science and Faith: The Anthropology of Revelation.* Savage, MD: Rowman & Littlefield Publishers, Inc., 1990.

———. *The End of Culture: Toward a Generative Anthropology.* Berkeley*Los Angeles*London: University of California Press, 1985.

Girard, Rene. *The Scapegoat.* Translated by Yvonne Freccero. Baltimore: The John Hopkins University Press, 1986.

Hayek, F.A. *The Fatal Conceit: The Errors of Socialism. The Collected Works of F.A. Hayek, Volume 1.* Edited by W.W. Bartley, III. Chicago: The University of Chicago Press, 1988.

On Firstness

Eric Gans

The semantician, and California Senator, S. I. Hayakawa belonged to a school of thought according to which all our conflicts stemmed from a lack of clear definitions. As opposed to those who, like Habermas, put their faith in *dialogue*, for *General Semantics* it was sufficient to construct a good dictionary once and for all and stick to it. Before we laugh at the naïveté of this perspective, we should reflect that it is not all that different from the practice of Plato/Socrates, for whom to define the Good is simultaneously to affirm its existence; similar too is the reasoning of Anselm's "ontological proof." What is implicit in this mode of reasoning is that the universal agreement about words characteristic of language is in itself the content of the word whose definition is being sought. If we all share the word "Good" then we all share the "same" idea of the good, and that sharing is the good itself. Socrates' argument against Callicles in the *Gorgias* is specious as a piece of logical reasoning, but it makes sense as a piece of *anthropological* reasoning: if we share on the meaning of a sign, that proves that at some point, the violence of our conflicting desires was deferred by a sign, and therefore that the conflict of these desires can in principle always be so deferred; to share the Idea of the Good is proof that this Good—the deferral of violence—exists.

What then of the vocabulary of generative anthropology (GA), which seeks to describe this originary event itself? From the standpoint of GA, the existence of *any* Idea affords the same demonstration of shared meaning as Plato's Good, with the proviso that the Good, or Anselm's God, are ideas that sum up the whole process and that, in the absence of an originary hypothesis that specifically affirms the reality of the originary event, serve to affirm its existence. Once the hypothesis has been formulated, however, we can examine the event more closely, even to the extent of including in our descriptive vocabulary elements of potential negativity that, taken by themselves, would appear to pose a danger to the event's positive outcome.

Such a concept is that of *firstness*, borrowed from the vocabulary of the American philosopher Charles Peirce and first applied to GA by Adam Katz. Unlike the Good, firstness is asymmetrical. We can all share in the Good, but we cannot all share in firstness; if I am first, you can at best be second. Thus implicit in the notion of firstness is the generation of *resentment*, which is precisely what the constructions of human culture have as their purpose to avoid. Yet by including the element of firstness in our minimal originary hypothesis, we strengthen the conceptual arsenal with which we seek to defend the historical reality of the human scene against the nihilism that affects to deny its validity. The ethical value of this operation is to affirm the unity of our species not in a celebratory mode, but minimally, as the descendents of beings who risked self-destruction through the ever-present possibility of mimetic violence, too powerful for pre-human social mechanisms to control, and which the human came into existence to prevent, or more precisely, to *defer*. It is by understanding and applying the concepts by means of which violence was deferred at the origin of our species that we have the best chance of deferring violence today.

In my earlier formulations of the originary scene I had not thought of specifying the individual who would *first* have had the idea of aborting his appropriative gesture and transforming it into a sign. However, Katz showed that we must hypothesize such a figure in order to maintain the minimality of the scene; to postulate that all participants acted "as one man" is clearly less parsimonious than to assume that a single individual took the initiative and that the others followed him. (Before the first aborted gesture "took" as a sign within the group, we may presume that countless similar situations ended in bloodshed.) Firstness fills an important lacuna in the elaboration of the "moral model" of reciprocal communication postulated by the originary hypothesis. Without firstness, the unanimity of the originary scene would appear to be devoid of real or even potential conflict, and as a result, *originary analysis*, which seeks the germ of a given human institution in the founding event, would appear to trace everything back to a moment, however ephemeral, of Edenic harmony. Firstness introduces into our model of the scene the internal time of the constitution/imposition of the sign, a time of potential mimetic conflict that we encounter in every subsequent event in the struggle to impose the new sign that—always temporarily—defers violence. In particular, and it is in this context that Katz formulated his modified hypothesis, the introduction of firstness provides a particular insight into the *political* scene, which we may define as constituted by the group's agreement in principle that it is necessary to act before it is known what action to undertake. The political choice between two or several alternatives, like the speaker's paradigmatic choice among two or more morphemes, derives from an originary choice where the sign was the sole well-defined alternative, the other being the mere absence of sign and sense, the return to the crisis that the sign alone could resolve.

In the originary scene and afterward, firstness attaches to the one who by first renouncing his desire inaugurates the becoming-meaningful of its object.

In the originary scene, the *first* begins the process of conversion whereby the aborted gesture of appropriation becomes the first sign. The asymmetry of originary firstness thus leads to the "equal" distribution of the central object of desire. In his seminal work, *Essai sur le don* (1923–24), Marcel Mauss describes the manner in which the reciprocity of the originary scene is extended to life as a whole in traditional society. If I give you something, whether it be a jewel, a banquet, or a girl in marriage, I do not expect an immediate counter-gift; on the contrary, to respond immediately would be a serious gaffe. The exchanges of our social life have remained Maussian: if you invite me to dinner this evening, you will find it odd if I invite you back tomorrow, and offensive if I offer you payment — but not if I bring you a propitiary bottle of wine. A society in which — outside the major rituals by which the community reconstitutes itself — gift-giving constitutes the entirety of the system of exchange exists permanently on a "virtual" originary scene where interaction takes place in slow motion; as one prestation leads to another, each person perseveres in the faith that he will eventually receive his due. A Maussian exchange is not, however, as the terms *gift* and *counter-gift* might seem to suggest, simply a postponed *transaction* in which the second offering cancels the debt created by the first one:

> When a Baruya (lineage) gives a woman and accepts another in exchange, both parties are not quits, their reciprocal debts are not cancelled. They balance each other and constitute the justification of numerous exchanges of property and services . . . By giving one creates an obligation in the other, by accepting one becomes in turn the giver's debtor. (Maurice Godelier, *Métamorphoses de la parenté*, Fayard, 2004, p. 70; my translation)

This absence of final closure must be understood as a consequence of the persistence of the founding scene; exchange extends to infinity because the real creditor of the "debt" contracted at every stage of the process is the sacred center rather than the gift's nominal recipient. Like the first participant in the originary scene, the author of the gift abandons the object in the name of the community; as a result, his partner owes the community a similar renunciation. What keeps the account of this debt is a *representation* of the object received, which is of the same order as the sign that allowed the originary community to defer possession of the sacred object.

This structure in permanent disequilibrium lacks the means to defend itself against the eventual usurpation of the center by the Big Man, who gives without the possibility of a symmetrical return. The implicit instability of this exchange system is revealed in the phenomenon of the *potlatch,* the analysis of which occupies a good portion of Mauss' little book. The man who possesses a surplus no longer seeks to return to equilibrium but to triumph by excess: my gift is so great that your counter-gift must be postponed for eternity, and at the limit — in true hierarchical societies — to offer a counter-gift is simply unthinkable. Originary equality is unstable because there is no obstacle inherent in the scene that can prevent the firstness that precedes this equality from persisting indefinitely. Insofar as it has a real locus in the world, the sacred center is not invulnerable to usurpation; the opposition between center and periphery remains absolute only in the ontological separation between the sign and the reality to which it refers. Because premodern society is constructed around a mode of exchange that never leaves the originary scene, it cannot prevent this scene from "evolving." But by the same token, because this evolution remains within the framework of the originary scene, the economic development that creates the surplus supports a "naïve" hierarchy in which economic power is directly linked to the sacred, so that nothing prevents the sovereign who occupies the state's redistributive center from presenting himself as a god.

From Mauss to Adam Smith

The subsequent evolution that leads to the market system characteristic of the modern age is too complex to be described here, but we must note a crucial stage: the Hebrews' invention/discovery of *monotheism.* The unique resentment that we call *antisemitism* attaches to the Hebrews' firstness in making "their" god the universal God. The unique divinity who occupies the center in relation to the entire human periphery, who names himself in Exodus 3 with a declarative sentence (*ehyeh asher ehyeh,* "I am that I am") rather than by an appellation to be called on, guarantees that even the most powerful king cannot claim to incarnate the sacred. But to deprive all men of incarnate divinity is tantamount to saying that the sacred resides in their "soul," which we can define without theology as the faculty of using signs. Christianity is not simply implicit in Judaism, but it is a natural development of it; since monotheism puts within reach of all the ideal of reciprocal exchange that is the moral intuition of the originary scene, we discover that we all bear within us the equalitarian moral model of this scene and that even the most extreme resentment generated by hierarchical society cannot efface it. The power of the cross is the persistence of the voice that announces the "good news," seemingly subversive of the social hierarchy but in the final analysis, its implicit guarantee: we are all equally bearers of the primordial moral intuition—as Girard said to me one day, "we all are sons of God."

Yet the certainty that each inherits from his culture and bears within him as a template the moral as well as the semiotic configuration of the originary scene makes possible the birth of a new exchange system that will eventually replace the one described by Mauss: the market system that defines modernity. What is new is that the commercial transaction is no longer an extension of the originary scene, but a minimal model of it. Instead of giving and counter-giving on a virtual scene whose temporality extends in principle to eternity, one gives and the other counter-gives *at the same time*, whereupon the transaction is complete. Each one abandons a thing in order to acquire another thing he considers more advantageous. But market exchange is not as a general rule symmetrical. One of the "things" exchanged is normally a more or less nonconsumable *medium of exchange* that confers a value on the other. We recall that in the system of gift/counter-gift the recipient's debt exists only in the form of a sign that recognizes a debt not to the other but to the sacred center. Money is the concrete realization of this sign of recognition; it bears a "meaning" but as opposed to the ordinary sign, it is a credit drawn on the sacred that cannot be freely reproduced. The scene of a transaction dissolves instantly because money allows the "gift's" recipient to pay his debt at once. In contrast, to barter one thing for another is to give and receive twice, incurring two debts that must annul each other. As Mauss points out, barter, although for common sense the most primitive form of exchange, is never its normal mode even in pre-monetary societies.

In market exchange, one typically exchanges a universal medium of exchange for a specific product chosen among many others. The firstness inherent in the process of production, in which the producer must renounce his own desire in order to satisfy the desire of his future customer, is revealed in the act of exchange. Unlike Maussian exchange, where (outside the potlatch competition) the firstness of the original gift has no permanent status but is answered with a new initiative that results in an indefinitely prolonged chain of "first" gestures, market exchange maintains a permanent distinction between production and consumption, creating a permanent asymmetry between the consumer and the producer. In the world described by Adam Smith, each finds it beneficial to produce what brings him the most profit, but the individual typically manifests his firstness as a producer within the context of a *firm* where he is not in the general case the leading figure. The emergence of "consumer society" with the maturing of market exchange does not modify the production-consumption distinction so much as *supplement* it; it makes consumption itself a "productive" activity that enforces what Jean Baudrillard calls the *discipline* of the modern consumer, the sum of whose purchases constitute a representation of a personal aesthetic that serves as a potlatch-like gift to his milieu. Yet the discipline by which one consumer demonstrates his firstness among others does not make him for all that the equal of the producer, whose marketable commodity is the prior result of the deferral of his desire in productive labor. The consumer who buys is obliged to affirm the producer's firstness; the market gives no assurance that he will do so without resentment. When we hear the recriminations that accompany an increase in the price of a gallon of gasoline, what shall we say of whole societies who reject the aesthetic of consumption and experience the "global" market as an enemy force?

The Misunderstood Holocaust

One cannot deny that a serious crisis of confidence — a loss of faith in the modern version of firstness — has prevailed in recent years within Western society. This loss of faith is especially visible in Europe, where it is reflected in a demographic deficit that is rapidly depopulating many European ethnic groups—a collective suicide occurring for the first time in history in the absence of famine or plague. This crisis may be traced back to the historical singularity that inaugurated a new era, moral as well as aesthetic: the Holocaust. The single-minded energy the Nazis devoted to this operation, often at the expense of military efficiency, shows that the Final Solution was not an "ordinary" genocide such as often occur in civil wars when one side gets the upper hand, as in Bosnia or Rwanda a few years ago, or in Darfur today. Given the absolute weakness of the Jews vis-à-vis German power, the antisemitic fear that motivated the Nazis seems incomprehensible. However, and it is here that this critical event is still misunderstood, the Holocaust cannot be reduced to the massacre of the "weak" by the "strong," even if one pins on the "weak" the label of "scapegoat." What the Nazis wanted to destroy in the Jews — with a historical nuance I will specify shortly — was the *firstness* of the inventors/discoverers of the One God who presides over the destinies of the "Abrahamic" religious family. Nazism was a consequent attempt, unique in history, to carry out systematically the antisemite's dream of a *judenfrei* world. When resentment leads to the systematic destruction of the sole object that gives it meaning, it has gone beyond the realm of possibility; by such an act this entire realm is reconfigured.

The postmodern era's historical "misinterpretation" of the Holocaust in victimary terms was not entirely disastrous. The victimary reading of the

Holocaust and more generally of the racism of the Axis powers precipitated the liberation of the European colonies, the abolition of racial segregation in the United States, and a generation later, the end of South-African apartheid, not to speak of numerous movements favoring other liberations — women, homosexuals, the handicapped, animals, the environment.... From the point of view of peoples or minorities who had been relegated to inferior status, the victimary model was an eternal but suppressed human truth that the horrors of the war had made too evident to continue to be ignored by Western consciousness. However, because the limited truth conveyed by this model does not touch on the Holocaust's core moral lesson, it predictably ended by turning into its opposite, as we observe in the current renewal of antisemitism, of largely but not exclusively Muslim inspiration. The *jihadis* at least know why they hate the Jews, and it is surely not because they are "weak." If today anti-Americanism has become amalgamated with the old antisemitism in a generalized hostility to the US-Israel axis, still largely imaginary but increasingly made real by the two countries' common enemies and false friends, this may once again be explained by a resentment of firstness that amalgamates the historico-religious and the politico-economic.

Since the beginnings of modern market society there has existed the obscure intuition of a bond between the religious firstness of the Jews and the market system. One can go so far as to say that it is the evocation of this bond that *defines* the modern form of antisemitism, inspiring its nineteenth-century adepts to invent a new term to designate this ancient phenomenon. The Nazis resented the firstness of the Jews more in the context of the market that in that of religion. Marx and Hitler were united in their hostility towards the market system, which both considered a fundamentally Jewish phenomenon. In this sense, despite all that separates them, both merit the title of "Socialist."

The identification of the Jews as the secret masters of the modern exchange system is only secondarily related to their former mediating activity in the exchanges between states in the early modern era; the causal link may even run in the other direction. In a market where each freely seeks his interest through the exchange of values, the system as a whole possesses more intelligence about these values than any individual participant and is therefore analogous to the divine Subject of the originary scene. Those economic agents who succeed better than their fellows appear to have *first knowledge* of the will of the Subject of the market; as in a Ponzi scheme, the latecomers are dupes who furnish the profit realized by the early arrivals. The continued proliferation of the century-old *Protocols of the Elders of Zion*, a work taught in schools throughout the Middle East, shows the power of this analogy in all its insane logic: those who were first to worship the universal god are necessarily first at the altar of the Subject of the market. Marx's *On the Jewish Question* says nothing else: the Jews, the "chosen people" of the abstract and universal God, are also the elect of the abstract and universal god of the market, *Money.*

Because the Jews of Auschwitz were, perhaps inevitably, understood as simple victims rather than as martyrs of *firstness,* the world's revulsion at the Holocaust did not rid it of antisemitism. If generative anthropology allows us to correct this misunderstanding, it is because it has been able to draw conclusions from postmodern history, the most important of which is undoubtedly the impossibility of creating or even conceiving in any concrete sense the resentment-free post-market social order called "socialism." From now on we are certain that no economic *Aufhebung* will transcend the market's "contradictions," even as we hope that the open economic market will generate an open political market.

Postmodern Romanticism

Postmodern victimary thinking differs from originary anthropology by its utopian refusal to accept the modern form of firstness. The term *postmodern* tends to be used within an exclusively aesthetic framework, when it should be understood literally. If modernity is defined by the substitution of market exchange for the Maussian system of traditional society, then postmodernism is an aspiration toward a beyond-modernity. Victimary thinking does not reject firstness as such; it aspires to the *originary* firstness of a renunciatory gesture that points the way to immediate reciprocity, while rejecting the firstness defined by the market as a hypocritical perversion. The capitalist renounces immediate satisfaction; but the capital whose consumption is deferred is augmented by profits reaped from the consumption that others will not or cannot defer. The Holocaust is only the final proof of the inequity of the asymmetrical market transaction. In contrast, the victimary gesture of renunciation seeks no personal material advantage. By symbolically renouncing my privileged status in the modern marketplace, I act so as to fulfill and thereby eliminate the resentment of the non-privileged. But this victimary "gift" that presents itself as a gesture of pure generosity is nothing other than a moral potlatch.

Victimary thinking is a latter-day variant of romanticism, which has from the outset denounced the bourgeois exchange system and its allegedly disastrous consequences for the "natural" order. This tie to romanticism sheds light not only on postmodernism's bond with environmentalism but on its connection, at first unsuspected but increasingly overt, to antisemitism. The victimary thinker dreams of emulating the renunciatory gesture of the originary scene in order to purge himself of *White Guilt*, the counterpart in the "victimizer" of the resentment of real or supposed victims. "White Guilt" refers only contingently to skin color; it is the guilt of the *unmarked*, of the non-minority, the non-victim — the WASP in a world of ethnics, the European (or Euro-American) in a world of Africans and Asians. As long as we have not renounced our privilege of non-markedness, we risk incurring the resentment of our victimized Others. White Guilt takes the initiative by adopting this resentment against ourselves. As if to illustrate how far White Guilt can be carried, British subject Andrew Hawkins recently presented himself on his knees in chains before an African crowd at Banjul, Gambia to implore the nation's vice-president to absolve him for the acts of a remote slaveholding ancestor.

For the bearer of White Guilt, the fact that this sort of renunciation is primarily symbolic rather than material is not a sign of hypocrisy but of authenticity. As in the beginning, reciprocity is initially manifested by the equal exchange of signs; the fact that today such symbolic gestures are predicated on the continued existence of the market system is ignored. The symbolic return to the origin confers on this self-accusing behavior a moral superiority to the current system at the same time as its situation within the framework of originary firstness protects it from the charge of seeking any permanent asymmetry for oneself. In the originary event, he who first converts his gesture of appropriation into a sign acts before the others without affirming any superiority to them; he is simply more afraid than they of mimetic conflict, whether or not he is the group's former *alpha*, as in the murder scenario in Freud's *Totem and Taboo*.

It goes without saying that a symbolic gesture of renunciation does not restore originary equality. The moral potlatch of the sufferer from White Guilt, addressed more to his fellows than his Others, effects no fundamental change in the exchange system. Far from provoking the "subalterns" to offer the hoped-for counter-gift of abandoning their resentment, this asymmetrical gesture is likely to encourage them to express it all the more. Victimary behavior implicitly presupposes that its renunciatory gestures will have no effect on the system that supports them, that the asymmetry will always endure. But today, by dint of repetition, the cumulative mimetic effect of these gestures has finally provoked an adversary determined to reverse this asymmetry for good. It is now clear that abandoning the asymmetrical firstness of the market does not lead to the renewal of originary reciprocity, but only to an asymmetry that is far more brutal and far less productive.

Firstness Today

The introduction of firstness into the conceptual vocabulary of GA goes far to clarify the issues raised at the outset concerning GA's place in its historical epoch and the "solutions" it offers to the problems of our time. As is clear from much of my own writing since 9/11, I believe that GA has an important part to play in what is shaping up as a "final conflict" between liberal market society and the remnants of the Maussian world, which in its oppositional stance acquires traits that accentuate its difference from what it opposes. The violence, implacable hatred, and fanatical intolerance that characterize our jihadist enemy are not so much inherent necessities of the traditional social order as possibilities latent within it that serve as advertisements for its distinction from the liberal social model it opposes. It is these sociopathic traits that radical Islam uses to recruit its followers. Nor should their passive appeal to the Muslim "silent majority" be underestimated. Ahmadinejad's apocalyptic ravings at the 56-nation Organization of the Islamic Conference in August 2006 were received with applause, as was Mahathir's somewhat less violent antisemitic diatribe at the Tenth Islamic Summit Conference in October 2003. One awaits in vain any repudiation of this venomous rhetoric from these supposedly representative Islamic groups. The silence of the representatives of "mainstream" Islam is symmetrical with the tacit "no enemies on the left" reticence of American academics to speak out against even the most hysterical anti-Westernism, just as the resentment of the marked is symmetrical with the White Guilt of the unmarked.

The underlying truth that drives victimary thinking is the universal human value of reciprocity, as embodied in the "moral model" of reciprocal exchange inaugurated by the exchange of signs in the originary event, a model we intuitively apply to all human interaction and for which linguistic exchange serves as a reminder. However one may justify a lack of reciprocity, every human being who is subjected to it will experience resentment, deferred compensatory violence. GA conceives of no apocalyptic end to resentment; the most we can hope for is to recycle its energy in productive activity by competing with a more successful rival in the marketplace rather than seeking to destroy him. Whereas the model of victimary oppression ignores social and economic productivity and holds up to any given inequality the touchstone of universal reciprocity in a utopian vision of the originary scene, our analysis of the function of firstness in the originary hypothesis allows us to interpret asymmetrical relations as *deferred reciprocity*. This model extends Maussian exchange beyond the social-welfare implications that Mauss, himself a good socialist, develops in his final chapter, to encompass the dynamic of historical evolution. The notion of firstness does not provide a blanket endorsement of social inequality; for an asymmetry to exemplify firstness, it must indeed be a *going first* that others may follow. The fact that it is not always possible to separate in advance genuine firstness from oppression or exploitation obliges us to judge each example on its merits.

The critique of modernity from the standpoint of the Maussian exchange of traditional society is that the market transaction abjures its broader social function, in which the firstness of the gift provides the recipient with an opportunity to advance in turn a firstness of his own. In this view, the asymmetries of market society are examples not of firstness but of victimization. This argument is not merely academic; since 9/11 it is being made forcefully and persistently "on the ground." GA's response is that because all human exchange is derived from the same model, originary firstness is not abolished in market society but transformed into a creative dynamic that transcends traditional society's alternative of the unchanging symmetry of the gift or the wasteful sacrifice of the potlatch. One responds to an innovation not by duplicating it but by innovating in turn.

Firstness and resentment may be seen as the symmetrical engines of history, moments of imbalance around an ever-deferred reciprocity. The "first" have always been resented, but only since the end of World War II have we come to listen directly to the voice of resentment, which had previously reached us filtered through cultural mediations. Now that we are no longer lulled by the dream of "transcending" the market, we risk being persuaded by this guilt-producing voice into viewing our advantages in the global economy as traces of past inequities rather than as resources for future reciprocity.

It is ultimately Europe's and our own misunderstanding of the Holocaust — of our own history — that has made us vulnerable to *jihad*. Only by accepting the necessity of firstness in our exchange system can we deal with the resentment it generates. Our enemies' murderous nihilism should awaken us to the urgent need to reject the victimary guilt this misunderstanding has engendered. We cannot afford to compromise with those who, more radical even than Hitler, intend not only to destroy "the first" but to erase from the earth the system that enables them to be so. There is a propaganda war to be won through demonstrating that there is no possible return from the modern exchange system, that it is not only vastly more productive economically — of public health as well as prosperity — but its ethic is far closer than that of resentment-filled traditionalism to the originary moral ideal. But before we can even think of winning the war for the "hearts and minds" of the developing world, we have to win the war in our own. It will be too late to recall nostalgically the joys and freedoms of the modern world after they have been destroyed.

If this victory is to be more than rhetorical, we, meaning the members of the academic *intelligentsia* who are the probable readers of this essay, must take seriously the task of articulating both the necessity of firstness and the problems posed by the resentment it invariably arouses. Because we are scholars first and persons of action second, our primary task is to examine the ways in which firstness, understood and misunderstood, is articulated in our institutions, not simply with the purpose of combating White Guilt and victimary resentment, but with an eye to possible avenues of reconciliation. We are indeed all heirs of the originary event, and the always-available possibility of dialogue is a result of this heritage. But the mere call for "dialogue" cannot suffice to bring enemies together productively. The rhetoric of resentment is by definition incoherent; the violence of its condemnations reflects its inability to admit to its dependency on what it attacks. The originary hypothesis offers the sole "neutral" ground, prior to any historical divisions, on which the analysis of this rhetoric may be carried out. Muslims and Jews may fight over the heritage of Abraham, but there is nothing they cannot share in the heritage of the originary scene.

The insights provided by the originary hypothesis have just begun to be applied to the cultural institutions that are ever more in need of them. It is when human beings seem to have the least in common that they most need to be reminded of the minimal core of humanity that we all share, the source of our hope that the violence that yet again threatens to destroy us may be yet again deferred.

Originary Aesthetics and the End of Postmodernism

Raoul Eshelman

One of the most exciting aspects of the originary aesthetics proposed by Eric Gans in his Generative Anthropology (GA) is that it allows an affirmative approach to the new epoch that is unfolding around us right now. As of this writing, in fact, GA is the only theoretical direction to have brought forth names and substantial definitions for the epoch after postmodernism: Gans's "postmillennialism" and my own "performatism."[1] Mainstream cultural criticism, by contrast, is caught in a vicious circle. Although the vast majority of academic critics realize on some level that both poststructuralism and postmodernism have run their course, they can react to this situation in only one way: by engaging in *still another* round of critical reflection that both places in doubt and reifies the original poststructuralist and/or postmodern point of departure. For this reason no counterproposal to Gans's and my own epochal designations has appeared from the poststructuralist camp and, indeed, none is to be expected. The posthistorical answer to the crisis of posthistoricism is to produce even more posthistorical criticism.[2] In the future, though, critics and students will be faced with an increasingly one-sided choice. Either they can continue to engage in an endless, increasingly sterile cycle of reflection on a no-longer operative aesthetic or they can turn to theories that share the semiotic monism, performative intuition, and set to transcendence that are typical of the new cultural turn. Among these new monist theories (which include Peter Sloterdijk's spherology and Jean-Luc Marion's phenomenology of givenness[3]), the originary aesthetics of GA has emerged as one of the most productive and versatile means of describing the sweeping paradigm shift that is now going on in world culture.

In the following remarks, I would like to outline briefly how GA's originary aesthetics differs from poststructuralism and postmodernism and how it can be used to break out of the posthistorical mindset that still hobbles most contemporary criticism.

Originary Aesthetics, Performance, and Intuition

One of the crucial features of the originary scene as described by Gans is that it necessarily includes an aesthetic moment. Given GA's postmetaphysical and minimalist pretensions this might at first seem odd. Traditional philosophical aesthetics — the study of the beautiful — involves the elaborate, after-the-fact definition of what is supposed to be an essential, self-revealing quality. In the twentieth century, the obvious normative and empirical problems accompanying this endeavor led to the disappearance of aesthetics as a discrete branch of philosophy. Similarly, in today's poststructuralism the discussion of beauty is possible only within the bounds of an ideological or deconstructive critique exposing its instrumental, derivative nature.[4] How, then, is an aesthetics possible that does not repeat the old metaphysical patterns or deflate under the first deconstructive reading *sous rature*?

It is important to emphasize that the aesthetic moment is intrinsic to the originary scene and does not arise belatedly, in the course of the more complex cultural development following the original discovery of language, the sacred, and the human. Let us quickly recall some of the basic features of the originary scene. In that scene, two rivalrous protohumans vying for a desired object abort their striving for that object when one protohuman intuitively emits a sound standing for the object and the other protohuman intuitively accepts it. The result is an *ostensive sign* — a sign that does not just represent a present object, but also consummates a *performance* or *event* enabling the two opponents to temporarily defer their strife by acknowledging a common sign representing the desired object. This strife can never be completely resolved, since the sign can never actually replace the object it represents. Accordingly, the originary scene, although temporarily pacifying the conflict, is always marked by mutual resentment and by an always unresolved, eminently political tension regarding the future distribution of the contested object. This way of deferring violence through representation is uniquely human; it requires a shared intuitive consciousness of the sign's representational power that no animal has been shown to possess. Because this originary intuition is so overwhelming the first two humans are themselves incapable of reflecting on the origin of their own performance; instead, they ascribe it a transcendent origin that Gans calls the Name-of-God. This originary act of belief in turn paves the way for the more complex institutions of ritual and religion that try to repeat the original scene of salvation.

In linguistic terms, the first ostensive sign marks only the success of its own performance and has no meaning in the usual sense (for the simple reason that is has no semiotic point of reference outside of itself). It acts as a point of departure for the development of language in the more complex imperative and declarative modes that form the basis of most of our practical transactions.[5]

Both language and ritual are readily identifiable institutions growing directly out of the originary scene. This is not the case with aesthetics or art, which, as Gans emphasizes, can't be directly linked with any originary institution.[6] Rather than arising in the later institution of art, the aesthetic moment is tacitly present in the originary scene as a necessary and free reference back to the minimal conditions governing that scene. As Gans puts it, the aesthetic moment resides in "the oscillation between the sign representing the central object and the contemplation of the object as referred to by the sign."[7] This means that the aesthetic experience arises out of our unavoidable awareness of the mediatedness of the object by the sign. In aesthetic experience the sign appears pleasurable to us because it "evokes its object without attempting to possess it";[8] it "drowns"[9] the resentment resulting from the substitution of the sign for the thing by switching our attention back and forth between the sign itself and the thing as mediated by the sign. The first sign is neither simply an index pointing to an object (linguistic deixis) nor an arbitrarily chosen sign that has been belatedly (and erroneously) ascribed a transcendent power, but a construct that is simultaneously divine, political, and beautiful. Rather than favoring one over the other, GA makes it possible to talk about all three within a single anthropological, onto-semiological framework. Moreover, GA is postmetaphysical in the sense that it explicitly locates this framework within the bounds of a semiotically defined intuition or *Anschauung* (the originary scene centered around the ostensive sign) and not in a privileged space outside the sign system.

Given this brief summary it is now possible to distinguish GA's innovative contribution from traditional Kantian aesthetics (to which it owes a great deal[10]), from the poststructuralist critique of that aesthetics, and from structuralist functionalism.

Because of its similarities with Kantian aesthetics and its insistence on the semiotic autonomy of beauty, it could first appear that GA is highly susceptible to a deconstruction demonstrating the contingent status of what purports to be a free, privileged relation. Like Kantian aesthetics, GA's concept of beauty in regard to the originary sign confirms the validity of Kant's four classic attributes: beauty in the originary scene is there without concept, is necessary, is pleasing, and is without a purpose. This concept of beauty however originates in an originary, intuitive semiotic performance and not in a free, extra-semiotic space that has been artificially cut off from the conceptual purposiveness (*Zweckmäßigkeit*) that is a necessary feature of the semiotic system that mediates it. This, indeed, is the gist of Derrida's deconstruction of Kant's aesthetics in *The Truth in Painting*.[11] As Derrida notes, the wild tulip (the example used by Kant) is "beautiful only by not entering into [the cycle of fecundation];" it is subject to a law, but a "law without concept"[12] that "furnishes a supplement of adherence."[13] As soon as the flower is conceptualized — which is to say drawn into the supplementary semiotic order — it will be instantly stripped of all privileges assigned to it by Kant; it can be shown to be beautiful (free, without concept, without purpose etc.) only insofar as it is artificially cut off from the purposeful, conceptual signs that mediate that beauty. Similarly, Kant's notion of the human emerges not as originary, but as a belated, artificial construct that is needed to reconcile the split between free natural beauty and the necessarily normative concept of that beauty in human reason.[14] In Gans's monism, by contrast, the human, the divine, and the beautiful emerge in an intuitive stage that *precedes* the concept but is nonetheless still semiotic. This application of semiotics to the realm of intuition must be regarded as one of GA's fundamental innovations.[15]

Although the originary scene is not entirely impervious to a Neo-Nietzschean deconstructive reading, such a reading would impoverish it by reducing the emission of the first sign to a grab for power masked by a fraudulent or at best illusionary representation. At the same time, it would insist on belatedly establishing the conceptual, semantic status of the ostensive sign, which in deconstructive terms could only be understood through the emission of a second, interpretative sign transcending intuition. By contrast, GA offers a rich originary scene that does not reduce the human to the capacity to seek truth or power. Rather, it grounds language, as well as the apprehension of transcendence and beauty, in the first discrete act of human intuition.

Regarding structuralism, there is a certain superficial similarity between Gans's definition of the aesthetic as an oscillation between the referent and the sign and Roman Jakobson's poetic function, which defines the poetic, self-referential function of language as existing in an ambiguous relation to the referential one.[16] Although formally similar to the GA definition, Jakobson's concept lacks an explicit ground in an originary context. Following in the tradition of Saussure, Jakobson's well-known six-part functional scheme introduced in "Linguistics and Poetics" assumes the preexistence of a complete, hierarchically organized linguistic system that is separate from the material world to which it refers. Upon closer examination, however, it can be shown that Jakobson locates the origin of the poetic function (and, by extension, of language as a whole) in an iconic, isotopic relation in which sound is congruent with meaning and meaning with sound.[17] In this regard Jakobson can be said to continue in the Kantian tradition defining the aesthetic sign without concept, purpose, and interest.[18] Projected onto the higher level of the text, this originary iconic relation between the phonic signifier and the signified acts to hold the structure together and set it off from its context. Poststructuralism reverses this by playing up indexicality and contextuality; in the process the iconic closure prescribed by Jakobson dissipates in a chain of contiguous signifiers and the text loses its "natural" cohesion.

GA avoids the problem of choosing between index and icon by positing a performative, ostensive sign. What is important is not the sign's indexical or iconic quality but its ability to effect intuitive, shared closure vis-à-vis the represented object. This closing of the first sign at the center of the originary scene in turn has an energetic rather than a functional or epistemological basis. Because of its ability to interdict violence the sign acquires and holds a charge that prevents the participants from falling back into the previous animal state prior to representation. The result is not a structure, but a *scene* which is held together by the originary intuition that the sign can provide a relief from mimetic violence. The scene, which is rooted in intuition, is sub-semantic and does not require a totalizing signified, archiseme, or semantic gesture[19] to summarize its performance, as is the case in classical structuralism.

Whatever one happens to think of GA, it should be clear that there are three things that it is *not*. First, GA's semiotic monism stands in direct opposition to poststructuralist, neo-Saussurean semiotic dualism and cannot be assimilated back into it without an act of violence that would destroy GA entirely. GA's monism is, in other words, the irreducible, monist Other of poststructuralism and stands in direct competition with it. As with all epochal shifts, this competition ultimately will be decided on a pragmatic, and not on a purely argumentative level. Secondly, GA is not renascent structuralism. Although it shares with structuralism the concept of phenomenologically mediated closure, its concept of closure is based neither on function, nor on linguistic hierarchy, nor on an iconic concept of the sign. Finally, GA is not a naïve repetition of Kantianism, even though it reinstalls the basic tenets of Kant's aesthetic in its own discourse. If anything, GA's aesthetics can be said to overhaul Kantianism by applying semiotic analysis to intuition (*Anschauung*) and by defining beauty through the performative quality of closure rather than through the relational tendencies of the first sign (iconic or indexical, tendency towards the material or the intelligible etc.). Perhaps the most accurate way to describe GA in positive terms is as postmetaphysical, performative Kantianism. It is a Kantianism that is acutely aware of the deconstructive critique and that situates aesthetics in the movement of intuition *per formam* rather than in form or in consciousness itself.

Performatism and GA

When I first started thinking about how to apply GA to the nascent monist epoch, the major challenge that presented itself was how to think of literature in scenic, rather than in structural or discursive terms. In effect, I asked myself what the main components of the originary scene were and how they could be translated into a working analytical metalanguage. One of the biggest practical problems involved was positioning the new metalanguage vis-à-vis the terminology of poststructuralism. Here, two tactical moves seemed possible. First, I could have chosen a set of neologisms stressing both the otherness of my analytical venture and its affinity to the terminology of GA — "scenism" or "closurism" or "ostensivism" or what have you. All these locutions, however, seemed clumsy and not well suited to encouraging debate on the aesthetic particulars of the new epoch. Because of this I opted for the second route, which was to use terminology close to or overlapping with that of poststructuralism (the one thing I *didn't* want to do was to use the prefix "post" in any of my coinages; there was to be no suggestion that the new direction was yet another ironic supplement to postmodernism or poststructuralism). Because the notion of performance is, among others, crucial to the originary scene, and because the Latin root hooks up comfortably with the suffix "-ism," I settled on "performatism." Like "Symbolism," "Romanticism," or "Realism," it was designed as a buzzword meant to make a short programmatic statement about the epoch's approach to reality; its actual content had to be spelled out using more familiar concepts that would convey the innovative quality of the new monism. Although in basic agreement with Gans's notion of postmillennialism, performatism as I understand it has a narrower focus. Where Gans sets forth a critique of victimary thinking that also addresses a broad spectrum of socio-political issues,[20] the concept of performatism is restricted to describing specific literary, cinematographic, and architectural devices. As I understand it, performatism is a practical application of GA that could eventually be extended to include all of the arts.

Obviously, it is not useful to imagine the originary scene literally, as a conclave of cavemen pondering a bone in their midst. Rather, it is necessary to break the scene down into its analytical components in such a way that they can be applied to different genres and types of art. Taking the poststructuralist (Derridean) notion of framing as a promising starting point, I found it possible to describe the originary scene in terms of a *double frame*. This refers to the two charged boundaries that establish the first sign on the one hand (the inner frame) and the closure of the scene around the sign on the other (the outer frame). The inner frame or scene provides a focus for the participants that at the same time attracts them (as a safeguard against further violence) and repels them (as a sacred object, or the Name-of-God). The outer frame, for its part, marks the boundary between the first human community and its unknown other, the transcendent. In the originary scene, the inside frame is perceived as being entirely congruent with the outside frame (the transcendent, outside Other, God, is thought to have emitted the ostensive sign). In their postmodern, secularized form, the inside and outside frames are perceived as contingent and are open to a never-ending critique in all directions. The inside frame, for example, can be undercut endlessly by asking what is being concealed by the emission of the sign; the question reveals a certain truth but generates still more signs open to the same sort of critique as to what they themselves conceal in revealing.[21] Similarly, the outer frame delineating the boundaries of the human can be extended infinitely by demonstrating its contingent character; it can always be shown that it could be placed elsewhere and produce different effects.

This skeptical, playful, or subversive attitude towards framing accurately describes the situation in poststructuralism and postmodernism today.[22] Frames still seem to exert a kind of archaic fascination on the postmodern mind, but only insofar as they can be easily transgressed, shifted, undercut, or surpassed. The frame, in effect, has lost its sacral charge and become a kind of plaything for the peripatetic, skeptical, and nostalgic postmodern imagination. Although this transgressive understanding of framing still dominates academic discussion, in aesthetic terms it has lost its appeal and is slowly but surely being expunged from all works of art pretending to any sort of innovation.

The epochal turn that I call performatism is no less fixated on framing than is postmodernism. The difference is that the performatist aesthetic — as a direct reaction to postmodernism — returns the originary charge to both frames in an *artificial* process of double framing. This means that both frames are presented as being charged and congruent, as in the originary scene. However, because this "loaded" congruence can no longer be experienced spontaneously or naively, it must be imposed on the reader using expressly artificial, and often patently implausible means that force us to believe intuitively rather than to know or understand. The result stands in direct analogy to the ostensive scene described by GA: the work acts as a kind of closed scene causing the viewer to experience beauty and belief without losing an eye for the referential or "political" dimension of the scene. And, because the viewer experiences the double frame as artificial or willed by an other, unified higher consciousness, it is possible to speak of performatism as marked by the return of authoriality or aesthetic theism: the author returns as a godlike, although not entirely omniscient authority inside and outside the scene of the work. On the side of viewer response, the double frame forces upon the subject a kind of minimal subjectivity, a constricted, artificially induced unity that however succeeds in setting itself off from the discursive matrix that effaces the performance of subjectivity in postmodernism.[23]

Following the minimalist credo of GA, I have tried to set forth the basic
formula of performatism in the most parsimonious possible terms. Although
the task of describing just how this new aesthetic is asserting itself in culture
cannot take place in the framework of a single essay, it is nonetheless possible to
point out some of its typical devices. In the following brief remarks on the new
directions in which culture is headed, I would like to touch on three basic things
that I think will be especially important for charting the future development of
performatism: the representation of ostensivity, the shift to authorial or theist
narrative, and the use of centering as a thematic and argumentative device.

Applied Performatist Aesthetics

The two basic problems involved in analyzing performatist works are to
establish the boundaries of the double frame and to describe the coercive means
employed to effect closure. As noted above, the frame is a kind of aesthetic trap:
it forces the viewer or reader to focus in on the work as a whole, wondrous performance rather than to reflect ironically on how it relates to the endless regress
of an irreducibly open discursive context. By coercively imposing "inescapable"
forms on us, the frame forces us to accept the closure of the work at hand and
to suppress any logical, ideological, or epistemological doubts that we may have
about how this closure comes about. In effect, we are made to "believe" in the
aesthetic scene created by the work in spite of our better judgment.

The most radical and inescapable type of framing occurs when communication takes place entirely within the realm of the ostensive. At first, this device itself seems hardly viable. Everyday ostensive signs like "fire" or "man overboard" are restricted to relatively simple situations, and it is hard to imagine how
they could be used to organize a complex work of narrative art. Nonetheless, a
deep-rooted desire to undercut the endless regress and the dualist semiosis of
postmodernism has resulted in new kinds of aesthetic scenes that create a common intuitive consciousness of presence and transcendence entirely below the
threshold of conceptual language.

The most radical example of a purely ostensive language that I have been
able to find so far is the Czech film comedy *Skřítek* (The Elf, 2005). In terms
of its story, *Skřítek* is a rather predictable comedy about how a family father has
an affair with a younger co-worker and then returns to his wife and family. The
catch to this full-length feature film is that it contains no real language whatsoever. The characters all speak a kind of gibberish bearing no relation to any
known idiom, including Czech. This "language" — it is really a string of speeded
up and distorted sounds — can however be intuitively understood by the viewer

because it relates to conventional, familiar scenes or situations (the funnier ones include a teacher explaining the digestive system of a cow in a vocational school classroom and a teenager bugging his mother for more pocket money). This lack of a conceptual, linguistic level forces us to engage in an intuitive, rather than conceptual, interpretation of what is present on the screen. At the same time, the performance of the movie demonstrates that it is possible to communicate perfectly well using purely ostensive signs, which by definition relate to present objects on an intuitive, group level but otherwise have no meaning.

The difference between the movie and the originary scene is, of course, that in the originary scene the appearance of consciousness and the birth of language occur simultaneously and before any sort of conceptuality whatsoever; this simultaneity is experienced as a respite from mimetic conflict as well as an act of beauty and of transcendence. Obviously, when watching the movie we are already tacitly familiar with the concepts involved due to the linguistic experience gleaned from our own everyday life. However, the film's lack of a conceptual language artificially forces us back into an ostensive or originary mode against our better judgment. And, perhaps more importantly, it also forces us to experience language as transcendent. Because the non-conceptual language of the characters can never be translated into our language it appears to be "magical" (it works perfectly well for them even though it doesn't have any meaning for us). This transcendent, semiotic inner frame is supported by the presence of an animated, antic elf on the fictional level who helps the various family members until they have been reconciled (this is the outer frame that makes the film's closure complete). The result is a double frame that not only suggests that it is possible to communicate and act intuitively and "magically" beneath the threshold of conceptuality, but also confirms that magic dimension on the authorial level by allowing an impish deity to intervene in the action.

Conceptuality, of course, still exists in a banal way and can easily be retrieved and deconstructed. However, its deconstruction would itself become trivial, since it would have to "translate" the movie back into the conventional linguistic concepts that the movie goes out of its way to avoid. This predicament can be made clearer still by imagining what would happen if all language or sound would be removed from the film. The result would either be a silent movie with a banal plot or a filmed pantomime (neither of which could make any claim to aesthetic innovation). By using ostensive signs as its main aesthetic device, a movie like *Skřítek* exposes deconstruction's blindness toward the intuitive, transcendent, and aesthetic dimensions of language and its one-sided focus on problems of truth-seeking. It is admittedly unlikely that *Skřítek's* creators thought in such highly theoretical terms while making the movie. However, it is evident that on an intuitive level they were trying at all costs to evade the typically postmodern fixation on discourse by eliminating the conceptual side of language entirely and by creating an autonomous, "magic" aesthetic space within the framework of the film.

Skřítek marks a radical limit of performatism in the sense that carries the minimal linguistic mode of ostensivity to a maximum level of saturation. As a device, *Skřítek*'s wall-to-wall use of the ostensive results in a unique performance that is unlikely to call forth any direct imitations. [24] The more usual situation is that ostensivity is mediated or narrated in some way. Here, too, we encounter different degrees of coerciveness in the way frames are set up and forced upon us.

One of the commonest devices in narrative double framing is what I have come to call first-person authorial narration. In Franz Stanzel's typology of narrative[25] there is normally only room for three narrative situations: authorial third-person narrative (the omniscient narrator), figural third-person narrative (free indirect discourse), and first-person figural narrative — the classic *Ich-Erzähler* full of inner contradictions and unaware of the greater ironies unfolding around it. Authorial first-person narrative has no place in Stanzel's typology because it would seem to result in a psychologically and logically unproductive conflation of the implicit author and the figural narrator. If a first-person narrator's ideology, emotional attitude and scope of knowledge are almost on the same level as those of the authoritative implicit author, the first-person narrator would dominate the proceedings to the detriment of everyone and everything else; there would be little or no ironic tension between the first-person narrator and the story he or she tells. The result, in effect, would be a text that is all literal, or all surface, and with only one possible way of reading it. This sort of text might well be encountered in dogmatic tracts prior to the Enlightenment, but not in classic works of psychological fiction lying between the age of sensibility and modernism.

Both postmodernism and performatism break with the psychological dialectic between authorial third-person narrative and figural first-person narrative, though for different reasons. Postmodernism deliberately creates undecidable situations that conflate the authorial and the personal. The unreliability of a narrator, for example, is typically duplicated on a higher, authorial level that presents us with an irreducible, endless irony: it turns out that the only thing that is authoritative is unreliability itself. Performatism, by contrast, creates narrative *decidability* by setting up a double frame that causes the reader to strongly identify with or believe in something transpiring in the framed center of the story. To be binding, this identification or aesthetically mediated belief has to be operative on something more than a psychological level (as is the case in realist fiction). Hence the tendency in many performatist works to bestow "magical" authorial powers on first-person figural narrators or, alternately, to confirm the insights of a first-person narrator on a higher authorial level and effectively nullify the ironic rift between narrator and implicit author.

Because I've treated problems of narrativity at length in two other articles,[26] it will suffice here to give a brief example of how authorial first-person narration works using Ian McEwan's suspenseful and cleverly constructed novel *Atonement* (2001). The novel begins by recounting in third-person style how a precocious twelve-year old girl named Briony Tallis ruins the lives of her sister Cecilia and her lover Robbie by falsely claiming he raped an underage cousin of Briony's. A second section then goes on to recount the painful separation and gradual reconciliation of the main protagonists during World War II, masterfully mixing psychological analysis of the characters with a gripping, detailed account of Robbie's successful escape to Dunkirk after the German invasion of France. The first two sections comprise around 350 pages of the book's paperback edition. In the third and final section, which is only twenty some pages long and is dated 1999, a first-person narrator appears and reveals herself to be Briony, who has since grown up to be a famous writer. In truth, she says, Cecilia and Robbie both perished in World War II and were never reconciled at all. The book we have been reading turns out to have been a fictional fabrication meant to atone for Briony's tragic real-life lie by presenting us with the uplifting, but factually untrue reconciliation between Cecilia, Robbie, and Briony. Having admitted this, Briony goes on to formulate her predicament in explicitly theist terms:

> [...] how can a novelist achieve atonement when, with her absolute power of deciding outcomes, she is also God? There is no one, no entity or higher form that she can appeal to, or be reconciled with, or that can forgiver her. There is nothing outside her. In her imagination, she has set the limits and the terms. No atonement for God, or novelists, even if they are atheists. I was always an impossible task, and that was precisely the point. The attempt was all.[27]

At first it might seem as if we are dealing with a standard postmodern device. The book, after all, encourages us to identify psychologically with the three main protagonists and then abruptly renders that identification void. The point of the book, it would seem, is a neo-Nietzschean critique of the author-as-God. The author can only achieve personal atonement by not telling the truth (by creating a fictional world in which everything is in accord with her subjective desires). In postmodern terms, the switch from third-person to first-person narrative simply exposes the impossibility of telling any truth authoritatively and underscores the contingent character of all narration. Even when you appear to occupy a transcendental, omniscient position you still have a figural status that is always contiguous to the world you are writing about and that is never "disinterested" in the work's outcome.

Such a reading is still no doubt possible. However, it has difficulty explaining the easy decidability of the novel's truth structure as well as the massive quantitative disproportion between the identificatory, but illusory third-person segment and the truth-revealing, but banal first-person segment. Why, of all things, spend ninety-five per cent of a book unfolding a fabrication only to expose it as such in a few short pages? The only point would seem to be to play a long-winded, cheap trick on the reader.

If the book is read in performatist terms, however, both the book's decidability and its focus on identification become readily understandable. For in the performatist reading, the two narrative segments (along with certain crucial scenes in the story[28]) create an ironclad frame that is meant to force the reader back into the moral problems involved in achieving atonement and forgiveness rather than to dwell on the insoluble ironies involved in fictional truth-telling. In effect, the book forces the reader to *believe* by objectifying the story at length in the third person, for it is only through the force of this objectified belief that forgiveness and atonement can be achieved (forcing belief upon the skeptical is the classic task of the theist God and the omniscient realist narrator). The reader who has been aesthetically "converted" by the gripping narrative performance unfolded in the first two segments is faced with a choice between a beautiful, reconciliatory outcome and a simple, ugly truth.

This is analogous in certain ways to the originary ostensive scene, in which the reconciliatory power of the first sign overrides and occludes the animalistic, unmediated "truth" of simple, applied force. Both in the originary scene and in *Atonement* it is the beautiful, transcendent ability to believe that dominate. The difference is, of course, that the book is a postmetaphysical performance which obligates us to reflect belatedly on the conditions of aesthetic belief that we have just experienced. This obligation can be made clearer by imagining what would happen if the author had simply eliminated the third, revelatory part of the book: the result would have been a spellbinding, but utterly traditional third-person realist narrative. (Similarly, the sole use of a first-person narrator would have resulted in a romantic, Rousseau-like, and completely disingenuous attempt to tell the truth about Briony's own misdeeds.) The belated insertion of a first-person narrative forces the reader to critically review once more the reconciliatory aesthetic performance of belief that he or she has just experienced.

It does not suggest, however, that the reader jettison this experience entirely or place it *sous rature*. In fact, rather than crossing out ninety-five per cent of the book in one grand sweep the last, revelatory segment underlines it by emphasizing the utter *necessity* of that aesthetic experience. Ultimately, you are faced with an aesthetic choice that is really not one: you can either opt for the beautiful experience of reconciliation and atonement or for the short, ugly experience of just knowing the truth.[29]

This is also why aesthetics per se is central to the performatist or post-postmodernist experience. If what is beautiful cannot outshine what is true, we will remain mired in postmodernism. However, because beauty cannot "naturally" impose itself on us (as is still the case in Kant), it must be imposed forcibly, using performative tricks like the ones described above. The result is a self-fulfilling prophecy or ostensive tautology: aesthetic, artificial means are used to create identifications that are experienced primarily as intuitively beautiful and secondarily as true or false conceptual judgments. The tension between beauty and truth is always present, but the performative work unashamedly strong-arms us into preferring beauty — and lets us know that it is doing so in the process. Elsewhere I have called this "Kant with a club," but one could also think of it as a kind of Nietzschean Kantianism: it marks a will to beauty and not to power.[30]

Ethics, Politics, and Aesthetics: Centering the Peripheral

I mentioned earlier that the concept of performatism is intended to focus on the aesthetic devices of the new epoch and not on its socio-political ramifications. This does not mean, however, that performatism is a theory of *l'art pour l'art* that blindly excludes political, social, and ethical issues. Instead, performatism marks both a continuation and reversal of postmodernist practice regarding politics and ethics. Like postmodernism, performatism emphasizes the *position* of participants in political or ethical situations over the content of their beliefs (in this sense it is post-ideological). However, unlike postmodernism, it valorizes the *center* position rather than the periphery or margin. More specifically, performatism works by taking a peripheral phenomenon and placing it squarely in the center of a double-framed aesthetic performance. This simultaneous act of framing and centering "recharges" the peripheral in unpredictable ways that as a rule are not consonant with traditional ethical or political norms. All in all, the act of centering shakes up, rather than shores up, the status quo, and conflates the political (or the ethical) with the beautiful and the divine under expressly artificial conditions.

Just how this centering works in regard to a current, eminently political issue can be made clearer using an example from the film *American Beauty*, which I've discussed at greater length in my first article on performatism.[31] The film accords a minor role to the "two Jims" — a friendly, healthy gay pair who are equally at ease chatting with the heroine about her roses and with the hero about his jogging technique (the two Jims are also the ones welcoming the homophobe and closet homosexual Col. Fitts to their neighborhood). Instead of emphasizing the peripheral or victimary status of gays, the movie places them at the epicenter of its moral universe: they are the only couple with a functional, happy relationship. Moreover, the two Jims may be thought of as twins, since they resemble one another in name, appearance, and sexual orientation. Notwithstanding René Girard's observation that twins are traditionally feared because they are thought to embody mimetic rivalry,[32] the two Jims act as examples of *successful* mimesis, demonstrating that doubling need not be dangerous, and, indeed, can lead to a transcendent unity of rival positions (here, too, they may be said to have a quasi-divine valence). The fact that the closet homosexual Col. Fitts will later murder Lester Burnham after Lester spurns his advances does not detract from the two Jims' moral ideality; Col. Fitts simply does not find the right "fit" in the heterosexual Lester and reverts to violence to erase his mistake. Col. Fitts doesn't murder because he's gay or because he's evil; he murders because he's a jilted lover unable to find his way back to the reconciliatory center marked by the two Jims.

The kind of centering described above is post-ideological in the sense that it does not predetermine what or who is placed in the center and made beautiful.[33] However, this doesn't mean that ideology isn't necessarily present in post-ideological discourse (just as metaphysics is still necessarily present in post-metaphysical discourse). An immediate example of just how ideology works in the context of GA is Eric Gans's discussion of gay marriage, which he carries out in direct reference to the originary scene.[34]

At first glance, it might appear that gay marriage is the real-life equivalent of the two Jims; it means participation of a heretofore peripheral, "other" social group in a divine, centered covenant accepted by the whole of society. In this regard, it would seem to find direct legitimation in the intuitively experienced moral reciprocity of the originary scene. Gans, however, rejects this assumption. Instead, he argues that what is at stake in marriage as an institution is not the originary ideal of symmetrical moral reciprocity, but rather the normative intent to privilege asymmetrical heterosexual relations, and ultimately child-bearing, over other forms of social contract ("the legitimation of heterosexual relations is the purpose of marriage[35]"). If marriage were extended to include other forms of cohabitation, says Gans, "its institutional specificity would disappear"[36] and society would "declare itself by default indifferent to the nature of child-produc-ing and -rearing arrangements."[37] Although unhappy with this situation, Gans doesn't explicitly come out against gay marriage, which he seems resigned to accept as a social fact. Yet even if we accept Gans's purely anthropological argu-ment that the institution of marriage is an adjunct to the originary scene that is not privy to its promise of moral reciprocity, his stance still has an easily identifiable ideological slant. Gans would like to preserve the tradition restrict-ing access to the power of the originary scene, even as his opponents are trying to break through that tradition to draw upon the powerful originary charge contained therein. This is a political (and sacral) issue as much as it is an anthro-pological one.

I don't pretend to have done justice to all of Gans's arguments, nor do I wish to embark here on an impassioned defense of gay marriage (which I happen to support). The point of this short excursion into the world of public policy is to show that the post-ideological framework provided by GA is neither neutral, objective, nor immune to ideological interpretations. Deriving value judgments from the originary scene depends heavily upon how you interpret both the scene itself as well as its normative and historical extensions. As Gans himself is aware, this type of scenic analysis is unavoidably circular:

> The primary point is that the establishment of a scenic model provides a heuristic for understanding the fundamental parameters of human institutions; conversely, this model can be modified in turn in order to fit more plausible sets of such parameters. The "hermeneutic cir-cle" thus described is more rigorous than that attainable from textual analysis alone, the distance between cultural texts and fundamental anthropological categories being inevitably mediated by the same meta-physical presuppositions from which the analyst is, or at any rate claims to be, seeking to liberate himself.[38]

To this one might also add that ideological presuppositions color this hermeneu-tic circle no less than metaphysical ones. And, as Gans himself notes, his own neoconservative political interpretation of GA is not identical with GA itself, which in his view is a "center" or "realist" viewpoint that is open to both "right" and "left" interpretations.[39]

The suspicion that GA may be a Trojan Horse for neoconservative ideol-ogy fades quickly anyway when GA is applied to art. For unlike the kind of discourse cited above, which is obligated to argue in an empirically plausible, purposeful way, closed or framed works of art are free to stack the heuristic deck any way they please. For example, *American Beauty* obviously sets up the two Jims' gay relationship as an ideal, central scene both for the other characters and for us. Even if you're a raving homophobe you have little choice but to accept this as an aesthetic fact. And, as if that were not enough, *American Beauty* also gives you a raving homophobe to identify with — but one who turns out to be homosexual himself. The relentless monism of *American Beauty* (which is typical of performatist works in general) suggests that there is no ideological, sexual, or metaphysical Other, only different degrees of participation in (or estrangement from) one larger scenic unity with which we cannot but help identify.[40] Regarding gay empowerment, *American Beauty* skews this unity to the ideological left by inserting a heretofore peripheral group into its moral center or scene. This also accurately describes how the aesthetic politics of performatism work in general. Depending on how the frames and scenes are set up, the work will assume a certain ideological stance, which it will however present as centered, unified, and capable of universal consensus. Just how "left" or "right" work is will have a great deal to do with what peripheral elements are centered, and under what conditions.

This can be seen more clearly in regard to the crucial problem of globalization. Based on my critical reading up to now I have identified both "right," "left," and "terrorist" works of performatism treating this theme. "Right" performatism attempts to create unified pockets of spirituality within global capitalism (as in Olga Tokarczuk's *Hotel World*), whereas "left" performatism (as in Arundhati Roy's *The God of Small Things*) centers oppressed others and presents them as beautiful. Finally, "terrorist" or "sublime" performatism, as exemplified by the Czech writer Miloš Urban's *Sevenchurches*, toys with the fantasy of destroying capitalism entirely.[41] Though rough generalizations, these categories do suggest the great breadth of ideological territory that has already been covered by performatist works.

In general, I have the impression that performatist works are no less critical towards society than postmodern ones (which incidentally also have the reputation among some left-wing thinkers of being unduly escapist, defeatist, and obfuscatory). The real major difference between the two is that performatist works use monist devices of centering and unification to promote their political agendas, whereas postmodernist ones insist on arguing from a peripheral or victimary position that would seem to guarantee a critical attitude towards capitalism. The fear on the part of leftist critics that leaving this position of institutionalized otherness will automatically result in capitulation to bourgeois ideology is, I think, unfounded. If anything, the aesthetic ideology of "left" performatism presents an alternative to victimary discourse by emphasizing a positive way of creating unified new identities or centers that compete with and unsettle the existing system. The movement for gay marriage is one case in point; another is the search of postcolonial societies for a positive regional identity that — *pace* Edward Said — does not simply consist in being the ineffable Other of the capitalist West.[42] Indeed, as the aesthetic practice of performatism becomes increasingly dominant, we are very likely to see a shift in how leftist ideology argues and presents itself (in fact, this turn can already be said to have taken place in the thought of the prominent Marxist critic Terry Eagleton, whose recent book *After Theory*[43] argues for the positive reassessment of such "taboo" concepts as normativity, morality, tradition, identity etc.).

Conclusion

The discipline of aesthetics collapsed after twentieth century modernism demonstrated its "eternal" values to be arbitrary norms and relocated the aesthetic act in the destruction of those norms. In place of aesthetics came phenomenology and semiotics, which described works of art in terms of intentionality and functionality rather than as expressions of a transcendental ideal. Postmodernism made the arbitrariness of aesthetic norms an ironic norm of its own and poststructuralism added to it an epistemological critique of all transcendental pretensions. In the postmillennial or performatist epoch, aesthetics returns, but in a postmetaphysical mode. Its focus is not a universal, transcendental beauty, but a double-framed, imposed beauty that arises involuntarily for the viewer on the restricted scene of a work of art. In the new epoch, beauty returns not as an essence, norm, or ideal, but as the effect of a singular, binding performance. The task of GA's aesthetics is to describe and analyze how this imposed beauty arises and how it interacts with the linguistic, transcendent, and political elements derived from the originary scene as described by GA.

Notes

1. Gans first proposed postmillennialism in *Chronicles of Love and Resentment* Nr. 209, 3 June, 2000 (www.anthropoetics.ucla.edu/views/vw209.htm). My notion of performatism, which uses his theory of ostensivity as its root concept, was developed independently of his *Chronicle* and first appeared in *Anthropoetics* 2 (2000/2001). <www.anthropoetics.ucla.edu/ap0602/perform.htm>
2. The prevailing practice is to affect a skeptical attitude towards postmodernism without offering a historically defined alternative to it. A representative collection documenting this is *Beyond Postmodernism. Reassessments in Literature, Theory, and Culture*, ed. by Klaus Stierstorfer (Berlin: Walter de Gruyter, 2003). A number of the authors (most notably Ihab Hassan and Vera Nünning) discuss unpostmodern trends toward subjectivity, faith, aesthetics and ethical solidarity in an approving way. None of them, however, is willing to conceive of, let alone name, an epoch that would lie beyond postmodernism.
3. I have treated the "new monism" in an eponymous English-language article that will appear shortly in a *Sonderband* of the *Wiener Slawistischer Almanach.*
4. For more on this (as well as a noteworthy attempt to rehabilitate Kantian aesthetics) see Tobin Siebers' "Kant and the Politics of Beauty," *Philosophy and Literature* 1 (1998), pp. 31–50.
5. See Gans's discussion in *The Origins of Language* (Berkeley: University of California Press, 1981) as well as in *The End of Culture* (Berkeley: University of California Press, 1985) Chapter 5, "The Elementary Forms of Culture," esp. pp. 105–128.
6. *Originary Thinking* (Stanford: Stanford University Press, 1993), p. 122. For example, one can only speculate on whether prehistoric cave paintings were intended as representations of animals for their own sake or as part of a magical ritual meant to aid the hunt.
7. *Originary Thinking*, p. 117.
8. *Originary Thinking*, p. 118.
9. *Originary Thinking*, p. 119.
10. Gans has acknowledged his debt to Kant at length in "Originary and/or Kantian Aesthetics," *Poetica* 35 (2003), pp. 335–353.
11. See *The Truth in Painting* (Chicago: The University of Chicago Press, 1987), esp. pp. 83–118. Here, it seems to me, Derrida imposes his own semiotic dualism on Kant. GA's monist interpretation is more in keeping with contemporary Kant scholarship, which stresses the mediating role of sensual intuition between the *Ding an sich* and the mind. See in this regard Arthur Collins, *Possible Experience: Understanding Kant's Critique of Pure Reason* (Berkeley: Univ. of California Press, 1999) as well as Otfried Höffe, *Kants Kritik der reinen Vernunft. Die Grundlegung der modernen Philosophie* (München: C.H. Beck, 2004), esp. pp. 81–86.
12. *Truth in Painting*, p. 95.
13. *Truth in Painting*, p. 94.
14. See *Truth in Painting*, pp. 114–118. As Derrida shows, natural, supposedly au-

tonomous beauty turns out to be contingent upon the reason that it has been "naturally" working to support.

15. This move has a direct phenomenological parallel in Jean-Luc Marion's phenomenology of givenness as outlined in *Being Given* (Stanford: Stanford University Press, 2002) and other works. For more on this see also my article "The New Monism" (forthcoming in a *Sonderband* of the *Wiener Slawistischer Almanach*). The only two semiotic concepts offering a comparable perspective are Peirce's notion of firstness and Mukařovský's concept of unintentionality (*nezáměrnost*). Peirce consistently emphasizes synthetic thirdness over intuitive firstness; Mukařovský set forth his concept in a 1943 article and never developed it further.

16. See Jakobson's remark in "Linguistics and Poetics," *Selected Writings. Vol. III. Poetry of Grammar and Grammar of Poetry* (Mouton: The Hague, 1981), 18–51, here p. 42: "The supremacy of the poetic function over the referential function does not obliterate the reference but makes it ambiguous. The double-sensed message finds correspondance in a split addresser, in a split addressee, as well as in a split reference [...]."

17. See his approving citation of Valéry's definition of poetry as a "hesitation between the sound and the sense" in "Linguistics and Poetics," p. 38. This can result in a rhetorical accentuation of conventional semantic relations (as in the famous "I like Ike") but also in a suggestive, Dada-like "transrational language" (*zaum'*) that remains beneath the threshold of semantic convention and hence conceptuality. The latter position is typical of Jakobson's formalist phase.

18. For a more detailed description of the Kantian elements in Jakobson's poetics see Peter Zima, *Literarische Ästhetik* (Tübingen: Franke Verlag, 1991), pp. 188-189.

19. Mukařovský tried to close the gap between the material signifier and in the reader's mental response to it by positing a totalizing "semantic gesture" that would unify both in a single performative sweep. In practice, the term inevitably tends to dissolve into an analysis oriented either toward form (the aesthetic *Ding an sich*) or towards reader-response (the thing as it is perceived in consciousness), thus confirming the pattern of dualism traditionally ascribed to Kant. For a dispassionate critical appraisal of this split in the concept of semantic gesture see Wolf Schmid, *Der ästhetische Inhalt. Zur semantischen Funktion poetischer Verfahren* (Lisse: Peter de Ridder Press, 1977), esp. pp. 25–27.

20. See, for example, *Chronicle* 40, April 27, 1996, "Victimary Culture."
          <www.anthropoetics.ucla.edu/views/view40.htm>

21. This is evidently the Hegelian-Heideggerian-Derridean tradition. It would be an interesting project to trace its antecedents back farther and compare them with the competing Kantian-Durkheimian-Goffmanian line of which GA and performatism are a direct extension.

22. The programmatic formulation of this notion of frame can be found in Derrida's discussion of the parergon in *The Truth in Painting*. However, it is implicit in such typical postmodern practices as narrative metalepsis and *mise en abyme* or in the entire notion of discourse, which demonstrates how the subject, rather than being

a fixed, "sacred" unity, is rather arbitrarily framed and determined by the energetic, linguistically transmitted power swirling around it.

23. This is the most obvious difference between the notion of performance in performatism and the way Judith Butler uses the term: her performance is always a failure, and the subject once more dissipates in the discursive matrix that constitutes it in the first place. For Butler's own definition of performance see her *Bodies that Matter* (New York: Routledge, 1993), in particular the "Introduction."

24. *Skřítek* is, interestingly enough, not entirely alone. A film comparable in technique is Aleksandr Rogožkin's *The Cuckoo* (2002), in which three people come together who don't understand one another's language. The difference between this movie and *Skřítek* is that overdubbing allows the viewer to understand the mutually opaque languages of the characters. For more on *The Cuckoo* see my "Performatism in the Movies (1997–2003)" *Anthropoetics* 2 (2002/2003). (www.anthropoetics. ucla.edu/ap0802/movies.htm)

25. See his *A Theory of Narrative* (New York: Cambridge University Press, 1984). Stanzel's terminology is still commonly used in the German-speaking world, but is often considered conceptually inferior to the more sophisticated system devised by Gerard Genette that breaks narrative down into abstract levels and dispenses with all personified terms. It is precisely the use of anthropocentric terminology that makes Stanzel's system interesting for performatism.

26. See "Checking out of the Epoch: Performatism in Olga Tokarczuk's „The Hotel Capital" vs. Late Postmodernism in Ali Smith's "Hotel World" (with remarks on Arundhati Roy's *The God of Small Things* and Miloš Urban's *Sevenchurch*)," Anthropoetics 2 (2004/2005) and "After Postmodernism: Performatism in Literature," *Anthropoetics* 2 (2005/2006).

27. *Atonement* (London: Vintage, 2002), p. 371

28. Both these scenes can be said to have an originary quality. In the first, Briony, watching from a distance, sees her sister undress and plunge into a fountain in the presence of Robbie; her imaginary interpretation of this silent scene is her first step towards becoming an author of psychological fiction. In the second crucial scene, the naïve Briony misreads a sexually explicit love letter by Robbie that leads her to make the false accusation of rape. In both cases there is an basic and unbridgeable disjunction between the originary force of these confrontations (made known to the reader through the older Briony's narrative) and the younger Briony's misinterpretation or misreading of them. The structure of the text doesn't rule out the possibility of a third and final misreading by Briony. However, it makes sure that it can't take place, quite simply because her theist narrative is the last point of reference, which we have to believe whether we like it or not.

29. In a certain, specifically Kantian sense it is not possible "not to like" a performatist work of art. Because the work of art imposes itself so drastically on viewers, it forces them to take an all-or-nothing attitude that either binds them to the immanent logic of the work or repels them entirely (one could also say that it "converts" them aesthetically or immanently to the belief system of the work at hand). This

is also why performatism does not aspire to be a theory of reader response like that practiced by Wolfgang Iser: the reaction of the "implicit reader" to a performatist work of art cannot be anything other than schematic (at least as a first reaction). In purely empirical terms, reader response to performatist works is often divided between spontaneous awe and utter rejection of the work in question as trivial or obvious. In the case of *American Beauty*, postmodern viewers tend to classify it as nothing more than a merciless satire of American life (an interpretation which is possible only if you completely ignore the narrative frame of the film, which specifically sets forth the possibility of a beautiful redemption).

30. I suggested the notion of "Kant with a club" in "Performatism in Literature," p. 2, though in regard to Nietzsche you might want to call this "Kant with a hammer." Gans has notes an affinity between performatism and Nietzsche in *Chronicle* 258, March 23, 2002, "On Esthetic Periodization."

31. See my "Performatism, or the End of Postmodernism," Anthropoetics 2 (2000/2001).

32. See, for example, the discussion in René Girard, *Things Hidden since the Foundation of the Earth* (Stanford: Stanford University Press, 1987), pp. 14–19.

33. Unlikely things that have been made beautiful in this way include an exposed penis (in Lars von Trier's movie *Idiots*) as well as a dead bird and a white plastic bag (in *American Beauty*). For more on this see my "Performatism in the Movies."

34. See his *Chronicle* 289, Aug. 23 2003, "Gay Marriage: An Originary Analysis" (www.anthropoetics.ucla.edu/views/vw289.htm)and *Chronicle* 296, March 6, 2004, "Gay Marriage II: The End of Kinship"
(www.anthropoetics.ucla.edu/views/vw289.htm>

35. *Chronicle* 289.

36. *Chronicle* 289.

37. *Chronicle* 289.

38. *Chronicle 289*, "Gay Marriage."

39. See *Chronicle* 324, October 22, 2005 "Questioning Generative Anthropology." (www.anthropoetics.ucla.edu/views/vw324.htm)

40. That is why there can be no victims in a monist world; there is only (temporary) estrangement from a center. In the case of *American Beauty*, even the nominal victim, Lester Burnham, is not one: his violent death leads to his deification and ability to grasp the beauty of the whole.

41. For more on this see my "Checking out of the Epoch," esp. the "Conclusion," p. 7.

42. As Gans himself has pointed out, postcolonial studies contain notions of reciprocity and dialogicity that have a certain affinity to GA (see in this regard *Chronicle* 163, March 20, 1999 "Deconstructing the Subject"). Unfortunately most, if not all, specialists in postcolonial theory remain stuck in the posthistorical mode.

43. New York: Basic Books, 2003.

Epigenetic Evolution of the Immaterial Intellect on the Originary Scene[1]

Christopher S. Morrissey

Introduction: The "Intelligent Design" of the Scapegoating Mechanism

The recent controversy over evolution and "intelligent design"[2] can help clarify what is at stake in the controversy between Eric Gan's account of hominization and that of René Girard.[3] That is, both controversies are fundamentally about the scientific resolution of effects to causes. The controversies arise over how *a variety of causal factors* are to be seen as inter-related and integrated into a whole account. In other words, these controversies involve a *philosophical* dimension that addresses manifold questions of causality. In this philosophical dimension, the causality debates cannot be settled by empirical evidence alone but ultimately only by the intellectual *interpretation* of that evidence within a causal nexus.

In the evolution and "intelligent design" debate, the philosophical interpretation concerns whether or not it is necessary for science to invoke God (the *First* Cause) on natural levels of *secondary* causality.[4] Such a controversy therefore reaches an intellectual impasse when the inter-related casual factors are poorly understood. Because of the poverty of their metaphysics, "intelligent design" proponents seem unable to grasp that their argument makes a philosophically inordinate invocation of divine causality. The confusion that accompanies their claims comes about because they don't realize their fundamental argument has more to do with bad metaphysics than with good science.[5] In making their case for "irreducible complexity" in biological phenomena, they in effect argue that some biological phenomena are irreducible to natural explanations. As their critics point out, this is tantamount to giving up on natural science.[6]

Something similar is happening in the hominization debate between Girard and Gans: in the interpretation of the data, all the possible causal factors involved need to be more explicitly sorted out. On the one hand, Girard's mimetic theory of a "scapegoating mechanism", like much of modern science, trains its theoretical focus on what traditional philosophy refers to as *efficient* and *material* causal factors. Girard does this in order to offer a reliable mechanistic hypothesis about how mimetic behaviour *effectively* leads to and is *materially* resolved by unanimous violence against a surrogate victim.[7] On the other hand, Gans' account of the origin of language (as a deferral of violence) aims to integrate Girard's insights into *the wider range of causal factors* that have come to be recognized in the evolutionary process. That is, to my mind, Gans' "generative anthropology"[8] takes up questions of what traditional philosophy would call *formal* and *final* causality, because these questions are not adequately treated in the Girardian account.

Therefore, in this essay, I offer an argument for how Gans' generative anthropology better accounts for the requisite single-step *epigenesis* of human nature.[9] I affirm the thesis that human nature must be defined by the distinct *formal* characteristic of language which can only have arisen *suddenly* from the material conditions of the "genotypic milieu".[10] Once generative anthropology is understood in terms all of the types of inter-related causal claims that it is making, generative anthropology's account of epigenesis may be recognized as having better explained the evolution of human culture's enormous *adaptive advantage* (i.e., human culture understood in terms of *final causality*).[11] For only generative anthropology has properly integrated the full amplitude of the insights into causality that neo-Darwinism has in fact achieved.

To my mind, Girard's theory resembles a combination of the worst philosophical tendencies of *both* sides of the controversy between the evolutionists and "intelligent design" proponents. In one respect, Girard's scapegoat mechanism owes much to the mechanistic and mathematical habits of mind that proved to be so successful in the early stages of modern science.[12] In that respect, it resembles the scientism of evolutionists who over-interpret neo-Darwinism in a mechanistic and materialist mode. (This kind of thinking argues that evolutionary theory means that the universe is unguided and unplanned; people like Richard Dawkins and Daniel C. Dennett wish to make the science say: no God is required.)[13] Yet in another respect, however, Girard's account of hominization resembles the Platonizing tendency of "intelligent design" theorists who argue both for the necessity of exemplary extra-natural Ideas of *formal* design and also for the necessity of divine causal intervention to achieve in nature the *final* (i.e., purposive) realization of that exemplary design. Ironically, while initially conceived as a "mechanism", Girard's "scapegoat" hypothesis is ultimately, in scientific terms, a kind of *Platonic Idea* that is formally imposed on the evolutionary process. In order to explain the genesis of the adaptive advantage secured by human culture, the "deified scapegoat" is a *deus ex machina* trotted out in Girard's account. Mimetic theory must be contrasted, however, with generative anthropology's consonance with neo-Darwinism.

In order to contrast generative anthropology's causal account with Girard's attempted explanation of the *genesis* of the *adaptive* advantage secured by human culture, I argue that human culture can only have arisen from the *exaptation* of language.[14] Language occurred first in, not the genesis, but rather the *epigenesis* of human nature. For this reason, generative anthropology gives a better *philosophical* account of what neo-Darwinism has *scientifically* established; that is, it offers the best account of how man (*anthropos*) was generated by *all* the inter-related causal factors involved in neo-Darwinian evolution. To demonstrate my thesis I will, in the first part below, outline how traditional philosophical terminology accurately describes the neo-Darwinian causal factors involved. In the second part, I will compare and contrast the implied inter-relation of causal factors: first in Girard's scapegoating mechanism, then in Gans' account of the origin of language, and finally in Adam Katz' proposed emendation to Gans' account. In conclusion, I will suggest the relation between causality and the anthropological insights of the Adam and Eve story because, as Gans has written, "The epistemology of this passage [Genesis 3:1–13] is far more subtle than that of its traditional readings."[15]

Part 1: Causal Analysis in Neo-Darwinism

In terms of causality, the neo-Darwinian account of evolution is a scientific achievement of such magnitude that its vindication of *nature's incredible dynamism* presents a long-overdue challenge to the philosophical prejudices of mechanism and materialism. These prejudices, which have accompanied the rise and success of modern science since Galileo, arise from a habit of mind that focuses solely on what the metaphysical tradition calls efficient and material causes. With evolution, formal and final causes once again come into full view for modern science, because efficient and material causes are no longer sufficient to account for the observed dynamism of the universe. Because the universe is now seen to be *dynamically* evolving (and not a billiard table of interacting *static* types writ large), the full range of causal factors must be discussed in interpreting the empirical data. Something beyond mechanism and mathematics is required to account for the observed evolutionary reality of mind-independent being. As John Deely has carefully and painstakingly argued, the neo-Darwinian account of evolution is "a return to the [classical] conception of science as reasoned facts, distinct from and superordinate to mathematized facts".[16]

Deely has shown how neo-Darwinism achieves knowledge of the evolution of species *as a reasoned fact*.[17] Benedict Ashley has remarked on how the full range of causality, in all its inter-related types of factors, comes into view for neo-Darwinism because its focus is on the evolution of the *species*:

It is not the individual that evolves but the species, and the species evolves not from some inner teleology but through interaction with the environment (*natural selection*). This environment is an *ecosystem* composed not only of geography and climate but also of other living things in mutual competition and symbiosis.[18]

From this wider context of inter-relations, neo-Darwinism has succeeded in bringing (if only implicitly, i.e., empirically yet still non-philosophically) to the forefront of scientific consciousness *all* of the traditionally recognized types of causality.

Aristotle's philosophy of causality articulates the scientific need for a full account of causal interactions.[19] Deely has clearly established that neo-Darwinism deploys the full range of traditional Aristotelian causal analysis in its demonstration of evolution as a reasoned fact.[20] Thanks to Deely's work,[21] Ashley recognizes that neo-Darwinism's significance in the history of modern science is that it "views evolution as due to *the interaction of several types of inter-related factors*" [emphasis mine].[22] Drawing upon Deely and Waddington, Ashley gives a usefully explicit summary of *the four types of causal factors involved in evolution* which, when seen together with the extensive modern empirical data, vividly exhibit Aristotle's complete account of causality:

(1) *epigenetic* factor: the tendency of interbreeding population to reproduce itself in a stable manner and increase in numbers ("formal causality," i.e., the maintenance of type).

(2) *genetic* factor: the tendency to variation resulting from constant small random mutations in the genetic code ("material causality," i.e., a variety of differing individuals within a species capable of transmitting their differences).

(3) *selective* factor: natural selection by the environment which eliminates those variants which are less effective in reproducing their kind ("efficient causality," i.e., the agent determining in which direction species-change will take place).

(4) *exploitative* factor: the flexibility of living things by which they are able to occupy new niches in the changing environment ("final causality," i.e., a feed-back mechanism which guides the selective process toward a new type which can exploit *new* environmental possibilities).

It is the directive bias of the selective and exploitative factors which biologists now believe is responsible for the *progressive*, apparently teleological, character of evolution. In spite of the many dead ends, the interaction of all these factors results not only in the increasing adaptation of each species to its environment but also in the direction of organisms which are more and more complex, highly integrated, and *relatively independent of their environment.* Higher organisms have an "internalized environment."[23]

Metaphysics, as conceived of by Aristotle, addresses itself in a special way to questions of causality by distinguishing these various types of causality.[24] The debate over evolution and "intelligent design" is, as Robert T. Miller has pointed out, ultimately not a debate between science and religion but really an argument over metaphysical questions of causality: "The truth is that Intelligent Design is metaphysics".[25] When Cardinal Schönborn wrote his opinion piece in the *New York Times* arguing that intelligent design in nature is visible to reason,[26] he seemed to be misattributing a *theological* notion of randomness (an "unguided, unplanned" universe) to neo-Darwinism's precise *scientific* understanding of how chance occurs amidst the causality of mutation and natural selection.[27] Schönborn subsequently claimed that his opinion piece was being intentionally provocative and clarified that his real argument was neither theological nor scientific but properly philosophical: i.e., that ever since Bacon and Descartes modern science has focussed on material and efficient causes, whereas an account of formal and final causes is also needed "to challenge the hegemony of scientism".[28]

Schönborn's philosophical point is well taken, but the difficulty comes when discerning when to have recourse to formal and final causes as proper explanations of the phenomenal dimensions; for the task is one of enormous intellectual labour.[29] Stephen Barr reminds those over-eager to import "intelligent design" into a scientific context as a causal explanation of "irreducible complexity" that "appearances of irreducibility can be deceptive" because "we simply don't know all of nature's tricks".[30] As Barr puts it, "God is not a scientific theory";[31] to seek natural explanations for phenomena is simply to do science (which is something that should not be confused with "naturalism", i.e., insisting that *only* natural explanations are valid explanations)[32]. In fact, a recent article, by applying information theory to neo-Darwinism, shows how biological complexity can be accounted for by the natural explanations of random mutation and natural selection.[33] Even so, such scientific truths "go hand in hand with the truths of natural philosophy, each depending on and making up for the limitations of the other", as Schönborn points out.[34] Schönborn thus reminds neo-Darwinism that there are philosophical problems concerning the *formal* origin and *final* purpose of human nature that remain unsatisfactorily addressed by much evolutionary theory; the attempt to answer the full set of causal questions in purely *material* terms is an illusory solution characterized by intellectual haste:

> the Thomistic philosopher would expect nature to exhibit an intrinsic teleology, an immanent, lawlike self-unfolding that would appear to the empiriological scientist as "self-organization," "emergent properties," and other such philosophically question-begging locutions, as if matter itself was the source of the ontologically prior (although not necessarily temporally prior) principles that organize and structure it.[35]

The neo-Darwinian theory of evolution, however, and its account of the operation of the panoply of natural causes, is not at odds with the Aristotelian-Thomistic qualification that God alone was capable of infusing the rational soul into the first human.[36] Properly understood, there is nothing otiose or magical about this metaphysical qualification;[37] it is the same qualification made about every subsequent embryo in human history.[38] From the metaphysical point of view, God alone infuses the rational soul of every human being who is conceived.[39] But as "intelligent design" proponents have noticed (and this is the truly *intelligent* observation for which they ought to be credited), neo-Darwinian theory is constantly tempted to overstep the bounds of its modelling techniques and step into the realm of *ontology*. Hence the talk of "God" and "soul" seems suspect and otiose to the scientific mind habituated only in *empiriological* thinking.[40] But what that talk represents is the transition *from the material to the immaterial*, as the rational form of man is infused at the point of hominization,[41] *activating his potential capacity* to achieve a new species form.

Deely sums up why the generation of the definitive form of the human is a clear and sudden transition, i.e., why it is an *epigenesis* between individuals (and not simply another evolutionary *genesis* of a new species) that evolves a new function, distinctively human:

> At the interior moment of man's initial emergence, we encounter an epigenic break in the unfolding evolutionary pattern.... For perhaps the only time in the history of biological development, a specific discontinuity arose and could only have arisen *between two individuals*: i.e., *either* the entire development of the anthropoid organism was circumscribed by the limitations imposed through the biological mechanism of gene transfer — in which case it did not possess a human genotype; *or* there was a reaction capacity in the organism which transcended the limitations of biological heredity — in which case it was endowed with a human genetic structure.[42]

Following C. H. Waddington, Raymond Nogar implicitly articulates the fourfold causal inter-relationship involved in this process by distinguishing the formal and final *effects of the environment* (the exploitive system and the epigenetic developmental system) from the material and efficient causes of random genetic variation (the genetic system) and the natural selection system:

> As the organism of one generation selects its possible environment, it *exploits* it and modifies it to suit its potentiality. The stresses reveal latent potentialities (perhaps of a new function) and *development* takes place. *Natural selection* takes place in reaction to stresses, and mutation modifies the selected potentialities. In reproduction, this modification is passed on to the second generation by replication.[43]

Deely explicitly articulates the fourfold causality involved:

> What Huxley…refers to as constitutive, differential, integrative, and analytic methods of approach to the question of the reasons for the differences within biological populations are in fact organizing evolutionary explanations according to the formal pattern of Aristotle's four causes. This is perhaps most easily seen in C. H. Waddington's analysis of the entire process of evolution as the intersection of four main sub-processes. According to Waddington, further developments of evolutionary theory require incorporating a circular concept of causality, consisting, as he explains, of four basic systems: the genetic system, corresponding analogously to Aristotle's sense of material cause; the epigenetic system, corresponding to formal cause; the natural selective system, analogous to efficient causality; and the exploitive system, corresponding to Aristotle's final cause.[44]

Deely cautions that the point is not to make a simple equation between Aristotle and Waddington; rather, "the point of the formal notion of the four causes is that they name a *set of relationships* necessarily involved in any phenomenon whatever as understandable".[45] Thus, in the set of relationships involved in evolution, it should be noted that the emergence of man needs to be accounted for in terms of *an epigenetic formal cause*, in addition to the causes of random genetic variation and natural selection. For the phenomenon of man to be understandable, all dimensions of causality have to be accounted for.

In other words, the philosophical point is that a true scientific hypothesis cannot be metaphysically incoherent. Thus human science needs to reach the best empiriological version of the originary scene so that it will have the least amount of difficulty in seeing it in harmony with a causally coherent ontology. This refinement process needs to be one of purging our scientific-causal account of any *mythical* metaphysics. To this task I now turn in the second part of this essay.

Part 2: The Epigenesis of the New Human Form

First, I note that because the epigenesis of the new species-form of human nature must be a sudden "break",[46] Gans' originary scene must be preferred to Girard's. Scientifically, there are many reasons why Gans' hypothesis is more minimal and therefore preferable.[47] But for my purposes here, i.e., for addressing the philosophical manner in which causal inter-relations on the originary scene must be considered, my main focus is on the metaphysical considerations. Metaphysically, Girard's scene inadequately accounts for the origin of the *immaterial intellect*. As Deely notes,

> The radical power underlying man's cultural capacities is the very capacity from which conjecture springs, and so hypothetical problem-solving — ... To this root capacity the term "intellectus" is traditionally applied.[48]

For Girard, the scapegoat serves as the material, mechanistic cause from which humanity is born.[49] That is, the body of the dead scapegoat becomes the locus of signification.[50] "The signifier is the victim."[51] But the philosophical and metaphysical problem with this scenario is that it postulates the activation of the *formal cause* by the *material cause*. In other words, for Girard language comes later and is "added on" to the dead scapegoat. The signification of the scapegoat as a deity (which signification is by definition "immaterial") is the *formal* representation of what has materially transpired: unanimous aggression has been discharged by the agency of the proto-humans, bringing about a *material* state of startling and unifying peace (which results upon realization of the communal unity now forged with the death of the scapegoat).

But this Girardian scenario of the formalization of humanity (through language) being activated *after* its material realization (the scapegoat mechanism bringing peace) is metaphysically incoherent. That is, it is unsustainable from the viewpoint of a rational doctrine of causality. The only reason Girard adheres to it is because of a resolute desire to keep his hypothesis "scientific" (in a mechanistic-mathematical sense) at all costs. He thereby adopts the materialist posture of the anti-metaphysical prejudices of contemporary scientific culture. But from the standpoint of the Aristotelian-Thomistic tradition, it is incoherent to educe formal causality from material causality. The potency of matter can only be actualized by the actuality of form. The principle of causality (which makes all scientific inquiry possible) is that *"nothing changes itself"*; *"something can act only so far as it is in act"*.[52]

In other words, something cannot give itself what it does not have. Something cannot cause itself to be what it is not. This does not mean, however, that evolution is impossible; far from it. It means only that when the potency of matter is reconfigured, by receiving a form of higher actuality, it requires a cause proportionate to that act of reconfiguration, i.e., capable of conferring the state of actuality of that new figuration. In an evolutionary transition, this means simply that the new form cannot arrive *after* the evolutionary change in the matter. Rather, it has to be coincident with that material change as its formal cause. The material development "calls for" its new form at the same time that it is ready for evolutionary advancement into a higher phase of final causality.[53] The reason for this is that form and matter are the correlative principles of material beings, since any material body is in its nature a compound of matter and form;[54] but since form is the higher principle (giving its actuality to the potency of matter), as Aristotle says, the nature of a thing is primarily its form.[55] Ashley gives a useful summary of how Aristotle's four causes articulate the inter-relationships of *potency and act* in any natural unit belonging to the dynamic, evolutionary universe:

> The natural unit has (1) some *organization* or order (formal cause) and (2) at the same time has *potentiality* (material "cause") for becoming other than it is. (3) This potentiality is actualized from outside by *another natural unit* (efficient cause), and this actualization is either destructive of the unit, or actualizes it in its own line of stability and actuality, and hence is (4) *teleological* (final "cause").[56]

The evolution of language after the originary scene is obviously a process with material components (additional sounds, gestures, symbols, etc.) that can be added on by the human community, by means of their own rational agency, to their material repertoire of signs after that first scene of hominization. But as part of that scene, the *mental act* by which an original human conceives of the *material scapegoat* as somehow *immaterially significant* has to be part of the scene.[57] In Girard's account of the scene, this corresponds to the deification of the scapegoat. But while this is a plausible materialist scientific hypothesis (i.e., insofar as it is restricted to material causality), it is unfortunately impossible to test empirically in material terms, since the originary scene is by definition unrepeatable. The plausibility of Girard's scenario derives solely from his classification of the structures of what he alleges are the distorted mythical memories traceable to that originary scene of persecution.[58] But his hypothesis does not articulate the epigenesis on the originary scene of man's formal dimension: viz., that the *mental act* generated on the scene is *immaterial* (i.e., that "understanding signifies one's projecting oneself upon one's current possibility of Being-in-the-world; that is to say, it signifies existing as this possibility").[59]

This immateriality is nothing magical or mythical, provided we resolve it in terms of its causal explanations. Girard purports to do so, but my critique is that his material cause *precedes* his formal cause, such that no causal motivation is given other than time. This is clear from Girard's remarks in *Things Hidden* answering the question about how the scapegoat victim would become the sacred signifier:

> It is necessary to conceive of stages, however, which were perhaps the longest in all human history, in which the signifying effects have still not truly taken shape. One would have to answer your question by saying that once the victim appeared, however dimly, the process leading toward the sacred has begun, although concepts and representations are not yet part of it.[60]

But the immaterial mental act Girard needs to explain is: "This [scapegoat] is our communal deity." Of course, I am expressing that mental act here with a metaphysical declarative sentence that strictly speaking is only a subsequent evolutionary mode of speech acts.[61] But on the originary scene, even without such a declarative sentence, there was generated the same *mental act* which this declarative sentence now attempts to represent using language. On the originary scene a mere gesture could have stood in for today's declarative sentence as the representation signing that mental act. The point is that the generative hypothesis explains the generation of an *internal mental act* that defines the human as human.

Therefore if the originary scene is generated by a host of material factors aligning in terms of material causality (e.g., unanimous violence against a scapegoat), the mental act that apprehends that alignment has to be coincident with that alignment. The reason for this is that a mental act cannot apprehend what it apprehends *after* it has apprehended it.[62] By definition the formal causality of the immaterial act of apprehension must be coincident with its material causes, otherwise no new *nature* of human consciousness has been formed.[63] Without the correlation of matter and form, no new nature has evolved, and the only event occurring is animals apprehending, with their indexical sensory activity, various material configurations on the scene. That animal apprehension would be devoid of any communal significance because no new symbolic *form* has been given to them.[64]

But in the originary scene of Gans, there is a correlation of form with matter in that the formal causality of the mental act of representation is generated *together with* the material causality of the scene. That is, in Gans' scene there is an epigenesis. The consequence of his modified scenic hypothesis is that a scapegoat need not necessarily be part of the scene,[65] which is fortunate, since it seems to be a needlessly dogmatic empirical claim to demand the material presence of a scapegoat on the originary scene.

Girard's universal scapegoating pattern does not exist in reality any more than Plato's Ideas do.[66] Rather, what is required is simply the correlation of a formally immaterial mental act with a plausible set of material conditions that could define a group as a community. Gans describes the requisite correlation of causal factors thus:

> ...a circle of protohumans, possibly after a successful hunt, surround an appetitively attractive object, for example, the body of a large animal. Such an object is potentially a focus of conflict, since the appetites of all are directed to something that cannot belong to all...at the moment of crisis, the strength of the appetitive drive has been increased by appetitive mimesis, the propensity to imitate one's fellows in their choice of an object of appropriation, to such a point that the dominance hierarchy can no longer counteract the symmetry of the situation.... Hence, in violation of the dominance hierarchy, all hands reach out for the object; but at the same time each is deterred from appropriating it by the sight of all the others reaching in the same direction. The 'fearful symmetry' of the situation makes it impossible for any one participant to defy the others and pursue the gesture to its conclusion. The center of the circle appears to possess a repellent, sacred force that prevents its occupation by the members of the group, that converts the gesture of appropriation into a gesture of designation, that is, into an ostensive sign. Thus the sign arises as an *aborted gesture of appropriation* that comes to designate the object rather than attempting to capture it. The sign is an economical substitute for its inaccessible referent. Things are scarce and consequently objects of potential contention; signs are abundant because they can be reproduced at will.[67]

Thus the communal understanding on the originary scene is metaphysical. By this we use the term "metaphysical" not in its pejorative sense, that is, as something scientifically otiose that invokes disproportionate principles of causality to explain states of material being. Rather we use the term in its proper causal sense, in that it denotes the immaterial being of something. The immaterial being on the original scene is *the mental act* by which the new humans recognize the *formal significance* ("a repellent, sacred force") of the *correlative material alignment* (a symmetry generated by the "aborted gesture of appropriation"). This correlation of matter with form thus arrives on the originary scene as an experience of the epigenesis of a uniquely *new nature*. That is, it is the inaugural experience of the human *as human*.[68]

Thus, given human nature (i.e., that it is actually constituted and defined by the potential for mental acts of such communal significance), it is impossible to maintain an evolutionary hypothesis that postulates either *the priority of a formal cause* (as "intelligent design" proponents do by inordinately invoking God's direct action) or *the priority of a material cause* (as the philosophically impoverished proponents of a dogmatically atheistic evolutionism and scientism do). To assert the priority of formal causality would be to assert something like, "God made man when he said, 'let there be man,' and there was man." That is, it would be to invoke *merely* divine causality on the originary scene. For what "divine causality" means in metaphysical terms here is simply the metaphysical causal doctrine of the priority of act to form (since the divinity of God is that, unlike any other being, he alone is pure act).[69] Therefore formal causality alone without material causality is what myths recognize about the originary scene, viz., the *formal* significance of the human; but they (like the mythology of "intelligent design") divorce this formal significance from a fully scientific account of the *correlative* material causes.[70]

Girard, on the one hand, has a universal scapegoating Idea that lends itself well to being a *deus ex machina* explanation of the sort favoured by radical leftists and other dogmatic moral equivalence theorists. This is the "idealist" side of Girard that resembles Plato's idealism. On the other hand, Girard also has a "realist" side to him that asserts the priority of a sudden material cause. The scapegoat generates communal peace, which in turn is misinterpreted and misrepresented as coming from the divine agency of that deified scapegoat. But it is impossible for Girard's model to causally account for this as a coincident event (i.e., in which the formal and material causes coincide) that causes the new human nature, because *the peace precedes the recognition of it as "divine" peace*. In the Gansian scene, however, the material cause (i.e., the communal symmetry of the aborted gestures of appropriation) is *inconceivable* in the scenic hypothesis apart from its coincidence with the formal causality (i.e., the recognition of the gestures as *ostensive*, that is, as indicating the sacred object of desire in the scenic center). In Girard's scene, because we can imagine a "time lag" between the material cause (the dead scapegoat bringing peace) and the formal cause (the recognition of the scapegoat as deity) this means that there is *no necessary connection between the material and formal cause.* Thus Girard has a gradualist evolutionary hypothesis that does not account for the formal epigenesis of human nature; as he puts it:

> There is no need to assume that the mechanism of awakening attention works right away; one can imagine that for a considerable period it produced nothing at all, or *next to nothing.* Nonetheless, even the most rudimentary signifying effects result from the necessity of controlling mimesis; as soon as we grant that these effects can be in the slightest degree cumulative, we will have recognized them as forerunners of forms of human culture.[71]

In Gans' scene, however, there is no conceivable "time lag" with *next to nothing* going on; in contrast, for him the formal and material causation is correlative. The formal significance is inseparable from the aborted gesture itself. The sacred center is designated by the communal sign: "This [central object of desire] is our communal deity." The participants in the scene do not require a "time lag" to reflect on the significance of their aborted gesture, because it is *the very act of their aborted gesture* that is significant: i.e., it has averted violence by means of a mental act in which the community *recognizes their representation of the sacred* as having averting violence.

In reply, a Girardian may wish to stipulate that the recognition of the scapegoat as deity could, at one chance event time, occur *simultaneously* with the generated peace. In other words, one could assert that the scapegoat mechanism would have resulted in the generation of the human when, on one occasion, there was no "time lag". That is, at some time, then, formal and material causality *had* simultaneously coincided. Perhaps this would occur after several "trial runs" of the scapegoat scenario, which eventually "clicked" simultaneously on this one occasion, finally resulting, at last, in the formal recognition that coincides with human consciousness: "This [immediately misrecognized scapegoat] is our deity." But this chance event would be extremely weak in its effect (as Girard rightly recognizes),[72] as weak as a chance genesis of genetic mutation. Genetic mutation never suddenly creates a new species (this is the "naïve, impoverished, and simplistic interpretation"; i.e., it is most emphatically *not* the evolutionary understanding of how mutation works with natural selection): for this reason, an epigenesis of *form* must mark the sudden transition to man.[73]

Note how this Girardian reply (viz., "imagine if 'on this one occasion' human nature happens") does not answer the metaphysical objection to the Girardian scenario. It is does not address the causal critique that requires an epigenesis, as evolutionary biology has demonstrated the data calls for.[74] That is, it does not address the major fault in the Girardian hypothesis: that the postulated recognition of the deity (i.e., the misrecognized scapegoat) has no *necessary* connection between the simultaneity of the formal and material causality as constitutive of the originary scene. The possible "time lag" that we can imagine on the scapegoat scene demonstrates the lack of causal necessity in the hypothesis. Only on the Gansian hypothesis is there a necessary connection between the material and formal causality, i.e., only on the Gansian hypothesis is there *an epigenetic activation from the material in the formal*. In other words, only the Gansian hypothesis is truly scientific, whereas the Girardian scenario still postulates the magic of storytelling (with regard to *formal* causality), i.e., the mythical intervention that "on this one occasion" humanity formally happened. The way to see this is to realize that the lack of a *necessary* correlation between matter and form in Girard's scenario is equivalent, in metaphysical terms, to postulating that, on one special day, God intervened (as in the "intelligent design" scenarios) to impose the divine exemplar, i.e., his Idea of a scapegoating pattern.

In other words, Girard's scenario, because it does not embrace the full Aristotelian causal dynamism that neo-Darwinism has rediscovered (and has factually fleshed out well beyond Aristotle's empirical imagination), is a scenario still (like "intelligent design") needlessly *mythical* in metaphysical terms. That is, it grants no autonomy or automatic causality to the workings of nature.[75] The scapegoat mechanism gives the illusion that Girard is explaining the scene like a scientific materialist would. But it relies on a shortcut to explain the *formal* cause of man, exactly as "intelligent design" does. At the last minute, Girard's originary scene relies on a mythical divine agency, because it is forced to postulate that everything aligned *causally* at just one happy moment in time and actualized the Platonic scapegoat Idea.[76]

The nature of causation, however, is that it related to the order of the *actual* natures of the beings involved. For the originary scene to align with a causal necessity, then, Gans' minimal hypothesis is preferable because it accords with a minimal account of human nature in epigenetic causal terms: that is, as formally immaterial (possessing minds in the *activity* of using language) but materially conditioned by an alignment of appetites, imaginations and gestures (which the activity formally signifies).

But there is, however, one valid objection that can be made to the Gansian scenario. And with my preceding explanation of what the objection from metaphysics (i.e., from the philosophical recognition of the dimensions of inter-relations in the types of causality) is to the Girardian scene, we can catch clear sight of it. For there is a possibility of making the originary scene more minimal, that is, of purging it of its last narrative residue in which one unnecessary mythical element asks us to suspend our disbelief and to postulate hominization "on this one occasion".

Adam Katz has already suggested an amendment to refine the hypothesis of the originary scene into its most minimal form. His amendment concerns the originary gesture, about which he suggests the following:

> ...the emission of the originary sign, the gesture of renunciation enacted in the moment when mimetic crisis threatens the existence of the community itself in a generalized paroxysm of violence, is enacted by a *single individual* in midst of the crisis, and the other members of the proto-community in turn *imitate and thereby register and confirm that sign as a sign*. On its own terms, it seems to me that this sharpens precisely the elements of the originary scene that originary thinking puts to work...[77]

After quoting the passage from Gans on the originary scene that I have already quoted above, in which Gans states, "The 'fearful symmetry' of the situation makes it impossible for any one participant to defy the others and pursue the gesture to its conclusion,"[78] Katz goes on to argue persuasively for his amendment with the following rejoinder:

> But then what makes the symmetry fearful, if not that somewhere in the group the violence has already begun, that is, that the ostensive sign wards off a mimetic contagion in process? In this case the aborted gesture becomes a sign *in distinction from* this contagion. While the aborted gesture might conceivably be made by several, even all of the participants, the necessary distinction from the process of contagion suggests that somewhere this distinction will be sharper, and that if the sign *qua* sign emerges someplace within the scene it is economical to assume that imitation of that singular gesture is more likely than a simultaneous discovery of its efficacy.[79]

In terms of my critique of Girard's scene, then, which demanded a metaphysically coherent account of causality of the scene, we can see how Katz' amendment refines Gans' scene in accord with the strictest scientific and philosophical causal requirements.

The Katz amendment purges the originary scene of its last mythical "occasion" postulate. That is, we no longer have to assume that "on this one occasion" everyone *just so happened* to abort their gestures of appropriation at roughly the same time, instantiating a Platonic Idea of a circle of finger-pointers all pointing at the divine center. We do not need any such mythical narrative requirement, in which protohumans stumble across the *formal signification of the sacred* because the "fearful symmetry" of the ostensive gestures *just so happened* to align with the *material configuration* of the extended arms on the encircling periphery (all arms being stretched towards the one desired object in the center).

Katz' amendment should be adopted and confirmed, then, for a reason in addition to the ones that he has already articulated (i.e., concerning all the possibilities that this more minimal hypothesis opens up for originary analysis).[80] That is, on the basis of the reasoning I have set forth regarding the metaphysical requirements of the scene, Katz' amendment is required if the originary scene is to be purged of any residue of mythical narrative. We have seen that "mythical narrative" is equivalent to *the inordinate invocation of divine agency* in any explanatory scenario. If change (especially the evolutionary change which is our subject matter here) can be accounted for by secondary causal factors other than direct divine intervention by the First Cause, then the principle of causality demands that we scientifically assign a proper cause proportionate to the activation of *the form on the scene.* The originary scene, in metaphysical terms, only requires one protohuman to abort his gesture as he recognizes a sacrality on the scene (the epigenetic moment of the formal cause) that is correlative to the appetitively desired object (material cause). The reason for this being the minimal metaphysical requirement is that only *one mental act* is required to be generated from the one correlative act of form actualizing the potency in matter. At minimum, only one protohuman on the scene is required to mentally "get it" (i.e., to represent "this is the deity") and to thus become human in nature by this first actualization of humanity. Let us name this first human in honour of the discoverer of the Katz amendment; let us call him "Adam."

Conclusion: Imagining the Garden of Eden

And thus we have arrived at last to the point where I can offer my suggestion about how to metaphysically understand the incorporation of "firstness" on the originary scene (that "firstness" to which Katz has drawn our attention) by giving a unitary empiriological and ontological account of the scene. I suggest the following originary scene:

The community of protohumans is threatened by a contagion of violence as they battle over an appetitive object. Before the mimetic crisis happened, "Adam" had been the dominant animal in the hierarchy. Now he again asserts his dominance, but in a new way. Whereas before he would physically defeat his rivals, it is now the case that, because the crisis of undifferentiation has led to too many simultaneous challengers for him to defeat, he throws a gesture in the direction of the desired object that he cannot possess. The gesture deliberately stops short of appropriation so that he does not incur the wrath of his now numerous undifferentiated challengers. (This apprehended potential danger, vividly illustrated by the contagious violence all around Adam, is the *efficient* cause of the aborted gesture.) With that aborted gesture of appropriation, he indicates the ostensive (*material*) object that is desired in the (*formal*)[81] imagination *and* also inadvertently indicates the sacred means of (*finally*) ending the mimetic crisis: viz., deferring appropriative action and instead contemplating the unpossessable sacred center.[82] It is an inspired moment. At this point, i.e., of the renunciation of mimetic contagion for *non-violent contemplation*, God can be said to have infused the rational soul, thus turning "Adam" into Adam, the first human. Metaphysically, God has *actually* set his seal upon what the necessary coincidence of matter and form has brought about in this scenario. Namely, not the subsequent *embryonic activation* of potential offspring, but rather the *originary activation* of the human: a mimetic gesture that begins with the leader, Adam, and is then copied from him, which as it is copied by the community moves the community from contagion to order in the manner of Gans' originary scene (a peaceful periphery united by an ostensive sign as they stand, in symbolic contemplation, around a sacred center).

Here we have a material evolution and adaptation from what was properly materially disposed. That is, a set of *material* conditions (the appetitive object) and *efficient* conditions (mimetic crisis and contagion) "called out" for the reception of a new *form* of which that mimetic protohuman potency was also capable at that evolutionary stage (viz., the first symbolic mental act). When the matter received its new form, the new *human community* (i.e., the event's final cause) was created in each protohuman who became human by copying the formal act of representation instead of copying violence. The evolutionary species with the material conditions to sustain this developmental capacity of representational non-violence was thus also, on the metaphysical level, i.e. formally speaking, granted the dignity of immaterial existence, which type of existence, so metaphysics reasons, can only come about from the direct creation of God who, as immaterial, is the only cause proportionate to the creation of formal immateriality.[83]

This metaphysical analysis may perhaps shed some light on what the Genesis text signifies by means of Eve and the serpent: "Eve" was the one who became Eve by being *the first to imitate* Adam's gesture. She was thus "born from his side" in the characteristic way that humans are humans: i.e., by copying the representational mimetic gesture of aborted appropriation, otherwise known as "language" (our species' adaptive advantage, the tool with the greatest potency for deferring violence). Note the suggestive figuration of Eve's origin in the Genesis text. A rib is an (interior) curved line, like the curve of the (exterior) outstretched arm: i.e., *like an aborted gesture of appropriation*. The interiority of the rib is perhaps Genesis' poetic way of mimicking the interiorization on the originary scene of the mimetic gesture that correlatively constitutes the mental act of representation. In other words, "Adam's rib" is *non-violence*. To say that Eve is created from Adam's rib, then, is not a misogynist myth; it is to credit a woman with being the first and primary helpmate in deploying non-violence. Eve probably sympathised with her mate Adam's non-appropriative gesture, expressing her solidarity with him by copying his gesture; together, their mimesis set a pattern for a new mimetic cycle, one that reversed the contagion and led to the new human community.[84]

As for the serpent, it is the "doubling" of human nature as the *rational animal* that suddenly becomes present on this originary scene. As an *animal*, that is, in its *lower* nature (i.e., metaphorically crawling "low" and serpent-like), the newly formed human nature still possesses animal appetite (i.e., the desire to appropriate the tasty object of desire, the food source in the sacred center over which the protohumans were likely fighting). But in its *higher* nature, that is, as the now-rational *human* (i.e., possessing the first sign), the new human understands that first sign as a symbolic interdiction on the sacred center. (In this regard, note that the tree is at the *center* of the Garden of Eden. In this way, the Genesis text profoundly reproduces the center-periphery structure of the originary scene.)[85]

The original sin was then committed by Eve, who first acted to appropriate the sacred center. It seems highly plausible that she would move to appropriate the sacred center first.[86] Usually an outsider from this circle of quarrelling males, she suddenly saw a new appropriative opportunity. Urged on by "the serpent within" ("Now's your chance! The men are all standing around enjoying this new activity of pointing at the god!"), she made her move. Her move was quickly imitated by Adam as he too "fell" from the circle of non-violence. And then the rest of the community fell into the "original sin" of the sparagmos that Gans has described so well in its evolutionary moment *after* the originary scene of hominization (and not *before* it as Girard would have it).[87] If anything, the sacred center is "scapegoated" in the sparagmos in a return to animal irrationality; but in spite of this fall (or better, because of it), the community is ever after haunted by the memory of the evolutionary moment of representation (just prior to it) *that made the sparagmos' "knowledge of good and evil" possible.*[88] The cycle can now repeat again and again: *formal* recognition of the sacred is ritually re-enacted again and again in the fundamentally characteristic human mode, and the deity is killed again and again in the feeding ritual of the sparagmos that also *materially* and *effectively* binds the community together in an adaptively advantageous socializing ritual (the communal feast as final cause). *"God is dead, and we ourselves have killed him"*: Nietzsche's great insight was into this fundamental anthropological moment, as Girard has so persuasively argued.[89]

Notes

1. This essay has appeared in earlier versions as a paper read at the Colloquium on Violence and Religion conference at Koblenz, Germany in 2005 (for which it won a Raymund Schwager Memorial Award) and also as part of the first chapter in my Ph.D. dissertation, *Mirror of Princes: René Girard, Aristotle, and the Rebirth of Tragedy* (Simon Fraser University, 2005).

2. Christoph Cardinal Schönborn's July 7, 2005 opinion piece in *The New York Times* ("Finding Design in Nature") gave new impetus to the controversy. The debate continued in successive issues of *First Things*: Cf. Robert T. Miller, "Darwin in Dover, PA", *First Things* 162 (April 2006): 9–11; Stephen M. Barr, "The Miracle of Evolution", *First Things* 160 (February 2006): 30–33; Christoph Cardinal Schönborn, "The Designs of Science", *First Things* 159 (January 2006): 34–38; Michael Behe, "Scientific Orthodoxies", *First Things* 158 (December 2005): 15–20; Stephen M. Barr, "The Design of Evolution", *First Things* 156 (October 2005): 9–12. The controversy swirling through these articles has spilled over onto the journal's letters pages: Cf. Robert T. Miller "Design, Science, and Philosophy: An Exchange", *First Things* 164 (June/July 2006): 5–11; Stephen M. Barr, "Evolving Darwin?", *First Things* 163 (May 2006): 2–6; Christoph Cardinal Schönborn, "Darwin's Designs", *First Things* 162 (April 2006): 2–6; Michael Behe, "Godly Science", *First Things* 161 (March 2006): 2–3.

3. Cf. Eric Gans, "René et moi", *Chronicles of Love and Resentment* 307 (Saturday, September 25, 2004): <http://www.anthropoetics.ucla.edu/views/vw307.htm>.

4. Thomas Aquinas advises against making this philosophical mistake; cf. *Summa Theologiae* I, q. 22, a. 4, ad 1.

5. Cf. Miller, "Darwin in Dover", 11: "Intelligent Design is metaphysics". Cf. also Joseph Fessio's observations at Miller, "Design, Science, and Philosophy", 6: "There is indeed a need for more clarity regarding what counts for science in today's academic community, what formal and final causes are and where they are legitimately employed in intellectual inquiry, and what the nature of metaphysics is and its relation to natural philosophy or philosophical cosmology".

6. Larry Arnhart, *Darwinian Conservatism* (Charlottesville, VA: Imprint Academic, 2005), 93–103, argues that "teaching the controversy" should happen in schools because "Darwin himself debated intelligent design theory in his writings" (102).

7. René Girard, *Things Hidden Since the Foundation of the World: Research Undertaken in Collaboration with Jean–Michel Oughourlian and Guy Lefort*, translated by Stephen Bann (Books II & III) and Michael Metteer (Book I) (London: Athlone, 1987), 3–138. Original edition, *Des choses cachées depuis la fondation du monde* (Paris: B. Grasset, 1978).

8. Eric Gans, *The End of Culture: Toward a Generative Anthropology* (Berkeley: University of California Press, 1985).

9. Cf. Raymond J. Nogar, *The Wisdom of Evolution* (New York: Doubleday, 1963), 292–294.

10. John N. Deely, "The Emergence of Man", in John N. Deely and Raymond J. Nogar (eds.), *The Problem of Evolution: A Study of the Philosophical Repercussions of Evolutionary Science* (New York: Appleton-Century-Crofts, 1973), 137.

11. Human culture furnishes the pre-eminent example of "exadaptation"; cf. Miller, "Darwin in Dover", 9. Cf. also Stephen J. Gould and Elisabeth S. Vrba, "Exaptation – A Missing Term in the Science of Form", *Paleobiology* 8.1 (Winter 1982): 4–15. The root of human nature is "the species-specifically human mode of apprehension underlying the exaptation of language for communicative purposes": John Deely, *Four Ages of Understanding* (Toronto: University of Toronto Press, 2001), 651.

12. Cf. Benedict Ashley, "Change and Process", in John N. Deely and Raymond J. Nogar (eds.), *The Problem of Evolution* (New York: Appleton-Century-Crofts, 1973), 267–278.

13. For a serious rejoinder, i.e., one that makes an invaluable philosophical clarification of what the concept of "evolution" properly means in all its significance, see John Deely, "Evolution: Concept and Content. Part I", *Listening* 0 (1965): 27–50 and "Evolution: Concept and Content. Part II", *Listening* 1: 35–66 (1966). For Deely's latest thinking, that ultimately evolution is identified more clearly in *semiosis*, cf. *Four Ages*, 429, 635, and 703 n. 53.

14. Cf. Deely, *Four Ages*, 488, 646, 651 and 680.

15. Gans, *The End of Culture*, 195. Cf. Gans' full discussion of Genesis, 190–202. Cf. also Eric Gans, *Science and Faith: The Anthropology of Revelation* (Savage, MD: Rowman & Littlefield, 1990).

16. John N. Deely, "The Philosophical Dimensions of the Origin of Species, Part 1", *The Thomist* 33.1 (1969): 132. See also John N. Deely, "The Philosophical Dimensions of The Origin of Species, Part 2", *The Thomist* 33.2 (1969): 251–342. Both parts are also published together in a reprint that follows the same pagination: John N. Deely, *The Philosophical Dimensions of the Origin of Species* (Chicago: Institute for Philosophical Research, 1969). Cf. John N. Deely, "The Impact of Evolution on Scientific Method" in John N. Deely and Raymond J. Nogar (eds.), *The Problem of Evolution* (New York: Appleton-Century-Crofts, 1973), 29–37. Cf. also Deely, *Four Ages*, 64–66, 79–81, and 491–509.

17. Deely, "Philosophical Dimensions", 127.

18. Benedict Ashley, "Causality and Evolution", *The Thomist* 36.2 (1972): 199–230, quoted from 211.

19. Deely, "Impact of Evolution", 47.

20. Deely, "Philosophical Dimensions", 127. The chain of reasoning is likened in Deely's diagram to the progression of syllogistic reasoning via major and minor premises: MAJOR: Reproductive Prodigality (1st Fact); MINOR: Population Constancy (2nd Fact); CONCLUSION: Struggle For Existence (1st Deduction); MAJOR: Struggle For Existence (1st Deduction); MINOR: Appreciable Variation (3rd Fact); CONCLUSION: Differential Elimination/Survival (2nd Deduction); MAJOR: Differential Survival (2nd Deduction); MINOR: Particulate Inheritance

(4th Fact); CONCLUSION: Evolutionary Selection (3rd Deduction) [leading to] EVOLUTION AS REASONED FACT.
21. Which follows that of C. H. Waddington, "Evolutionary Adaptation" in Sol Tax (ed.), *The Evolution of Life* (Chicago: University of Chicago Press, 1960), vol. I, 381–402 and *The Ethical Animal* (New York: Atheneum, 1961), 84–100.
22. Ashley, "Causality and Evolution", 211.
23. Ashley, "Causality and Evolution", 212–213. Cf. Deely, *Four Ages*, 65–66 on modern biology's preference, for historical reasons, for speaking now of teleonomy rather than teleology.
24. Cf. Aristotle, *Metaphysics* I.7, 988a18–988b21.
25. Miller, "Darwin in Dover", 11.
26. Schönborn, "Finding Design in Nature".
27. Barr, "Design of Evolution", calls this Cardinal Schönborn's "central misstep".
28. Schönborn, "Designs of Science", 38.
29. Cf. Robert Sokolowski, "Formal and Material Causality in Science", *Proceedings of the American Catholic Philosophical Association*, Supplement to *American Catholic Philosophical Quarterly* 69 (1995): 57–67.
30. Barr, "Miracle of Evolution", 32.
31. Barr, "Miracle of Evolution", 33.
32. This is Barr's rejoinder to Colson in "Evolving Darwin?", 4–6.
33. Christoph Adami, Charles Ofria, and Travis C. Collier, "Evolution of biological complexity", *Proceedings of the National Academy of Sciences* 97.9 (April 25, 20): 4463–4468.
34. Schönborn, "Darwin's Designs", 5. In defence of this traditional Aristotelian-Thomistic insight, Schönborn cites the recent article by Michael Augros, "Reconciling Science with Natural Philosophy", *The Thomist* 68.1 (2004): 105–141. The best contemporary book on the issue, however, is in my opinion William A. Wallace, *The Modeling of Nature: Philosophy of Science and Philosophy of Nature in Synthesis* (Washington, D.C.: Catholic University of America Press, 1996).
35. Schönborn, "Darwin's Designs", 5.
36. Cf. Dennis Bonnette, *Origin of the Human Species*. 2nd ed. (Ypsilanti, Michigan: Sapientia Press, 2003). Original edition 2001.
37. On Girard's extreme degradation of the status of natural reason (i.e., as proper to human nature), which leads to a hasty denial of the possibility of properly metaphysical knowledge, cf. Hans Urs von Balthasar, *Theo-Drama: Theological Dramatic Theory (Volume IV: The Action)*, trans. Graham Harrison (San Francisco: Ignatius Press, 1994), 308–309. Original edition, *Theodramatik: Dritte Band: Die Handlung*, 1980.
38. Cf. Norman M. Ford, *When Did I Begin? Conception of the Human Individual in History, Philosophy and Science* (Cambridge: Cambridge University Press, 1988), 57–64.
39. Thomas Aquinas, *Summa Theologiae* I, q. 90.
40. The contrast between the empiriological and the ontological comes from the terminology of Jacques Maritain, *The Degrees of Knowledge* (Collected Works of

Jacques Maritain, vol. 7), trans. Gerald B. Phelan (Notre Dame, Ind.: University of Notre Dame Press, 1995). Cf. John Deely's caveats about the terminology in Deely, "Impact", 33 n. 53, 35 n. 61, 59 n.142, and 70 n.174.

41. Anthony Rizzi, *The Science Before Science: A Guide to Thinking in the 21st Century* (Bloomington, Indiana: Institute for Advanced Physics Press, 2004), 254.

42. John N. Deely, "The Emergence of Man", in John N. Deely and Raymond J. Nogar (eds.), *The Problem of Evolution: A Study of the Philosophical Repercussions of Evolutionary Science* (New York: Appleton-Century-Crofts, 1973), 136.

43. Nogar, *Wisdom of Evolution*, 298–299.

44. Deely, "Philosophical Dimensions", 105.

45. Deely, "Philosophical Dimensions", 107.

46. Deely, "Emergence of Man", 136.

47. Cf. Eric Gans, "Differences", *Modern Language Notes* 96.4 (1981): 792–808, esp. 799–806; Gans, *The End of Culture*, 19–38; and Gans, "René et moi".

48. Deely, "Emergence of Man", 136.

49. Cf. Walter Burkert, René Girard, and Jonathan Z. Smith, *Violent Origins*, edited by Robert Hamerton-Kelly (Stanford, California: Stanford University Press, 1987), 73–105.

50. Girard, *Things Hidden*, 99–104.

51. Girard, *Things Hidden*, 103.

52. Rizzi, *Science Before Science*, 123.

53. Cf. Rizzi, *Science Before Science*, 251–254. Cf. also Thomas Aquinas, *Summa Contra Gentiles*, 3, 22; and Jacques Maritain, *Untrammeled Approaches* (Collected Works of Jacques Maritain, vol. 20), trans. Bernard Doering (Notre Dame, Ind.: University of Notre Dame Press, 1997), 116–118.

54. Cf. Rizzi, *Science Before Science*, 41–50, 81–85, 370, 374–375.

55. Aristotle, *Physics* 2.1, 193a9–193b18.

56. Ashley, "Change and Process", 294.

57. On the immaterial component of mental acts, see Rizzi, *Science Before Science*, 68–74.

58. René Girard, *The Scapegoat*, trans. Yvonne Freccero (Baltimore: Johns Hopkins University Press, 1986), 12–44. Original edition, *Le Bouc émissaire* 1982; English trans. reprint edition, Johns Hopkins paperback, 1989.

59. Martin Heidegger, *Introduction to Metaphysics*, as quoted in Deely, "Emergence of Man", 135–136.

60. Girard, *Things Hidden*, 100.

61. Cf. Eric Gans, *Originary Thinking: Elements of Generative Anthropology* (Stanford, California: Stanford University Press, 1993), 62–85.

62. Notice that the metaphysical critique of any theory of causal inter-relations relies critically on the principle of contradiction, as Aristotle has established; cf. *Metaphysics* IV.3–4, 1005b8–1009a5.

63. Cf. Vincent Edward Smith, "Definitions", in *From an Abundant Spring: the Walter Farrell memorial volume of* The Thomist (New York: Kenedy, 1952), 337–362.

64. Cf. Terrence William Deacon, *The Symbolic Species: The Co-evolution of Language and the Brain* (New York: W.W. Norton, 1997), 376–410.

65. Eric Gans, *Signs of Paradox: Irony, Resentment, and Other Mimetic Structures* (Stanford, California: Stanford University Press, 1997), 8.

66. That Girard's theory is more *ideological* rather than *empirical* is shown by the left-wing "politically correct" moral equivalence typical of so many of mimetic theory's enthusiasts (e.g., when they compare political phenomena as distinct as the motives of George W. Bush and Mahmoud Ahmadinejad or of Israel and Hezbollah). Like Plato's Ideas, this is the ultimate failure of all rationalist ideological schematisms: i.e., to purport to have discovered a higher reality that is always to be idealistically *read into* reality itself.

67. Gans, *Originary Thinking*, 8–9.

68. But as Robert Sokolowski warns, the intentionality involved in human mental acts should not be misunderstood so that we might erroneously postulate otiose mental entities that have no real existence; cf. "Exorcising Concepts", *Review of Metaphysics* 40 (1987): 451–463.

69. Thomas Aquinas, *Summa Theologiae*, I, qq. 2–3.

70. Cf. Deely, "Impact", 74–80 on the world-view of *mythos*. Note Deely's classification of the evolutionism of Teilhard de Chardin as a *mythos* (77), marked by an idealist notion of truth (77 n. 199), being ultimately of the same genre as Plato's *Timaeus* (79).

71. Girard, *Things Hidden*, 100.

72. Girard, *Things Hidden*, 100.

73. Deely, "Emergence of Man", 137.

74. Cf. Nogar, *Wisdom of Evolution*, 292–294.

75. Cf. Benedict Ashley, "Research into the Intrinsic Final Causes of Physical Things", *Proceedings of the American Catholic Philosophical Association* 26 (1952): 185–194.

76. The irony is that it is Girard who accuses *Gans* of relying on a mythology (that of a "social contract"); cf. Gans, "René et moi". As we have seen, however, it is Girard's hypothesis that is marked by an inordinately idealist mythology, in a fashion similar to the inordinate hypothesis of "intelligent design".

77. Adam Katz, "Remembering Amalek: 9/11 and Generative Thinking", *Anthropoetics* 10.2 (2004): <http://www.anthropoetics.ucla.edu/ap1002/amalek.htm>, 1.

78. Gans, *Originary Thinking*, 8.

79. Katz, "Remembering Amalek", 2.

80. Katz, "Remembering Amalek", *passim*.

81. As Richard van Oort puts it, "After this hesitation, the 'division' of the kill follows in the ensuing sparagmos. But this sparagmos is forever haunted by the memory of the sign, which demonstrated to each individual that his relationship to the central appetitive object is mediated by the other's desire. Henceforth each individual will be unable to appropriate the central object without realizing that he is participating in a social act that is mediated by the other's desire." *Anthropoetics*

11.1 (Spring/Summer 2005): <http://www.anthropoetics.ucla.edu/ap1101/sparag-mos.htm>.

82. Cf. Gans, *The End of Culture*, 23–32.

83. Thomas Aquinas, *Summa Theologiae*, I, q. 90, aa. 2–3. Cf. Deely, "Emergence of Man", 141 n. 28 and 144 n. 99. Cf. also John Deely, "The Immateriality of the Intentional as Such", *The New Scholasticism* 42 (1968): 293–306 and John Deely, *What Distinguishes Human Understanding?* (South Bend: St. Augustine's Press, 2002).

84. As a necessary and moderating antidote to the many influential feminist read-ings that do ideological violence to the Biblical texts, cf. Benedict Ashley, *Justice in the Church: Gender and Participation* (Washington, DC: Catholic University of America Press, 1996).

85. *Genesis* 3:3. Cf. Gans, *The End of Culture*, 19–23.

86. Again, the primacy of this feminine "original attempt to appropriate" divinity need not be interpreted as a misogynist element but rather as the "firstness" on the originary scene of *the impulse of the most marginalized participant* on the scene to gravitate first to the sacred when given the opportunity.

87. Gans, *Signs of Paradox*, 133–136.

88. Cf. Gans, *Signs of Paradox*, 142–151.

89. For Girard's superb, sustained treatments of Nietzsche, see René Girard, "Strate-gies of Madness – Nietzsche, Wager, and Dostoevski", in *"To double business bound": Essays on Literature, Mimesis, and Anthropology* (Baltimore: Johns Hopkins Univer-sity Press, 1978), 61–83; "Nietzsche and Contradiction", *Stanford Italian Review* 6.1–2 (1986): 53–65; "The Founding Murder in the Philosophy of Nietzsche", in Paul Dumouchel (ed.), *Violence and Truth: On the Work of René Girard* (London: Athlone Press, 1988), 227–246; and "Nietzsche versus the Crucified", in James G. Williams (ed.), *The Girard Reader* (New York: Crossroad), 243–261 (originally published as "Dionysus versus the Crucified", *Modern Language Notes* 99 (1984): 816–835). Cf. also "The Twofold Nietzschean Heritage", in *I See Satan Fall like Lightning* (Maryknoll, NY: Orbis Books), 170–181.

The Question of Originary Method: The Generative Thought Experiment

Adam Katz

> What I have called the heuristic function of the originary hypothesis may also be put in terms of dialogue: whether or not we agree that it took place, or even that it is meaningful to ask the question, the originary event provides us with a minimal subject of conversation. (*Signs of Paradox* 6)

Originary method presupposes that all human phenomena can be found on the originary scene upon which language, the sacred, and humanity emerge. In the originary event, the sign emerges as an aborted gesture of appropriation in the midst of a mimetic crisis triggering a breakdown of pre-human hierarchies in the convergence upon the central object, threatening the self-destruction of the community in a convulsion of violence. This gesture is the first sign — it "means" something, the deferral of violence, and it refers to something, the object, or "God," who repels the attempt at appropriation, it is irreducible to any "signal" embedded in instinctual practices, and it is iterable. Eric Gans presents the scene in minimal, parsimonious terms — but it is clear that, if we are to locate all that humanity is capable of on this scene, minimality is a sign of inexhaustibility, not reductionism.[1]

Scenic thinking furthermore implies that we can only locate phenomena on the originary scene from within another scene, which is itself an iteration of the originary one. Any such iteration, meanwhile, is itself merely a sign of all other iterations, actual and possible: since the event is closed with the emission of the sign, the iteration implies the possibility of infinite iterations already present within the scene. It follows that our account of any given scene in terms of the originary scene, within the scene of accounting itself, must read the scene under investigation as "touching" all the others through however many mediations. Our own inquiry, then, is a sign, and therefore a deferral — the "goal" of inquiry is also the deferral of violence which maintains the possibility of future scenes of inquiry.

The principle of minimality — that we introduce no more elements into our explanation than are absolutely necessary to offer a plausible account, always preferring the more parsimonious account — itself derives from the originary scene, wherein a slight modification of the gesture guiding the convergence of all upon the object constitutes the scene, which is to say, "reality," in its inexhaustibility.[2] The scene of inquiry can be located in the minimal distinction on the originary scene between whoever first emits the gesture in minimal distinction from the emerging crisis and those who imitate the gesture and thereby both render it effective and normalize it. The possibility of sustaining a focus upon the relation between sign and object, and hence of categories such as "beauty," "good," "holy," "truth," and so on, can all be located in the act of deferral — and we would then examine the more fully developed forms of these categories as more concrete signs which appeared as saving revelations at some moment of crisis for the prevailing communal sign, drawing, as any iteration must, upon the resources of the originary scene — which is to say, by deriving a sign from the scene.

All this means that originary method does not privilege any particular category of transcendence, such as "truth," as traditional metaphysics does. Rather, originary method is interested in the conditions of articulation of the saving sign, and seeks to situate itself in that infinitesimal instant when the exponentially increasing range and intensity of desires and resentments generated by the latest version of the sign (or, more precisely, by the field of mimetic activity constituted by that version) can and must be given a new articulation. So, what we can expect from originary method is not new rules or procedures for determining the true, or the good, or the beautiful, but rather examples and maps for constituting scenes of thinking that both iterate external scenes of action and provide for their own iteration — in this way what is otherwise the fatal flaw in all such attempts at rule giving, that the attempt to establish such rules, procedures, criteria, etc., simply generate the need to devise rules, procedures and criteria for interpreting the rules, procedures, and criteria, ad infinitum, can itself be made both wholly explicable and generative on the terms of the paradoxical form of the originary sign which, in a Godelian manner, constitutes the system within which it cannot be adjudicated.[3]

The originary hypothesis proposes a theory of meaning, but a very distinctive theory, one which situates itself within the generation of meaning: the hypothesis itself as method is ultimately nothing more than the enactment of the steps leading from the everyday question "what does it/she/he/you mean" to the boundary between the central object and everything else, meaning and meaninglessness, precisely where the originary scene is located. In other words, originary thinking has only provided its answer to that everyday question once it has restored the scene at the root of meaning. If such a restoration is the answer, though, then it follows that "meaning" is itself nothing more than the retrieval and restoration of the sign as a beginning, or, more precisely, the experience of the sign as initial conditions. Meaning ultimately resides in what Charles Sanders Peirce called "feeling" or "Firstness": the "state, which is in its entirety in every moment of time as long as it endures" (1955 82), in the ostensivity of the originary sign, which "means" nothing more than the boundary between the self-induced consummation of the human community in nothingness and the symmetrical, reciprocal equipoise in relation to the articulation of the central object with the iterable form of the sign. This account of meaning deliberately conflates the notion of meaning in its more "existential" sense with its conventional senses as paraphraseability, referentiality, or consequentiality: meaning is nothing more than the unthinkability of anything being any different than it is right now and it is the experience of the sign as confirmation of such that we are, unwittingly or not, requesting when, with whatever level of sophistication, we try to "make sense" of something. And the proof that one has understood is that they emerge as the sign guaranteeing that sign and instigating its iteration.

The sign must be iterated to produce this experience, though: repeated, but repeated under the conditions initiated by the problematized sign, repeated so as to actually complete that sign, so as to resolve the doubt that has crept into its meaning, repeated so as to introduce the outlines of a discernable design or pattern that will have constituted that questionable sign in relation to the full range of desires and resentments it defers. This iteration is always hypothetical and experimental: it must evoke the desires and resentments implicated in the sign's dubitability in order to test out a new way of deferring them and it can never fully hedge against the risks involved in doing so. The only difference between everyday uses of languages and disciplinary inquiries into the constitution of meaning is that in the everyday we rely upon the results of past experiments to secure a range of predictable consequences, to have the iteration already contained in the original; whereas in inquiries — whether theoretical, pragmatic or aesthetic — we locate ourselves on the boundary, first, between differing shades of meaning but, in the end, between meaning and the concrete threat of meaninglessness it wards off. And the boundary between what I will call "normal" and "disciplinary" ways of engaging signs is itself an effect of the distinction between (borrowing from Peirce) "firstness," "secondness" (clashing, immediate effect from the outside) and "thirdness" (law, generalization) on the originary scene, which can thus account for the ongoing metamorphosis of engagements on one side of the normal/disciplinary boundary into engagements on the other, thus warding off meaninglessness.[4]

It is precisely with this metamorphosis that originary method is concerned: the shading and then cascading of everyday emissions of signs into full scale boundary explorations finally recedes back into the everyday. This metamorphosis, once it becomes self-reflexive and self-directed inquiry, is the generative thought experiment. I have already alluded, and will return, to the debt the generative thought experiment accrues to Peirce's pragmaticism, or "critical commonsensism." I will begin, though, by acknowledging an even more profound debt, to the late thinking of Hannah Arendt. Perhaps originary thinking is uniquely qualified to remedy the astonishingly scandalous neglect of Arendt's final masterpiece, *The Life of the Mind*.[5] In one of the few even minimally extended discussions of the "thought experiments" Arendt took to be the only manner of arriving at lasting results in conceptual inquiries, she provides us with their essential features in a discussion of Duns Scotus. Her interest in Scotus, here in connection with her inquiry into "Willing," is with his unequivocal defense of "contingency," extremely rare among philosophers who, as Arendt makes clear elsewhere, have a vested interest, as "professional thinkers," in "necessity." ("Scotus is the only thinker for whom the word 'contingency' has no derogatory association" [134]).[6] Just as important is Scotus' "surprising proof of the existence of contingency" (134): "let all those who deny contingency be tortured until they admit that it would be possible not to be tortured."

What, exactly, constitutes "proof" here, and, moreover, in a manner completely different from the coercive uses of the "truth" that Arendt elsewhere associates with the metaphysical tradition?

> Their validity, according to Scotus, depends on the *experiential interna*, an experience of the mind whose evidence can be denied only by those who lack the experience, as a blind man would deny the experience of color. The dry, tindery quality of such remarks could suggest flashes of insight rather than thought-trains, but these abrupt flashes usually occur only in the thought-thing, a single pithy sentence that is the result of long previous critical examinations. It is characteristic of Scotus that, despite his "passion for constructive thinking," he was no system builder; his most surprising insights often appear casually and, as it were, out of context; he must have known of the disadvantages of this, for he warns us explicitly against entering into disputes with "contentious" opponents who, lacking "internal experience," are likely to win an argument and lose the issue at stake. (134)

We can see here that Arendt's insistence on the validity of thought experiments is of a piece with her claims on behalf of the experiential basis of conceptual modes of understanding: as for originary thinking, concepts are always grounded in events, or, rather, in the internal iteration of the signs that are the issue of events.[7] The thought experiment either brings to a head such an iteration, which is to say it either "resonates" experientially, generates an internal scene, or it doesn't. It follows a long "train" of internal testing (iterations), while being sharply distinguished from that train to the point of appearing to stand alone, to come out of nowhere, and to be pared down to the minimal unit of intelligibility, the "single pithy sentence," a formulation that at its best will be both paradoxical and axiomatic. And, finally, the thought experiment is, we might say, "allergic" to "disputes" and "contentiousness," which is to say, the instrumentalization of thinking by pre-established interests and positions.

The "internal experience" one would be lacking to the extent that one rejected the proof of the thought experiment is that of thinking, or "internal experience" itself. It is in the nature of thought experiments, or, at least, what we might call their "issue," that further analysis is beside the point: the ultimate proof is one's ability or willingness to participate in the scene generated by the thinker's re-entry into the world as a sign of that internal experience. The thought experiment is what Gans calls "auto-probatory": it "describes something that must have taken place in order for the discourse to have been composed" (*Science and Faith*, 50). In Scotus's thought experiment, the burden is put on the denier of contingency to provide a plausible hypothetical situation in which one being tortured would not consider, not even for the tiniest millisecond, the possibility of not being tortured; or, what it would mean to consider such a possibility without, even to the most infinitesimal extent, believing in it. The "cruelty" of the thought experiment is itself suggestive of the sheer impossibility of the denial of contingency: we can say that they "should" be tortured precisely because no one can actually deny contingency; such denials are meaningless. The "threat" of torture is dissolved in this very utterance, which at the same time implicates the believer in "necessity" in the belief of the "necessity" of the practice of torture, which in actuality seeks to abolish contingency. Finally, the forcible destruction of contingency is thereby exposed as the true meaning of its denial (if anyone were to genuinely deny contingency, it would mean that torture would be "the only language they understood"). The proof of contingency is simply the impossibility of thinking without presupposing it — the revelation of contingency is what must have taken place for the discourse to have been composed.

The thought experiment is the declarative sentence shading over into ostensivity.[8] At the end of a long line of conversations set in motion by the uncertainty over what someone or something means there issues the statement that one either gets, assimilates and enacts, or doesn't. But this either "getting or not" is itself meaningful only to the extent that the scenic conditions of getting it have been set. These conditions are what I will later call the "doubled scene" wherein the scene of inquiry or disciplinary scene iterates the original scene of meaning such that stances within the "discipline" become only minimally distinguishable from the object (about which one asks, what is it?), and the sign (about which one asks, "what does it mean?") around which the discipline has been founded. But I will stay with Arendt a little while longer as she provides the only compelling reminder that I am familiar with that the internal space of thinking must itself be distinguished from conversation, even (or especially) insofar as it is an iteration of dialogue. The "pithy sentence," the declarative becoming ostensive, is the digressive thought train returning from the invisible to the apparent public world, from whose contentiousness it originally departed.

For Arendt, the plurality of the world is converted into the "two-in-one" (the inner, silent dialogue between me and myself) that is thinking. Thinking is a basic human need, akin to "living"[9] — generative anthropology can account for the need to dwell with signs, deliberately unmoored from their relation to objects (while thereby referring to the entire world of objects, actual and possible), placed in a sheer dynamic relation to each other — while generating "conscience" as a side effect. This is because the "only criterion of Socratic thinking is agreement, to be consistent with oneself" (187), not as in the logical "law of non-contradiction" but as in being able to "live together" (occupy the same scene) with oneself. Thinking aims at meaning; meaning is the reconciliation of oneself with oneself and with the world; and for this purpose thinking withdraws itself into a timeless space, between past and future, where one moves "diagonally," against the grain of linear temporality, carving out a distinct present.

This suspended present is produced through the deferral of the infinite past pushing me forward and the infinite future blocking my way; it is possible insofar as "life is a boundary affair," and "my worldly existence always forces me to take account of a past when I was not yet and a future when I shall be no more." This "transcend[ence of] my own lifespan" leads to the political centrality of thinking in "political emergencies," "When everybody is swept away unthinkingly by what everybody else does and believes in, those who think are drawn out of hiding because their refusal to join in is conspicuous and thereby becomes a kind of action" (192). And it leads to the cultural centrality of thinking insofar as thinking, as a "small non-time space in the very heart of time" is the birthplace of "great works," whose

> Relative permanence throughout thousands of years, is due to their having been born in the small, inconspicuous track of non-time which their author's thought had beaten between an infinite past and an infinite future as directed, aimed as it were, at themselves — as *their*

predecessors and successors, *their* past and *their* future — thus establishing a present for themselves, a kind of timeless time in which men are able to create timeless works with which to transcend their own finiteness. (211)

Since thinking is essentially derivative of the stance of the spectator on the margin who becomes an actor on the inner scene, it involves the mutation of the world into signs most worthy of viewing (and the possibility of a renewal of the center). The more thinking is itself the more it informs its own ongoing dialogue with inrushing signs of distinction, signs of *your* predecessors demanding recognition, commemoration, rededication and offering gratitude for the new turn in the conversation; signs of *your* successors demanding spiritual nourishment and precedents of initiative and courage and, again, gratitude for having drawn a line that articulates existence as a sign.

If we view the thought experiment in scenic terms, we can simply describe it as the process of founding and entering; constituting and reifying; exiting and indexing this space of thinking. It might seem anachronistic to see the originary scene itself as such a "timeless" space because the means for making predecessors and successors present in this way were unavailable. Still I would submit that we, as successors of the originary scene cannot help but attribute at least a tinge of such timelessness to it, and we have a firm basis for this in the originary scene, insofar as each participant must see himself emitting the originary sign in the emission of each of the other participants in a reversal of the mimetic contagion which led one participant to ever so slightly convert the gesture of appropriation into one of renunciation: in that present, each participant is nothing other than a sign in a sheer relationship to other signs — nothing but mimetic contagion rushing toward non-distinction from behind, and unchanging dead space looming ahead, our path toward which might nevertheless be deflected within this suspended instance. Thought experiments are iterations of this originary experience at the same time as they are interventions in and refinements of boundary distinctions in everyday sign-usage, and the criterion for judging them is the emergence of their author as sign now iterated in the iterations of the experiment.

To return again to Arendt, for the thinker located between past and future

[t]he antagonistic forces of past and future are both indefinite as to their origin seen from the viewpoint of the present in the middle. The one comes from an infinite past and the other from an infinite future. But although they have no known origin, they have a terminal ending, the point at which they meet and clash.

This strikes me as a perfect description of what appears at the instant just on the verge of the emission of the sign: from that imminently human standpoint, the possibility of infinite extension, which equates with the universal indifference indicated by impending extinction, can appear as the other of the preliminary moves toward the sign:

> The diagonal force, on the contrary, has a definite origin, its starting point being the clash of the two other forces, but it would be infinite with respect to its ending since it has resulted from the concerted action of the forces whose origin is eternity. This diagonal, whose origin is known…but which exerts its force toward an undetermined end seems to me a perfect metaphor for the origin of thought. (209)

And, I will add, it is a perfect metaphor because the origin of thought is itself nothing more than the virtual enactment of the generativity of the originary scene as a moment of the scene itself.

In presenting originary method in dialogue with Arendt and Peirce, I am suggesting that the development of originary thinking will draw upon similarly originary thinkers, thinkers who take a minimal faith in the articulation of sign and reality as an experiential given. In the case of Peirce, whose thought provides us with a way of configuring the disciplinary space upon which the (Arendtian) thought experiment depends, out of which it emerges, and to which it returns, what allows us to construct a simplified model of Peirce's semiotics-as-logic as a kind of map for the generative thought experiment are the following. First, Peirce's insistence on a basic, unbreakable faith in reality as a ground for precisely the furthest reaching and freest inquiry, in which meaning emerges from the demands of life and is defined in terms of the standpoint of the scientific, or disciplinary community (what will withstand the most trained scrutiny in the long run) — and in which one's own signifying activity is simultaneously the object of the inquiry. Second, Peirce's articulation of logic with semiotics, and both with nothing less than the salvation of the "unlimited community." Third, Peirce's insistence upon a belief in the reality of God, understood in terms that not only do not contradict, but necessarily follow from the logic of free inquiry; and, in terms that suit both the hypothetical character of originary thinking's positing of the sign and, ultimately, of the sign itself. All of these points of contact with originary thinking, which similarly articulates sign, the ethical urgency constitutive of the human, and hence of thought, and the name-of-God, will enable us to use Peirce's semiotics to construct the originary scene as both source and object of thinking.[10]

In originary terms, disciplinary inquiry seeks to restore the sign, which shifts our attention from the truth to the sacred, and aligns truth with ever more minimal representations. The original iconic sign is the first "signifier" himself, the first to emit the originary gesture, who "resembles" his own activity as sign-giver as the gesture becomes sign in the cascading imitation of the at first tentative, not-quite-meaningful gesture; becomes sign, that is, in the initial signifier's imitation in turn of the group's confirmation which encloses the sign and the scene. Meaning is unthinkable without iconicity in this sense: "I will meet you tomorrow at 8 in the usual place" means nothing without my representing ("resembling") something like "trustworthiness." The iconic dimension of the sign I emit has the character of both immediate experience and a hypothesis — in some distribution of proportions, you "know" me, and also recognize that whether or not you see me (can "point" to me) tomorrow at 8 at the "usual place" (which can also be "pointed to") constitutes a "test" of that knowledge. (While, of course, the sign's character as hypothesis only becomes apparent if I don't show up — if I don't show up ten straight times, what does "I'll meet you tomorrow at 8" mean?) And all this presupposes the symbolic dimension, the sign's general iterability — but the symbolic, meaning in general, depends completely upon the personal "backing" given to any sign: only then can the same set of signs be used to arrange a meeting between anyone, anywhere, any time (and have it always be just as much "this time").

Any sign, then, involves a "disciplinary" dimension: I must be interested in the meaningfulness of the signs I emit, and so I must be interested in exploring, testing and embodying "trustworthiness" as I seek to locate the boundary between some new sign that will resolve the scene and the disarticulation of signifying elements along with the collapse of the scene (and thereby commemorate the initial signifier, our ancestor, who maintained his gesture long enough for it to return to him when he couldn't have been completely sure, not only of its eventual success, but even about what, exactly, he was doing). This disciplinary dimension need be only minimally reflective — my concern that the sign signify (an act which requires minimal consciousness) already derives from the originary scene. And any sign contains a "normalizing" dimension: whatever makes my sign reducible to infinite other proposed assignations insofar as its distinctiveness is really (also for a disciplinary mode of intelligence) irrelevant because what is relevant is the totality of mimetic interactions that resolve themselves into norms (regularities) enabling each interaction to not be infinitely open and hence infinitely dangerous. The generative thought experiment is situated in this relation between disciplinary and norm; allied with the disciplinary, of course, but wanting nothing more than the friendliest relations and most open field of transactions with, the normal.

The disciplinary scene opens with the deliberate iteration of the sign whose normal iteration has revealed and generated some convergence which the sign itself does not defer; this iteration is simultaneous with some perceived distance between the sign and its meaning. The agent here has one foot in each scene: this is the condition Peirce described as the actual doubt that initiates any inquiry.[11] We can call this the initial scene, which opens the boundary between the normal and the disciplinary. We will have left the initial scene once we get a glimpse or feel of the originary scene, through however many mediations, actually touching the initial scene, restoring and extending the dislocated meaning. First, though, "doubt" involves the opening of the originary scene, insofar as the originary scene has not yet been closed — and to the extent that we can never be certain whether the originary scene has "worked," because deferral is by definition tentative and provisional, the originary scene is never definitively closed. If signs only mean to the extent that they are iterable, and iterability needs actual iteration to be demonstrated, what will have happened to all signs, signification as such, once we get to the sign that "doesn't work," and there is no more iteration? This opening of the originary scene renders uncertain all meanings, making inquiry possible by rendering existence problematic.

If the originary scene is now open, the maintenance of meaning depends upon the current, initial scene, which now has the burden of establishing its own closure as a sign of the closure of the originary scene. This articulation of the initial with the originary scene, meanwhile, must take place on yet a third scene, what we can call the constitutive scene: the constitutive scene is populated by icons of inquirers who in a kind of controlled or virtual mimetic rivalry set up trials to determine the new form of the sign. These trials involve representing the simultaneity of the initial and originary scene: this simultaneity is the representation of the originary scene as verging upon closure, and hence as both extending into and infiltrating the no longer fully present initial scene, generating fluctuations between different and reciprocally modifying possible closures. Thus, both scenes are coequal, complementary signs of each other: each scene is transformed into a resource for representing the possible closure of the other. The issuing of the constitutive sign involves exiting the disciplinary scene and re-entering the normal (distributing the sign); this closes the initial scene, incorporating it as sign, and re-establishes the priority of the originary scene (*its* closure, generating provisional certainty) as the essence of the initial scene, making "doubt" again possible. The iconic intelligence who finds a way out of the constitutive scene reaches back and touches the initiator emerging from the originary scene and merges with him moving forward into the yet uncreated (and soon to be troubled) scene.

Re-establishing the normal/disciplinary boundary is equivalent to rendering it invisible: either something means, and there is no doubt, or we see the sign in relation to other possible meanings and its contingency becomes visible; and this despite and because of the infinitesimal distance between the two conditions, considering that the experience of the sign as initial conditions is a mark of distinction between the signifier and everyone else. The disciplinary scene, then, is set up within the constitutive scene as the enhancement of the visibility of the emergent boundary and the doubling of the initial scene. What is involved here is boundary detection: where, exactly, is the boundary separating that meaning from other meanings (including of course, the distinction between various shades of meaning associated with a single sign — which we can speak about here as different meanings). The disciplinary emerges as a representation of the decomposition of the imminent convergence upon the object (mimicking the repulsion exercised by the object/God); thus, it involves establishing boundaries distinguishing and deferring each step or motion toward convergence from the next; indeed, boundaries within what appears as a "step" or "motion," and the disciplinary representation proceeds in constituting those boundaries as follows: the disciplinary scene is saturated by a set of indexes that, to the normal spectator, would be aligned with a meaning on one side of the boundary, while being visible to the disciplinary intelligence as pointing to one located on the other side of the boundary. A simple example: let's say we want to establish the boundary between "sanity" and "insanity," in order to determine what someone means by these terms (or, more strictly, whichever has been thrown into doubt — although, of course, doubt about one could hardly be completely separated from doubt about the other). The thought experiment here would populate the scene with indexes that would lead the normal spectator to indict or convict on the side of madness; and would lead the disciplinary observer to arrive at the opposite conclusion (or vice versa). Of course, the more intertwined the two judgments are, the better the experiment — one would want to know exactly what kind of insanity could so easily pass as sanity, what form of sanity could be so easily mistaken for insanity. But even in this simple example we can see a paradoxical result — the thought experiment itself must be on the boundary, pushing toward the enactment of a kind of sanity that would appear insane to all but a few, maybe even one other person (and that at a particularly lucid moment), and a kind of insanity that is so uncannily like sanity that only under improbable, accidental circumstances could the real insanity be revealed.

We must introduce a slight complication here. Since the disciplinary scene has emerged precisely because the normal scene has become problematic (precipitating the doubling of the initial scene), this process of inquiry and construction

of the constitutive scene is both deepening and resolving the crisis generated by
the normal scene. So, the disciplinary is in fact the agency of pluralizing the
normal, and proposing more fit versions to transcend the current one which has
been rendered less fit, placing indexes, then, on the side of the boundary populated by icons of a possible normality. Such forays involve serial articulations of
the originary with the initial scene, different modes of the kind of provisional
reciprocal closure I discussed earlier. The disciplinary agency distributing and
scrambling the indexes finds that it has populated the scene by subtracting itself,
as an inquirer, from it. In closing the (constitutive) scene and the boundary
inquiry, then, we add this iconic inquirer, stepping back into the originary and
forward into the constitutive scene, as the final element of the equation. This
iconic inquirer, or mode of intelligence enters the scene by having the disciplinary observer convert the normal observer, producing the reversal that yields a
perfectly commonsensical and completely unexpected axiom out of the material
of the initial scene (for example: once the harm done in the present by the pursuit of one's resentment exceeds reparations available for the damage done in the
past it is time to donate that resentment to the center). And so the new sign will
be some relatively marginal normal sign, minimalized to its originary dimensions and adapted to conduct the iconic disciplinary intelligence.

The thought experiment enacts the paradox of self-reflexivity, that self-
knowledge (and, especially, the more acute the self-knowledge) cancels itself
insofar as the self known is no longer the self that knows. It is therefore not
surprising that so many crucial thought experiments address the question of
human capacities for which no "proof" can be given, but which we nevertheless find we can't make sense of anything without presupposing and enacting.
Scotus's thought experiment is one example: on the face of it, the better we get
at scientific thinking the better bet "necessity" seems to be, while "contingency"
appears to be nothing more than a hunch, if not wishful thinking. And, yet,
science would come to a halt without an implicit, commonsensical belief in
contingency (one has to, at the very least, be prepared to see something radically
new). Similarly, Nietzsche's "eternal return" thought experiment (the focus of
which is not the "hypothesis" of the "eternal return" but on what *your* answer
would be to the demon) is interested in nothing more than representing what
it would mean to really "mean" what one says and does (what would it mean to
"affirm" one's existence) — again, something for which no visible proof is forthcoming.[12] And we can say exactly the same thing about Wittgenstein's thought
experiments regarding, for example, the claim that I can never "really" know
another's pain, which Stanley Cavell has generalized as the modern problem of
"skepticism." Indeed, we must posit an "inside" to others because we experience

THE QUESTION OF ORIGINARY METHOD: THE GENERATIVE THOUGHT EXPERIMENT   *113*

one in ourselves, but our experience of our own leads us to resist any claims upon the other insofar as we would like there to be something, let's call it "x" (*this pain* [pointing emphatically to one's chest, etc.]) that can't quite be "captured" by others about ourselves and which we therefore can't capture in others.[13]

We might say that positing such an "x" is itself a kind of sign, a deferral of the violence implied in such claims upon the other; it would make sense to see this agreement as a component of the pact founding modernity, relegating the sacred to the private, or, more precisely, deferring the sacred center as if it were the source of violence, since even private sacrality proves too dangerous. Insofar as modernity is an attempt to forget our reliance upon the ostensive, and the postmodern further extends this forgetting by iterating and intensifying the terror of the sacred center, the generative thought experiment restores the ostensive as the opening to thought by representing that "x" as "just" an array of signs, but an array that can never exhaust what it refers to even while that array's distinctiveness is not only in the signifier's attempts to do so but to solicit the participation of others, as signs of one's signs, in the process. I can know the other's pain, indeed, I can represent the other's humanity, insofar as I contribute to their "array" — perhaps by seeking to mitigate their pain without claiming to have exhausted its consequences for them, or exhausting the full meaning of them for others. After all, if you have really tried to help me understand your pain, in all its uniqueness, we can at least distinguish between what I have understood and what I haven't (otherwise, what was the point of your trying? And if you didn't try, how could you declare the failure of any such attempt?); or at the very least, between what indicates to *you* serious concern and what strikes you as a mode of denial — and if we can establish even that minimal boundary, who is to say that more effort won't enable us to push it "upwards," towards understanding; and if we can push it upwards, on what grounds could we place a priori limits on how far?

It is also highly significant that the strongest thought experiments implicate the audience in some kind of double bind, demanding, in order to understand (iterate) the thought experiment, the exercise of capacities that could only result from that iteration. The thought experiment tries to gauge the "reach" of the sign in question: at what point does its meaning dissolve into meaninglessness, become a cliché, a sheer prompt to plug in a particular habit? The only way to carry out such a test is to place yourself inside the sign — completely, inescapably inside — and insist that you find a way out. And the only way out is into some other sign, whose very existence is both precluded and anticipated by the present prevailing one. The Wittgensteinian thought experiment helps us to see how such apparent incommensurabilities become generative. If there is something about you intrinsically incommunicable (our "x") you must be able to communicate that incommunicability (a thorough and unmistakable marking of the spot where the "x" is to be found). And doing so will be possible only under the condition — while at the same time the effort will generate — a new mode of individual distinction predicated on such a process of "marking," rather than upon the substance "x," is generated. Since this process of inquiry into distinctiveness is necessarily initiated (if it is a real inquiry) by some imminent mimetic rivalry aimed at possessing the essence of another (or possessing the general possibility of such possession), the new mode of distinction will be a new mode of deferral, keeping that "essence" enough out of everyone's reach and in some iterable form point to the unreachability of *everyone's* "x" so as to generate a shared resentment toward the center, a resentment that simultaneously maintains the center.

I am suggesting that claims to the incommensurability of some meaning, the impenetrability of some sign, which is to say, the direct mapping of that sign onto a reality the experience of which is nothing more than the "ether" through which subjects and objects move and collide with each other are deeply embedded in the very ontology to which the thought experiment is response: the denial of contingency and the denial that a sign could add anything to the brute experience of pain, which you either have or not, are one and the same, a belief in the thorough, reciprocal saturation of sign and reality. At the same time, such claims must be asserted, over and over again: they are never secure. And through such assertions we are taught something essential about signs and meaning, which is that they are about securing the world, which we will always prefer to its deconstruction. Indeed, I myself can't experience the pain in my representation of it and vice versa. I will return to this issue in my discussion of the "mimetic fallacy," but for now I will just suggest that the incommensurability of meaning and impenetrability of the sign might be associated with a kind of iteration of the sign that seeks to abolish all instants between each successive iteration; that such a continuous iteration is itself best associated with an attempt to remain within demarcated imitative practices; and that originary method, by associating such practices with the mimetic crisis at the root of the sign provides us with a new way of opening up such practices.

A scene is known from within another scene which articulates the known (initial) scene with the originary scene. So, if the central, really only, question that we are interested in in terms of originary method is, how we might generate plausible candidates for the sign that will serve as the aborted gesture of appropriation (including, of course, how to preserve, enhance, embed ritually, and so on, that gesture) in relation to whatever mimetic crisis is most imminent, the scene on which we answer that question is directly transformed into a new scene in which the question arises anew. Gans' account of the originary scene already provides a way of discussing how one scene is closed and represented through the emergence of another scene in the doubling of the first: the originary scene is immediately closed by the sparagmos, in which the central object is distributed equally and consumed, and this scene is itself doubled or represented in the first ritual, which iterates the scene.[14] We would have to say that the originary scene is not complete until, like any sign, it demonstrates its iterability. It is only then that genuine, human resentment toward the center, which is to say human scenes, emerge. So, to borrow from Peirce, we have "firstness," or the originary scene in which the iconic signifier emerges; "secondness," in which the iconic scene is embedded in the indexical relation to the object; and "thirdness," in which the entire scene is iterated, "generalized" and, in a sense, reduced to those elements that will make future iterations possible, that will eliminate any sense of contingency in the scene.

Even more, we can bring Peirce's ternary back into the originary scene itself — it must itself have contained a firstness, secondness and thirdness in order to generate these relations. On the originary scene, firstness is the gesture of renunciation issued "unintentionally" by the "alpha" animal at the height of the mimetic crisis (we would have to think of this more as a gesture of surprise and resignation at the break down of the pack's hierarchy — he sees himself in the others' grasping and they see his seeing himself as a slowing down, i.e., as renunciation): this instant contains the crucial elements of firstness and iconicity, especially in its utterly hypothetical and retrospectively miraculous while seemingly inevitable character, both of which "color" all sign usage hereafter.[15] "Secondness" would be the moment when the gesture begins to circulate: it might "catch on" and "take," it might not: single individuals within the group are indexing each other as icons, but as yet there is no generality. Finally, we must imagine a "tipping point" at which the imitation of the gesture cascades throughout the group, finally returning to the first signifier, who repeats, in a more refined form, his own gesture, thereby making it "meaningful," and creating the frame wherein the entire process will now proceed at a higher level.

A scene of inquiry, then, always contains an irreducible firstness; the knower takes off iconically, transforming a minimal perception of some element of mimetic contagion in the normally operating transcendent sign or dispensation into a map co-extensive with the experience of that crisis. An object emerges as a potential site of mimetic rivalry insofar as it is not "covered" by the ritualistic or habitual reduction of all available objects; and the rivalry thereby instigated is over the object whose possession indicates possession of the sign itself. So, there is a kind of (mimetic) knowledge of how to secure the object and promote awareness of one's possession; but there is also a more profound knowledge of how to detect the elements of mimetic crisis implicit in such rivalry and consequently represent the object as divisible or sharable. It is the desire for such knowledge that is opened along with the disciplinary scene, in which the inexhaustibility of the sign is affirmed. Paradoxically, the effect of mimetic contagion is to call into question what counts as a genuine imitation of the transcendent sign, requiring that disciplinary knowledge seek to save that sign by properly imitating it (through self-representations as a hypothesis regarding the proper mode of imitation). This initiates a process of closing the existing transcendent sign (of course, like the originary scene itself, the odds are vastly opposed to any such hypothesis genuinely "taking"); in fact, once a given transcendent sign has emerged, the process of selecting a successor has already begun. The secondness of the scene of knowing is the construction of the disciplinary space, where each member indexes the other as potential icon of the new transcendent sign: here, as well, the possibilities of failure are far higher than those of success, and the possibility exists of mimetic rivalry infiltrating and destroying the discipline as well. Finally, the thirdness of the scene of knowing is the various more or less institutionalized (and ritualized) disciplinary spaces contending with each other on a scene erected before and streaming into (through the latter's more crisis-ridden elements) the normal, producing new modes of firstness.

The test of originary method, then, is, in a sense, rhetorical[16] — whether or not it can constitute scenes that are iterations of the originary scene and that are open to everyone — everyone, that is, willing to accept that their own hypothesis of origins could be made more minimal, which is itself a very minimal requirement. And originary method can meet anyone halfway by recognizing that iterations of the originary scene will necessarily be diverse since the scene itself is never really closed — each iteration elicits another so far undisclosed element or dimension of an element on the scene, and the iteration must itself be made available for other iterations within other scenes with their own "criteria" for an appropriate gesture. The thought experiment is always an attempt at reconciling two forms of the sacred being within a more originary, minimal representation; part of the work of doing that, though, is acknowledging the plausibility of each of the competing versions.

Originary method is, then a form of commonsensism: it assumes that our intuitive sense of the center is adequate for the purpose of aligning ourselves on the margin in relation to everyone else. No one can genuinely act under the assumption that it is impossible to improve their account of the provenance of claims they have a stake in, or to more or less reliably ascertain the trustworthiness of witnesses, or find better ways of reducing the influence of distractions and preconceptions that would interfere with one's judgment. For that matter, there is no culture or genre in which these concerns would be utterly unintelligible, without even the most minimal vocabulary capable of registering them, at the very least some way in which something might be pointed to together. The elemental intuitions we carry with us whenever we have to, in practice, decide upon the truth of a particular claim, testify to our faith in the originary sign. Anyone who, in any given situation, refuses to participate in the process of determining the conditions of proof does so for other than skeptical reasons — they wish to shed doubt on this particular scene, perhaps for good reasons, but certainly not due to any conviction regarding the impossibility of a scenic revelation as such. And the locally skeptical participant performs a useful service by carrying out counter-intuitive speculations regarding conditions under which the most solid facts might start to fray at the edges. Even here, though, the "faculty" at work derives from the intuition that the mimetic crisis calling for the saving gesture might very well appear in some guise that makes it unrecognizable until it is too late.

In originary terms, we might consider the truth the parallel progression of form and object: the sign gives the object form as the object holding the scene together through our gesture toward it, so there will never be an object without form at the same time as no form will ever exhaust any object, leading us to the conclusion that our search for truth is a mode of activity aimed at minimalizing form so as to generate new worlds of appearance open to new modes of disciplinary activity. Since this also means that the disciplinary scene will be running ahead of the norm the nature of truth is such that it always arrives "too soon," before the groundwork has been prepared for the shattering of the present version of the sacred sign that the truth always entails. Nevertheless, generative anthropology is also supremely optimistic insofar as it presupposes that there are ample opportunities (if no guarantees) for the truth to be in the hands of those who can do something with it when something needs to be done with it and that its efficacy will be acknowledged after the fact sufficiently so as to sustain the attachment of truth to the sacred center, as the original revelation averages out across the various social scenes and is normalized. So, for originary method, the question is not so much how to provide rules for how to establish the truth (which one discovers as the form of the sign that limits disputation once the scene has become plural and there are elements of reality unaccounted for ritualistically or habitually) but how to prepare for and then present revelations so as to make them viable as instigators of new events and capable of permeating, gradually, a range of cultural scenes.

The pragmaticist account of the originary scene that I have been proposing also enables us to account for the source of error, which becomes a new kind of problem in terms of originary thinking. If we are all inscribed with the results of the originary scene, shouldn't the discovery and implementation of the needed sign come naturally, be self-evident, a result of intuition? As I have been suggesting, yes — but the possibility for losing contact with this self-evidence is also inscribed within the scene. We can reconstruct what I am calling the threefold scene theoretically, and our spontaneous interest in meaning and the spontaneously scenic nature of all thought make the trails of speculative inquiry leading to that reconstruction of perpetual interest, but this very description implicates our access to the originary in the originary nature of our interest. That is, there is no memory of the originary scene, and there are powerful interests on the constitutive scene to erase the miraculous and tenuous character of the not-yet-significatory elements of the scene. More precisely, the processes I have just described in terms of the "ritualization," "averaging out" or "normalization" of the scene embed in the event/sign's thirdness the completed form of what in the initiatory and originary scenes is merely a preliminary iconicity. This is the source of the "mimetic fallacy" insofar as the ground of that fallacy is the assignment of transcendence to the subordination of the copy to the original and hence the assumption that a representation is determined by its resemblance to its object: this accounts for the retrojection of an origin that is really an effect of the legitimacy needs of the scene positing the origin. In this case, the unanimity which closes the scene is posited as origin, so that whatever origin one posits merely registers the "faculty" or "capacity" which originary analysis discloses as a result of the scene.

In other words, for those clustered around the exit of the constitutive scene, all one knows is that one has imitated the sign emitted by another and that it "worked" — there is the appearance of a seamless trail of mimetic influence, from the convergence toward the central object and then the successfully implemented deferral. As with Bergson's "intuition," firstness cannot be grasped within thirdness (just as firstness cannot appear, even to its bearer, other than through its declensions into secondness and thirdness) — the transcendent sign, which is an articulation touching (indexing) the elements of contagion and thereby transforming them is a free, new, spontaneous act that imitates nothing, and therefore can only be experienced as a re-entering of the scene which is incommunicable because it's the foundation of communicability. Gans accounts for the transcendence of imitation through imitation in terms of a shift from the participants on the scene imitating each other to their imitation of the object in the gesture itself.[17] Since the attractive power of the object becomes evident as a quality exceeding its appetitive interest through the mediation of each one's desire through the others' desire, its repulsive power is the attribution to the object of the power producing the deceleration resulting from the reciprocal observances of the participants' movements toward appropriation. The object becomes God, compelling the participants on the scene to remain equidistant from it, in which case the shift from imitating the others to imitating the object is a shift toward imitating God — but what does God do other than constitute and guarantee the scene, which is therefore what one is doing, and which we still have no better way of describing than in the language of prayer: God, grant us this power. Such imitation has crossed over into participation. Now, since thirdness is the accumulation of imitations, it takes firstness's articulation to itself be an imitation of the (meaningful) reality it has in fact constituted. Thirdness, that is, softens the radicality of the break effected by the sign; it naturalizes the miracle of the sign by finding its structure everywhere and articulating that structure as ritual. In other words, it seeks to render imitation necessary, to eliminate the contingency it always entails, which is ultimately to present imitation as simultaneous, as in the ritual. But only in this way is iconicity possible, so there is no "critique" of normalization that will make any sense, since there would be no meaning without the crystallization, reduction and portability provided by thirdness — rather, originary method seeks to solicit the articulation of the threefold scene by shaking what is already coming loose within a ritualized, normalized scene.

The mimetic fallacy, that is, only becomes a fallacy when it is imported into the disciplinary scene: there, it appears as the reduction of the articulation of transcendence and immanence (the sign and mimetic rivalry, the vertical and horizontal) to its mimetic dimension. And what it does there is violate the "sliding scale" implicit in the event/sign relation, wherein neither element can appear other than as a complement of the other: we could imagine an event so tremendous that it would so thoroughly transform reality so as to fill it with signs that are only the barest fragments and slightest indicators of the transformation itself, and we could imagine an event so liminal, adding just the slightest tendency to an emergent configuration so as to be no more than the "signness" of the sign mapping that configuration — but either way, or in any situation in between, both sign and event subsist as the obverse of the other.[18] The mimetic fallacy allows for no event that could lead the recipients of the sign to swerve and eddy back to its origin — any reality outside of the sign is encompassed in the sign. In other words, the mimetic fallacy is a result of resentment against and the consequent attempt to copy "significant" reality.

The mimetic fallacy is an attempt to strangle the eventness of the sign, the scenicity of the human imagination, and the intuitions of firstness we retain

even at the far end clustering of thirdness: reversing cause and effect, the mimetic fallacy posits the sacred center constituting the scene as the source of
violence, and hopes to transcend this violence by eliminating the convergence
it indirectly refers to (whether this fear of the sacred center is pervasive, as in
Enlightenment movements, or more localized, aimed at "unregulated" access to
the sacred by the "many," in more authoritarian doctrines, is irrelevant to my
argument here). To be fair, this is not simply a "mistake": those on the disciplinary scene constructing idols plausibly fear both the violence of those within the
arena of the normal for whom opening up the distance between sign and object
is intrinsically problematic; and the rivalry within the scene itself; and both
insofar as competition over the desire (even if illusory) of possessing the sacred
sign is, in fact, the source of violence. But to eliminate that convergence is to
eliminate mimesis itself, or, rather, to subordinate mimesis to a model abstracted
from and immune to event-fulness. Since an absence of scenicity is impossible,
the various forms of metaphysics, formalism, nominalism, gnosticism and idolatry are constituted by an anti-scenic scene, at the sacred center of which is the
keeper of the sign, the specialist who comes to know the sign inside and out, who
knows how indispensable and irreplaceable each detail is, for whom the sign is
a complete system, and who protects the transcendent sign from tampering, or
renewal. The responsibility of the disciplinary intelligence is to resist the temptation to empower such caretakers of the sign and take up the difficult work of
retrieving, modifying and expanding the sign in response to exigencies generated by the very success of the sign. The mimetic fallacy is the intensification of
the desire to possess the sign, as opposed to inhabiting, enacting and devising
modes of measuring it: it uses the analytical decomposition of the scene to cer-
tify the sign rather than deploying that decomposition to disclose the elements
of a new scene/sign.

So, if the generative thought experiment is a response to some marginal
imminent mimetic crisis, it establishes a disciplinary scene upon which we immediately confront the mimetic fallacy. This reveals to us the stakes of the disciplinary scene: the mimetic convergence intensified there will either turn into
a struggle toward possession of the sign itself, to occupy the center of a social
authority that can no longer provide for the required circulation and redistri-
bution of signs and goods or it will unfold as an imitation of the sign that is
simultaneously a renunciation of such possession, liberating the iconic effects
inscribed in the sign. The thought experiment takes us through a series of barely
perceptible, infinitesimal steps from degenerate idol to preliminary icon, and
these infinitesimal steps involve intuitions ("contact" with via a series of infinitesimal steps, minimal distinction and maximal tangibility) of what is outside

of mimesis: on the one hand, the sheer indexicality of the other, the feeling of motion — ultimately the suspended scenes prehended in the open scene one acts on, and the suspended scenes prehended through those scenes, all opened, all providing minimal "proposals" for closure — that   flows through others' feelings through one's own, prior to any "imitable" act, what Peirce calls "percepts." On the other hand, the cataclysm of the community, the point at which, as a result of the acceleration of mimetic contagion beyond the point of reversal, violence can no longer be given a "form" (and therefore can no longer be reframed via the gesture of aborted appropriation) because one would be consumed by it. These twinned intuitions, which by definition can't be signified, are what guides one through the articulation of the doubled scene.

The sacred center always was, and is increasingly evidently, a central intelligence, in which we all participate, regarding transactions on the margin. I see others' moves toward the center, which become increasingly complex as they see and incorporate my seeing. Something must be at the center, something recognizable as given to possession, but, from the large animal presented by the hunting group on the originary scene to accumulated wealth, fame, political power, moral authority, and so on, the central object has always had an immaterial dimension (which is always increasingly dominant, but never to the exclusion of some thing that might be pointed to and divided) that depends upon each recognizing the other's recognition of it as the common object. The center, that is, is more and more what enables us to see each other seeing each other and we must attribute to it the power of refusing to us the power to foreclose the unfolding of the scene on which the other discloses him/herself as sign. This power is God, and we pay tribute to it by representing the center (which, perforce, we must do), but representing it as representable by all who pay this tribute, and in unprecedented and so far unimaginable ways. In this way, fierce devotion to the cause of the center is identical with both disinterested study of the full range of "cause/effect" and "subject/object" relations and the taking of one's own becoming sign as the initial object disclosing the world of objects.

Coupled with our adherence to the center is a belief in the reality of evil. The contestants on the scene of mimetic rivalry aim at possession of the sign, occupation of the center, and convergence toward the center under the aegis of the sign maintain an equilibrium between deferral and appropriation unless and until one of the rivals sees the opportunity for possessing the sign evaporate and hence adopts an attitude of enmity toward the system of deferral itself, proceeding to study its weaknesses, particularly those lurking in the delicate balance itself. Deferral can always be represented as appropriation, and appropriation as deferral: the project of any sign of deferral must clear a certain space and claim a certain "privilege" (at the very least the privilege to defend the space itself, a kind of resentment on behalf of the center), generating resentment; the gathering force of that resentment itself requires some internal order and hence some deferral. Only in confrontation with good do the signs of evil become evident — in such confrontations evil comes to define itself increasingly through boundless resentment, while good comes to renounce the possession of the sign it sees exemplified by evil and thereby discovers new resources of transcendence, becoming capable of proposing a pact that can even include the repentant, excluding only those who have irredeemably contaminated the sacred center. While evil seeks to defer such confrontations until it imagines its advantages are decisive by drawing upon the inherent preference for deferral among the good and the ultimate symmetry between all forms of resentment.

If the originary scene relies upon firstness, is follows that it must also generate "lastness": as the sign spreads to the point where it has become irresistible insofar as the resources now exist for physically preventing any one from appropriating the object, there will be at least one for whom the sign is an external imposition, directly and arbitrarily blocking *their* access. For the last, overturning the entire system and violating (by claiming, and claiming to represent the heretofore hidden truth of) the sacred center is elemental justice. As I hypothesized earlier, the "first" is in a sense "last" insofar as his imitation of his "returned" gesture "seals" the scene — indeed, therein lies the possibility of deferring evil, insofar as the last receives a symmetrical exchange. At the same time, while the last must be at least minimally included for the sign to take effect, the exclusion from voluntary participation is exacerbated insofar as the fleeting possibility of evasion from the sign is taken away.[19] (Perhaps the last initiates the sparagmos, raising the question of whether the sign will be implemented through his restraint.)

Originary method, then, participates in the ethical, the cognitive, and the revelatory: it models the scene it seeks to repair and is willing to present itself as a set of indexes pointing to both heuristic and sacred openings. The confrontation with evil forces us to reconcile these obligations by distinguishing between symmetry and reciprocity, which are not only undermined by evil, but upon which evil is parasitical. Symmetry, as a mode of secondness, involves the iteration of the dubitable sign in its idolized form so as to generate an icon to index relation, or a relation between mutually adapting forms, with regard to elements of the scene which have taken on an apparently extrinsic relation to each other. Seeking out and constructing symmetrical relations once operative boundaries have been destroyed is, in fact, the source of those indexes with which the disciplinary inquirer populates both sides of the boundary separating shades of meaning. It makes sense, for the long run at any rate, to assume the active presence of all elements of the originary scene, including those disclosed by the inquiry itself: the dissolution of the sign into meaninglessness, then, is probably composed, in some combination, of the emergence of new objects generated by new modes of mimetic interaction along with new modes of idolatry and evil seeking to contain and exploit the openness of the scene. The moment of secondness is the establishment of as many points of contact between all these elements as possible, to provide the conditions for establishing an immanent hierarchy of nexuses capable of iteration and sustenance and to gather such nexuses precisely at those points where they threaten to degenerate (instantly and irremediably) into the contraction of the entire scene into the sparagmos, where unbounded resentment can always make a living by calling for a new redivision.

Symmetry might involve inimical as well as cooperative relations — at a minimum it involves the incorporation by one agent on the scene of self-determined modifications introduced by another agent. In seeking to construct symmetries we confront the full range of attractions, repulsions and immunities objects and agents hold for each other — and this provides the best medium for representing the kind of contained flux we need for boundary inquiries. Symmetry, for this very reason, contains the possibility of reciprocity — at a certain point it becomes (if it will become at all) reciprocity, that is, an open-ended relationship in which the participants of the relationship continue to generate new and increasingly voluntary layers of the relationship. The imposition of symmetry, in the form of basic "ground rules," or what we might call a "cap" on mimetic rivalry, a relatively controlled environment allowing for at least minimal predictability all around, is the initial, iconic gesture; the struggle for reciprocity is the sustained form of that gesture, manifesting a willingness to see it assimilated within thirdness, covenants and relations between relations. (We might hypothesize that the ritual emerges in the course of the sparagmos, as the tendency of each to try to gain more than their share is resisted through the iteration of the sign; and, in turn, everyone's willingness to accept their share is similarly signaled.)

Originary method involves a bias toward qualitative categories or the study of essences — whatever makes a sign intelligible, its transcendence is incomparable within the system of resentment and desire it articulates. The qualitative category can be understood as a particular way of closing the originary scene in its articulation with the initial scene on the constitutive scene. The originary scene allows for a very wide range of articulations without violating its basic parameters. For example, I previously represented the first extension of the gesture as resigned reaction on the part of the "alpha" animal to the breakdown of the group's hierarchy; here, the emphasis is on the completion and in an irreducible sense the inclusion of firstness within thirdness. An inquiry into a category like "disinterestedness," though, might close the originary scene around the equilibrating function of the sign — it must have "taken," in other words, because it in effect measured, and was perceived as measuring, and thereby deferring, the otherwise immeasurable contagion. There can't really be contradictions between various representations, any more than in a cubist painting that seeks to include a range of perspectives simultaneously; rather, originary method continues to bring out new dimensions of the scene as we locate ourselves, quite literally, within it. Originary method in this case teaches respect for the ancient categories of honor, excellence, courage, holiness, and love, among others, that both provoke and defer resentment, while quantitative measurements taken alone can only incite it — but, ultimately, anything counts as the qualitative or an essence that traces a possible path from firstness through to thirdness.

We must refer the quantitative back to the equal division of the sparagmos, a process iterated and complicated with each new sign and each step away from the originary egalitarian community. Part of the new transcendent sign is the determination of units of divisibility which provide a frame for the resentful policing of distribution. We therefore find the quantitative reaches its limits at those points where the determination of equal shares itself generates unintended and perhaps intangible differences which produce more resentment than any distribution could facilitate. This process takes shape in originary method in the form of the infinitesimal: resentment and desire have a comparative dimension — they are intrinsically comparative — and hence are measurable: x has more than me, y is more talented...; but, in the end, such comparisons are drawn into the qualitative and immeasurable: x and y are *in my place*. At this point, we are beyond "more" and "less" — having the house next to mine, with a slightly better view of the river, can be more enraging than the gulf between billionaire and pauper. This means that we can speak about "marginal resentment" — that tiny "bit" that tips things over from healthy competition to sheer hatred. This distance is immeasurable because the transition is intuitive and imperceptible; but the attempt to measure it nevertheless produces crucial knowledge: was it building that fence just above eye level, the party to which I wasn't invited and yet *he* was...whatever we can propose as the tipping point into "asymptotic" resentment (or, contrarily, whether it is, say, memory of my parents' struggling against far more difficult conditions that operates as a sign deferring this outcome) is what sets up the space of inquiry which moves beyond the quantitative into different possible scenic articulations. The effort to measure the infinitesimal (ultimately a mode of warding off evil) is the origin of the indexes the iconic intelligence distributes on either side of the falling or disintegrating sign in conducting its boundary inquiry. The completion of the inquiry comes when the ending of another scene is revealed (brought from mediate to immediate relation) in minimal form in the middle of the present, open one (in the midst of its secondness, in the flux of index/icon interactions), providing the latter scene with the sign that will retrieve the origin and close the scene.

The more closely we look at any sign, the more we iterate it so as to reveal its ground in the invisible, the more we convert the sign into a set of indexes pointing to the disciplinary space, the more the elements of permanence in signification as such are shaken free from those elements of the sign that are closed along with the more specific threat they originally warded off. The disciplinary space comes into existence as a kind of exodus from the social and institutional investment in precisely those elements of the sign that worked best and are therefore now especially irrelevant. This move involves a desire for minimality and a resistance to certainty: it is in the nudging of absolutist assertions so that what appears 100% true might be made to appear less so, even 99.9%, because that's enough to play with variations on the scene frozen behind the certainty. This is not to say that originary method is more skeptical or less confident in its claims than any other method; rather, it is aware that underlying every concept there is an event that can be represented yet more minimally, and that in effecting that minimalization one retrieves and restores the category in question in some new relationship (now opened) between that category and all others and that this new relationship is only crystallizing in the very event of inquiry. We move more and more, as Peirce recommended, towards claims formulated in hypothetical and probabilistic terms along with increasing faith that the "threefold universe" is becoming more complex, more articulated, more unified — and that to the extent that it isn't, or in accord with the marginal probability that things are developing or disintegrating otherwise, it is in the signs resulting from our inquiry that such degenerations will be visible and resisted.[20]

On the disciplinary scene, exploring the region of doubt opened up with the normal, initial, scene promotes, simply in the interest of maintaining the scene and seeing what it gives us to see, an attitude of doubt toward all signs. Deliberately seeking out some minimal degree of uncertainty in fixed beliefs, even formulated as "if I'm wrong about this the intelligibility of the world comes to depend upon the following highly improbable scene," enables us to set up a distinction between "meaning" and "information" (a distinction which is itself a form of the distinction between the originary and the generative). "Meaning" I have amply defined and described: it is the relation to the sign as initial conditions, a firstness. Meaning is the minimal distinction of the sign from the scene, even as the sign takes center place as the constituent element of the scene.

Information, meanwhile, is rendering the entire scene maximally meaningful: every element of the medium, environment, and accumulated references to prior and co-existing scenes, indeed, the entire sign system, becomes detachable as sign. Where, after all, does the sign begin and end? With the first gesture toward the object? The first disturbance introduced by the contagion of desire? The first recognition of this disturbance, perhaps manifested in its exacerbation? How could we definitively isolate the gesture from these preliminaries and the aftermath that "legitimate" the sign, make it real: the sparagmos, the ritual iteration? The sign must be understood as the fingertip of the first outstretched/ withdrawn hand and the entirely new configuration of the (now) community and every "point" in between. So, the sign *qua* sign is the very distinction between the faintest "profile" of the sign and the entire articulation in which that profile is embedded, through which it ramifies and echoes. And the more the sign is put to work registering all the possible boundaries separating each point in between from every other point the more it transforms each of these boundary markers into signs whose relation to all other signs is increasingly regulated by shifting probabilities: think about a public opinion poll that is constantly modified by introducing the results of the previous poll so that ultimately what is registered is opinions about possible opinions about... and interestingly, the effect of this is to maximize faith in the possibility that at the very least (which is at the same time the "very most") these transactions are intensifying our relations to one another and to the sacred center, itself now no more and no less than this habit of attunement to the information in our surroundings. Information is a thirdness, but whereas the thirdness of normalization closes the scene, the thirdness of information articulates one scene as the sign of another, and, potentially, all others. Information is the disciplinary scene itself as origin, it is rendering questionable as a mode of generating effects.

Participation in originary inquiry naturally implies belief in origins — at one point there was no sign and at another point there was, and nothing "in between" those two points sufficiently accounts for the difference: something genuinely new has happened, something that wasn't "contained" in the existing. One could imagine such transitions occurring gradually and unconsciously, but this would ultimately serve only (potentially quite valuable) heuristic purposes — however many steps you imagine between a sign, i.e., a representation of what is not present, and the various modes of signaling available to the higher animals, in this case at least Achilles never catches the tortoise — there will never be enough steps. The same goes for an alternative hypothesis that language emerged suddenly but essentially accidentally[21]. In both cases what can't be accounted for is the recognition of the sign by others, its iteration qua sign.

The most parsimonious assumption is that the sign emerges deliberately, even while deliberateness only emerges as an effect of the sign, as, in fact, acknowledgment of the sign. The very appearance of the internal scene of thinking itself — which comes unbidden even as we enter it deliberately — irresistibly testifies to the reality of the origin as a guarantee of thought.

The implications of the originary for inquiry is that inquiry itself aims at the originary, i.e., that the purpose of locating origins is to generate a new one. However sophisticated your critical methods, your inquiry is only complete when something emerges that is qualitatively different from what existed previously, this qualitative difference shapes what comes, and this is sufficient proof , not in every instant, but of the general possibility of the emergence of a new sign. What does that sign, only that sign, and that sign in its entirety, make visible? In thus locating beginnings to discover fresh ones we inscribe that track of time Arendt speaks of. It also follows, then, that our disciplinary spaces seek to map the events they metamorphose into signs and the signs they dissolve back into events by transforming scenes into signs which map and generate other actual and possible scenes. In thus shaking loose signs and events and setting up observation posts from which possible articulations of maps and territories can be tried out, there is both absolute free play for the intellect and, insofar as the disciplinary scene gravitates toward closure (albeit a closure that simultaneously represents a new opening), rigorous discipline: only a real scene can close the scene of inquiry, a real scene in which virtuality (the thirdness of the icon) comes into alignment with the indexes it brings into view and power is articulated with accountability. What is sacred on the scene of thought is the perpetual interchange of subject and object as we enter the things we think and in turn are possessed by those objects as signs of the sacred; resentment on the disciplinary scene is providentially interrupted by external demands (disputes); the sign defers these rivalries by enacting thinking becoming action and thereby action becoming sign.

It follows that originary social theory and politics is most at home in a setting that is rich in "significance," where signs represent in a wide range of settings and for a wide range of audiences, encouraging both the formation of disciplinary spaces and normalizing mimetic spaces wherein one sign can always serve to defer some rivalry organized around another sign. In such a setting, originary thinking would become a cultural reality in its own right as a generalized semiotics, enabling sign users to trace the diversity of signs back to their origins in some mode of sacrality so as to force open "blockages" and render signs capable of representing new modes of transcendence. Such a dialogue between the normal and the disciplinary would enable the continued unfolding of those modes of sacrality best suited to a secular order in which we acknowledge the irreducibility of the contribution humans themselves make to the constitution of the human precisely insofar as humanity is also the species that poses the greatest threat to its own survival. What is necessarily sacred under such conditions is whatever sign, object, habit, or institution testifies simultaneously to our common origin and our (as a species and each individual's) essentially contingent future. (That *you* take this to mean x itself means y to *us* — what do you mean, "us," I don't recognize myself in your "us" — very well, that you distinguish "yourself" from "us" in these terms in relation to x means z to us — wait just a minute...)

The generative thought experiment produces a newly distributable object: that object is the enhanced participation of signs on both sides of the dubitable boundaries, made contingent upon that very participation. Take, for example, the dispute in the U.S. over illegal immigration: suppose we were to offer U.S citizenship to all illegal immigrants who provide evidence and testimony contributing to shutting down the notorious "coyote" worker transport rackets. Illegal immigration is a (metaphorically, too) "boundary question," insofar as the illegal immigrant has an inescapably dubitable meaning: as both transgressor of explicit norms and object of real interdependence and possible solidarity (the same person who demands a strict enforcement of border laws will recoil at seeing his/her neighbor hauled away) the meaning of the illegal immigrant is a pole of mimetic attraction and hence rivalry and crisis from which a path might be imagined to the self-destruction of the American community or to the scapegoating of the illegal immigrant as a means of deferring same; so, we are driven to discover ways of representing the illegal immigrant on both sides of that boundary simultaneously, until we find a way to represent precisely what renders the illegal immigrant vulnerable to being neglected, despised or persecuted as that which might reveal new modes of solidarity.

This is a good thought experiment, not insofar as it solves the problem or elicits broader consent (this is the mimetic fallacy, the assumption that a better situation need only be imagined — and then re-imagined in conformity with the original, now a "plan," by every wider circles of the community to become "real"; such formulation can usually be deflated by simply asking "who goes first?" — the thought experiment just gives us the "first") but to the extent that either enacting or rejecting it would be more meaningful than present formulations. And the "moves" the thought experiment proposes would be thus generative of meaning insofar as it presents a new object which can be more widely shared and yet equally (if not increasingly) valuable than the one currently productive of crisis. The thought experiment effects this by slightly and yet decisively enhancing the visibility of contributions everyone is already making to the coming crisis: asymmetries are transformed into symmetries (the double bind currently entangling the Mexican immigrant, of having to be either outlaw or subversive of the rule of law itself is transformed into a more revealing and generative double bind, in which entering the American polity requires the disavowal and undoing of the very mechanisms through which he or she has "entered" it and others to whom that immigrant might consider themselves to yet be more obliged might still do so), while symmetries are pointed toward possible reciprocities (moral obligations and real yet "shadowed" relationships can be given a legal form; the sheer "necessity" driving economic exchanges brought within the scope of a political "covenant"; and citizens and non-citizens thereby made participants in a possible exchange of generosity for bravery, transforming the status of the latter and the meaning of being the former). One can hope that the newly possible reciprocity will outweigh the new symmetrical antagonisms that current, increasingly inadequate modes of deferral have allowed to fester (such as the possible nation to nation conflict between the U.S. and Mexico, with the latter now deprived of an economic and political safety valve — but also, thereby, compelled to transform its own conditions) but the very uncertainty here is essential to the experiment. (On the American side, meanwhile, we also commit ourselves to a precedent which will make a relapse into current convenient habits overtly shameful.) And, finally, it is a good thought experiment to the extent that it generates equally or more productive "follow ups," which I believe the one I have just presented, upon some reflection, will be shown to be quite capable of.[22]

The commitment of the thought experiment to locate the "first," the domino at the front of the line, so to speak, means that originary method gladly embraces its partial nature, even while making, as is surely apparent here, the most ambitious claims: our starting point is always some preliminary sense of gathering crisis and a kind of reaching around of elements of signification to match that sense; certain articulations of these elements seem to provide some islands of symmetry, ordering the onrushing swirl and providing us with the minimal revelations needed to proceed further along in articulating the material. Furthermore, each articulation we manage to piece together makes the shape of the crisis more visible, along with an expanded sense of potential, preliminary responses — we are at best just ahead while almost always feeling ourselves falling behind and so all we can do is stick to and continually refine and render more sensitive the instruments and line of inquiry we find ourselves having more or less fortuitously stumbled upon. Acting as an iconic figure capable of carving out provisional beliefs (becoming a sign complementing the scene of becoming) out of the flux of experience — demonstrating the patience, nimbleness, courage and alertness to do so and to present our results to the world — is the best criterion for knowledge we have, because an ensemble of claims about the world that index such experience will support future iterations, along with the covenants, conversations and collaborations in which lie the germs of future signs.

Scenic thinking aligns an icon (the signifying person) with an index (something that, in the end, after however many assignations, can be pointed to) through a symbol (the iterability of such alignments and assignations) in response to the recession in the reach of some presiding sign. In more Gansian terms, some ostensive-imperative/interrogative articulation is embedded in a declarative. Sceneless thinking remains within thirdness, symbol attaching to symbol, declarative following declarative according to either logical rules aimed at banishing paradox or associative patterns affirming the presumed pre-existent symmetry among equivalent "signifiers," who, in the absence of the sacred center can only appear in repellent symmetry.

The generative thought experiment places the sceneless sign in a scene that sign might plausibly have emerged from. All thoughtlessness is the mutual repulsion of such signs from the very scenes they have been dispossessed of; the generative thought experiment, in asking, "what does that mean," exposes this repellent force that leads one declarative to hinge upon another, until the successive signs at least come to refer to themselves and each other, thereby establishing an attractive pole toward the ostensive. What we point to on this, disciplinary, scene, is what now appear as different possible index-icon articulations on the scene whose sacred center has been repelled by the sceneless sign. To the extent that a particular icon-index articulation takes hold, which is to say to the extent we are forming a circle around a center-periphery configuration, we discern the boundary between meaning and self-induced collective cataclysm. To that extent, other articulations appear to be held together by force, or they evaporate — they don't lead us from scene to more minimally inscribed scene. In dissolving that force, all originary method can do is to point, if the reader or interlocutor will face in the same direction and thereby at least intimate a circle, at where we should be pointing at any instant in order to inscribe whatever (percept, gesture) will set the sign off from (as, commemorating) the event.

Notes

1. For a few locations where Gans discusses the originary scene, see *Science and Faith*, 3-5; *Originary Thinking*, 7-9; *Signs of Paradox*, 15-29; *The End of Culture*, 19-21; and his very helpful introduction to Generative Anthropology at http://www.anthropoetics.ucla.edu/gaintro.htm. For a discussion of originary analysis, see *Originary Thinking*, 7-9, and the "Introduction" to *Signs of Paradox*.

2. Gans' insistence that his account of the originary scene be "construed according to the primordial rule of scientific discourse that requires the *minimality of the hypothesis*, a rule often formulated in terms of "Ockham's Razor" — that mental entities not be multiplied beyond necessity" (*Science and Faith* 13) has been long-standing and consistent. For a very interesting example of Gans re-articulating the originary event in accord with the rule of minimality, see the opening chapter of *Signs of Paradox*.

3. See *Signs of Paradox*, especially Chapter 3, "The Necessity of Paradox": "There is a difference between formal and informal knowing that cannot itself be formalized within a given system. My declaration about your knowledge is a piece of information that contributes to a knowledge beyond the reach of that declaration" (50). More broadly, Gans grounds paradox itself in the sign: "with signing comes true paradox: the sign cannot represent the object-as-such, only the object-represented-by-the-sign…. Only the signification-relation establishes within the world the vertical separation of levels of being that makes paradoxical self-referentiality both possible and necessary. The category of paradox designates what signification is created to avoid or, more precisely, to defer: the reimplication of model and obstacle. The sign is to be imitated; the referent is to be avoided. It is already clear from this dichotomy why the danger of paradox arises when a sign is taken as a referent…. Originary paradox…takes the pragmatic form of the double bind of model and obstacle" (39).

4. There are a lot of places where Peirce articulates his tripartite phenomenology. One place where one finds it discussed in relation both to Peirce's semiotics and logic is in "The Categories Defended," in *The Essential Peirce*, Volume 2, 160-178.

5. Another enormous debt must be acknowledged even though its explicit inclusion into this essay would have led to unworkable complexity is the one I owe to the innovative novelist, the late Ronald Sukenick. A great deal of my analysis and performance of scenic thinking, in particular the notion of the "doubled scene" and the division of the scene into "originary," "initial" and "constitutive" scenes results from my study of Sukenick's work. For readers interested in pursuing these connections further, see Katz (2005a), Katz (2005b) and Katz (2007), with more hopefully forthcoming.

6. "*Could it be that professional thinkers, basing their speculations on the experience of the thinking ego, were less 'pleased' with freedom than with necessity*" (*Willing* 33, italics in original). It is noteworthy that Gans' focus on paradox, along with his continued "minimalization" of the hypothesis in *Signs of Paradox*, led him to intensify his

focus on the question of freedom. The paradox for Gans, as I will suggest later in my brief discussion of his analysis of the shift, through the logic of mimesis itself, on the originary scene, from imitation of the other to imitation of the object indicates, that point at which something new, something not exhausted in its essentials by its precedents and conditions, enters the world: "Like the birth of the vertical from the horizontal, the birth of freedom from necessity is another statement of the paradox of originary signification. Its explanation can never be complete; as the birth of a new level of complexity, it is irreducible to any earlier configuration. But rather than lament the futility of intellectual bootstrapping, we should take such paradoxes — and all paradox reduces to this one, the paradox of the human-as-such — as guarantees of the inexhaustibility of originary thinking" (24).

7. Arendt describes her *Between Past and Future* as follows: "these are exercises in political thought as it arises out of the actuality of political incidents...and my assumption is that thought itself only arises out of incidents of living experience and must remain bound to them as the only guidepost from which to take their bearings" (14). Even more, as we can see from Arendt's analysis of Kafka's thought-experiment "He," undertaken here and returned to in Thinking, thinking itself is simultaneously an event and a complex analysis of the same "cessation of action in the situation of mimetic crisis" (*Signs of Paradox* 20) that issues in the sign.

8. Gans first traced the development of the sign from the ostensive, through the imperative and to the declarative statement in his first book exploring the hypothesis, *The Origin of Language.* He returned to the question in the chapter, "A Generative Taxonomy of Speech Acts," in Originary Thinking, as part of a critique of speech act theory (62-85). See also his essay, "Originary Narrative," where he theorizes the origin of narrative in these terms. For my purposes here, most important is Gans' definition of metaphysics as the assumption that the declarative statement is the primary linguistic form (seem especially, "Plato and the Birth of Conceptual Thought," *Signs of Paradox* 175-191). The implication, it seems to me, is that the transcendence of metaphysics involves restoring, within the declarative, the irreducibility of the ostensive, which is activated by the self-referentiality of language, the sign pointing to itself.

9. "The only possible metaphor one may conceive of for the life of the mind is the sensation of being alive. *Without the breath of life the human body is but a corpse; without thinking the human mind is dead*" (*Thinking* 123, italics in original).

10. Peirce's "Critical Commonsense" is perhaps the best reference point for his view of thinking, disciplinarity and reality: "the propositions and inferences which critical common-sensism holds to be original, in the sense one cannot 'go behind' them are indubitable in the sense of being acritical" (1955 290). Elsewhere, he writes: "for instance, we must think that there is an element of order in the universe. Could any laboratory experiments render that proposition more certain than instinct or common sense leaves it? It is ridiculous to broach such a question. But when anybody undertakes to say precisely what that order consists in, he will quickly find he outruns all logical warrants" (376).

On logic and the unlimited community, this remarkable passage: "...death makes the number of our risks, of our inferences, finite, and so makes their mean result uncertain. The very idea of probability and reasoning rests on the assumption that this number is infinitely great. We are thus landed in the same difficulty as before, and I can see only one solution to it. It seems to me that we are driven to this, that logicality inexorably requires that interests shall *not* be limited. They must not stop at our own fate but must embrace the whole community. This community, again, must not be limited, but must extend to all races of beings with whom we can come into immediate or mediate intellectual relation. It must reach, however vaguely, beyond this geological epoch, beyond all bounds. He who would not sacrifice his own soul to save the world is, it seems to me, illogical in all his inferences, collectively. Logic is rooted in the social principle.

...Now, it is not necessary that a man should himself be capable of the heroism of self-sacrifice. It is sufficient that he should recognize the possibility of it, should perceive that only that man's inferences who has it are really logical, and should consequently regard his own as being only as far valid as they would be accepted by the hero. So far as he thus refers his inferences to that standard, he becomes identified with such a mind.

Finally, from his "A Neglected Argument for the Reality of God": "...from what I know of the effects of Musement [i.e., the Pure Play of the Intellect] on myself and others...any normal man who considers the three Universes [i.e., of Firstness, Secondness and Thirdness] in the light of God's reality, and pursues that line of reflection in a scientific singleness of heart, will come to be stirred to the depths of his nature by the beauty of the idea and by its august practicality, even to the point of earnestly loving and adoring this strictly hypothetical God, and to that desiring above all things to shape the conduct of life and all the springs of action into conformity with that hypothesis. Now to be deliberately and thoroughly prepared to shape one's conduct into conformity with a proposition is neither more nor less than the state of mind called Believing that proposition, however long the conscious classification of it under that head be postponed." (1958 366).

I would simply ask the reader to see the centrality of deferral to meaning in each of these formulations, and to add that Peirce's notion of the "deliberately formed, self-analyzing habit" (1955 286) as the "Final Interpretant" of any sign is a perfect definition of the mode of internal and external appearance of the originary thinker in a post-ritual world.

11. "Thus, both doubt and belief have positive effects upon us, though very different ones. Belief does not make us act at once, but puts us into such a condition that we shall behave in some certain way, when the occasion arises. Doubt has not the least such active effect, but stimulates us to inquiry until it is destroyed." 1955 10).

12. I imagine the reader is familiar with Nietzsche's thought experiment, which is readily available at any rate (indeed, I have just pasted it in from the Internet), but here it is:

The greatest weight. — What, if some day or night a demon were to steal
after you into your loneliest loneliness and say to you: 'This life as you now
live it and have lived it, you will have to live once more and innumerable
times more; and there will be nothing new in it, but every pain and every
joy and every thought and sigh and everything unutterably small or great
in your live will have to return to you, all in the same succession and sequence — even this spider and this moonlight between the trees, and even
this moment and I myself. The eternal hourglass of existence is turned
upside down again and again, and you with it, speck of dust!' Would you
not throw yourself down and gnash your teeth and curse the demon who
spoke thus? Or have you once experienced a tremendous moment when
you would have answered him: 'You are a god and never have I heard
anything more divine.' If this thought gained possession of you, it would
change you as you are or perhaps crush you.

13. I have in mind, of course, Wittgenstein's sustained thought experiment in *Philosophical Investigations* regarding the possibility of a "private language," especially
sections 243-317; and Stanley Cavell, *The Claim of Reason: Wittgenstein, Skepticism,
Morality and Tragedy*, in particular Part Four, "Skepticism and the Problem of
Others."

14. *Signs of Paradox* 144 — which refers us back to *Origin of Language*.

15. It can not be sufficiently stressed that a wide range of modes of configuring
the originary scene are compatible with the pragmaticist form I am proposing.
One might say that that articulating the originary scene with the initial scene
in the way I have proposed requires "inflecting" the originary scene, making it
slightly (minimally) less minimal, in the interest of transforming the originary
scene into a "razor" minimalizing all other scenes, and the pragmaticist form
provides the best way of doing so. With regard to the specifics of the scene I
construct here, see Gans' discussion early in *Signs of Paradox*, where he rejects
this focus on the "alpha" animal, suggesting that the "lesser" animal signs first,
"persuading" the alpha. My description here is indebted to an earlier version of
Christopher Morrissey's essay included in this volume, which itself is a reading
of my "amendment' of the scene in terms of a "first signifier" in an earlier essay
(Katz 2004/5).

16. See Gans' discussion of the relationship between "thought" and "rhetoric" in
Signs of Paradox, Chapter 2 ("Mimetic Paradox and the Event of Human Origin"
13-36): "Thinking is the distancing, the deferring of mediation.... Rhetoric, in
contrast, is the foregrounding of mediation. The subject persuades the other to
imitate his use of the sign by emphasizing not the sacrality of the object but the
appropriateness of his own gesture. The addressee of rhetoric is the "late" participant in the scene who observes that other(s) is/are already using the sign. He
converts his gesture of appropriation into a gesture of signification in the interest not of representing the object but of imitating his fellows.... Rhetoric comes

after thought, which it can never wholly expel. In this, it is analogous to the violence of the sparagmos, which it paradigmatically serves to incite" (34). This discussion is a development of the distinction Gans had made earlier between the "thoughtful" emission of the sign and the "rhetorical" one "under the mimetic influence of the model" (24).

17. See *Signs of Paradox*, 23-29.

18. I have in mind here Jean-Francois Lyotard's illuminating thought-experiment regarding the possibility of representing the Holocaust, from his *The Differend*:

> You are informed that human beings endowed with language were placed in a situation such that none of them is now able to tell about it. Most of them disappeared then, and the survivors rarely speak about it. When they do speak about it, their testimony bears only upon a minute part of this situation. How can you know that the situation itself existed? That it is not the fruit of your informant's imagination? Either the situation did not exist as such, or else it did exist, in which case your informant's testimony is false, either because he or she should remain silent, or else because, if he or she does speak, he or she can bear witness only to the particular experience he had, it remaining to be established whether the experience was a component of the situation in question. (3)

Needless to say, the point is not that testimony on events like the Holocaust is not to be regarded (Lyotard is opening a discussion here on the controversy of the "revisionist historians" of the 1980s); rather, I would suggest, what is involved is a hypothesis concerning the needed modification of our capacities of judgment to respond to an event aimed at expropriating all capacity to represent it.

19. In his discussion of evil in "Originary Violence" in *Signs of Paradox* (131-151) Gans associates evil with the tearing apart of the central object in the sparagmos. But it seems to me that an account of evil that would not be limited by the closure of the scene but would rather aim at its destruction, which is to say the kind of radical evil he analyzes in terms of the Nazis in "The 'Jewish Question'" (152-67), an "evil so great that it has no figure whatsoever" (163), must be located on the originary scene itself.

20. In his "A Neglected Argument for the Reality of God," Peirce writes:

> From speculations on the homogeneities of each Universe, the Muser will naturally pass to the consideration of homogeneities and connections between two different Universes or all three. Especially in them all we find one type of occurrence, that of growth, itself consisting in the homogeneities of small parts.... In growth, too, we find that the three Universes conspire; and a universal feature of it is provision for later stages in earlier ones. This is a specimen of certain lines of reflection which will inevitably suggest the hypothesis of God's reality. (1958 364)

By "probability," I mean the process of drawing inferences regarding interrelations within a group according to interrelations within a sample drawn from that group, in faith that existence and therefore experience are sustained by regularities, "so that if experience in general is to fluctuate irregularly to and fro, in a manner to deprive the ratio sought of all definite value, we shall be able to find out approximately within what limits it fluctuates" (1955 327), understanding, of course, that our own inquiry (the process of "sampling") is itself part of the fluctuation insofar as we are ourselves always part of the group from which the sample is drawn.

21. For some of Gans' most important defenses of the assumption of an origin, and a consequential origin, to all things human, to the human itself, see *Science and Faith*, 1-17; *Originary Thinking*, 1-18; and *Signs of Paradox* 1-9; see also the "Introduction" to this volume.

22. While I assume that she didn't compose it as such, Marianne Pearl's call upon the Pakistani people to erect a memorial to her husband, murdered (by jihadis) journalist Daniel Pearl, nevertheless functions as such a thought experiment (I have been unable to find the original op-ed piece in which Mrs. Pearl made this proposal). As soon as the call is taken up (that's the question, of course, who will do so?), everyone's evolving responses will be far more revelatory than most other scenes one could imagine, much less induce.

Works Cited

Arendt, Hannah. *The Life of the Mind.* San Diego*New York*London: Harcourt Brace & Company. 1978.

———. *Between Past and Future: Eight Exercises in Political Thought.* New York: Penguin Books, 1977.

Cavell, Stanley. *The Claim of Reason: Wittgenstein*Skepticism*Morality*and Tragedy.* Oxford*New York*Toronto*Melbourne: Oxford University Press, 1979.

Gans, Eric. *Signs of Paradox: Irony, Resentment, and Other Mimetic Structures.* Stanford, CA: Stanford University Press, 1997.

———. *Originary Thinking. Elements of a Generative Anthropology.* Stanford, CA: Stanford University Press, 1993.

———. *Science and Faith: The Anthropology of Revelation.* Savage, MD: Rowman & Littlefield Publishers, Inc., 1990.

———. *The End of Culture: Toward a Generative Anthropology.* Berkeley*Los Angeles*London: University of California Press, 1985.

———. *The Origin of Language: A Formal Theory of Representation.* Berkeley*Los Angeles*London: University of California Press, 1981.

Katz, Adam. "'A Little Direct Intervention by the Author is Called For': Textual Identity in the Work of Ronald Sukenick." *Angelaki: Journal of the Theoretical Humanities*, 11:2, August 2006, 63–80.

———. "Narrative Thinking and Experiential Knowledge: The Example of Ronald Sukenick." *Texas Studies in Literature and Language* 47.3, Fall 2005a, 189-212.

———. "Iconoclastic Commitments: Idolatry and Imagination in Cynthia Ozick and Ronald Sukenick." *Mosaic: A Journal for the Interdisciplinary Study of Literature.* Vol. 38 No. 3, September 2005b.

———. "Remembering Amalek: 9/11 and Generative Thinking." *Anthropoetics: The Journal of Generative Anthropology.* Fall 2004/Winter 2005. (On-line)

Lyotard, Jean-Francois. *The Differend: Phrases in Dispute.* Translated by George Van Den Abbeele. Minneapolis: University of Minnesota Press, 1988.

Peirce, Charles Sanders. *The Essential Peirce: Selected Philosophical Writings.* Edited by Nathan Houser and Christian Kloesel. Bloomington and Indianapolis: Indiana University Press, 1992.

———. *Charles S. Peirce : Selected Writings (Values in a Universe of Chance).* Edited with an Introduction by Philip P. Wiener. New York : Dover Publications, 1958.

———. *Philosophical Writings of Peirce.* Selected and Edited with an Introduction by Justus Buchler. New York: Dover Publications, 1955.

Wittgenstein, Ludwig. *Philosophical Investigations.* Translated by G.E.M. Anscombe. Oxford: Basil Blackwell, 1967.

Generative Anthropology and Bronx Romanticism

Eric Gans

I have been arguing for the past twenty-odd years for the superiority of Generative Anthropology over other anthropologies, implicit and explicit. But the current trend of autobiographical "witnessing" reflects a central question of anthropological epistemology. However little must be taken on faith in accepting the originary hypothesis and however impersonally it is presented, its presentation is an *act* performed in the context of an *event* — and so there is always a point in asking the question *"D'où parlez-vous?"* [Where are you speaking from?] The potential interest of examining the invention/discovery of GA from the standpoint of my own socio-psychological predispositions is not primarily biographical, nor even ultimately sociological, since sociology has no means for evaluating the anthropological significance of social formations — their historical adaptation of and to the scene of representation. My purpose in providing the social background for my own ideas is not to pigeonhole them in a sociological grid but to demonstrate the anthropological generativity of my — and by extension, of others' — social origins. Some moments of historical space-time are privileged, and the present exploration begins with the assumption that whatever truth is revealed in GA has been distilled from my specific social experience, not put into question by it.

The ethical models or *anthropologies* that we create are framed as solutions to our personal situations in the world. These situations are generally described in terms of something like the Marxist notion of socio-economic class, which our era has enlarged to include gender, ethnicity, race, and the other "ascriptive" qualities of physique, age, handedness, sexual orientation.... Yet the narrow understanding of anthropological theories as group ideologies is a perfect example of what this understanding itself purports to denounce; it would be dismissed as sophomoric pseudo-sophistication were it not so effective in serving the self-interest of those who proclaim it. By denouncing "bourgeois universality" as the ideological instrument through which the bourgeoisie dissimulates its power, one dissimulates the far cruder will to power of strident particularism. If indeed "all is political," then all that should matter is the degree to which the nakedness of political power is deferred. It is one thing to attempt to justify one's values as universal, another to justify them simply as one's own. In this regard, postmodern victimary thinking lacks — deliberately renounces — the crucial nuance that separates sacrificial from post-sacrificial thought. Now that a century scarred by victimary resentment has come to a close, perhaps we can retrieve something of our former appreciation for the bourgeois virtues.

I hope this analysis can contribute to GA itself by shedding light on the preconditions for the emergence of the originary hypothesis. In particular, I hope to examine in what sense GA's transmutation of René Girard's mimetic anthropology into a hypothesis of the origin of representation reflects what Lucien Goldmann would have called the *praxis* of a well-defined social group. But what praxis is likely for the members of a group consisting of individuals who define themselves by their *no-longer*-membership in it? Such is the perverse situation of the *Bronx romantic.*

The "Bronx" I refer to as the homeland of my romanticism is less a place than a state of mind, specifically that of my generation who were expected to find success in prosperous postwar America not only for themselves but for their parents, whose advancement had been slowed by the Depression. (Those for whom this was not the case were most likely no longer living in the Bronx.) The Bronx High School of Science (BHSS), when I attended it from 1954 to 1957, was composed in large majority of such persons, mostly male, and overwhelmingly Jewish. Very few of these people still live in the Bronx, where not long ago we sought in vain a Jewish delicatessen. The Bronx is a place of transition, and in the case of this particular generation, of transition deferred and thereby intensified.

Not all the inhabitants of this particular Bronx could be called romantics. The typical BHSS graduate became a doctor or engineer and made a good living without suffering too much angst as to his or her uniqueness. American society in the 1960s, quite a bit more than today, was *la carrière ouverte aux talents* [careers open to people of talent]; there was a shortage of MDs and PhDs, and there is always a shortage of people with 150 IQs. But given that the intense pressure to succeed generated by the failed parental dreams of the Depression was comparable to that faced by the post-Revolutionary bourgeois youth depicted in Balzac's novels, it was not surprising that at least some of us would be more attracted to the structure of transcendence itself than to any possible worldly incarnation of it. To define oneself as unique in a mimetic world is Girard's *mensonge romantique*, but to *seek* this uniqueness is not a lie but a paradox, one Girard himself has lived as well as I.

***

Without experiencing any kind of discrimination, many third-generation lower-middle-class Americans like myself were nonetheless not altogether integrated into the mainstream of American culture. In 1941, when I was born, ethnicity was still something one divested oneself of; some ten years previously, my uncle had gone to the trouble of de-Judaizing his (and my mother's) family name. Although I was comfortable enough with cultural matters to eventually abandon the mathematics of my high-school days for a college major in the Humanities, I did not feel enough at home in my own culture to study English literature, whose ex-colonial status arouses my unease to this day. Whence the attraction of a foreign culture, particularly that of the country that had helped us — *Lafayette, nous voilà!* — to throw off the English yoke. Nor, when I began my French studies, had France yet abandoned its postwar affection for *les Américains* to become the exemplar of European resistance to American *hyperpower.*

The acquisition of culture in general and of French culture in particular was of too great consequence for someone of my modestly respectable social status not to treat these acquisitions with a certain reverence. Whence my intense and durable hostility to modernism — and the reason why I became a *dix-neuviémiste* rather than a *vingtiémiste*. I was a latecomer to the "universal" high classical Western culture that absorbed and survived the Romantic revolt, but on whose decadence the modernists avidly fed. Modernism is the extreme form of the esthetic aristocracy's war against the *bourgeois* market system. It is a distillation of everything about culture that excludes the Bronx romantic, including a generous helping of antisemitism. The modernist, typically of upper bourgeois stock, affects to despise the culture of the bourgeoisie and above all the "white collar" aspirants to this culture who cannot afford to treat it with the contempt of those who already possess it. The modernist is continually in the process of renouncing, nearly always symbolically, his cultural and economic privileges in order to recapitalize this renunciation in a new post-bourgeois utopia. The postmoderns have retained the renunciation but have rejected both the newness and the utopia as disguised forms of bourgeois ambition; the point is now to celebrate the marginal and the victimized, not as new centers of social cohesion but as archetypes of eternal marginality and victimization.

My particular place in and relationship to the "white collar" class reflects that of my parents. My father finished college and law school and passed the New York State bar examination, yet never practiced law. In the depth of the depression there were few paying jobs for law school graduates; in order to remain gainfully employed he clung to the security of the Post Office, where he had worked at night throughout his college years. His youthful sacrifices having exhausted his ambitious energies, he remained all his life a postal clerk, unwilling to take on the pressures and inconveniences of even the lowest supervisory position. My father was an educated man, but not a cultured one: the refinements of university education never really sank in. My mother, an orphaned member of a better-established family, was attracted to the trappings of culture and "gentil-ity," yet unwilling to push my father to help her acquire them.

Does this analysis suggest a mimetic relationship between father and son, mediated by the mother's tentative cultural snobbery? The attempt at "class" analysis dissolves in a mist of socio-psychological detail, which Sartre alone of major thinkers had the self-confidence to try to sort out by means of his *progres-sive-regressive* method. But while honoring the reflection that culminated in his immense study on Flaubert (*L'idiot de la famille*), I would prefer to find in my own (auto)biography not infinite detail but a simple heuristic by means of which to show how the ideas of GA both reflect and universalize the fundamental rela-tionships to the world that I absorbed from my early milieu.

My white-collar stratum, resentful of the notion of intrinsic superiority that is the hallmark of both aristocracy and nativism, was both meritocratic and liberal: advancement should be based on merit alone, with no consider-ation for either family connections or ethnic identity. In today's more victimary atmosphere, liberalism is opposed to meritocracy, considered a *neoconservative* concept because of its incompatibility with compensatory group privilege. Curi-ously enough, the Jews of my generation who have been associated with neocon-servatism are for the most part of a more privileged background than my own, whereas the large majority of the members of my own class — even defined in the most literal sense as the Bronx High School of Science class of 1957 — have remained loyal to liberalism long after having ceased to be its beneficiaries. Ac-cession to higher cultural and financial standing than their parents has gener-ated in my classmates a susceptibility to White Guilt that, despite my own mod-est worldly success, I have never shared.

The idea that we are all bound to particularity in the same degree, that we all universalize our personal experience with the same naive insistence, denies the conditions necessary for its own emergence. One's adherence to one's own culture always takes place against a background of cultural attitudes that offer models of both imitation and distancing. The dual nature of mimetic desire as a universal human characteristic makes both attraction and hostility inex-tricable. As soon as I take on a cultural attitude of belonging, I permit its the-matization by myself or by others, and consequently its "antithetical" denial. The Hegelian dialectic, like all other operations of human culture, is a figure of mimesis.

The "universal" or better put, the *originary* position in culture cannot be the privilege of any class. But there are social classes whose members' relation to culture is more abstract, and therefore more "minimal," than others'. At the center of the continuum between affirmation and denial lies not equilibrium but a neutrality that reflects the failure of affective bonding. One predisposed to disaffection from his milieu of origin is more likely than another to become the purveyor of a universalist anthropology. To step back from the concreteness of culture is to privilege resentment over love and its power of identification. In contrast with the "humanistic" gestures of the privileged toward Man in general that mask their disdain for humanity in particular, the movement of abstraction reflects a tentative relationship to one's social milieu, geographical place, and level of achievement.

What most distinguishes GA from other secular ways of thinking is its insistence on starting from an explicit rather than an implicit hypothesis of origin. (Although religious thought denies its hypothetical nature, the religious "act of faith" in fact poses its own originary hypothesis.) By naming the hypothesis and consequently naming itself as a "doctrine," GA offers a target to resentment that empiricist *in medias res* approaches avoid. GA eschews both the self-serving "smallness" that Doug Collins has persuasively enthroned as the essence of modernism, and marginality, its postmodern avatar. Proclaiming that "small is beautiful" or denouncing *phallogocentrism* are strategies for acquiring power in the most hypertrophied of institutions. Each modernist had his own originary hypothesis; the postmodernist has everyone else's *but* his own. GA's democratic universality, which imposes a minimal constraint on the human, is confronted with an anarchy of ostensibly unconstrained particularity. But intellectual democracy, in its minimality, appeals to a meritocracy of the spirit, whereas the anarchic denial of universality demagogically allows each participant to retain the myth of his or her victimary group's inviolate self-substantiality.

Just as the market operates by exchanging values ostensibly independent of it and even hostile to it, most people in democratic society would rather be implicit aristocrats than explicit democrats. The minimal hypothesis, because it is a part of the culture to which it applies, cannot escape the laws of desire even as it defines them. Hence this new anthropological paradigm is neither adopted nor suppressed but simply ignored because it lacks a clientele among the groups that form the liberal-democratic social order. There is no class of persons, beyond the occasional Bronx romantic, for whom GA can serve as an ideology; it remains confined to the marginal position that the apostles of postmodern marginality always flee in practice. Its truth-claim remains confident, however, if only because it is the one way of thinking that dares to affirm, without falling into the Nietzschean abyss, the fundamental role of *ressentiment*, which lurks behind Jacques Derrida's perverse abstractions of *supplement, margin, remainder, hymen, frame,* and *différance.*

Bronx Romanticism and Theoretical Minimalism

GA's minimalism reflects the *tabula rasa* of a class lacking any real cultural baggage beyond intelligence and self-discipline. In opposition to modernist mystification, GA simplifies. Just as in putting forward general intelligence as its criterion, the meritocratic social model espoused by the white collar class privileges and encourages the trait that best correlates with the generation of new degrees of freedom, so GA's minimal model is rich in potentiality because its understanding of the human is bound by the fewest possible constraints. The creation of one from the Bronx, the exemplary non-place with no culture of its own, GA sets a single group of human equals at the origin of all cultural phenomena. Because the path by which the universal reciprocity of the originary scene leads to these phenomena is always historically reversible, there is no culture, however aristocratic, from which the humble Bronxian is in principle excluded. The opening-up of the cultural sphere to one defined only by the desire and capacity to acquire it — one representative of white-collar respectability as opposed to blue-collar resentment — is an essential element of GA. But it is only one half of a diptych.

Why add to "Bronx" the qualifier of *romantic*? The romanticism of originary thinking depends on the simplest of paradoxes: in imposing the requirement of a minimal theory, which I am at the same time the first to create, I leave minimal room for competition. The richer the original content of a theory, the easier it is to participate in it; the quirks and absurdities of psychoanalysis have only stimulated its adoption and further elaboration. GA's generative structure makes this maximally difficult. Its minimalism requires a commitment from those who would develop it — and minimize it — still further: that they acknowledge its origin.

The situation of the "Bronx romantic," lacking in social standing but desirous of acquiring cultural knowledge, is a pretty good approximation not only to the indefinite status of the participants in GA's hypothetical originary scene but to the attitude toward society that those under the "veil of ignorance" in John Rawls' liberal-democratic "original position" should be but are not obliged to share. The institutions of human representation that we call *culture* are *for* everyone, and whether one seeks to understand how culture arose or wishes to sketch the "good society" to which it presumably tends, the best model of "everyone" is one that eliminates a priori privilege *yet at the same time requires a genuine commitment to the social order*. It is the lack of this commitment in both Rawls' "worst off" and Sartre's "least favored member of society" that obliges us to reject their versions of the social contract. No social order can be driven by the needs and desires of those with the least ability or commitment to offer it — but it can rely on those of the Bronx romantic.

***

One consequence of living in the postmodern era is that it is no longer possible to dismiss ethical attitudes as simply out of date. We are obliged to justify our actions by their ethical content and not by their apparent conformity to the direction of history. For example, one no longer hears very often the once popular Nietzschean mantra "God is dead." It is no longer as obvious as it seemed a century or even half a century ago that modernity goes hand in hand with *secularization*. Similarly, we have reason to doubt the demise of a secular but supposedly equally obsolete notion: that of the unique individual Self and its destiny.

The self's search to be recognized by others as unique might seem to be the ultimate in self-centeredness, but seen in a different perspective it is the essential post-millennial, or to use Raoul Eshelman's term, *performative* ethical act. The Bronx Romantic can define himself only through the creation of a message of uncontestable originality. At the same time, in a world that suffers less from the positive-sum and therefore solvable problems of poverty, hunger, and pollution than from the intractably zero-sum game of mutual recognition, the viability of this message in the marketplace of ideas is dependent on its capacity to contribute to other people's messages; the individual's search for unique self-definition can be rewarded only insofar as it benefits the self-definition of others. Whence my hope that my minimal idea may serve as the point of departure for a "new way of thinking."

The durability of the online journal *Anthropoetics*, now in its twelfth year, testifies to the appropriateness of the Internet as the locus of the Bronx Romantic's appropriation of European culture to American placelessness. Think of the postmodern self as a WWW site, an extension of the quasi-ubiquitous personal home page. Your site contains links to other sites; you choose which to link to, but not which link to you. In this model of human self-representation, the "recognition" reflected in these links is granted in function of one's own self-image. Each person constructs his own page, and links do not signify adoration of another's, but auxiliary means of enhancing one's own. No one wants his page to be nothing but a conduit to other pages. The user who follows a link is not supposed to remain on the linked page, but to return to the page on which the link was found; if he doesn't hit the Back key, your page must be redone. Hence the more *I* might strive for substantive celebrity by loading my site with striking images, the less likely *your* user is to return from my site to yours, and therefore the less useful it would be for *you* to link to my site in the first place. In order to obtain maximal recognition, I must provide a service that enhances the interest of your site while minimizing its chances of becoming an obtrusive rival. The most effective service, according to these criteria, is GA.

This simply stated goal of efficacy determines the key feature of GA: its *minimalism*. Minimalism is not merely an empirical feature of GA in contrast with other systems, in the sense that the mimetic theory of desire is more parsimonious than the psychoanalytic theory of desire. Ockham's razor not only determines the evolution of the theory, it is the horizon of the theory itself. Rightly considered, there are no "personal features" of GA by which I as its "creator" could wish to be remembered. GA as a theory of culture is vanishingly cultural and maximally theoretical — vanishingly creation and maximally discovery. The Bronx romantic, like all romantics, wants to be remembered. But because the Bronx contains nothing memorable, he devises a theory that allows him to be remembered for having reduced memorability to a minimum. Minimization is close to Collins' useful concept of *prehumiliation*. But the difference is that whereas prehumiliation reenacts (or "preenacts") the primordial passage from victim to divinity, minimization reduces the divinity/victim differential to a minimum. GA is not so much prehumiliated as preshrunk. The Bronx romantic seeks recognition for providing the least obtrusive mediation between the personal imageries of others.

The usefulness of such a theory is in the adaptability of its explanatory model to all the phenomena of human culture, to all uses of representation. Representation is never simply *expression*: even when one "says what one feels," one represents oneself as... Erving Goffman was one of the rare social scientists to appreciate the paradoxality of this structure; Gregory Bateson, in a very different mode, was another. Cultural interpretation is the creation of models for what lies behind or rather *within* the process of representation-as. Today we have put aside the old naive models of cultural expression, but the new cynical models, simplistically associated with postmodernity, suggest that because there is nothing but representation-as, there is nothing to represent. In *The Transparent Society* (Johns Hopkins, 1992/1989), Gianni Vattimo feels obliged to reject "patriarchal" monism for "chaotic" pluralism. But what we represent is not our fixed human essence but the focus of our mimetic interaction. We represent the object of our common desire in such a way as to avoid coming into conflict over it. We make it alternately the victim of our violence and the divinity that has deferred this violence. GA fosters respect for the minimal necessity of this deferral that makes human existence possible.

The Pursuit of Amateurism

The minimalism of GA reflects that of the Bronx itself, its status as a way station for my father's or my generation between the Lower East Side and Scarsdale or Beverly Hills. The attraction to transcendence fostered by life in this non-locus is reflected in a persistent — and perverse — personal trait: *amateurism*.

Early in my study of French literature, I was struck by a key sentence in that quintessential portrait of the romantic soul, Chateaubriand's *René* (1802):

> Il fallut quitter le toit paternel, devenu l'héritage de mon frère.... *Arrêté à l'entrée des voies trompeuses de la vie, je les considérais l'une après l'autre, sans m'y oser engager.*

> I had to leave my father's house, which had become my brother's inheritance....
> *Paused at the entry-point of the deceitful paths of life, I contemplated each one in turn, without daring to start out on it.* (My emphasis.)

The image of the *entrée des voies trompeuses* suggests a central intersection or *rond-point* from which they all diverge, like the avenues around L'Etoile. The deceitfulness is not that of any given path, but of the general condition that once one path is chosen, you must abandon all the others. To pause at the *entrée*, in contrast, is to retain the possibility of choosing any one of them and thereby to make the latent choice of all. To remain at this universal intersection is to remain within the unity of childhood while grasping the variety of options open to the adult. This is the configuration of adolescence, conceived as an extended moment of transition and apprenticeship. Beyond his creator's own experience of exile, René's new cultural-psychological attitude reflects and reacts to the beginning of post-Revolutionary bourgeois society. The young man — and today the young woman as well — can no longer, as in the pre-Revolutionary era, pass from childhood to adulthood in a moment of sexual initiation; he must acquire a profession, a qualification with which to enter the marketplace. If there is one thing that the members of market society share, it is their prolonged and therefore *romantic* adolescence.

In this context, maturity may be defined as abandonment of the transitional space of adolescence and successful advancement along one of the *voies trompeuses*. Maturity is the normal goal of adolescence, but for the romantic, it is a horizon one never wants to reach, a spiritual death one seeks to defer until the end.

According as we reject or accept the romantic perspective, we will choose very different professions. In the first case, serious engagement with the "real world" is of the essence; at best we may hope to succeed well enough to retire early and enjoy a second adolescence before it's too late. But in the second, we choose our professional activity with an eye to preserving adolescent *disponibilité* as fully as possible; professional life must remain maximally amateurish. The amateur does not stand inactive at the center of René's intersection, but although he takes a few steps along one or several of the *voies,* he never goes far enough to lose sight of their common starting-point.

For the original Romantics, to make a profession of the deferral of maturity meant "expressing oneself" in art. But in today's world, dominated by the neo-romantic youth culture that Chateaubriand already anticipated in horror, adolescent self-expression competes in a well-established marketplace; youth too has been professionalized. The path of the professional adolescent may lead to fame and fortune, but it takes one far from René's crossroads. In our culture, the most effective way to defer maturity indefinitely is rather to remain in the institution *par excellence* of adolescent universality, which is not coincidentally called the *university.* A professor is someone who has never left school, who refers to everything outside *the academy* as *the real world.*

As its departmental structure suggests, the academy is itself professionalized, but in some domains more than others. The amateur's choice of field must be made with this in mind. The question is not whether one can do without knowledge and discipline. The intellectual amateur is not a noble savage; there is no "natural" way of thinking. But he must seek a mode of thought that can remain productive without being particularized into a technique or *methodology.* Every field of study, most definitely including philosophy itself, risks professionalization as either a set of techniques for the manipulation of nature or worse, a set of rhetorical devices for the manipulation of others. The problem posed by the professionalization of thought is as old as Plato's critique of the Sophists. For Plato, the legitimate professionals are the artisans, the shoemakers and carpenters who deploy their technical knowledge in manipulating the natural world for human purposes. In contrast, human interaction is not in essence an instrumental activity, and the art that manipulates this interaction is not a true profession but a means of deception. The profession of the true philosopher, like Socrates, is to have none.

The study of French literature in 1960 — this is no longer true today — involved very little pressure to conform to a given critical methodology or to focus on any particular field of specialization. French culture's universalism, concerned more with principles than concrete details, is reflected in the modes of scholarship it favors or at least, tolerates. It is no accident that Girard's theory of mimetic desire and subsequently, GA emerged within the field of French Studies. To the extent that GA has become a field of study in its own right, its minimality insures that it offers the maximal resistance to its transformation into a marketable technique. Just as no formulation of the originary hypothesis can ever be definitive, there can never be a well-defined, delimited body of knowledge that will provide its context. An originary theory of the human can neither ignore any given aspect of the human nor become dependent on it.

The Bronx Romantic is drawn to amateurism because he preserves the most radical Romantic intuition: that life is adolescence and maturity is death. In order to remain at the originary center, he must remain vigilant toward the seductions of professional life. In this respect, it is no doubt fortunate that the professionalism of today's academy is so different from what I encountered at the beginning of my career forty years ago. In those days, the academic world was small and expanding, jobs were easy to come by, and status, on a playing field where all the players were acquainted, was obtained through seniority and publication — that is, by doing one's job. Today the profession is large and static, if not contracting, jobs are difficult to obtain, and status is a function of networking and a trendiness that must be fought for as a value in itself, most often with victimary weapons. This situation, although disheartening to new entrants in the field — particularly to those attracted by the anti-victimary mode of originary thinking — is not without its charms for the tenured Bronx Romantic: it makes full absorption in professional life impossible.

The true amateur never sells his soul to the crowd, above all to his professional crowd. He theorizes the operations of the collective and the sacrificial with all the generosity of which he is capable, but he forbears to tailor his ideas to the fluctuations of the intellectual marketplace. The more we respect the market as the determiner of value, the more vigilantly we must resist its judgment as to our understanding of it. The truth of the market at any given moment is never what the market at that moment wants to hear.

The power of the Romantic attitude lies in permitting us to assimilate the contours of our individual life to the originary unity of the human. This is a unity that remains virtual and can never be fully actualized. Darwinians who propose a unitary explanation of the human within the confines of their field, be it sociobiology or evolutionary psychology, inevitably fail to grasp the paradox inherent in reducing the human invention/discovery of the transcendent realm of the sign to the model of natural adaptation. But the Bronx Romantic remains faithful to the intuition that if one is to understand how humanity and its culture might have come into being, one must not stray far from the central singularity from which all roads diverge.

Hamlet's Theater of Resentment

Richard van Oort

I

In a series of important and original commentaries on Shakespeare's "theater of envy," René Girard argues that Hamlet is caught in the tragic double bind of mimetic desire.[1] Hamlet defers his usurpation of the center in the face of the ghost's demand for revenge. Girard argues that this nonviolent deferral, in which Hamlet lurks on the periphery of a scene infected with the mimetic violence of both the old king Hamlet and the new king Claudius, is the true "hidden" meaning of *Hamlet*. Shakespeare was tired of the sacrificial assumptions of revenge tragedy and so composed a tragedy that held two messages, one for the groundlings who desired the blood and guts of the traditional revenge story, and one for an elite circle of intellectuals who would appreciate the double entendre of an anti-revenge theme within the revenge genre. When Hamlet ultimately consummates his revenge in the final bloodbath, this is a concession to the general audience and to the genre that fulfills the audience's bloodthirsty expectations. But we miss the deeper point Shakespeare wished to make, Girard insists, if we accept this as the main point of the text itself.

As Eric Gans points out, it is in fact possible to retain the essential insight of Girard's theory of mimetic desire without further burdening the argument with the assumption that tragedy either succeeds or fails depending on how forcefully it sides with the renunciation of violence.[2] For ultimately all tragedy fails when it comes to representing nonviolence, for the simple reason that a tragedy is not a doctrine but an aesthetic work. The biggest difficulty for Girard's theory is that it cannot explain the difference between aesthetic and ritual representations of what Girard, like Freud before him, takes to be a founding act of violence. For Girard, both religious and aesthetic works stand or fall depending on the clarity with which they reveal the scapegoat mechanism that Girard explicitly situates at the very origin of the human and cultural order.[3]

Girard's ambivalence concerning the discovery power of the artwork reflects a deeper ambivalence concerning the status of the aesthetic in his anthropology. Generative anthropology confronts this ambivalence head on; the aesthetic is a category of the originary hypothesis. What makes the artwork anthropologically "revelatory" is its reproduction within the individual of the aesthetic effect, an effect that can be traced to the originary event. "Esthetic experience," Gans writes in *Originary Thinking*, "is our only socially unmediated link with the originary event."[4] Whence the intuitive sureness of our experience that a particular art work possesses fundamental anthropological content.

Let us briefly recall Gans's analysis of the aesthetic in the originary event. The originary sign defers the conflict of exacerbated mimetic attention. But this deferral does not enable humanity to transcend mimetic conflict once and for all, as must be assumed by Girard in his apocalyptic interpretation of the art work "against itself." Generative anthropology's more minimal notion of the "deferral of violence through representation" is an "etic" description of the aborted gesture of the originary scene. What makes the aborted gesture a specifically aesthetic sign is not the self-conscious desire to defer conflict, but the desire to imagine oneself the sole occupant of the center. But this desiring representation of the center can only be experienced by the individual if the original appetitive goal remains unfulfilled. The experience of this unfulfillment, or in other terms, of the self's necessary exclusion from the center is the "second moment" of desire, powerfully described by Gans as the moment of "originary resentment." Aesthetic experience is the individual's attempt to cope with resentment. "The source of [aesthetic] pleasure in the sign," Gans writes, "is the temporary relief (or deferral) it provides from originary resentment. Through the sign, we replace, or supplement, our originary alienation from the center" (*OT* 118).

This account of the aesthetic moment of the originary event has significant consequences for understanding the passage from ritual to market society. Only in the latter does literature become the central cultural institution, and only in the West has there developed an aesthetic "high culture" distinct from ritual. From the cave paintings of the late Paleolithic to the monumental sculpture of ancient Egypt, humans have decorated sacred sites with aesthetic images. But only in relatively recent human history, beginning with the artistic experiments of the ancient Greeks, has the aesthetic evolved to found institutions of its own. The history of the aesthetic is the history of art in the West since the Greeks.

Though Girard certainly grasps the radicality of the Western aesthetic experiment, he ultimately subordinates it to its moral counterpart in Judeo-Christianity. For Girard, literature must always ultimately fail because it depends for its full force upon a misrecognition of the victimage mechanism. Hence Girard's insistence that his literary analyses are grounded in Judeo-Christian revelation and, in particular, in the text of the gospels. Only an anthropology informed by an awareness that scapegoats are innocent is able to demonstrate the historical truth of the victimage mechanism. More secular and more resolutely anthropological than Girard, Gans argues that humans are aware of their own violence from the beginning. The originary desire to imagine oneself in the center is the first step in recognizing the dependence of the center on the desires of the periphery. For most of human history, aesthetic experience remains a necessary but subordinate element of ritual, which is by definition suspicious of individual desire. But beginning with the ancient Greeks, desire is released from its containment in ritual to become the explicit object of an independent cultural institution. The classical aesthetic does not restrict individual desire by sacralizing the center in order to guarantee its inviolability outside the collective context of ritual distribution. On the contrary, it encourages you to imagine yourself in the center by presenting fictional models of the center's usurpation by the periphery. In classical tragedy, this imaginary usurpation is "punished" when the protagonist's occupation of the center is demonstrated to be the result of a monstrous crime, as when Oedipus discovers that his heroic rise to the throne of Thebes is in reality the fulfillment of the prohibited narratives of parricide and incest. Having released desire from its stasis in collective ritual, the classical aesthetic opens the center to increasingly profound explorations of it.

Aesthetic history tells the story of this expansion from center to periphery. When drama reemerges as the central cultural institution in the Renaissance, Shakespeare thematizes the classical protagonist's relationship to the center by representing it as a contested space among equals rather than as inherent to the being of the protagonist. Whereas Oedipus unselfconsciously believes his existence to be synonymous with the center's immortality, Hamlet imagines the center as permanently divorced from him. Hamlet understands, where Oedipus does not, that the achievement of central being is a dream rather than a reality. Hence the preponderance of soliloquizing in the play, the most famous example of which is Hamlet's reflection on the gulf between peripheral selfhood and central immortality in the "To be or not to be" speech. The classical aesthetic is historicized and ultimately anthropologized. Aesthetic history becomes a history of increasingly developed thematizations of the center-periphery configuration of the originary event. The rise and fall of literature as the central cultural institution in the West reflects "the rise and fall of the aesthetic as an anthropological discovery procedure" (*OT* 25).

This is ultimately a less sensational account of modernity than Girard's. In his essay on *Hamlet*, Girard argues that we are poised precariously between absolute violence and absolute nonviolence. We continue to be fascinated by revenge, but we are also too self-conscious of its immorality to carry it out in good faith. "Like Hamlet," Girard says, "we are poised on the brink between total revenge and no revenge at all, unable to make up our mind, unable to take revenge and yet unable to renounce it" ("HDR" 298). In an arch-romantic move, Girard suggests that Hamlet's predicament resembles that of modernity:

> In *Hamlet*, the very absence of a case against revenge becomes a powerful intimation of what the modern world is really about. Even at those later stages in our culture when physical revenge and blood feuds completely disappeared or were limited to such marginal milieux as the underworld, it would seem that no revenge play, not even a play of reluctant revenge, could strike a really deep chord in the modern psyche. In reality the question is never entirely settled and the strange void at the center of *Hamlet* becomes a symbolic expression of the Western and modern malaise, no less powerful than the most brilliant attempts to define the problem, such as Dostoyevsky's underground revenge. Our "symptoms" always resemble that unnameable paralysis of will, that ineffable corruption of the spirit that affect[s] not only Hamlet, but the other characters as well. The devious ways of these characters, the bizarre plots they hatch, their passion for watching without being watched, their propensity to voyeurism and spying, the general disease of human relations make a good deal of sense as a description of an undifferentiated no man's land between revenge and no revenge in which we are still living. ("HDR" 296)

Girard's sense of the devious voyeurism at the core of *Hamlet* accurately describes both the prince and the play. As the romantics were the first to realize, it is in fact impossible to separate the two. The dramatic action is an externalization of the prince's mind. The celebrated "play within a play" at the center of the work is a self-conscious staging of a violent scene that Hamlet first *imagines*.

II

Many spectators and readers still accept Hamlet's representation of the murder in the "Mousetrap" play as a straightforward reproduction of Claudius's crime. But the only evidence Hamlet has for the latter is the testimony provided by the ghost. And why should the ghost be trustworthy? In a subtle and closely argued reading published almost a century ago, W. W. Greg underscored this point when he remarked that Claudius's failure to respond to the dumb show that precedes the Mousetrap play — and which graphically depicts a usurper pouring poison into the king's ear and then making love to the queen after her husband's body has been dragged offstage — suggests that Claudius cannot have murdered his brother in the manner reported by the ghost.[5] When Claudius does eventually react and call for light, Greg concluded, it is not because his guilt has been discovered, but because he has been threatened by Hamlet, who has indicated during the ensuing performance that it is the king's *nephew* who murders his uncle.[6] In a reading of the play that was published thirty-four years after Greg's, but which confirmed and developed many of Greg's original intuitions, Harold Goddard pointed out that Hamlet's aggression toward Claudius, Gertrude, Polonius, and Ophelia reaches a truly menacing pitch during the play within a play.[7] Far from holding the "mirror up to nature," he is literally throwing himself into the role of vengeful destroyer. It is worth recalling that the next time we find Polonius, Gertrude, and Hamlet in the same room, Hamlet kills Polonius (whom he mistakes for the king) and then has the gall to accuse Gertrude of her supposed "crime" of sexual infidelity! Clearly this is a man who has lost all sense of proportion. Greg's reading does not, of course, excuse Claudius of the original murder, but it certainly throws into question the objectivity of the ghost. Hence Greg's controversial conclusion that the ghost, who only ever talks to Hamlet and who is invisible to Gertrude, must be a "hallucination."

Greg's 1917 essay sparked considerable debate.[8] I have no wish to revisit its various polemics except to observe that most of Greg's original critics believed the problem to be settled by pointing out that since Horatio, Marcellus, and Barnardo have also seen the ghost it therefore must be real and the ghost's testimony be granted a similar objective status. But this objection misses the point. The ghost is not an instrument of metaphysical objectivity, a camera on the wall passively recording whatever data passes before it. It exists as a representative of the sacrificial violence of the center.[9] The images of disease, pollution, and death that run through the play emanate from this center. The hint that the ghost also seems to come from purgatory, a Catholic institution much ridiculed by Protestants, is no doubt suggestive for those interested in reconstructing the religious controversies of the period.[10] But no amount of historical research will tell us why Hamlet is so attracted to this "questionable" shape's sacred ambivalence:

> Be thou a spirit of health or goblin damn'd,
> Bring with thee airs from heaven or blasts from hell,
> Be thy intents wicked or charitable,
> Thou com'st in such a questionable shape
> That I will speak to thee. (1.4.40-44)[11]

The rapid oscillation between positive and negative images of the ghost mirrors the oscillation of the originary aesthetic sign. The sign points to the object we desire. But the sign without the object is insignificant, so we return to the sign. In the first moment, the sign appears to be a blessing because it promises deliverance of the center. As in Hamlet's most famous soliloquy, the self dreams of the paradise of occupying the center, which appears as "a consummation / Devoutly to be wish'd" (3.1.63–64). This moment is reflected in Hamlet's positive designations of the ghost as "a spirit of health," "charitable," and bringing "airs from heaven." But since the center's significance cannot be delivered in reality but only imagined, the subject experiences the center as a locus of dispossession. This is the second moment of desire — what Gans calls "originary resentment" — and it is reflected in Hamlet's negative designations of the ghost as a "goblin damn'd," "wicked," and bringing "blasts from hell."

Readers tend to forget that Hamlet's contact with the ghost follows rather than precedes his first stage appearance. We first find the prince dressed in black, sulking on the periphery of Claudius's court. In 1930 Wilson Knight remarked that Claudius's villainy pales in comparison to the violence of the center imagined by Hamlet.[12] Only Hamlet imagines a violence that knows no bounds. Calling Hamlet the "ambassador of death," Knight interpreted the tragedy as documenting the path from life to death, from peaceful periphery to violent center. Unable to defer his resentment any longer, Hamlet gives full vent to his imagination and drags his fellows into death. By the end of the play he is responsible for six of the play's eight deaths. The Danish royal family is annihilated and the Norwegian threat, so adroitly averted by Claudius in his first act of international diplomacy, reappears menacingly on the doorstep. The "leperous distilment" (1.5.64) that transforms the old king's "smooth body" into a "lazarlike," "vile and loathsome crust" (1.5.72–73) figures the absolute monstrosity of the center, which infects all those who dare to come into contact with it.

Like Knight, Goddard, and Greg before him, Girard emphasizes the disease of the center's violence. Hamlet's failure is a failure to extricate himself from the cycle of violence represented by the ghost. But Hamlet's failure, Girard says, is also our failure. As long as we ignore the message of the gospels, as long as we ignore the choice between revenge and no revenge, we will be caught in the same vicious cycle as Hamlet. Thus Girard advocates an apocalyptic transcendence of representation altogether, a veritable end of history: "Hamlet is no mere word game. We can make sense out of *Hamlet* just as we can make sense out of our world, by reading both against revenge. This is the way Shakespeare wanted *Hamlet* to be read and the way it should have been read long ago. If now, at such a time in our history, we still cannot read *Hamlet* against revenge, who ever will?" ("HDR" 302).

Girard's specific target here is poststructuralist nihilism ("Hamlet is no mere word game"). But one can preserve the essential insight of deconstruction without also accepting its nihilism. In his more polemical moments, Girard would have us believe that language *is* a mere word game, that beneath the words there is a reality that transcends the human scene of representation. But this reality — if it really is an anthropological reality and not a biological mechanism — is as dependent upon the scene of representation as humanity itself.

Girard ultimately demands too much of the texts of the aesthetic tradition. On the one hand he requires them to demonstrate his theory. On the other he rejects them as a partial truth on the road to full mimetic disclosure. In Girard's analyses one sometimes gets the impression that his anthropology exists *despite* the misleading games played by poets.

Gans's originary hypothesis avoids — or more accurately, minimizes — this paradox of the "end of history" by returning it to its source in the originary scene. "The postmodern esthetic," Gans writes, "is constituted by its exit from esthetic history, by its rejection of the idea that a vision exists that transcends all other visions, or at least all previous ones. But this refusal of art is an invitation to science. What cannot be figured as an object of experience must become the object of a hypothesis" (*OT* 219). The postmodern aesthetic is characterized by its radical skepticism concerning the status of the referent: "it rejects the very term 'representation' as implying a presence prior to the sign. Since there is no prerepresentational state, signs point back only to other signs, not to a preexistent referent" (*OT* 218). The postmodern "invitation to science" is thus not to be understood as an invitation to empirical science. On the contrary, it is an invitation to an anthropology that grasps the irreducibly hypothetical and symbolic status of its object. The originary hypothesis is a bootstrapping operation that seeks to conceptualize its own emergence in the minimal human scene of symbolic interaction. The existence of generative anthropology as a disciplinary "method" or "practice" — what Gans calls "originary analysis" — is interpreted in terms of the coming into existence of humans in general. A rule of thumb rather than a scientific or empirical "methodology," its guiding assumption is that the most powerful anthropological explanation begins by situating itself within the context of the minimal condition of human existence. And the minimal condition of humanity is simply presence on the originary scene of representation. Humans are symbolic creatures, in the sense that their existence is defined not by their physical and biological make-up, but by their participation in and reflection on the "symbology" of the originary scene.

The privileged position of the aesthetic in generative anthropology's conception of human history derives from the deferring function of the sign in the originary scene. The sign defers the conflict of exacerbated mimetic attention. In René Girard's original conception of the "mimetic crisis," violence is not deferred but rather unleashed by the victimage mechanism. Collective rivalry among undifferentiated "equals" is vented upon an "unequal" scapegoat. The latter's marginality with respect to the group allows the majority to inflict violence without fear of mimetic reprisal. In this passage from violence to peace, universally replayed by different societies in their diverse myths and sacrificial practices, the scapegoat is transformed into a god, the bringer of peace and therefore of collective life. Hence the ambivalence of the victim, who is both scapegoat and god, both periphery and center.

Gans accepts the historical significance of Girard's theory of sacrifice, but he disputes its originary or foundational status. For Gans, the ambivalence of the victim is not in the first place a founding misrecognition on the part of the community concerning the source of its own violence. Ambivalence or "mimetic paradox" describes rather the very condition in which humanity comes into being. Humans are aware of their own violence from the beginning. This does not mean that we must attribute to the first sign-users a hyper-rational "etic" awareness that they are inaugurating an anthropology in which human origin is explained as the "deferral of violence through representation." Human history is not predetermined by the originary hypothesis. The openness of human history is the openness of symbolic representation, which is without precedent among animal communication systems. Whence the paradox of the "end of history." If history really were at an end it would mean that the mimetic conflict of the originary hypothesis had finally been transcended. But then humans would no longer require representation to defer it. Historical consciousness of the originary would be forgotten, and any attempt to formulate either its beginning or end would be superfluous. The need to formulate the end of history assumes that we have yet to reach it.

Thus no theory of the aesthetic can begin by expelling the aesthetic. Hamlet indeed defers his relationship to the center, but this deferral is not an end in itself. The specifically aesthetic moment of originary signification is the oscillation between the sign and the central object. This oscillation, which implies minimally the cognitive construction of a purely symbolic image of the object, delays rather than triggers the kind of motor response characteristic of nonsymbolic "genetically assimilable" patterns of behavior, including so-called "Skinnerian" or behaviorist modes of perceptual conditioning.[13] Hamlet does not merely seek models to imitate. He seeks to represent those models aesthetically in his "mind's eye" (1.2.185), as he says to Horatio, echoing Horatio's own characterization of the ghost as a "mote... to trouble the mind's eye" (1.1.115). This internalization of the public space of collective ritual is the source of the historicity of the aesthetic, which influences individual behavior not by communal coercion, but by eliciting an aesthetic response in the individual hearer/specta-tor/reader. In relying exclusively upon the dynamic of symbolic deferral for its aesthetic effect, the aesthetic work makes clear, in a way that its ritual precursors cannot, this dependence of the divine figures of the center on the representations constructed by the periphery. Hamlet's obsessive fascination with "this too too sullied flesh" (1.2.129) which nonetheless contains "that within which passes show" (1.2.85) — that is, a mind capable of counting itself "a king of infinite space" (2.2.255) — reflects an awareness that sacrality is an anthropological rather than transcendent or otherworldly phenomenon.

III

Hamlet's ambivalent relationship to the center is explicit from the beginning. But this ambivalence is not reserved for Claudius alone. It is directed at all who appear to accept the status quo of the center, which for Hamlet includes every-one in the Danish court. Even an outsider like Horatio is not free of suspicion. When the latter unexpectedly appears in Denmark, Hamlet's response is am-bivalent. On the one hand he is genuinely pleased to receive into Elsinore an old school friend; on the other, suspicious that his friendship with Horatio has been compromised by the latter's proximity to the center. Why has Horatio come to court? For several anxious moments Hamlet fears that his closest friend has aligned himself with his imaginary persecutors. Might Horatio be a secret spy for Claudius? As in his subsequent treatment of Rosencrantz and Guildenstern, Hamlet wants to know if this is a "free visitation." Hence the menacing edge to Hamlet's ostensibly joking remark, "We'll teach you to drink deep ere you de-part" (1.2.175), which is not simply a comment on the drinking habits of Danes, but also a probe to uncover Horatio's underlying intentions. Is he just another party guest like Laertes come to enjoy Claudius's open-handed generosity in the celebration of the king's marriage and coronation? When Horatio's reply contra-dicts this suspicion — "My lord, I came to see your father's funeral" (1.2.176) — Hamlet's response contains the paradoxical emotion of the man who sees the object of his resentment suddenly disappear, so denying him the satisfaction of indulging his appetite for irony: "I prithee do not mock me, fellow-student. / I think it was to see my mother's wedding" (1.2.177–78). On the one hand Ham-let is relieved to hear Horatio is not a "spy"; on the other, disappointed that his paranoia has been so effortlessly brushed aside.

In a kind of perverse reverse snobbery, Hamlet tolerates only those who can demonstrate their credentials as fellow resenters of Claudius's court. Hence the disproportionate degree of vituperation he directs at Gertrude, which is

motivated simply by the fact that she is closest to Claudius.[14] The same bench-
mark is used to measure the loyalty of his one-time circle of friends and inti-
mates. Horatio passes. Ophelia, Laertes, Gertrude, Rosencrantz, and Guildenstern fail (and they suffer rather massively for it). Through the course of their
first exchange, Hamlet manages to ask Horatio three times why he has visited
Elsinore, so he obviously is dissatisfied with Horatio's initial answers. It is only
when Horatio reveals the secret of the ghost that Hamlet lets his guard down
and desists from interrogating Horatio about his reasons for playing truant
from his studies. What enables Horatio to enter so thoroughly into Hamlet's
"heart of heart" (3.2.73) is that he has seen the ghost. The ghost is a mark of
conspiratorial membership; it signifies the privileged status of this small "band
of brothers," who stand alone in recognizing the injustice of the new king's
reign.

The ghost is an index of the level of resentment in Denmark. Whoever is
capable of seeing it is guaranteed a spot in Hamlet's "theater of resentment." As
fellow witnesses of the ghost, we are automatically included among the conspir-
ators. This group includes at most five members: Hamlet, Horatio, Barnardo,
Marcellus, and the audience. But really there are only two significant parties:
Hamlet and the spectator/reader.[15] We alone are fully of Hamlet's party because
we alone are willing to see him die for his cause. The contrary position that
the ghost does not exist is represented by Gertrude. She cannot see the ghost
because she has no reason to invent one. Like all the others in the opening court
scene except Hamlet, she is happy with Claudius as her king.[16]

But the play very pointedly begins not with the court scene but on the
cold, dark battlements of Elsinore castle. In this ghostly mist-bound scene,
resentment appears to exist only on the furthest margins of the Danish court,
among a few grumbling guards who cannot understand why they are patrol-
ling the new king's borders. Horatio and the two guards are the only ones to
see the ghost, and their creditability is subtly undercut by the presence of the
third guard, Francisco, who has seen nothing, not even a mouse stirring. We
never hear of Francisco again. His incapacity to see the ghost makes him a poor
candidate for mediating our desire, and Shakespeare dispatches him from the
scene altogether. The task of mediating our desire instead falls to Barnardo and
Marcellus, the original witnesses of the ghost. Horatio functions as a proxy
for the audience, when he sits down to listen to their story. Horatio is also the
mediating figure between the original witnesses and Hamlet, to whom he decides to communicate their tale. Hamlet thus arrives "late" on the scene, but
he turns out to be the ghost's strongest and most eloquent interpreter. Only
Hamlet is sufficiently self-conscious of his difference from the center to be able

to interpret this center as a locus of usurpation. Hamlet's celebrated capacity for soliloquizing is directly linked to his ability to conjure the ghost, to make it speak where to all others it remains either invisible or mute.[17]

Hamlet's soliloquies have justly received a great deal of critical attention, most notably after the romantics first saw in them evidence for the entire play as a "tragedy of thought."[18] But what is easily forgotten if too much emphasis is placed on the interior life of the prince is that this expression is not purely verbal. On the contrary, it first manifests itself theatrically in Hamlet's wordless overshadowing of Claudius's marriage and coronation. Dressed in black and pointedly turning his back on the festivity, our eyes cannot fail to be attracted by the stance of this singular individual. Not until we are well into the scene (after Claudius has thanked the court, dispatched Voltemand and Cornelius to Norway, and attended to Laertes's suit) does Hamlet deign to speak. And his words are intended not for those who share the stage with him, but for us. As curious spectators of this scene, we too eye it with ironic and critical detachment. Reacting to a scene he affects to dismiss but really requires for his own sense of being, Hamlet's first words depend for their force not on their literal meaning, but on their ironic undercutting of Claudius's:

> *King.* But now, my cousin Hamlet, and my son —
> *Ham.* A little more than kin, and less than kind. (1.2.64–65)

If I am both your cousin and your son, Hamlet ironically implies, then this is a little more kinship and a little less kindness than I am prepared to accept. By expressing this sentiment in an aside to the audience, Hamlet implicitly identifies us as "equal" resenters of Claudius. Only we, fellow masters of aesthetic irony, are able to appreciate the ironist's superiority over the object he ridicules. When Hamlet finally does address Claudius directly, the tone has been set. The literal meaning is for Claudius (and the court), the ironic meaning for us:

> *King.* How is it that the clouds still hang on you?
> *Ham.* Not so, my lord, I am too much in the sun. (1.2.66-67)

When Gertrude sides with her husband and admonishes Hamlet for taking excessively to heart the "common" fact of death, Hamlet reduces the strategy of the ironist to its bare minimum. Like a master deconstructor, all that is necessary is to notice the subtle addition of quotation marks around the word he effortlessly repeats: "Ay, madam, it is *common*" (1.2.74; my emphasis).

But if today's postmodern ironists have taken Hamlet's strategy to its minimal originary source in the play of the differing and deferring signifier, Hamlet
himself is far less minimal in his conclusions about the ultimate source of his
significance. What enables him to ironize Claudius repeatedly is quite simply
his sense that he is more authentic than those he ironizes. It is no surprise that
Hamlet's first sustained speech comes as a vehement defense of his authenticity
when he detects (mistakenly, as it happens) a criticism of it by the queen. In
response to her query, "Why seems it so particular with thee?" (1.2.75), Hamlet
pounces on the word "seems" rather than the word Gertrude stresses, which is
"particular." (Imagine if Gertrude had instead said, "Why *is* it so particular with
thee?") Hamlet the pun-master needs no further encouragement:

> Seems, madam? Nay, it is. I know not 'seems.'
> 'Tis not alone my inky cloak, good mother,
> Nor customary suits of solemn black,
> Nor windy suspiration of forc'd breath,
> No, nor the fruitful river in the eye,
> Nor the dejected havior of the visage,
> Together with all forms, moods, shapes of grief,
> That can denote me truly. These indeed seem,
> For they are actions that a man might play;
> But I have that within which passes show,
> These but the trappings and the suits of woe. (1.2.76–86)

We should not let our identification with the protagonist's resentment lead
us to overlook the self-serving and moral self-righteousness implied by this bit-
ter attack on the majority, who, as Claudius notes, have "freely gone / With this
affair along" (1.2.15–16). Hamlet's frustrated outburst to Gertrude amounts to
the now all-too-familiar claim of the victimary other: "How dare you presume
to speak for me since you cannot possibly know what I'm feeling!" To which of
course there is no possible argument except to be struck dumb.[19]

Hamlet's desire to plumb the depths of his inner soul in order to locate a
personal scene more significant than the public one monopolized by his uncle is
genuine enough, but it remains trapped within the only context Hamlet knows:
the ritual context of sacrificial violence. In the letter he writes to Horatio after
he returns from his abortive trip to England, Hamlet promises to strike Horatio
dumb: "*I have words to speak in thine ear will make thee dumb*" (4.6.22–23). This
promise echoes his earlier reaction to the player's Pyrrhus speech (which echoes
the ghost's account of a sacrificial tale so terrible it would make Hamlet's blood
"freeze" [1.5.16] and his hair "stand an end" [1.5.19]):

> What would he do
> Had he the motive and passion that I have?
> He would drown the stage with tears,
> And cleave the general ear with horrid speech,
> Make mad the guilty and appal the free,
> Confound the ignorant, and amaze indeed
> The very faculties of eyes and ears. (2.2.554-60)

In seeking to strike his audience dumb, Hamlet hopes to reproduce the asymmetry of the reader's/spectator's aesthetic relation to the text, in which reciprocal dialogue between the text's authorial or narrative "voice" and its audience is impossible. In attending to the play, we have no choice but to be engaged, to be momentarily struck dumb by its spectacle. This is not to deny the possibility that an aesthetic work may fail to sustain our interest. Inattention occurs precisely when the work fails to live up to the asymmetry granted to it by the subordinate position required by the spectator or reader. In opening a novel that we have never read before, or sitting down to a movie we have never seen, we expect this self-enforced asymmetry with respect to the text to be rewarded by a satisfying aesthetic experience, where this experience is itself ultimately a descendent of the originary mimetic paradox upon which all representation depends. In the most revelatory cases, in which category we can certainly count *Hamlet*, this aesthetic experience becomes the object of reflection by the work itself.[20]

If we are to understand the ultimate source of Hamlet's moral indignation, we must go beyond the sterile opposition of victim and victimizer that motivates the traditional interpretation of *Hamlet*. In his reading of "*Hamlet* against revenge," Girard goes a long way to unsettling this orthodoxy, and this places him in an important counter-tradition that includes earlier twentieth-century critics like W. W. Greg, Wilson Knight, and Harold Goddard. Greg's attempt to counter the traditional reading, however, was largely unsuccessful, partly because of limitations within his own theory, which tended to interpret the problem of the dumb show in terms of the question of the ghost's ontological objectivity, but also partly because of the weight of the tradition itself, which was unprepared for the heresy implied by a Hamlet more resentful (and thus also capable of more virulent forms of violence) than Claudius himself. The significance of Wilson Knight's and Harold Goddard's subsequent interpretations was to point out the degree to which this early modern tragedy is structured around a form of violence that begins not with Claudius, nor indeed with the heroic man-slayer King Hamlet, but with the displaced prince, whose festering resentment haunts his mind for three acts before exploding in a series of murders that culminates in the final bloodbath.

As the romantics understood in their idolization of the Danish prince, Hamlet is the prototype of the modern individual, for whom personal value is the basis for all ethical action. But Hamlet's tragedy is that he has no real possibility for integrating his personally held difference from the center into a publicly marketable personal identity that can circulate freely (and bloodlessly) on the periphery. There are doubtless a few highpoints that indicate the promise of a fulfilling "career" functioning on the margins of the Danish court, for example, Hamlet's brief career as director of "The Mousetrap." Here the prince's function as an "author" offers a brief liberation from the ritual constraints of the Danish monarchy. But this freedom, exhilarating while it lasts, is also short-lived. The scene of Hamlet's triumph as a writer of fiction is immediately followed by a reminder of his inadequacies as a participant in the old ritual agon, when he passes up on the opportunity to kill Claudius. The latter's iconic position of penitence at the altar reminds Hamlet all too vividly of the sacrificial context he wishes to escape. Hamlet's private "theater of resentment" is destined to remain subordinate to the sacrificial context figured by the ghost and his command to revenge. Hamlet delays for as long as possible, but ultimately he cannot extricate himself from a scene that assumes the absolute sacred/profane hierarchy of the old ritual center. As Nietzsche understood, in the face of the cultural monopoly exerted by the ritual center, the peripheral protagonist's attempt to assert his independence becomes a tragic impossibility.[21] But if this monopoly was already weakening in the Greek world so admired by Nietzsche, in the Christian world of Renaissance England it had experienced an irreversible revolution. By the time of the romantics, Hamlet had become an icon for the alienated self-consciousness of the peripheral subject, whose dependency on the old ritual center is now seen to be a mere contingency. What made Hamlet such an attractive figure to romantics like Goethe and the Schlegels in Germany and Coleridge in England was that they understood Hamlet's delay on the model of this alienated self-consciousness. But even before Goethe wrote *Wilhelm Meisters Lehrjahre* (but not before *Die Leiden des Jungen Werther*), Rousseau had already set the agenda for romantic Hamlets all over Europe in his *Rêveries du promeneur solitaire.*[22] With the romantics, Hamlet's posture of alienation from the center had become a form of praxis to be carried out in real life.

Notes

1. See René Girard, "Hamlet's Dull Revenge," *Literary Theory / Renaissance Texts,* eds. Patricia Parker and David Quint (Baltimore: Johns Hopkins University Press, 1986), 280-302; hereafter cited in the text as "HDR." For the full argument as applied to Shakespeare's career as a writer for the stage, see Girard, *A Theater of Envy* (Oxford: Oxford University Press, 1991).

2. See Eric Gans, "Form Against Content: René Girard's Theory of Tragedy," *Revista Portuguesa de Filosofia* 56 (2000): 53–65.

3. It is nonetheless worth reminding ourselves that were one to seek from the social sciences today a theory that was as attentive as either Freud's or Girard's to the heuristic power of literature, one would be sorely disappointed. This attentiveness to the specifically anthropological knowledge provided by literature is especially true of Girard, whose fundamental ideas concerning mimesis were drawn from a study not of ethnography but the modern novel. See René Girard, *Deceit, Desire, and the Novel: Self and Other in Literary Structure,* trans. Yvonne Freccero (Baltimore: Johns Hopkins University Press, 1965). Generative anthropology's differences with Girard, and to a lesser extent Freud, are thus differences of emphasis rather than ontology. From the perspective of a fundamental historical anthropology, it is the empirical sciences, not psychoanalysis or mimetic theory — or indeed the ubiquitous contemporary discourse of "theory" — that presents the biggest stumbling block. Current scientific thinking cannot countenance the notion of a minimal originary hypothesis that works "backwards" (deductively) on the basis of existing cultural institutions rather than "forwards" (inductively) on the basis of more elementary categories that are held to be transparently empirical rather than mediated by cultural representation.

4. Eric Gans, *Originary Thinking: Elements of Generative Anthropology* (Stanford, CA: Stanford UP, 1997), 123; hereafter cited in the text as *OT.*

5. See W. W. Greg, "Hamlet's Hallucination," *Modern Language Review* 12 (1917): 393-421.

6. As Greg points out, Claudius rises only *after* Hamlet intervenes: "The murderer empties his poison into the sleeper's ears, and — the King rises? Not a bit of it. Hamlet is unable to restrain himself any longer; he breaks out, hurling the crude facts of the story in the King's face, shouting, gesticulating, past reason and control. It seems as though the next moment he must spring at his throat. Naturally the court breaks up, the King rises, calls for lights, and retires to his private apartments, convinced — not that his guilt has been discovered, but that Hamlet is a dangerous madman, who has designs on his life, and must, at all costs, be got quietly out of the country, and, if possible, out of the world" (406).

7. See Harold Goddard, *The Meaning of Shakespeare* (Chicago: Chicago University Press, 1951), 331-86, esp. 362-68. Goddard identifies this scene as the critical turning point of the play as a whole: "There are many crises in *Hamlet,* but this is the crisis of crises — this, and not the sparing of the praying King or the killing

of Polonius, which are the inevitable outcome of what happens here. Now, for the last time, Hamlet is free. A second more and he will be bound by the fatality of his act…. The second passes, and Hamlet's blood finally overwhelms his judgment. Seeing Lucianus pour poison, he must pour poison too — all that is left in the vial" (367). Though Goddard explicitly acknowledges Greg's precedent, he insists that his reading evolved independently. From my point of view, it hardly matters who was the first to discern the radical ambiguity of a scene in which both Claudius and Hamlet merge into the single murderous figure of Lucianus. The point is that this dedifferentiation between villain and hero, persecutor and persecuted, exists at the core of the play, in a scene that is explicitly presented as an aesthetic doubling of the revenge genre. Hamlet's mimetic attraction to the spectacle of revenge mirrors our own attraction to it, with the notable difference that our release from it comes not with death but, rather less violently, with the last lines of the play.

8. For an overview of the debate, see Harold Jenkins's long note in his Arden edition of *Hamlet* (London and New York: Methuen, 1982), 501-505. In 1935 J. Dover Wilson published *What Happens in "Hamlet"* and dedicated it to Greg, with whom he vehemently disagreed. Not many people read Greg's essay anymore, but Dover Wilson's book has become a classic and is still in print today. As I hope to show in this analysis, I think we can still learn something from Greg's unorthodox and controversial interpretation.

9. Compare Girard on Shakespeare's use of the supernatural: "Supernatural apparitions in the tragedies are assimilated to monsters; it can easily be shown that, more or less discreetly, they are all rooted in the context of the mimetic crisis and the hallucinations that go with it. This is true of Caesar's phantom in *Julius Caesar,* of old Hamlet's phantom in *Hamlet,* as well as of the Weird Sisters and the other apparitions in *Macbeth*" (*A Theater of Envy* 70).

10. See, for example, Stephen Greenblatt, *Hamlet in Purgatory* (Princeton: Princeton University Press, 2001). In an earlier attempt to address the same problem, J. Dover Wilson, in *What Happens in "Hamlet",* 3rd ed. (Cambridge: Cambridge University Press, 1951), counters W. W. Greg by suggesting that a historical reading of Elizabethan "demonology" will settle the debate concerning Shakespeare's ghost.

11. William Shakespeare, The Arden *Hamlet,* ed. Harold Jenkins (London and New York: Methuen, 1982). All *Hamlet* quotations are from this edition.

12. Knight's essay "The Embassy of Death" was first published in 1930 in the first edition of *The Wheel of Fire.* In the fourth edition, published in 1949, Knight included a second essay on *Hamlet,* "Hamlet Reconsidered." See G. Wilson Knight, *The Wheel of Fire: Interpretations of Shakespearian Tragedy with Three New Essays,* 4th ed. (London: Methuen, 1949), 17–46, 298–343.

13. For the impossibility of genetically assimilating the symbolic function, see Terrence Deacon, *The Symbolic Species: The Co-Evolution of Language and the Brain* (New York: Norton, 1997), esp. 331-32. The aesthetic oscillation between sign and object is the anthropological correlate of the kind of interactional paradoxes that Gregory Bateson proposed as the source for schizophrenia and which Anna K.

Nardo, in "Hamlet, 'A Man to Double Business Bound," *Shakespeare Quarterly* 34 (1983): 181-99, finds depicted in Hamlet's relationship to his uncle-father and aunt-mother. See also Paul Watzlawick, Janet Helmick Beavin, and Don D. Jackson, *Pragmatics of Human Communication: A Study of Interactional Patterns, Pathologies, and Paradoxes* (New York: Norton, 1967). I have discussed the similarity between generative anthropology and Deacon's evolutionary notion of "symbolic reference" in "Cognitive Science and the Problem of Representation," *Poetics Today* 24 (2003): 237-95.

14. In 1919, T. S. Eliot suggested, in a now notorious essay, that *Hamlet* was a "failure" because it lacked an "objective correlative" for Hamlet's resentment, which consequently appears excessive and irrational. For Eliot, the ostensible object of Hamlet's resentment was Gertrude, but Gertrude's sins hardly justified the enormity of Hamlet's disgust: "Hamlet is up against the difficulty that his disgust is occasioned by his mother, but that his mother is not an adequate equivalent for it; his disgust envelops and exceeds her. It is this feeling which he cannot understand; he cannot objectify it, and it therefore remains to poison life and obstruct action" (125). Eliot put his finger, as Shakespeare did before him, on the fundamental problem of resentment, but he gets it backward. Resentment does not merely react to its object, it defines it. Eliot is right that "Hamlet (the man) is dominated by an emotion which is inexpressible, because it is in *excess* of the facts as they appear" (125). But this expression is "in excess of the facts" because representation is from the beginning in excess of the empirical reality of the appetitive object. Desire is not the same as appetite. And the denial of desire leads to a resentment that is by definition in excess of objective reality. See T. S. Eliot, "Hamlet and his Problems," *T. S. Eliot: Selected Essays* (New York: Harcourt, 1932), 121-26.

15. A case could be made to add Horatio to this elite company. (Compare Henry V's unforgettable lines of victimary resentment in *Henry V*, which Shakespeare wrote just before he began work on *Hamlet*: "But we shall ... be remembered, / We few, we happy few, we band of brothers.") An interesting question to ask is, Why is the foreigner Horatio so well informed of recent Danish and Norwegian history? Horatio's characterization of Fortinbras's army as a "list of lawless resolutes" (1.1.101) bears a clear parallel to his own position vis-à-vis Hamlet. The big difference of course is that Horatio, like the audience, does not lift a finger for Hamlet (unlike, for example, the rabble that forms around both Fortinbras and Laertes). In this sense, Horatio functions as a model of our aesthetic relationship to Hamlet's "theater of resentment." Like Horatio, we participate in the protagonist's resentment, but we do not suffer the consequences of it. Our function, like Horatio's, is merely to "consume" Hamlet's theater with pleasure, and then to pass on our good report of it to others, as Hamlet begs Horatio to do at the play's end. Hamlet's death is not a model to be imitated, as Horatio attempts to do by drinking from the poisoned cup, but a spectacle to be observed with ironic — which is also to say, theatrical — detachment.

16. For a brilliant interpretation of the events leading up to the opening court scene, I recommend John Updike's *Gertrude and Claudius* (New York: Ballatine Books,

2000).

17. The passage of desire from periphery to center is illustrated by the progression of the narrative as it passes from the guards, to Horatio, and thence to the prince. Shakespeare takes great care to underscore the point that the ghost appears only to those who are prepared to accept the asymmetry of the aesthetic sign. Though most readers regard Horatio as a philosophical "skeptic" whose conversion proves the reality of the ghost, it is in fact Francisco who most undermines the significance of the ghost; this workmanlike figure removes himself with minimal fuss and evident relief from the mystery of the scene that is about to unfold. Horatio, on the other hand, has not only agreed to accompany the original witnesses, but he responds favorably to Barnardo's insistence that their "originary" narrative be related once more for his (and our) pleasure:

> Bar.   Sit down awhile,
> And let us once again assail your ears,
> That are so fortified against our story,
> What we have two nights seen.
> Hor.   Well, sit we down.
> And let us hear Barnardo speak of this. (1.1.33–37)

No sooner does Barnardo begin his narrative than the ghost, as if waiting for its cue, usurps the stage, its sudden appearance designed to "freeze" our blood, make our "eyes like stars start from their spheres," and "each particular hair to stand an end / Like quills upon the fretful porpentine" (1.5.16–20). The story has begun.

18. August Wilhelm Schlegel, *Lectures on Dramatic Art and Literature,* 1810, quoted in *Critical Responses to "Hamlet," 1600–1900,* ed. David Farley-Hills, 4 vols. (New York: AMS Press, 1996), 2:49.

19. For a recent reading of this scene quite different from mine, see Paul A. Cefalu, "'Damnéd Custom . . . Habits Devil': Shakespeare's *Hamlet,* Anti-Dualism, and the Early Modern Philosophy of Mind," *ELH* 67 (2000): 399–431, esp. 403–5. Cefalu's main objective is to counter the "innatist" readings of *Hamlet* that, since the romantics, have dominated the critical tradition. I applaud this desire to return the self back to the public scene from which it emerges, but I think that there is a simpler explanation for Hamlet's strategy of authentification than either the romantic or historicist readings of Hamlet's psychology are capable of grasping. When Hamlet says he has "that within which passes show" he is indeed referring to his difference from the rest of the court, but this difference is not in the first place a difference between outward appearance and inner being. It is, more fundamentally, a difference between the multiple beings of the human periphery and the singular being of the sacred center. For Hamlet, what "passes show" — what is unrepresentable or, more precisely, sacred — is this originary difference between center and periphery. The ghost is Hamlet's attempt to represent the unrepresentable, a task that is paradoxical but not historically or culturally impossible. On the contrary, it is mimetic paradox

that generates the ghost and Hamlet's theater of resentment.

20. For a provocative interpretation of literary history as founded on the paradoxical supplementarity of representation, see Howard Felperin, *Shakespearean Representation: Mimesis and Modernity in Elizabethan Tragedy* (Princeton: Princeton University Press, 1977). Felperin's deconstructive intuitions serve him well in his readings of Shakespeare and Homer, but without a hypothesis for the origin of what Felperin at least implicitly accepts as a necessary (aesthetic) category of language, he is forced to place this origin, rather implausibly, in the Homeric text rather than in the origin of language, where it belongs.

21. Friedrich Nietzsche, *The Birth of Tragedy*, trans. Walter Kaufman (New York: Vintage, 1967).

22. Compare, for example, the opening lines of the *Rêveries*: "I am now alone on earth, no longer having any brother, neighbor, friend, or society other than myself. The most sociable and the most loving of humans has been proscribed from society by a unanimous agreement" (Jean-Jacques Rousseau, *Reveries of a Solitary Walker*, trans. Charles E. Butterworth [Hanover, NH: University Press of New England, 2000], 3). In *Originary Thinking* Gans argues that the resentment of the (modern) subject, thematized in such early modern tragedies as *Hamlet* in England and *Phédre* in France, is a response to the scandal posed by the old ritual center, the asymmetry of which toward the peripheral subject could not survive the challenge brought to it by universal Christian morality. In Rousseau, this asymmetry is understood to be a contingency with respect to what the romantics accepted as more foundational, namely, the private scene of representation within the originary self.

"The reforming of Reformation itself": Public vs. private scenes of representation in Shakespeare's *Measure for Measure*

Peter Goldman

1. The Question of Method

The challenge posed to the humanities by French Post-Structuralism has for the most part still not been answered. Most literary scholars have side-stepped this challenge by turning their attention to race, gender, and class in an attempt to justify their work on moral grounds. But defending the victims of "patriarchal oppression" does not substitute for a solid theoretical grounding. The humanities must begin by defining their object of study: the human, in broadest terms, and language more specifically. Jacques Derrida's deconstruction of Rousseau's *On the Origin of Languages* is meant to demonstrate that language cannot be defined without self-contradiction, and that humanistic inquiry depends ultimately upon an unjustified act of metaphysical faith.[1] While insisting upon its "undecidability," Derrida still analyzes language in metaphysical and structural terms; Post-Structuralism is a development of Structuralism even as it questions the foundations of those structures.

Metaphysics, however, is an invention of humans which is not coterminous with our origin. Anthropology can and should explain the existence of metaphysics, along with the human, even if this explanation involves the paradox of self-reference. With his originary hypothesis, Professor Eric Gans alone has taken up the gauntlet thrown down by Deconstruction. Humans, Gans observes, are the species for whom the main threat to our survival is other humans — not the environment, as with other species (*OT* 2). Language exists in order to ameliorate this fundamental ethical problem, to mediate our relationship to other humans. Gans therefore advances beyond the referential theories of language which have been so thoroughly deconstructed. Language is primarily ethical in function, "the deferral of violence through representation."

As a methodology, Generative Anthropology insists that we analyze human culture in terms of its ethical functionality. How does any particular instance of culture help the human community to survive, deferring the violence that threatens its existence? Among anthropologists, functional analyses of human culture are often rejected as reductive. But this is so only if functionality is narrowly conceived. The function of any specific instance of culture also exists in dialogue with other forms of culture and, indeed, the entire history of culture including its origin. This brings us to the second crucial feature of Generative Anthropology as a methodology. The origin of language, Gans argues, was an event, and the history of culture is a genetic or generative development of this originary event. This means that the fundamental categories of culture can be traced to our common origin, and they exist as a historical development of that event. In Gans' hypothesis of the originary event, language is constituted by a *scene* composed of a sacred center and a human periphery. All language is therefore scenic in character, and the scene of representation is the basic model for cultural analysis. The exchange of signs at the originary scene functions to defer the potential for violence by attributing divine significance to the center, originally occupied by an appetitive object. The divinity of the center is a function of the convergent desires of the participants as mediated by the sign. (In the "secular" culture which develops later, significance is equivalent to sacrality, in attenuated form.)

The scene of representation, however, is capable of infinite permutations and historical development. Since language functions as a relatively durable record of its own past, this history tends to be more or less irreversible. The transition, for example, from feudalism to a free market economy is a one-way road. The iconoclasm of modern historians refuses to grant that historical changes are "progressive," but the larger long-term developments are successful because they are more effective at recycling the resentments of the periphery into productive cultural forms.

How, then, does Gans's originary hypothesis inform this essay? In broadest terms, my topic here is Shakespeare's relationship to modernity, especially in reference to the opposition between the public and private. According to Gans, "the appropriate method for dealing with any significant cultural distinction . . . is to trace its component elements back to a hypothetical originary scene" ("Art and Entertainment" 25). At the originary event, the public scene is the total configuration of sacred center and human periphery. Each individual present, however, reproduces the public scene privately, representing it to him or herself.[2] The private scene is the imagination or memory.

The distinction between public and private is not originally problematic. The whole point of the originary event is to subordinate the individual to the public, sacred center. Without such subordination, no human community is possible. Despite individual variations in intelligence and sensitivity, each human present must interpret the originary event in roughly the same way in order for the event to function ethically. And, of course, the mimetic basis of the scene works to ensure uniformity among the participants.

But the potential for conflict between public and private is inherent to the originary event, because there are in effect two centers: the social (public) and the individual (private). In fact, the individual perceives him or herself as *alienated* from the sacred center as the divine Other. Originally, the distinction between public and private corresponds to the distinction between center and periphery. But the private scene is also by definition composed of a sacred center and human periphery, even if these are constituted imaginatively and not in social reality. Therefore, the individual has in effect a personal sacred which is capable of competing with the public sacred. Modernity is characterized by precisely the development of this originary potential. Gans's theory of modernity is too large a subject to explicate fully here, but it involves a devaluation of the public scene and a corresponding valorization of the private scene. This is problematic to the extent that the private center can be validated only through public recognition; hence the hypocrisy of the romantic who despises the public yet still seeks recognition as one who despises. Shakespeare's *Measure for Measure*, as we will see, explores the paradoxical relationship between public and private.

In the early modern period, the public scene is associated with ritual, ceremony, hierarchy, and public office — scripted spectacles governed by king or priest. (The medieval/Renaissance public scene is thus the opposite of what Jürgen Habermas calls the modern "public sphere," which is characterized by public debate or rationalized conflict.[3]) The private scene, on the other hand, includes the imagination, the memory, and the voice of conscience, so important for Protestant reformers. The private also encompasses the domestic, romantic love, the personal and individual, the scene of reading for example, or the scene of aesthetic judgment in which we decide individually whether we approve of an artistic work or not. As defined, public and private are not an absolute opposition, but rather relative terms. What is private from one perspective might well be public from another. Every scene of representation can be understood as more or less public or private. Nevertheless, the distinction is real and valid. I argue here that the opposition between public and private deeply informs the many interpretive problems posed by the Shakespeare's *Measure for Measure*, including the multiple substitutions.

2. Shakespeare and Modernity

The opposition between public ritual and private conscience is generally recognized as central to the Reformation, but has not yet been explored in reference to *Measure for Measure*, arguably Shakespeare's most radically Protestant and progressive play. No other Shakespeare play evokes the New Testament so insistently as *Measure for Measure*, and many recent critics have recognized that the play engages with contemporary Reformation debates in England. Huston Diehl, for example, sees the well-recognized "problems" of the play as representative of the problem of knowledge in Calvinist theology. The contrived nature of the ending, she argues, reveals the inadequacy of human efforts to re-present divine perfection on earth, and thus the "infinite space" between humanity and God (402–3). I agree with Diehl that the play exposes the limitations of reform, but I also explore how the play contributes in a positive way to the development of modernity by authorizing the private scene of representation. Diehl fails to recognize how the problem of representation is always intimately connected to the problem of authority — and, in this play, the conflict between public and private authority. As I have pointed out previously in another context, "Since any and all *forms* are subject to the iconoclastic critique, the real question is what legitimates any particular form" (Goldman 465). Deborah Shuger also examines the Protestant context of the play in some detail, arguing that Duke Vincentio represents an ideal of sacral kingship (60, *passim*). In contrast, I maintain that the play questions and undermines all public authority, including the Duke's. In what follows, I will argue that the play is not as contradictory as commonly thought, that it presents a coherent program for "the reforming of Reformation itself," to use Milton's pregnant phrase (*Areopagitica* 1019).

Measure for Measure critiques the Puritan agenda for public, legal reform, while affirming the alternative, Miltonic program of personal reform through testing and temptation. Furthermore, Shakespeare explores the limits of all efforts at reform, both public and personal. The critique of legal reform is based on a radical questioning of all public authority by which such reform could be accomplished. Ultimately, the subversion of public authority extends even to the playwright's authority over his creations and for his audience.

3. Testing, Temptation, and Reform: The Case of Angelo

In the opening scene, encouraging Angelo to take on the leadership of government during his absence, the Duke says, "Heaven doth with us as we with torches do, / Not light them for themselves; for if our virtues / Did not go forth of us, 'twere all alike / As if we had them not" (1.1.33-36). The reference here of course is to the Sermon on the Mount, in which Jesus states, "A city that is set on a hill cannot be hid. Neither do men light a candle, and put it under a bushel, but on a candlestick, and it giveth light unto all that are in the house. Let your light so shine before men, that they may see your good works, and glorify your Father which is in heaven" (Matt. 5.14–16).[4] The revealing of things hidden is a major theme of the New Testament as well as *Measure for Measure*: "For there is nothing hid, which shall not be opened; neither is there a secret, but that it shall come to light" (Mark 4.22; cf. Matt. 10.26, Luke 8.17, 12.2). The Duke suggests that heretofore Angelo has been a light hid underneath a bushel, and he proposes to let Angelo's light shine by having him govern in his absence. Angelo's private or secret self will be tested and revealed by taking on a position of public authority. This, I propose, is what the play does consistently: to take that which is private and make it public. To take another, minor yet revealing, example of this general pattern, in the second scene, when Claudio is first brought on stage by officers, he protests, "Fellow, why dost thou show me thus to the world?" (1.2.116). Similarly, Mariana is brought from the moated grange, Isabella from the nunnery, and Barnardine from prison.[5]

The play reveals what is private in order to test, reform, and ultimately authorize it. The paradox here, of course, is that the private can be tested and reformed only by making it public, that is, no longer private. This paradox derives from the essentially social or public nature of representation itself. There is no such thing as a purely private or autonomous authority. Authority depends upon recognition. The private is thus dependent upon the public, and public authority is likewise dependent upon an audience of private persons. While both the public and private aspire to autonomy, the play reveals them as mutually interdependent.

The opening scene of *Measure for Measure* is mildly ceremonial. The Duke appears in his public role as ruler, and as such he commands both Angelo and Escalus. Angelo, a previously marginal figure, is brought into a central, public role. At the same time, the Duke, a central figure, withdraws to a marginal position from which he will watch over the action and intervene when needed in order to bring about the desired result. This dual action (revealing and concealing) is emblematic for the play as a whole. The Duke, like Hamlet, prefers to operate from the margins, apparently finding greater authority there.[6]

The question posed by the opening scene, however, is whether Angelo really is a "light," as he seems to think he is, or not. Both Escalus and the Duke initially suggest that Angelo is virtuous and worthy of trust (1.1.23-25, 28-41). But the action of the play reveals him as a hypocrite, publicly virtuous but privately corrupt. The difficulty here is that the Duke seems to suspect as much from the beginning. Explaining why he is returning in disguise to Vienna, the Duke tells Friar Thomas, "Lord Angelo is precise, / Stands at a guard with envy, scarce confesses / That his blood flows, or that his appetite / Is more to bread than stone. Hence shall we see, / If power change purpose, what our seemers be" (1.3.50–54). A "seemer" is a pregnant characterization of Angelo, pointing to the tension between his public appearance and private self. The Duke's description of Angelo as "precise" suggests that he is to be associated with the Puritans and their attempts to legislate draconian punishments for adultery and fornication.[7] The stereotype of a Puritan, then as now, was a hypocrite. The Duke is also aware that Angelo has broken his promise of marriage to Mariana upon the loss of her dowry, "Left her in tears, and dried not one of them with his comfort; swallowed his vows whole, pretending in her discoveries of dishonor" (3.1.227–229).

The Duke's foreknowledge of Angelo's character defects raises problems for the Duke's motivation which I will consider at more length below. For now, I will note that Angelo's private self is tested by being placed on a public stage and given power, and that testing and temptation are consistent actions of the play.[8] His inner weakness is revealed first to himself; he is clearly surprised at his reaction to Isabella (2.2.169-194). In his attempt at blackmail, Angelo also reveals himself to Isabella, who then exposes him to Claudio, the Duke, and finally to the entire city in the last scene. The action of the play reveals Angelo's inner self as in need of reform.

Unlike the ritual humiliation of Malvolio or other comic villains, Angelo's mortification is not simply cathartic for the audience. He goes through a process of temptation, sin, and education which conforms to Protestant paradigms for conversion. The deeper meaning of Angelo's humiliation can be found by considering the Reformation context of the play.

In opposing traditional authorities, Protestant reformers required a new locus of authority, which they found with the private scene: the individual's personal relationship to God. The difficulty was how to authorize the private scene, to make it a new center of sacrality. For us as moderns, the private has a certain accepted authority. But for Shakespeare and his audience, the private stands in need of authorization. At this point in history, the very idea of a purely private or individual authority, apart from any public office or role, is quite radical. This problem comes into focus with the example of Angelo, who is corrupted by sexual desire when tempted by power. Desire was the problem, and sexual desire is paradigmatic in this regard, as the most stubborn and socially disruptive example of desire, the one most deeply rooted in our biological constitution. Augustine and his Protestant followers associated sex with sin (Ozment 26). Luther, for example, saw a link between original sin and sex (Wiesner-Hanks 63). The English theologian William Perkins speaks of "lust and concupiscence" as synonymous with "Original sinne" ("Whole Treatise" 92).

Sexual desire, in this play, appears in need of discipline or reform. In his conversation with Friar Thomas (1.3), however, the Duke does not mention the discipline of sexual license as the specific legal reform of which Vienna is in need; yet in his dialogue with Pompey he characterizes the bawd's trade in very harsh terms (3.2.20-28). And in the final scene, when he describes Vienna as a place "Where I have seen corruption boil and bubble /Till it o'errun the stew" (5.1.326-7), he clearly has sexual corruption in mind. A central action of the play is the attempt to discipline unruly sexual desire — for the city as a whole, but especially in the person of Angelo. Pompey, as well as Lucio, questions the limits of this attempt in general terms, asking whether fornication and prostitution can be controlled at all (2.1.229-34; 3.2.100-1), a point to which I will return. The more imperative question within the play is *how* to discipline the sexual desire of those in power, for this governs the fates of Angelo, Isabella, and Claudio.

Discipline, of course, was always a keyword among Protestants. Martin Bucer and other leading reformers emphasized discipline as one of the distinguishing "marks" of a true or reformed church (Hill 183-4; Shuger 10ff.). But there were many different kinds of discipline, depending on who was to enforce this discipline — whether the King, Church, or the individual — and where exactly discipline was needed. Initially, when reformers talked about discipline, the locus was the church itself: many reformers wanted to limit Communion to those who could demonstrate a godly life, a life free from, for example, sexual scandals. Even though discipline involved individuals ultimately, the main context was institutional. For most of the sixteenth century, there was little notion of a personal discipline which might substitute for institutional discipline, little notion of the public and private as separate spheres. As William Lamont has demonstrated, many early reformers in England envisioned the King as the leader in ecclesiastical discipline and church reform (28–55). When these hopes were disappointed, ministers saw themselves as the leaders in church reform (Lamont 56–77). It was only when the attempts at institutional reform were disappointed that ministers turned their hopes for reformation toward the individual.

When the Puritan authors of "An Admonition to the Parliament" wrote in 1572, they distinguished between public and private discipline, but private discipline was dismissed as "impertinent to our purpose" (264). By the end of the century, however, the leading Puritan theologian William Perkins wrote mainly about the problem of individual salvation, not church government. Diarmaid MacCullogh comments,

> by 1600, Puritanism seemed to have abandoned its vision of transform-
> ing the institutional structures of the English Church. As in the Neth-
> erlands, it gave priority in the manner of William Perkins to cultivating

the individual soul in pilgrimage to the blessings promised to the elect of God. (380)

The reform of individuals was becoming the primary imperative. Perkins and his disciple William Ames were the leading theoreticians of the emergent primacy of conscience as the locus of reform. When personal conscience came into conflict with traditional ecclesiastical or political authorities, Perkins insisted that conscience came first: "Inferior authorities cannot bind the superior: now the courts of men and their authorities are under conscience"; to reverse this hierarchy would be "Popish opinion" ("Discourse" 32). Public authorities were simply not to be trusted with the imperatives of personal salvation. The Puritan hopes for institutional reform were revived by the events of the Civil War, but Cromwell's rule proved a major disappointment, and the Restoration sounded the death knell for the Puritan's desire to reconstruct the English Church on a New Testament model. My point here is that there were two contrasting models for discipline, institutional and individual, which had currency in England at the time of *Measure for Measure*. Furthermore, the play stages both these models for us.[9] Angelo's strict enforcement of the law represents the Puritan ideal of "Godly rule," the civil discipline for which some Puritans lobbied.[10] He represents this ideal also in his own person, his appearance as "a man whose blood / Is very snow broth; one who never feels / The wanton stings and motions of the sense, / But doth rebate and blunt his natural edge / With profits of the mind, study, and fast" (1.4.57–61). On the other hand, the testing employed by the Duke represents an attempt at discipline and reform at the level of the individual.

Angelo fits into the debate over discipline in a complex way. He seems to be following the Puritan program: first, by ostensibly being morally pure himself, and, second, by insisting upon discipline in the political order. He would set up a utopia in which the problem of desire is eliminated, either voluntarily by individuals or forcefully by the State. Angelo represents the moral aspect of Puritanism but without the spiritual content. His ascetic appearance is completely superficial, since he immediately gives in to temptation. Angelo proves Milton's point that a virtue which is not tested is fatally vulnerable to assault. Thus Angelo seems to demonstrate the weakness of the Puritan program: first, because his punishment of Claudio is totally out of proportion to the "crime," and second, because his own discipline is revealed as superficial and ultimately hypocritical. The play thus could be seen as a simple critique of Puritanism in favor of traditional monarchical authority in the person of the Duke, albeit an authority which includes Christian forgiveness.[11] I want to resist this traditional interpretation of the play for a number of reasons, including the fact that the Duke is extremely problematic as an authority figure, a point to which I will return. Instead, I will show how the play dramatizes the power of personal reform, the authorization of the private scene, as an alternative to public, external discipline.

For Puritan reformers, temptation was a necessary part of the Christian life. Milton argues as much in *Areopagitica* — "Assuredly we bring not innocence into the world, we bring impurity much rather: that which purifies us is triall, and triall by what is contrary" (1006) — and *Paradise Lost* embodies this insight. Even in heaven, in the absence of any external agent, Satan discovers temptation. And in paradise, God himself tempts Adam and Eve by forbidding the freely accessible fruit of the "tree of knowledge." William Tyndale emphasizes that suffering and temptation are part of God's plan for individuals. The tribulation imposed by God works as an agent for the individual's moral reform:

> The spirit of tribulation purgeth us and killeth our fleshly wit, our worldly understanding and belly wisdom, and filleth us full of the wisdom of God. Tribulation is a blessing that cometh of God, as witnesseth Christ (Matt. 5). (Tyndale 9)

In Covenant theology, testing and temptation are God's means for preparing the soul for grace, as well as sanctifying the soul after conversion. Ames writes, "temptations are part of that warfare to which the faithfull are called, Eph.6.12." (Bk. 2, p.43). It was necessary to "wrastle as it were with God, by faith" (Ames 2.17). The endurance of suffering and temptation authorized the self in conversion as a member of the elect.

Harold Goddard rightly emphasizes that Angelo is tested by power rather than simply sexual desire (50-68). For Shakespeare, in contrast to his Puritan contemporaries, sexual desire is a serious social problem only when combined with political power. The public scene, where power is located, serves in this play mainly as a stage for testing and reforming the private self — not, as in traditional rituals, for the confirmation of an existing hierarchy. In what follows, we will examine in detail the process of Angelo's temptation and disgrace. What seems like a simple downfall actually conforms to a larger pattern of Protestant self-authorization in the play.

Angelo's initial actions upon gaining power are narrated for us secondhand by Lucio and the "underworld" characters (1.2). We learn that Angelo begins by arresting Claudio under an old law against fornication which has been not enforced for nineteen years (1.2.162–166). He also gives a proclamation that "all houses [of prostitution] in the suburbs of Vienna must be plucked down" (1.2.95–6). In Shakespeare's sources for the play, the character equivalent to Claudio is guilty of seducing an innocent young woman, or even raping her in some versions (Bawcutt 12–22). But Shakespeare makes Claudio and Juliet engaged so that Claudio's punishment appears so much more arbitrary and unjust. Claudio speculates that Angelo is motivated by the desire to make a "name" for himself, or simply to exercise his power, as a horse-rider, "Who, newly in the seat, that it may know / He can command, lets it straight feel the spur" (1.2.158–9). Angelo's downfall begins with a destructive abuse of power even before his encounter with Isabella.

The first time we actually see Angelo exercising his authority in person, however, is when Elbow brings Pompey and Froth before him and Escalus (2.1). Angelo's practical limitations are revealed in this scene. This case represents a comic example of what real-life judges face every day on the bench: a confusion of conflicting and obscure reports. Angelo has no patience for the detailed investigation required for the actual practice of legal judgment. He leaves abruptly in the midst of the proceedings, commenting that he hopes Escalus will "find good reason to whip them all" (2.1.138), carelessly conflating the innocent and guilty. Escalus, by contrast, is patient and flexible. He has been criticized for being ineffectual and doing nothing in this scene, yet it is not clear that any official action is really appropriate for this situation. Elbow's pregnant wife has apparently been propositioned after entering a house of prostitution in search of stewed prunes. Is this really a case for legal punishment? Warnings for Pompey and Froth are probably the only practical action for this case. This episode tests Angelo and reveals him as impatient with the practical details of ruling.

Angelo's main test, however, comes in his first interview with Isabella. He maintains a public appearance of rigid strictness, yet late in the interview he confesses to the audience, "She speaks, and 'tis such sense / That my sense breeds with it" (2.2.147–8), punning on "sense." Angelo's desire for Isabella seems to come suddenly and without any conscious seeking on his part. According to Ames, a devilish temptation "invades the mind suddenly, with a kinde of vehemency, after the manner of flashes of lightning,…repugnant to the light of nature, or to reason itselfe, and to our naturall inclination" (2.45).

After Isabella leaves, he attempts to understand his unexpected reaction. Angelo's several monologues are among the dramatic highlights of the play, and they serve effectively as an anatomy of the Protestant psychology of sin:

> What's this, what's this? Is this her fault or mine?
> The tempter or the tempted, who sins most, ha?

> Not she, nor doth she tempt; but it is I
> That, lying by the violet in the sun,
> Do as the carrion does, not as the flower,
> Corrupt with virtuous season. (2.2.170–75)

He begins by rationalizing his sinful desire, trying to place the blame on Isabella, characterizing her as the "tempter" and himself as the innocent "tempted." Angelo immediately recognizes, however, the sophistry of blaming the victim. He, like a dead carcass, rots in exposure to the sun, the same sun which nourishes the pure violet Isabella.

Angelo continues,

> ...Can it be
> That modesty may more betray our sense
> Than woman's lightness? Having waste ground enough,
> Shall we desire to raze the sanctuary
> And pitch our evils there? O, fie, fie, fie!
> What dost thou, or what art thou, Angelo?
> Dost thou desire her foully for those things
> That make her good? (2.2.175–82)

René Girard has analyzed well the mimetic nature of his attraction to Isabella. It is her purity, her very inaccessibility that makes her contagiously desirable to him. For Shakespeare, in contrast to the Puritans and the many modern critics who follow their lead, the problem is not sexual desire as such, but rather *mimetic* desire. Girard comments, "Her indifference to men matches his own haughty indifference to women. He sees her chastity as a personal affront, an act of cruelty, an irresistible challenge, a deliberate obstacle placed in his path, the ultimate scandalon" (295). Angelo exemplifies perfectly Augustine's thesis about the perversity of the human will.[12] Angelo sins deliberately, in full knowledge that his actions are wrong. In Puritan faculty psychology, the will was capable of acting in opposition to rational knowledge. Ames writes, "When the will doth first begin, to draw away the understanding from that, which it hath judged to be good, it doth it, by its own inclination without any judgement that it should doe so" (1.24). The fact that even the unregenerate, perhaps reprobate Angelo has this innate knowledge of good and evil confirms the existence of the conscience, the voice of God within his soul. Even, or especially, in its weakness and fall, Angelo's soul is revealed as a locus of sacrality and a compelling subject for theatrical representation.

The action of this monologue is Angelo's confrontation with his own sinful nature. He comments, "Even till now, / When men were fond, I smiled and wondered how" (2.2.193–4). Angelo had no previous knowledge of his own corruption! From a Calvinist viewpoint, this complete lack of self-knowledge is a dangerous form of pride. Calvin argues that self-knowledge and knowledge of God are inextricably tied together (37). When a person looks within, he finds an inner lack which impels him towards God and Christ as the only remedy: "Thus, from the feeling of our own ignorance, vanity, poverty, infirmity, and — what is more — depravity and corruption, we recognize that the true light of wisdom, sound virtue, full abundance of every good, and purity of righteousness rest in the Lord alone" (Calvin 36). The confrontation with one's inherently sinful nature is the necessary first step towards self-reformation.

Angelo's inner conflict is a well-developed theme of the play. As he anticipates his second interview with Isabella, he muses to himself,

> When I would pray and think, I think and pray
> To several subjects. Heaven hath my empty words,
> Whilst my invention, hearing not my tongue,
> Anchors on Isabel; Heaven in my mouth,
> As if I did but only chew His name,
> And in my heart the strong and swelling evil
> Of my conception. (2.4.1–7)

Like Claudius in *Hamlet*, he finds himself unable to pray, finding in his heart only "strong and swelling evil." His soul is the site of a psychomachia, a battle between conflicting desires. The fact that he wants to pray at all again confirms the presence of conscience, an inner voice that persists no matter how deep he sinks in corruption, warring against his unregenerate desires.

He continues,

> The state, whereon I studied,
> Is like a good thing, being often read,
> Grown sere and tedious; yea, my gravity,
> Wherein — let no man hear me — I take pride,
> Could I with boot change for an idle plume,
> Which the air beats for vain. (2.4.1–15)

Angelo recognizes here the emptiness of his ambition. He finds his public office "sere and tedious." His external "gravity" is merely another vanity, a form of "pride." He could just as easily live as a vain sensualist wearing an "idle plume" like Lucio. His thoughtful self-analysis seems unnecessary simply for plot development; rather it develops the centrality of the private scene.

He goes on with a general critique of public authority:

> O place, O form,
> How often does thou with thy case, thy habit,
> Wrench awe from fools and tie the wiser souls
> To thy false seeming! Blood, thou art blood.
> Let's write "good angel" on the devil's horn,
> 'Tis not the devil's crest. (2.4.12–15)

He progresses from his particular case to a general statement that "place" and "form," public authorities, are merely empty roles that "Wrench awe from fools" independently of any inherent worth. His sin has led him to a deep understanding of the vanity that underlies public authority, including his own. Underneath the public role, even the most "awesome" ruler is equally governed by passion or "blood." Writing "good angel" (a pun on his name) on the devil's horn will not change the inner reality of sin — again highlighting the radical discrepancy between public appearance and private conscience.

His third major monologue, delivered after his nighttime rendezvous with Mariana and his second order for Claudio's execution, reveals him as in the grip of a foreign power that seems to control him. Sin possesses him as a destructive, soul-destroying alien force. Shakespeare confirms Luther's comment that the unregenerate will "is the permanent prisoner and bondslave of evil, since it cannot turn itself to good" (187). Like Macbeth, Angelo finds that sin is its own punishment:

> This deed unshapes me quite, makes me unpregnant
> And dull to all proceedings. A deflowered maid,
> And by an eminent body that enforced
> The law against it! But that her tender shame
> Will not proclaim against her maiden loss,
> How might she tongue me! Yet reason dares her no,
> For my authority bears of a credent bulk
> That no particular scandal once can touch
> But it confounds the breather. He should have lived,
> Save that his riotous youth, with dangerous sense,
> Might in times to come have ta'en revenge,
> By so receiving a dishonored life

> With ransom of such shame. Would yet he had lived!
> Alack, when once our grace we have forgot,
> Nothing goes right; we would, and we would not. (4.4.20–34)

This time, he does not even try to rationalize his actions; he can find no other justification than self-interest, the avoidance of honorable revenge. This speech confirms Perkins' statement that "The effect of the accusing and condemning conscience, is to stirre up sundrie passions and motions in the heart, but specially these five...shame, sadnes and sorrow, feare, including Terrours of conscience, desperation, and perturbation or disquietnesse of the whole man" ("Discourse" 39–40). While Angelo himself stands under heavy condemnation, the power and authority of conscience on his private scene of representation is vindicated. Like Milton's Satan, he paradoxically becomes more worthy of dramatic representation in his fall. His profound self-awareness compels our attention. We should note that the action of his conscience is completely independent of any external influence. The private scene stands firm as a locus of sacrality even in its conflict and despair. In fact, the inner battle itself authorizes the private scene, just as the agon between heroic warriors authorizes the epic scene of battle in Homer and Virgil.

In the final scene, his inner soul, which has already been effectively revealed to himself, Isabella, Claudio, the Duke, and the audience, is finally revealed to the whole city. In response to the Duke's revelations, he confesses:

> ...O my dread lord,
> I should be guiltier than my guiltiness
> To think I can be undiscernible,
> When I perceive Your Grace, like power divine,
> Hath looked upon my passes. Then, good prince,
> No longer session hold upon my shame,
> But let my trial be mine own confession.
> Immediate sentence then and sequent death
> Is all the grace I beg. (5.1.374-382)

He publicly acknowledges his crimes here, acknowledging their sinful nature and recognizing the justice of any punishment which he might receive. Stephen Greenblatt has argued that there is no individual or social reformation in the play, that all the Duke's efforts toward change are ineffective (141). Significantly, however, Greenblatt completely ignores Isabella, who, as I argue below, exemplifies the human potential for forgiveness. In the case of Angelo, it is true that we have no promise to be better in the future, as Caliban makes at the end of *The Tempest*, nor does Angelo beg for mercy, but all this is beside the point. The important thing is that he fully recognizes and acknowledges his sin as sin. He has undergone a humiliating journey of self-knowledge and is now profoundly altered. Furthermore, Angelo is sincerely repentant. A little later in the scene, he admits,

> I am sorry that such sorrow I procure,
> And so deep sticks it in my penitent heart
> That I crave death more willingly than mercy.
> 'Tis my deserving, and I do entreat it. (5.1.485–88)

Angelo has been confronted with the truth of his inner self. What he does with that knowledge, however, is up to him. In this, Shakespeare recognizes the futility of Angelo's program at the beginning of the play, the attempt to fundamentally change human nature by legal proclamations. Reform must take place on the private scene of the individual soul. Only a complete and deep inner transformation will command public respect. The final outcome of Angelo's repentance is left undefined by Shakespeare in recognition of the limits of public authority.

4. Measure for Measure

The encounter between public and private in the play can be traced back to the New Testament ideal of reciprocity referred to in the title. The private is able to challenge the public because they are felt to be in a reciprocal or symmetrical relationship. The Passion story effectively levels all traditional hierarchical distinctions, since Jesus was executed as a lower-class criminal yet resurrected as the Lord of the universe. The Passion teaches, in effect, that anyone may occupy the central position. The public center and private periphery of the scene of representation are essentially equal, because equally human. In its most elementary form, reciprocity takes the form of the golden rule — "whatsoever ye would that men should do to you, even so do ye to them" (Matthew 7.12) — the ideal of mercy in the play.

In the Sermon on the Mount, Jesus commands his followers to give their alms in private, to pray in private, and to fast in private, "and thy Father that seeth in secret, he shall reward thee openly" (Matthew 6.4). God takes the private and makes it public, in recognition of its intrinsic worth. For Jesus, the integrity of the private scene of devotion is prior to the public reward of the Father. Sacrality here is essentially private — not a function of public ritual, the traditional locus of sacrality. Jesus radicalized the Old Testament law by demanding an internal obedience, not just external, ritual conformity. For Jesus and his followers, the public scene is suspect, contaminated by hypocrisy — "the leaven of the Pharisees and of the Sadducees" (Matt. 16.6). The public recognition of private virtue, while not eliminated, is typically deferred.

Angelo is an example by contrast of Jesus's teaching: the revelation of Angelo's inner self does not lead to public reward but rather serves to undermine his public role and the moral authority of his reform efforts. Angelo's political authority is dependent upon his private integrity, and the revelation of his private lust has the effect of completely destabilizing and subverting his public character. The private thus challenges the authority of the public. The public authority of Angelo cannot stand alone because it has a private side; the private, then, has become culturally essential; but when revealed, it stands in need of reform. The Christian ideal of reciprocity has corrosive effects on public figures because privately we are all sinners, at least by the standards of the Sermon on the Mount. As a result, all public authorities become suspect, a trend which has escalated in recent history.

The play draws explicitly upon the New Testament teaching. Asking Angelo to reconsider Claudio's punishment, Escalus tells him,

> ...in the working of your own affections,
> Had time cohered with place, or place with wishing,
> Or that the resolute acting of your blood
> Could have attained th' effect of your own purpose,
> Whether you had not sometime in your life
> Erred in this point which now you censure him,
> And pulled the law upon you. (2.1.10–16)

Escalus, in other words, asks for reciprocity between Claudio and Angelo based on their common tendency to sin, which is confirmed by Angelo's fall. Angelo responds that his judgment of Claudio is completely irrelevant to his own potential for sin; he argues for the traditional distinction between his public office as judge and his private person.[13] According to this interpretation, Jesus's command to forgive applies only to the private person. In other words, for Angelo, there is no reciprocity between public and private but on the contrary a complete separation, or rather a hierarchy with public authority on top. While there is much to be said for Angelo's argument, the play clearly favors Escalus's view here, in favor of mercy, since Angelo's actions are portrayed as scandalous in light of his own corruption.

In Angelo's hands, the law serves to justify what is simply an arbitrary sacrifice. Claudio is unfairly singled out in a city in which sexual corruption is so widespread it extends even to the de facto head of the government, Angelo himself. In this situation, Claudio's punishment can only be understood as a form of scapegoating, the opposite of impartial justice. The problem then is that legal justice as enforced by a public institution is not reciprocal; the judge offers judgment, but without himself being subject to the same standard. Angelo is able to judge Claudio for a crime of lust because of his position of authority, but that same authority gives him immunity to standards of justice.

This ideal of reciprocity is consistently the basis of Isabella's plea to Angelo for mercy. "Go to your bosom," she pleads,

> Knock there, and ask your heart what it doth know
> That's like my brother's fault. If it confess
> A natural guiltiness such as is his,
> Let it not sound a thought upon your tongue
> Against my brother's life. (2.2.141–146; see also 2.2.69–71,
> 2.2.78–84)

Again the appeal is based on a shared human tendency towards sin that levels all earthly hierarchies. The Duke makes a similar point in the final scene, pretending to defend Angelo against Isabella: "If he had so offended, / He would have weighed thy brother by himself / And not have cut him off" (5.1.115–17; see also 3.2.254–63, 4.2.79–85). From this New Testament perspective, the public authority is not inherently more valuable than the private person; in fact, as the case of Angelo reveals, the public authority is ultimately revealed as always already a private person.

Angelo's abuse of power provokes a profound questioning of all public authority within the play. Claudio complains,

> Thus can the demigod Authority
> Make us pay down for our offense by weight
> The words of heaven. On whom it will, it will;
> On whom it will not, so; yet still 'tis just. (1.2.120–123)

Claudio sees authority here as comparable to a pagan idol, a "demigod" whose actions are completely arbitrary and therefore unjust. His last line is heavily ironic: with no principle for discrimination, how can the actions of "Authority" be just? Political authority as such is called into question here. Later in the same scene, Claudio suggests that Angelo's actions represent his personal desire simply to exercise his new-found authority, just as a horse rider "Who, newly in the seat, that it may know / He can command, lets it straight feel the spur" (1.2.158-9).

Isabella memorably challenges Angelo:

> ...man, proud man,
> Dressed in a little brief authority,
> Most ignorant of what he's most assured,
> His glassy essence, like an angry ape,
> Plays such fantastic tricks before high heaven
> As makes the angels weep; who, with our spleens,
> Would all themselves laugh mortal. (2.2.122–28)

The pride of man is here revealed as laughable in view of the majesty of God. Humans are all equal before God, and the attempt of one to judge another is comparable to the tricks of an angry ape. Angelo himself questions his authority when considering his own corruption:

> ...O place, O form,
> How often dost thou with thy case, thy habit,
> Wrench awe from fools and tie the wiser souls
> To thy false seeming! (2.4.12–15)

In the final scene, the Duke threatens to execute a primitive form of reciprocity upon Angelo: "'An Angelo for Claudio, death for death!' / Haste still pays haste, and leisure answers leisure; / Like doth quit like, and measure still for measure" (5.1.417–19). This reciprocity is the Old Testament *lex talionis*, an eye for an eye, the basis for sacrifice. It works by reducing everything to the same level of violence. But the New Testament, drawing on the anti-sacrificial prophetic tradition of the Old Testament, attempts to transcend violence through mutual or even unilateral forgiveness. New Testament reciprocity requires imaginatively placing oneself in the position of the other. The play stages these competing forms of reciprocity in the last scene. The Duke's threat to punish Angelo is the sacrificial form of reciprocity, but Isabella's plea represents unilateral forgiveness, based on a recognition of common human failing. The latter is morally progressive, while the former is archaic and ultimately self-defeating, although still potent in our modern world. The latter accounts for the private person, while the former focuses on external public actions. Sacrificial reciprocity is based upon a superficial emphasis upon "honor," while New Testament reciprocity recognizes that underneath our public appearance, we are all equally sinners. The human community can transcend the vicious circle of sacrificial violence only through mutual forgiveness. There is no reason to think that the final scene is intended as a realistic model of legal justice; it serves rather to dramatize the historic alternatives of revenge and violence on the one hand and love and forgiveness on the other.

5. "The tempter or the tempted, who sins most?"

Isabella begins the play by withdrawing to the privacy of a nunnery, and she ends it on the public stage, pleading for mercy for the man who attempted to rape her. In this sense, she exemplifies the play's main action, making the private public. In contrast to Angelo, however, she is no hypocrite. Publicly, she presents an appearance of utmost purity. And unlike Angelo, she does not find sex a serious temptation. Despite the Duke's marriage proposal in the last act, there is no sign that she is tempted by sexual or romantic love. In that sense, her public appearance corresponds to her private or inner character. Her chastity is tested, like Angelo, and she proves true to her ideals. She appears chaste and she is chaste. The problem here is that the play does not recognize sexual purity as a value. Even in a world of overwhelming sexual corruption, there is no hint that complete abstinence, *virgin* chastity (as opposed to married chastity, the alternative Protestant virtue celebrated by the end of the play), is the answer to the problem of sexual desire.[14] Isabella's pride in her chastity during the dialogue with her brother (3.1) is presented as inhumane. Her character is revealed decisively with her statement, "More than our brother is our chastity" (2.4.186).

For Isabella, chastity itself is a temptation. Her problem of course is spiritual pride, which leads her to consign unfeelingly her brother to death. Her pride is manifested early in the play, in her initial interview with a nun of St. Clare's. Far from resisting the rules of the convent, Isabella tells Franscisca that she wishes "a more strict restraint / Upon the sisterhood" (1.4.4–5). She desires stricter rules as a way of demonstrating her inner strength. In other words, she wants to be tested so that she can prove her extraordinary purity. In her second interview with Angelo, she insists that she would willingly undergo death or torture before sacrificing her vow of chastity: "were I under terms of death, / Th' impression of keen whips I'd wear as rubies, and strip myself to death as to a bed" (2.4. 100–102). She repeats the point in the subsequent dialogue with her brother: "O, were it but my life, / I'd throw it down for your deliverance / As frankly as a pin" (3.1.105–107). She seems the character the least in need of inner reform, but spiritual pride, what Luther called the "white devil," was a well-recognized problem of reformation literature.[15]

Her first encounter with Angelo, when she seems reluctant to plead effectively for her brother's life until urged on by Lucio, is also revealing. At Angelo's first refusal, she says simply, "O just but severe law! / I had a brother, then" (2.2.45–46). Not until Lucio prods her, "Give 't not o'er so. To him again, entreat him!" (2.2.47), does she return to her pleading. Lucio is forced to chide her repeatedly for being "too cold" in her pleas (2.2.49, 61). Likewise, at her second interview, she begins to leave at Angelo's first refusal (2.4.34). It is true that Lucio praises her at their first meeting (1.4.34–37), and the Duke recognizes her basic goodness, saying, "The hand that hath made you fair hath made you good" (3.1.182). But this is more in recognition of her good intentions than her moral development. Spiritual pride is a subtle vice, and one of the hardest to root out. It has been well argued that for Shakespeare's audience her monastic vocation and insistence on her virginity would be associated with foreign "papistry" and thus morally suspect (Gless 97–141). Protestant theologians famously held marriage to be a higher spiritual calling than virginity. The play calls her private self into question because it lacks the warmth, humility, and compassion of true virtue.

As many critics have noted, she is Angelo's mimetic double. They are two sides of the same coin, and they represent the dual weakness of moralistic legalism. On the one hand, Angelo represents the vulnerability of an untried virtue. Isabella, on the other, represents the temptation of spiritual pride. The authority of the private scene cannot be based simply on moral purity, since, as the play argues, with Luther and Calvin, temptation and sin are the human condition. This does not mean, however, that the private scene cannot effectively serve as a locus of sacrality, but such authorization requires active testing and inner combat, an internalization of the drama of the crucifixion.

The crucial scene, and undoubtedly the most difficult to interpret, is her interview with Claudio. She speaks to Claudio initially in riddles, while he, facing death, seeks a straightforward answer. There is no way to save his life, she says, "none but such remedy as, to save a head, / To cleave a heart in twain" (3.1.60–61). He replies desperately, "But is there any?" (3.1.62). She appears to be playing with him, as she withholds the awful bargain proposed by Angelo. She explains, "O, I do fear thee, Claudio" (3.1.73). When finally confronted with Angelo's attempted blackmail, Claudio says simply, "Thou shalt not do 't" (3.1.104). But after a long and fearful meditation on death, he reverses himself and pleads, "Sweet sister, let me live" (3.1.135). This is Isabella's crucial test, and her exaggerated reaction is revealing: "O you beast! / O faithless coward! O dishonest wretch! / Wilt thou be made a man out of my vice?" (3.1.138–140). The point here is not that Claudio is justified in his demand, or that Isabella should sacrifice her body for Claudio's life. In moral terms, both Isabella and

Claudio are being asked to choose the lesser of two evils, and it is not at all clear which is which. This is a messy, complicated moral situation, and that, I believe, is Shakespeare's point, that life in this world often presents us with complex moral problems that force us to choose the lesser of two evils. This recognition is in contrast to the moral absolutism of both Angelo and Isabella, who seem to think that good and evil can never mix. As Harold Goddard points out, echoing Milton, "Good and evil get inextricably mixed throughout *Measure for Measure*, for virtue is no exception to the rule, and pushed to the limit, turns into vice" (55). What Isabella's reaction reveals is her lack of compassion for her brother's very human fear of death; despite her speeches to Angelo, she seems to lack the capacity to imaginatively put herself in the place of the other, essential for true reciprocity. In addition, she seems overly concerned not just for her virginity, but for her public reputation and honor before men, another example of pride (Gless 143–9).

At this point in the play, the Duke intervenes with the idea of the "bed-trick" as a way of saving both Isabella's virginity and Claudio's life. Some critics have found her involvement in the bed-trick to be compromising because she seems to be sanctioning premarital sex after having just argued strenuously against it. But the play switches decisively here from tragedy to comedy, and within the world of comedy, a substituted bedmate is completely conventional and acceptable. Questioning the bed-trick imposes a foreign set of generic expectations upon the play. Significantly, no one within the play questions the substitution of Mariana for Isabella, and there is no reason to think that Shakespeare's contemporary audience would find it doubtful. We need to remember also that the bed-trick allows her to maintain her two most important values: her chastity and her brother's life; other considerations pale in comparison.[16] But the bed-trick is more than just an easy solution to a difficult moral problem; her involvement is part of her education. Lever has noted that the Duke could have easily managed the bed-trick without Isabella's help (by means of a message to Angelo and a visit to Mariana); "In keeping with the tenor of the Duke's first speech to Angelo, Isabella is being reeducated in the function of virtue as an active force in the world" (Lever lxxxii). Yes, the substitution ploy is messy and compromising in moral terms, but this is the point: life in this world is messy and compromising; we are constantly called upon to choose the lesser of two evils. Isabella is "called," in the Protestant sense, to a life in this world, a life which involves many compromises and entanglements, not least of which is the marriage proposal at the end.

Isabella immediately falls in with the Duke's proposal of the bed-trick, too easily, according to many critics. Furthermore, while she is initially reluctant, she agrees quickly to the Duke's suggestion that she accuse Angelo publicly (4.6).

She seems completely passive in relation to the Duke. There is no hint of an inner struggle comparable to Angelo's, and no outward repentance for her pride. But her sin is of a more subtle nature, and so is the cure. We must remember also her dramatic moment of conversion in the final scene, when, after a long hesitation, she joins Mariana's plea to save her new husband (more on this below). The problem, however, is not just that her conversion to humility is not fully dramatized, but also the nature of the Duke's plans for her. He asks her not only to set up the bed-trick but also to play a very compromising role in the final scene. She proclaims herself there as a fallen women to the assembled city, and she must bear the scorn and ridicule of Angelo, Escalus, and the Duke himself. We should understand her role-playing as a needful exercise in humility, an exorcism of the demon of spiritual pride. In addition, this action works dramatically because her private scene remains inviolable. In religious terms, she exists primarily *coram Deo*, before God, who sees into the heart. Ultimately, she is accountable only to God. The fact that she is able to discount the public's judgment at the end is a remarkable testimony to the integrity of her private scene.

The Duke reserves one more test for Isabella in the final scene. Her role-play in this scene could be motivated simply by revenge. The Duke, therefore, threatens to have Angelo executed (5.1.411–421). Mariana pleads for his life and asks Isabella to join her. The temptation here for Isabella is to give in to the spirit of revenge which the Duke seems to be encouraging. Far from leading Isabella into reform, he tempts her to mortal sin. When she goes down on her knees to plead for Angelo's life, we can see that her pride has been completely destroyed, and that she is a very different, radically reformed woman from the naïve and vain novitiate of the first part of the play. Her plea is not particularly persuasive in rational terms. It seems rather doubtful that her "brother had but justice," or that Angelo's attempt to blackmail Isabella should be dismissed as merely an unacted "bad intent" (5.1.456, 459). More persuasive than the content of her plea is the fact that she makes this plea at all. That Isabella should plead for Angelo's life is what impresses in this scene.

Many critics have noted that the Duke's marriage proposal at the end is not completely satisfactory in dramatic terms, but this difficulty is mainly a result of the generic confusion of the play. Isabella progresses from the world of tragedy to romance and comedy, and such a transition can never be completely smooth. Her silence reflects the general difficulty of this moment, its implausibility. But I would point out that marriage to the Duke would be compatible with her general development in the play, from a novice nun to an active, worldly life. In terms of the progress of her character, the marriage proposal is dramatically necessary and typically Protestant.

6. Duke Vincentio and "the life removed"

The events of the play clearly undermine Angelo's public authority, but what about the Duke? He is often seen as the play's answer to the problem of authority, for good or ill, even in many recent New Historical analyses of the play.[17] On the other hand, critics who question the Duke's authority (both within the play and for the audience) tend to be rather perverse, imposing standards foreign to the play. Critics who delve too deeply into the Duke's motivations typically apply the generic conventions of novelistic realism to a Jacobean comedy.[18]

The Duke is rather different from any other prince or monarch in Shakespeare. Nevertheless, he is essentially from the world of comedy.[19] Even Lucio could serve as comic relief in a tragedy; and Angelo, Isabella, and Claudio all fit more or less comfortably in a tragic landscape. The Duke, however, is unimaginable within a tragic setting, since he serves largely to bring about the happy ending. Lucio constantly pokes fun at him, and his plans are often comically frustrated. While other monarchs in Shakespeare tend to self-destruct (Girard 183–4), the Duke withdraws only to play a more central role. The authority figures in romance and comedy usually function mainly as obstacles to the love matches, or they are magical figures who help bring about the desired marriages. The Duke is clearly in the later category, comparable to Oberon or Prospero. Insofar as he functions as a figure for testing and education, he could also be compared to Portia, Rosalind, or Viola. In contrast to tragic figures, there is no hint of inner conflict in the Duke. He never laments his choice of Angelo as deputy, or any of his actions. As a comic figure, he does not have any well-developed inner side. Unlike Angelo and Isabella, we need to look at the Duke primarily in terms of the functions that he serves within the play.

His primary function is to test all the other characters, and his disguise can be understood in this light. As Martin Wiggins points out, in the "Disguised Ruler" plays popular during the early seventeenth century the common element is that the ruler's "disguise enables him to expose vices that would otherwise remain hidden, or at least unspoken" (107). The Duke tests Angelo by placing him in charge and then secretly watching him. Claudio, Juliet, the provost, Escalus, Pompey, and Isabella all do not know that they are dealing with the prince of the realm, and that their actions and words are being examined from a position of authority. Lucio's loyalty and honesty are tested and found wanting. When the Duke lets Claudio think that he must prepare for death, this tests his spiritual health, since during the medieval and Renaissance periods the encounter with death was held to be a key sign of one's eternal destiny. His deception of Isabella about her brother's death similarly tests her faith and prepares for the major trial of the final scene.[20] Even in the last scene, in which he appears as himself, he serves to test the other characters who do not yet know his identity with the Friar.

His role as confessor can be understood from this perspective; confession takes the private and makes it (relatively) public, bringing it before the scrutiny of the priest, church, and God. The institution of confession at the Fourth Lateran Council of the Church in 1215 contributed to the development of modernity by authorizing the private scene, even as it attempted to bring it under discipline and control.

As a figure for testing, he requires a certain authority for the audience. The play's title makes clear that the Duke cannot effectively judge the other characters if he is guilty of the same faults himself. As a result of this plot imperative, the Duke claims to be immune to flattery: he does not "relish well" the "loud applause and 'aves' vehement" of the crowd (1.1.71). Similarly, he cannot be accused of sexual corruption: "the dribbling dart of love / Cannot pierce [his] complete bosom" (1.3.2–3, see also 3.2.118–9). In case we think the Duke a biased judge of his own case, his evaluation is echoed by Escalus, who characterizes the Duke as "a gentlemen of all temperance" (3.2.232).[21] It's true that he proposes to Isabella in the final scene, thus apparently contradicting himself on this point. The plot imperatives here come into conflict, and Shakespeare never bothers to reconcile them. On the one hand, this play is about exposing hidden vices, and the chosen plot for doing so requires a disguised ruler with a certain authority for the audience, including immunity to sexual temptation. On the other hand, the development of Isabella's character, as well as the comedic happy ending, requires the marriage of the Duke and Isabella.

The Duke's motivations, however, need to be considered, insofar as the play itself raises them as an issue. His reasons for pretending to leave Vienna and delegating authority to Angelo are famously problematic. He tells Friar Thomas that he intends to reform the enforcement of law in Vienna (1.3.19–43). He considers himself unqualified by his previous leniency, and Angelo seems like the best person for the job. But at the same time, he suspects that Angelo may not be as incorruptible as he appears, and so he remains in Vienna to monitor events. This, in itself, is not inconsistent. His main function in the play, I argue, is to test the other characters, but this is not overtly his primary motivation as a character. The Duke simply states that Angelo will be tested by power, and "Hence shall we see, / If power change purpose, what our seemers be" (1.3.50–54).

Many critics have claimed that he actually "expects Angelo to fall," and that this expectation renders his decision to give him power incomprehensible.[22] Students of Milton's *Paradise Lost* will find this a familiar issue, and I believe that

Reformation theology is a relevant context here: first, because the play is about the explicitly Christian themes of sin and forgiveness; second, Angelo himself compares the Duke to "power divine" (5.1.377). While I disagree with those critics who see the play as a Christian allegory, I believe that the Duke functions, at least in part, as a figure for testing and temptation which is analogous to God and Christ. Christ is God in human form; therefore he tests everyone with whom he comes into contact insofar as they are unaware of his real authority. His divine identity is not decisively revealed until the resurrection. The New Testament Gospels are the ultimate "disguised ruler" tale. The parallel to the Duke is instructive here if not taken to the point of full identity. Likewise, in Reformation theology, God tests Adam and Eve in Genesis with a full knowledge that they will fail the test.[23] Milton develops this idea in *Paradise Lost* when God permits Satan to enter Paradise and tempt Adam and Eve. The Miltonic argument is that virtue which is untested is fatally vulnerable, and that temptation is unavoidable (*Areopagitica* 1006). Even in heaven Satan, as an angel of light before his fall, could not escape the temptation to sin. In a similar way, Isabella succumbs to spiritual pride even in her attempt to avoid temptation by entering a convent. Temptation is in effect the human condition. God, therefore, cannot be charged with "setting up" Adam and Eve; nor, given the pervasive Biblical context, can the Duke be charged with setting up Angelo. Temptation and sin are inevitable; the question posed by *Paradise Lost* is how will we respond? *Measure for Measure* poses for its audience the same question, although there are no Satanic figures in the play. Sin is emphatically human in nature (which is also the point of Milton's very human portrayal of Satan). For Milton, as in *Measure for Measure*, testing and temptation are God's methods for educating humanity and cultivating our virtue, authorizing the private scene. Milton suggests that the fall is indeed fortunate for Adam and Eve. In similar fashion Angelo and Isabella learn about themselves through their trials, and this is a necessary step in their spiritual development.

Another important question regarding the Duke's motivation is whether he really wants to reform Vienna or not. This seems to be his primary motivation in the opening scenes, but this goal drops out as the play progresses. And in the final scene, he does not uphold the strict enforcement of the laws that he had characterized earlier as "needful bits and curbs to headstrong steeds" (1.3.19–21) but rather forgives everyone, even the murderer Barnardine.

First of all, it is not clear that Vienna is really as lawless as the Duke suggests. He tells Friar Thomas, "liberty plucks justice by the nose; / The baby beats the nurse, and quite athwart / Goes all decorum" (1.4.29–31). Likewise, in the final scene, as Friar, the Duke says, "I have seen corruption boil and bubble /

Till it o'errun the stew; laws for all faults, / But faults so countenanced that the strong statues / Stand like the forfeits in a barber's shop, / As much in mock as mark" (5.1. 326–330). But earlier in the play, when Escalus asks the Friar/ Duke, thinking he has come from afar, "What news abroad i' in the world?" the Duke answers, "None but that there is so great a fever on goodness that the dissolution of it must cure it.… This news is old enough, yet it is every day's news" (3.2.217–225). This suggests that the lawless "anarchy" he describes elsewhere is not specific to Vienna, nor is it new. In other words, this is the general condition of the world that people, including him, have been complaining about forever without effect. If so, it is not evident that Vienna's corruption is as bad as described, nor is it clear that it can be reformed at a general level. René Girard, no doubt, would see the Duke's descriptions as evidence of a sacrificial "crisis of degree" which is "the context of all Shakespearean plays without exception" (351). This play actually parodies such a view in the person of the Duke, suggesting that Shakespeare's view of modernity is not as dire as Girard's.

What evidence do we have of Vienna's corruption apart from the Duke's description? We see Lucio slandering the Duke, but this mainly wounds the Prince's vanity rather than causing any serious disorder in Vienna. Lucio is also held accountable for having refused support to Kate Keepdown, the prostitute who is mother of his child (3.2.194–98; 4.3.168–72; 5.1.520–24). Lucio's refusal to post bail for Pompey is also significant in this regard (3.2.42–84). But Lucio does not really pose any serious threat to the security of the state, and he is in fact forced to take responsibility for his bastard by marrying the prostitute, so the Duke cannot be charged with ignoring this particular case of corruption. The fact is, we do not see any specific examples of this crisis in decorum spoken of by the Duke. The real problem of Vienna is not rampant sexual fornication but rather corruption in high places; power is at issue here more than prostitution. The main example of corruption in Vienna, tellingly, is Angelo himself, and the Duke does deal effectively with him.

The other significant case of corruption is Pompey and Mistress Overdone's house of prostitution. The diseases spread by prostitution, however, are treated as a matter for good-natured humor by Lucio and friends rather than a serious cause for concern (1.2). Pompey and the other "low-life" characters are all portrayed sympathetically. It is true that the Duke chastises Pompey severely and characterizes his trade in savage terms:

> Fie, sirrah, a bawd, a wicked bawd!
> The evil that thou causest to be done,
> That is thy means to live. Do thou but think

What 'tis to cram a maw or clothe a back
From such a filthy vice; say to thyself,
From their abominable and beastly touches
I drink, I eat, array myself, and live.
Canst thou believe thy living is a life,
So stinkingly depending? Go mend, go mend. (3.2.20–28)

Pompey is forced to reform to some extent by becoming an executioner instead of a bawd, but this is Angelo's doing, not the Duke's. Why, then, doesn't the Duke do more to reform prostitution in Vienna? The answer is memorably given by Pompey and Lucio: "Does your worship mean to geld and splay all the youth of the city?" Pompey asks Escalus. Since the answer is "no," then "Truly, sir, in my poor opinion, they will to 't then" (2.1.229–33). Similarly, Lucio comments, "it is impossible to extirp [lechery] quite, Friar, till eating and drinking be put down" (3.2.100–1). This is a case in which the cure would be worse than the disease. And this is in fact the position of many governments: prostitution is illegal but usually tolerated to some extent because it would cost too much to eliminate it. It is only an apparent contradiction that the Duke evaluates vice harshly, yet judges it leniently. It is perfectly coherent to abhor the unsavory aspects of prostitution while at the same time recognizing the impossibility of ever eliminating it. This is in fact the implied position of the Duke in his general leniency both before the play and in the final act: an acknowledgment of the limits of the law. His general pardon for all concerned in the last scene represents a humane recognition of the limits of reform.

As ruler, the Duke clearly functions as an authority figure in the play, and this function is compatible with (indeed, necessary for) his testing the other characters. The question is whether the play finally upholds his authority or questions and undermines it. Good arguments can be made for either position (Shakespeare may have required some ambiguity here given his royal audience), but considering the opposition between public and private will help us to clarify the issue here.

In the opening scene the Duke withdraws from the scenic center which is the traditional locus of authority for princes. He becomes instead a private person with secret powers, sort of like Clark Kent or Bruce Wayne. In this, the Duke can be compared to Hamlet, who finds the center stage suspicious, a scene of flattery and hypocrisy. Hamlet actually prefers the margins of the Danish court, where he can make fun of the other characters and play with freedom a variety of creative roles.[24] In the same way, the Duke clearly and rather ostensively favors the "dark corners" of the kingdom. He simply doesn't *like* the public stage. He prefers to work behind the scenes, never revealing himself publicly until the final act. The Duke explains to Angelo, "I'll privily away. I love the people / But do not like to stage me to their eyes; / Though it do well, I do not relish well / Their loud applause and 'aves' vehement, / Nor do I think the man of safe discretion / That does affect it" (1.1.68–73). For the Duke, then, the public stage is a scene of flattery and vanity, of false appearances and hypocrisy, just as in *Hamlet* or *King Lear*. Later in the first act, the Duke comments to Friar Thomas, "I have ever loved the life removed / And held in idle price to haunt assemblies / Where youth and cost witless bravery keeps" (1.3.8–10). The witless or stupid bravery of public assemblies is supported by ignorant, idle youth and wasteful costs. The Duke's questioning of the public stage effectively undermines an important basis for political authority during the early modern period: ceremony, ritual, and spectacle.

Significantly, the Duke seems unable to reform Vienna from his public role; only as a private figure can he work effectively. The public laws are ineffective in reform; only privately and individually, by moral suasion and trying circumstance, can reform be accomplished. As a private person his authority is of a radically different quality than as a public figure.

The play also questions the Duke's authority through the figure of Lucio. He calls the Duke "A very superficial, ignorant, unweighing fellow" (3.2.136), one who would "mouth with a beggar though she smelt of brown bread and garlic" (3.2.176–7). "The Duke," Lucio claims, "yet would have dark deeds darkly answered; he would never bring them to light" (3.2.170–172); before "he would have hanged a man for the getting a hundred bastards, he would have paid for the nursing a thousand. He had some feeling of the sport" (3.2.113–116). Lucio's slanders serve not only to comically deflate the Duke's pretensions; they also illustrate the main problem with the public scene: its susceptibility to resentment from the periphery. The Duke's sensitivity to public opinion is often taken as an inexplicable character quirk or even as a serious flaw indicating personal insecurity. In fact, the main function of Lucio's slander is to illustrate the vulnerability of the public scene in the early modern period. The reason why the Duke avoids the center stage, as his comments suggest, is that the flattery found there is only a superficial cloak for an underlying resentment towards those in power.

Lucio's characterization of the Duke as given to lechery associates him with a long line of comic and corrupt friars going back at least to Chaucer and Langland.[25] The corrupt Friar is a staple of late medieval anticlerical literature, both serious and comic. It's highly significant that Friar Thomas at first assumes that the Duke wants to assume the Friar's robes to make a secret romantic tryst, perhaps even to seduce a woman (1.3.1–6). The last scene also serves to mock the Duke/Friar, at first when Lucio keeps interrupting the Duke; later, when he appears as the Friar again before his unveiling, he becomes subject to the combined abuse of Lucio, Angelo, and Escalus. These episodes seriously undermine his public authority as prince.

Further subverting his authority for the audience, establishing him as comic figure, is when his elaborate plan to save Claudio by substituting Mariana for Isabella is frustrated. When the letter from Angelo arrives to the prison, the Duke confidently predicts to the audience, "This is [Claudio's] pardon" (4.2.108). It is a moment of comic bathos when the expected pardon turns out to be an order for Claudio's immediate execution.

One of the major themes of the play, of course, is the abuse of authority, the arbitrary and unjustified nature of its exercise. We have already considered Isabella's speeches against authority, as well as similar comments by Claudio, Lucio, and Angelo. These comments are mainly directed at Angelo of course, but they are also aimed at the very being of public authority. They tend to undermine our respect for public authority, and thus reflect indirectly upon the Duke in his public office.

In the final scene the Duke seems to reassume whatever authority has been lost during the play, but I would argue that his final authority has been redefined by the events of the play. When he appears as Duke at the beginning of Act Five, he begins by falsely accusing Isabella and Mariana of deception, thus throwing doubt upon his plans, which at this point still remain obscure to the audience as well as to the other characters. He then delegates his authority to Angelo again, and escapes (5.1.268) so that he can reappear in his disguise as Friar, a private person. As the Friar he is roundly abused by Lucio and commanded to prison by Escalus. When he refuses to be led off the stage, Lucio lays hands on him at Angelo's suggestion and pulls off his hood. This is a key moment in the play; again, the private is revealed and made public; what is revealed is that the most despised and abused person in this scene is actually of the greatest potency and authority. This is emblematic for the larger thematic meaning of the play: the authorization of the private. The abuse that he suffers during the play authorizes him, just as Christ is authorized as the resurrected Lord by the suffering of his Passion. In effect, the Duke is endorsed here for the audience not through his public office, but through his actions during the play — a radically different form of authority, one which is earned, not bestowed by birth and rank. His final marriage proposal to Isabella establishes that he is subject to desire just as the rest of the characters in the play. This humanizes him and enables us to see him as a private person, not just an impersonal authority figure.

The marriages at the end of the play have seemed contrived and artificial to many critics. But in Isabella's case, a marriage to the Duke is consonant with her movement away from the convent to an active life. Claudio's marriage to Juliet is not problematic since they are already engaged. Lucio's and Angelo's marriages are presented as justice for the women whom they have wronged. We do not find, however, the typical joyous marriages of traditional romantic comedy, since Angelo and Lucio are forced to marry, and the Duke's proposal to Isabella is not anticipated by the audience. This ending results in part from the artificial and contrived combination of comedy and tragedy. If Isabella and Angelo start out as tragic characters, then the happy ending is bound to seem unnatural. But the awkwardness of the ending is more than an artifact of the play's generic confusion; the ending functions to question the Duke's authority once again and the authority of the public stage in general. The audience is reminded at the end of the artificiality of the traditional comic ending, which results from the interventions of the omnipotent author (in relation to the artistic work) rather than a natural and realistic dramatic result. The ending of *Measure for Measure* is in effect metatheatrical and ironic. Just as the artist functions as a *deus ex machina* in order to bring about the desired dramatic ending, so Duke Vincentio attempts to script carefully every aspect of the final scene. While we may have been tempted to think of the Duke as comparable to a playwright in earlier scenes, the final scene virtually demands this comparison.

In *The Tempest*, Shakespeare makes an explicit analogy between Prospero and the dramatic artist. Similarly, in *Measure for Measure*, the Duke functions as an artist-figure which gives us Shakespeare's commentary on his art. Like a playwright, the Duke works from behind the scenes, scripting a performance which is put on by others. Yet the nature of the artist's creation is intrinsically public, performed on the public stage for anyone with a penny in his pocket. In performance, the product of the artist's private imagination is made public, and *tested* before an audience, who may approve (or authorize) it or not. So the process of artistic creation parallels the main action of the play, making the private public, in order to test and authorize it. As such, the play could be seen as attempting to authorize the private artist and his creation, in parallel with the play's general attempt to authorize the private. However, the irony of the ending, the generally unsatisfactory reception of the final marriages, works against this interpretation. What the ending actually points to is the limits of the author's authority.

Considered as a playwright, the Duke is not particularly effective. We have noted that he seems unable to enforce the law in Vienna. And his plans for reforming Vienna have completely unforeseen consequences: Angelo does not act as expected, especially in his second order for executing Claudio. Lucio, Pompey, and Barnardine do not follow the scripts laid out for them. Barnardine's refusal to be executed is notable in this regard. And in the last scene, the Friar/Duke's seeming triumph, Lucio is stubbornly unrepentant, interrupting the Duke and resisting his final judgment even when faced with death. The Duke's artistic "creations" prove doggedly independent. This suggests Shakespeare's awareness that the artist's materials are subject not only to the imagination, but also to the constraints of real life, from which they ultimately derive. While the artist seems like the public god of his creation, he cannot constrain the private subjectivities of his creations.

The similarities between Prospero and Duke Vincentio are worth exploring briefly for the considerable light they throw on *Measure for Measure*. Like the Duke, Prospero is inept in his public role as ruler, allowing his brother to usurp him. In addition, Prospero's creations stubbornly resist his government: Caliban revolts openly, Ariel cries out against his servitude, and even his own daughter questions his actions repeatedly. Also like the Duke, Prospero tests those around him, and the results of this testing are decidedly ambivalent. While King Alonso is reformed, Sebastian and Antonio refuse to repent. Finally, at the end, Prospero releases his spirits with an acknowledgment of his personal weakness, and he forgives everyone, refusing to take revenge. I disagree with Girard that Prospero represents or parodies Shakespeare himself (343–353); rather I would say that *The Tempest* comically questions the power of the dramatic artist and his role in Renaissance society. Both *Measure for Measure* and *The Tempest* are ironic reflections on the demise of the godlike artist.

It was a commonplace of Renaissance literary criticism that the artist is a god in relation to his creation. Sidney, for example, in his *Defense of Poesy*, compares the poet to a prophet (*vates*) or creator (935–6). While Nature creates a "brazen" world, "the poets only deliver a golden" (Sidney 937). Shakespeare started out as a relatively unknown writer whose name was not even mentioned on the title page of his first published works. By 1603, however, when *Measure for Measure* was written, he had achieved considerable fame, and for his later works, his name was often larger than the title in publication (Erne 56–77, Honan 263–65). Unlike Jonson or Spenser, however, Shakespeare apparently had an ironic perspective on his fame, since he never bothered to leave behind any personal statements or records for posterity (apart from his art), and his later plays parody the artist in the persons of Duke Vincentio and Prospero.[26]

The ending of *Measure for Measure* anticipates Shakespeare's farewell to the stage in *The Tempest*. Although the Duke has attempted to control and reform everyone in the play, in the end he forgives and releases everyone to their individual consciences. He tells Barnardine, "Thou'rt condemned; / But, for those

earthly faults, I quit them all, / And pray thee take this mercy to provide /
For better times to come" (5.1.493–95). When Claudio is revealed as alive, the
Duke says to Isabella, "If he be like your brother, for his sake / Is he pardoned"
(5.1.501–2). Heeding Isabella and Mariana's pleas, he tells Angelo, "Look that
you love your wife, her worth worth yours. / I find an apt remission in myself"
(5.1.508–9). And to Lucio, he says, "They slanders I forgive," commanding him
merely to marry the mother of his child. Just as Prospero releases all his spirits
in recognition of his weakness and their independence, so the Duke forgives
everyone and leaves them to their own devices. Although he remains Duke, he
in effect abjures his power. His proposal to Isabella reveals him as human in his
desires, and equal to the rest of the characters. His marriage joins with the rest of
marriages, and puts him at the same level as the rest of the forgiven "sinners."

At the end, then, the Duke virtually abdicates his art in recognition of its
limits; the authority of the private scene ultimately trumps the public, with profound consequences for literary history. Even the greatest of artists is dependent
ultimately on the approval of his audience, as we see when Prospero begs for
applause in the epilogue to *The Tempest*. Unlike a real Duke, the artist has no direct political power. He presents dramatic actions for an audience who respond
according to their various inclinations. The artist works with individuals at the
level of persuasion and suggestion, not legal force. So too, the Duke prefers to
work by trying circumstance rather than direct force. While the artist can attempt to reform his audience, ultimately individuals must cooperate. There are
limits to rhetorical persuasion just as with legal reform. As Shakespeare became
familiar with personal fame, he resisted its allure, recognizing that the artist, in
proportion to his fame or centrality, is vulnerable to resentment from the periphery. Like the Duke, Shakespeare would prefer to operate from the margins,
as an anonymous playwright, but his fame is beginning to make that position
impossible for him. The central position of the "great artist" is also increasingly
problematic, as the disintegration of rigid hierarchies during the seventeenth
century multiplies reciprocity (and thus resentment) between the center (the artist) and the periphery (his audience). After Shakespeare, ambitious artists would
have to find new ways of legitimating their authority.

7. Substitutions

The opposition between public and private illuminates the much-noted substitutions of the play. Substitution is associated with public roles. When it comes
to performing the Mass, for example, one priest is as good as another, assuming
certain basic qualifications are met. Likewise, when a public official leaves office,

a new one is designated. Private persons, however, are not interchangeable. Family members can't be simply replaced like appliances. Shakespeare's comedies play with and even undermine this distinction. The romantic beloved is always valorized as absolutely singular and irreplaceable, yet the lovers in the comedies often switch partners with dizzying speed, thus demystifying the rhetoric of romantic love (Girard 30–39, *passim*). Comedy tends to focus more on social roles and community rather than the unique individual subjectivity, the subject of tragedy.

Measure for Measure, as its contemporary generic confusion indicates, fits uncomfortably into this scheme. The ending of course fits the comic mode. Everyone is married, and to whom does not apparently matter. Yet, at the same time, audiences and critics have always felt that the choice of partners in this play does matter. We have questioned whether Angelo and Mariana or the Duke and Isabella will be happy together. Lucio regards his marriage as a punishment worse than death. In Shakespeare's sources, the analogues to Isabella and Angelo marry each other at the end, but Shakespeare introduced Mariana as a partner for Angelo, apparently in recognition of Angelo's and Isabella's recalcitrant individuality which prevents them from working together as a romantic pair. Angelo and Isabella are presented as singular individuals who cannot simply pair off indifferently in the interests of social harmony.

Unlike a pure comedy, the multiple substitutions in this play simply do not work.[27] Angelo is not an effective substitute for the Duke. Mariana does not substitute for Isabella, as Angelo learns in the last scene; if she did, there would be no need for Angelo to marry her. Even Barnardine, a clownish figure, is an irreducibly singular individual who cannot be executed in place of Claudio. The play's questioning of the public scene extends to an undermining of the logic of substitution.

Substitution is also evoked by the play's title and the theme of reciprocity. Legalistic, sacrificial reciprocity assumes that people and offenses are substitutable: an eye for an eye, the logic of sacrifice. But the New Testament concept of reciprocity demands that the singular private scene be recognized as uniquely valuable, a locus of authority. According to the traditional Catholic doctrine of Atonement, Christ's suffering substitutes for our deserved punishment in the eyes of God, just as the scapegoat carries off our sin. The sacrificial interpretation of the crucifixion suggests that God's "honor" demands a payment for sin, indiscriminately as to victim. Protestant reformers argued against the sacrificial interpretation of the Atonement, demanding instead that each individual work out his or her own salvation in fear and trembling. Of course, even in Protestant theology, Christ mediates between the individual and God, but this is an individual relation, not a communal, public ceremony. For this reason, individuals must learn to forgive, and not to rely on sacrificial public systems of law, since each individual will be held responsible to God: "if thou bring thy gift to the altar, and there rememberest that thy brother hath ought against thee; Leave there thy gift before the altar, and go thy way; first be reconciled with thy brother, and then come and offer thy gift" (Matt. 5.23-24). Individuals cannot be expected to be saved simply on the basis of any sacrifice or substitution. Christ's sacrifice is one which demands the individual's reciprocal sacrifice. Just as the play contrasts two different models of reform, so it contrasts two different models of reciprocity and justice.

8. Conclusion

Shakespeare recognized the popular "disguised ruler" motif as a valuable vehicle for dramatically exposing hidden vices, and he targeted the hypocrisy and pride of those dedicated to moralistic legal reform, the Puritans. *Measure for Measure* participates in contemporaneous debates over the means and ends of reform. Whether Shakespeare read William Perkins or not, his play follows Perkins' agenda for individual reform while dramatizing the problems with legal reform. The play is skeptical of institutional reform, but it still affirms the alternative, more modest, Puritan agenda for reforming the private scene.

The problem with legal control of sexual vices is that the enforcement is in practice hypocritical, since no one is so free from vice as to enforce it effectively without crippling self-culpability. There are distinct limits to reform given the stubbornness of human nature. While individuals may undergo more or less radical conversions, there is no way to enforce such change at the collective level. And even when the individual does reform, there is no guarantee against backsliding.

While simply exposing hypocrites makes for good theater, individual reform is a much more difficult action to dramatize. It does not fit the tragic paradigm, which calls for a fall ending in death. Nor does it fit the comic mode, because the need for reformation in *Measure for Measure* is presented seriously, in-depth, and at length. Dramatically, this is not one of Shakespeare's greatest works. The story of individual development, education, and reform is really novelistic in character (although Shakespeare used it effectively in his later romances, *The Winter's Tale* and *The Tempest*). Milton had similar problems adapting this theme to the epic mode.

While Shakespeare's play is very topical, its significance transcends the local debates over reform. What is ultimately at stake in this play is an issue of central importance for the development of modernity: the authorization of the private scene of representation and the concurrent subversion of all public scenes. Critics who concentrate on character and genre issues miss this point, as do those who focus on historical issues narrowly conceived. The scene of representation is an anthropological category and a true cultural universal. At the same time, its specific articulation is subject to historical evolution. The larger importance of the action of the play is not simply the reform of Isabella and Angelo, but the reconstruction of the private scene as a locus of sacrality, which requires taking the private and making it public. If the conscience can serve as an internal divinity, then, potentially, any and all of us are similarly divine. We take the authority of private scenes for granted as moderns, but for Shakespeare and his audience the authorization of the private scene requires a new and radical sublimation of mimetic desire. Shakespeare views the private scene here not from a romantic Rousseauvian but rather a realistic Hobbesian perspective.[28] Modern critics like Foucault who see all discipline as sinister and repressive operate on utopian assumptions about human nature that ignore history.

The authorization of the private scene also involves the iconoclastic deconstruction of all public authority figures. The play does this primarily by exposing the hypocrisy of Angelo. The Duke's public authority is also questioned in various ways; he is unable to effectively reform Vienna, or to reform completely Angelo, Lucio, and Barnardine. The Duke is presented as a comic character, subject to Lucio's ridicule and the whole city's in the final scene. When the friar is finally revealed as the Duke, his authority takes on a radically different quality, as a private character transformed and authorized by his struggles. A superficial reading of the play sees the Duke in his public role as the answer to the problem of authority, but this interpretation misses the ironic and comic aspects of the Duke's character. As a figure for testing the Duke does require a certain limited authority, but only in terms of plot. The different roles played by the Duke prevent him from being a fully rounded character, and he is best viewed in functional terms. Again, this is not entirely satisfactory in dramatic terms and seriously limits the play's aesthetic power. Interestingly, *Measure for Measure* often works better for reading and discussion than in performance. But despite these dramatic limitations, the play does present a coherent model of reform, and it contributes to the development of modernity by authorizing the private scene.

Notes

1. See Jacques Derrida, *Of Grammatology* (Baltimore, MD: Johns Hopkins UP, 1976).

2. This description is not meant to imply any particular theory of perception. The point is simply that through language individuals have the capacity to remember (or represent privately) specific events, as such, and that such individual representations, while based on objective events, have a subjective dimension.

3. The public sphere begins to emerge in the 17th century, especially with the public debates surrounding the English Civil War. The public sphere is a *marketplace*, rather than a hierarchy, as with the early modern public scene. Milton's *Areopagitica* is the perhaps the most important theoretical statement of the importance of a public sphere. Shakespeare's late plays do contribute to the development of the public sphere, an argument I plan to make in another place.

4. All Biblical references are to the 1599 Geneva Bible, available online at <www.genevabible.org>.

5. Critics have commented on the multiple scenes of enclosure and confinement, but they interpret them anachronistically in terms of sexual repression. See Katherine Eisaman Maus, *Inwardness and Theater in the English Renaissance* (Chicago: U of Chicago P, 1995) 158–164; and Marjorie Garber, *Shakespeare After All* (New York: Pantheon, 2004) 568.

6. On *Hamlet*, see Gans, *Originary Thinking* (Stanford: Stanford UP, 1993) 156–7.

7. "Precise" was virtually a Renaissance euphemism for Puritan. Almost all critics agree that Angelo would be recognized as a Puritan by Shakespeare's audience, although some critics prefer to see him primarily as an example of the dramatic/literary tradition of the "corrupt magistrate." On Angelo as Puritan, see Victoria Haynes, "Performing Social Practice: The Example of *Measure for Measure*," *Shakespeare Quarterly* 44.1 (1993): 18–20. On Angelo as "corrupt magistrate," see J.W. Lever, introduction, *The Arden Shakespeare: Measure for Measure* (London: Thomson, 1965) xxvi-xliv.

8. Many critics have noted that testing is a dominant theme of the play — see, for example, Louise Schleiner, "Providential Improvisation in *Measure for Measure*," *PMLA* 97.2 (1982): 227–236 — but no previous critic has connected testing to the authorization of the private scene.

9. Debora Kuller Shuger makes a similar point, although she articulates the play's resolution of this debate in different terms from myself. See *Political Theologies in Shakespeare's England: The Sacred and the State in* Measure for Measure (New York: Palgrave, 2001) 117–25.

10. On the Puritans' attempt to legislate the death penalty for adultery, see Keith Thomas, "The Puritans and Adultery: The Act of 1650 Reconsidered," *Puritans and Revolutionaries*, eds. Donald Pennington and Keith Thomas (Oxford: Oxford-Clarendon Press, 1978) 257–282; Christopher Hill, *Society and Puritanism* (New York: St. Martin's Press, 1997) 206; and Haynes, 14–17.

11. Critics who see the play as an argument for monarchical authority include Franco Moretti, *Signs Taken for Wonders* (London: Verso, 1983) 57–61; and Leonard Tennenhouse, *Power on Display* (New York: Methuen, 1986) 155–169.

12. See for example the pear-stealing episode of his *Confessions* (London: Penguin, 1961) 47.

13. See Elizabeth Marie Pope, "The Renaissance Background of *Measure for Measure*," *Twentieth Century Interpretations of* Measure for Measure, ed. George L. Geckle (Englewood Cliffs, N.J.: Prentice-Hall, 1970) 55–72. But cf. Stacy Magedanz, "Public Justice and Private Mercy in *Measure for Measure*," *SEL* 44.2 (Spring 2004) 317–332; and Darryl J. Gless, Measure for Measure, *the Law, and the Convent* (Princeton, NJ: Princeton UP, 1979) 44–49.

14. *Pace* Barbara J. Baines, "Assaying the Power of Chastity in *Measure for Measure*," *Studies in English Literature* 30.2 (Spring 1990): 284–301; Maus, 159–61; and Marilyn French, *Shakespeare's Division of Experience* (New York: Summit Books, 1981) 186–91.

15. Luther's *Commentary on Galatians*, chap. one, verse four; available online <eword.gospelcom.net/comments//galatians/luther/galatians1.htm>.

16. Critics have also observed that Isabella's and Mariana's situations are not equivalent. Mariana was engaged to Angelo, and a promise to marry was almost equivalent to marriage in Renaissance England. See Lever, liii–lv.

17. Recent critics who take this line include Shuger, 102–117; Moretti, 57-61; and Tennenhouse, 155–169.

18. An example of this approach is Harry Berger Jr., *Making Trifles of Terrors* (Stanford: Stanford UP, 1997) 335–426.

19. On the Duke as a comic figure, in accordance with his roles as "duke-in-disguise and the intriguing friar disguise," see Haynes, 23–25. I agree with Haynes that the Duke is "Utterly unmimetic of anything in the social world outside the play" (23), although I do not agree that audience identification with the Duke's interventions constitutes the central aesthetic pleasure of the play.

20. G. M. Pinciss develops this point persuasively in "The 'Heavenly Comforts of Despair' and *Measure for Measure*." *Studies in English Literature* 30.2 (March 1990): 303–313.

21. Some critics have seen Duke Vincentio's questioning of Escalus about the Duke's "disposition" (3.2.225-6) as symptomatic of a deep personal insecurity (See, for example, Berger, 340–41). But there is little evidence that the Duke's "psychology" is a concern of the play at all. His question to Escalus serves merely as a comic way of introducing Escalus' comments in this regard, as well as testing Escalus's loyalty.

22. For the view that the Duke "obviously expects Angelo to fall," see David Bevington, introduction to *Measure for Measure, The Complete Works of Shakespeare*, 5th ed. (New York: Pearson-Longman, 2004) 415. On the possible implications of the Duke's apparent foreknowledge, see Berger, 342ff.

23. Calvin goes so far as to claim that God wills Adam and Eve to fall (*Commentary on Genesis*, chap. 3: available on-line <www.ccel.org/c/calvin/comment3/comm_

index.htm>). The Geneva Bible merely comments that God allows Satan to tempt them by means of the serpent (margin comment to Genesis 3.1). Milton, of course, insists on freedom of will, while still granting God foreknowledge of the fall.

24. See note 5 above.

25. On the comic aspects of the Duke's disguise as friar, see Haynes 24–26.

26. Lukas Erne has argued persuasively that Shakespeare consciously set out to craft a recognized body of printed works for posterity. See *Shakespeare as Literary Dramatist* (Cambridge: Cambridge UP, 2003). I would distinguish, however, Shakespeare's attempt to create an enduring literary heritage from a concern for the fickle "glory" of personal fame.

27. Alexander Leggatt develops and supports this point persuasively. See "Substitution in *Measure for Measure*," *SQ* 39.3 (Autumn 1988): 342–59.

28. See Gans on Hobbes, *Chronicles of Love and Resentment* ##176, 206, and 215 at <www.anthropoetics.ucla.edu/views/home.html>.

Works Cited

Ames, William. *Conscience with the Power and Cases Thereof.* 1639. Amsterdam: Theatrum Orbis Terrarum, 1975.

"An Admonition to the Parliament." 1572. *The Protestant Reformation.* Ed. Hans. J. Hillerbrand. New York: Harper & Row, 1968. 258-266.

Augustine, Saint. *Confessions.* Trans. R.S. Pine-Coffin. London: Penguin, 1961.

Baines, Barbara J. "Assaying the Power of Chastity in *Measure for Measure.*" *Studies in English Literature* 30.2 (Spring 1990): 284-301.

Bawcutt, N.W. Introduction. *Measure for Measure.* Oxford: Clarendon-Oxford UP, 1991. 1-63.

Berger, Harry Jr. *Making Trifles of Terrors: Redistributing Complicities in Shakespeare.* Ed. Peter Erikson. Stanford: Stanford UP, 1997.

Bevington, David. Introduction to *Measure for Measure. The Complete Works of Shakespeare.* (New York: Pearson-Longman, 2004). 414-417.

Calvin, John. *Institutes of the Christian Religion.* Ed. John T. McNeill. Trans. Ford Lewis Battles. Philadelphia: Westminster Press, 1960.

Diehl, Huston. "'Infinite Space': Representation and Reformation in *Measure for Measure.*" *Shakespeare Quarterly* 49.4 (Winter 1998): 393-410.

Erne, Lukas. *Shakespeare as Literary Dramatist.* Cambridge: Cambridge UP, 2003.

French, Marilyn. *Shakespeare's Division of Experience.* New York: Summit Books, 1981.

Gans, Eric. *Originary Thinking: Elements of Generative Anthropology.* Stanford: Stanford UP, 1993.

———. "Art and Entertainment." *Perspectives of New Music* 24.1 (Winter 1985): 24–37.

Garber, Marjorie. *Shakespeare After All.* New York: Pantheon, 2004.

Girard, René. *A Theater of Envy: William Shakespeare.* 1991. South Bend, IN: St. Augustine's Press, 2004.

Gless, Darryl J. Measure for Measure, *the Law, and the Convent.* Princeton, NJ: Princeton UP, 1979.

Goldman, Peter. "Living Words: Iconoclasm and Beyond in John Bunyan's *Grace Abounding.*" *New Literary History* 33.3 (Summer 2002): 461–489.

Greenblatt, Stephen. *Shakespearean Negotiations: The Circulation of Social Energy in Renaissance England.* Berkeley: U of California P, 1988.

Haynes, Victoria. "Performing Social Practice: The Example of *Measure for Measure.*" *Shakespeare Quarterly* 44.1 (Spring 1993): 1–29.

Hill, Christopher. *Society and Puritanism in Pre-Revolutionary England.* 1958. New York: St. Martin's Press, 1997.

Honan, Park. *Shakespeare: A Life.* Oxford: Oxford UP, 1998.

Lamont, William L. *Godly Rule: Politics and Religion, 1603–60.* New York: St. Martin's-Macmillan, 1969.

Leggatt, Alexander. "Substitution in *Measure for Measure.*" *Shakespeare Quarterly* 39.3 (Autumn 1988): 342–59.

Lever, J.W. Introduction. *The Arden Shakespeare: Measure for Measure.* London: Thomson, 1965. xi–xcviii.

Luther, Martin. "The Bondage of the Will." *Martin Luther: Selections from his Writings.* Trans. J. I. Packer and A. R. Johnston. Ed. John Dillenberger. New York: Anchor-Doubleday, 1962. 167–203.

MacCulloch, Diarmaid. *The Reformation.* New York: Viking-Penguin, 2003.

Magedanz, Stacy. "Public Justice and Private Mercy in *Measure for Measure.*" *SEL* 44.2 (Spring 2004): 317–332.

Maus, Katherine Eisaman. *Inwardness and Theater in the English Renaissance.* Chicago: U of Chicago P, 1995.

Milton, John. *Areopagitica. The Riverside Milton.* Ed. Roy Flanagan. Boston: Houghton Mifflin, 1998. 997–1024.

Moretti, Franco. *Signs Take for Wonders: Essays in the Sociology of Literary Forms.* Trans. Susan Fischer, David Forgacs, and David Miller. London: Verso, 1983.

Ozment, Steven. *The Age of Reform, 1250-1550: An Intellectual and Religious History of Late Medieval and Reformation Europe.* New Haven, CT: Yale UP, 1980.

Perkins, William. "A Discourse of Conscience." 1596. *William Perkins, 1558-1602: English Puritanist.* Ed. Thomas F. Merrill. Nieuwkoop, Netherlands: B. De Graaf, 1966. 3–78.

———. "The Whole Treatise of the Cases of Conscience." 1604. *William Perkins, 1558-1602: English Puritanist.* Ed. Thomas F. Merrill. Nieuwkoop, Netherlands: B. De Graaf, 1966. 79–240.

Pinciss, G. M. "The 'Heavenly Comforts of Despair' and *Measure for Measure.*" *Studies in English Literature* 30.2 (March 1990): 303–313.

Pope, Elizabeth Marie. "The Renaissance Background of *Measure for Measure.*" *Twentieth Century Interpretations of* Measure for Measure. Ed. George L. Geckle. Englewood Cliffs, N.J.: Prentice-Hall, 1970. 50–72.

Schleiner, Louise. "Providential Improvisation in *Measure for Measure.*" *PMLA* 97.2 (1982): 227–236.

Shakespeare, William. *The Complete Works of Shakespeare*. 5th ed. Ed. David Bevington. (New York: Pearson-Longman, 2004).

Shuger, Debora Kuller. *Political Theologies in Shakespeare's England: The Sacred and the State in* Measure for Measure. New York: Palgrave, 2001.

Sidney, Sir Philip. *The Defense of Poesy. The Norton Anthology of English Literature.* 7th ed. Vol. One. Eds. M.H. Abrams and Stephen Greenblatt. New York: W.W. Norton, 2000. 934–954.

Tennenhouse, Leonard. *Power on Display: The Politics of Shakespeare's Genres*. New York: Methuen, 1986.

Thomas, Keith. "The Puritans and Adultery: The Act of 1650 Reconsidered." *Puritans and Revolutionaries*. Eds. Donald Pennington and Keith Thomas. Oxford: Oxford-Clarendon Press, 1978. 257–282.

Tyndale, William. *The Obedience of a Christian Man*. 1528. Ed. David Daniell. London: Penguin, 2000.

Wiesner-Hanks, Merry E. *Christianity and Sexuality in the Early Modern World: Regulating Desire, Reforming Practice*. London: Routledge, 2000.

Wiggins, Martin. *Shakespeare and the Drama of His Time*. Oxford: Oxford UP, 2000.

The Dispensations of Moira:
Matter, Mind, and Culture from Thales of Miletus to Walter Pater

Thomas F. Bertonneau

To such a tremulous wisp constantly re-forming itself on the stream, to a single sharp impression, with a sense in it, a relic more or less fleeting, of such moments gone by, what is real in our life fines itself down. It is with this movement, with this passage and dissolution of impressions, images, sensations, that analysis leaves off – that continual vanishing away, that strange, perpetual, weaving and unweaving of ourselves. (Walter Pater, *The Renaissance,* the 1893 edition)[1]

The saint, and the Cyrenaic lover of beauty, it may be thought, would at least understand each other better than either would understand the mere man of the world. Carry their respective positions a point further, shift the terms a little, and they might actually touch. (Walter Pater, *Marius the Epicurean,* 1885)[2]

I

Dead matter is paradoxically a vital or even a pregnant symbol, always straining to give birth to something from its dumb abyss. Consider Thales of Miletus (Seventh Century BC), who inaugurates the paradox at the dawn of differentiated non-mythic thinking. After founding the discourse of rigorous materialism by asserting that "water is the first principle"[3] (that water is the primordial stuff of which everything else is a trans-substantiation), Thales adds matter-of-factly that "the universe is shot through with soul,"[4] or in the *variorum,* that *everything is full of gods.* This gesture does seem arbitrarily to put back what its author has just deliberately taken away; yet even that might be significant. As Friedrich Nietzsche writes in *Philosophy in the Tragic Age of the Greeks* (1870), "Thales is a creative master who began to see into the depths of nature without the help of fantastic fable."[5] Thales' insights arise, as Nietzsche adds, from "a sharp savoring"[6] of reality and thus stem sensuously by direct *esthesis* from the broad object of his contemplation. Heraclitus of Ephesus (flourished *circa* 500 BC), a successor of Thales in the Ionian Enlightenment, argued that "all things change to fire, and fire exhausted falls back into all things,"[7] another kind of materialism; but he also identified fire with lightning, lightning with Zeus, and Zeus with the *Logos*, the immaterial substrate of the fluctuating material domain of our common conscious existence. In Thales, divinity dwells within matter; in Heraclitus, matter outwardly betokens its insubstantial but overwhelming and quasi-divine opposite: the formative intellectual principle in its concealment from the senses. We note, however, that in Heraclitus' discourse, a vocabulary of taste ("moisture makes the soul succumb to joy" or "dry, the soul grows wise and good,"[8] and on occasion the soul is *smoky*), joined with a lexicon of moral strictness, points to the identical ability directly to savor of existence, which Nietzsche ascribes to Thales. Discrimination with regard to the qualities of nature, inward or outward, likely translates, in Heraclitus, to discrimination about the qualities of people, as in the irate assertion that having expelled Hermodorus, known for his "excellence," the Ephesians should "go hang themselves."[9]

A refinement of Thales' *hylotheism*, the *atomic theory* first promulgated by Democritus of Abdera (Fifth Century BC), explains all phenomena on the basis of infinitesimal units, in a variety of kinds each kind containing an infinite number, which transiently agglomerate and disintegrate in a perpetual exhibition of determinate thing-ness. The behavior of these indivisible units must obey an intelligible limit because it produces no monsters and accomplishes the same *here* as it accomplishes *there* despite the fact that its tendency produces *here* the green earth and *there* the barren moon. According to atomic theory green earths and barren moons proliferate and beyond a doubt also green moons and barren earths — "infinite worlds…composed of numerically infinite atoms."[10] As Walter Pater noted in *Plato and Platonism* (1893), while ancient materialism rejects teleology *qua* itself, it nevertheless from its beginning proposes the substitute of evolutionary process as a manifestation of inherent natural law working toward a consummation more elevated than the inception. The Darwinian themes of "extinction and renewal," Pater writes, appear by anticipation in the Ionian doctrines of flux.[11] That time shall sweep away the evolutionary consummation, whether it be *Nous* or *Logos*, makes it no less, formally speaking, a type of consummation; rather, its ephemeral quality heightens its value. Thus Democritus believed that the human animal had developed over the ages from a primitive fish, the simple form anticipating its later perfection, the later form justifying the initial primitiveness. Since knowledge, for Democritus, qualifies as good, although rare, and since human beings better navigate the domain of knowledge than their piscine cousins, it follows that existence has a meaning, which it articulates in the emergence of reason or intelligence. Knowledge remains even when the knower dies, as die he must along with everyone else, for "worlds are destroyed by colliding with one another."[12]

Democritus' critics charged against him a denial of the gods, as they would again in the case of Socrates, but like that of Heraclitus the physics of Democritus formed the background for an ethics that even his contemporaries found hard to impugn: "Contentment," he said, "comes to men from a moderate amount of enjoyment and a life of concord"[13] and "it takes courage to overcome pleasure."[14] Democritus' critical comments on religion, again like those of Heraclitus, belong to the incipient critique of inherited ideas and established customs that assimilates both thinkers to a generalized Ionian *éclaircissement*. Among these first philosophers, Matter and Mind seem locked in a peculiar dialectic, with Mind struggling to extricate itself from Matter.

Take Anaximander (Fifth Century BC): a Milesian like Thales, Anaximander wrote of no units but rather of a mass of undifferentiated *stuff* (the *Apeiron*) that passed into and then back out of *form (peras)*, as in a mute parody of moral reciprocity; but the Anaximandrian theory by no means excludes the particulate character of the *stuff* and perhaps presupposes it. Justice *(Dike)*, the principle of his system, entails measurement, which a reckoning in units best quantitatively assures. The earliest Ionian coinage, as from Ephesus and Miletus, is thus contemporary with the earliest Ionian (meta-) physics; Eric Havelock, responding to a parenthesis in Lucretius, links atomism to the alphabet, which signifies the "atomic" (phonetic) components of uttered words by visible material marks. The unit-idea reappears as the *geometric atomism* of Plato's *Timaeus*. A certain irony clings to the incorporation because Plato's mouthpiece, Socrates, although launching his career as a physicist in the manner of Thales and Democritus, later rejected both materialism generally and atomism specifically as fit objects of meditative interest. Evidently he could not do without atomism of some kind although the dialogue ascribes the theory to Timaeus, with Socrates as a mostly silent auditor. With Epicurus (341–270 BC) and with Lucretius (99–55 BC), whose *De rerum natura* remained incomplete at its author's death, we find ourselves once again in the presence of a rigorous and influential atomism-materialism, which seeks its end in the formulation of an ethical *modus vivendi*. By a partial misunderstanding, Epicureanism has lent its name to the apology for pleasure as the primary motive of reason, and has given rise to pseudo-philosophies of hedonism and gastronomy. Even W. F. Hegel's airy system in *The Phenomenology of Spirit* (1802) begins with *sinnliche Gewissheit*.

How is it that mentality, tasting the flavors of the worldly *stuff*, draws from wood and stone, as by a syllogism, the Q.E.D. of spirit? In his study *From Religion* to *Philosophy* (1912), F. M. Cornford traces the whole category of ancient physical speculation back to Bronze Age ethics. "In Homer," Cornford writes, "and in Ionian thought generally, we find a profound belief in Destiny *(Moira)* as an ordinance which limits all individual powers, whether human or divine; and we see, moreover, that this ordinance is even more a decree of moral obligation than a barrier of sheer physical impossibility."[15] Behind the *Moira*-concept, Cornford further detects the theme of *division:* "the separation of the world into elemental provinces," which basic parceling "is older in time than the birth of the Gods."[16] Myth gives out that *Moira* granted to the gods, once they emerged, their special privileges within the cosmos, as either elementally or pragmatically defined; in the human world, too, which is the real subject of this "first representation,"[17] the same apportionment obtains, forming the background of consciousness both collective and individual. The injunctions of law tell a person on what he may or may not lay his hands, incising the hitherto undifferentiated space of the world into its lawful pattern of touchable and untouchable portions, of paths where one may freely go and of admonitions that say, "keep off the grass" or "no usufruct of this tree."

In Milesian discourse and its successor-discourses, the name for that which falls subject to division is *physis* or *natura,* an item of vocabulary by which the user tries to abstract his concept from the tangled world of all-too-human behavior, but with limited success. It comes as no surprise, in Cornford's words, that: "The 'Nature' of which the first philosophers tell us with confident dogmatism is from the first a metaphysical entity; not merely a natural element, but an element endowed with supernatural life and powers, *a substance which is also soul and God.*"[18] While, in the atomistic development of early physics, "science turns its back on theology," so that "the supernatural has all but disappeared,"[19] yet a persistent anthropomorphism in speculation resurrects the original moral impetus that, as myth, for example, shows Marduk carving up the corpse of slain Tiamat or Zeus burying the Titan enemy in the earth, in both cases because the malefactor has overstepped the settled limits. Cornford's *"all but"* will dog materialism more than he himself allows. In a remark that antedates Cornford's comments by twenty years, Pater reminds his readers that Heraclitus' stark moralism, while holding fast against that "very law of [physical] change which it asserts,"[20] thoroughly imbues the later doctrines, otherwise entirely materialistic, of "the Cyrenaics [and] the Epicureans," which would detach themselves from normative or fear-based moral strictures by detaching themselves from all non-materialistic explanations of phenomena.[21]

The strangeness of it gives rise, for example, to several odd features of *De rerum natura,* the epic-didactic poem that constitutes the main source of modern knowledge about Epicureanism. Lucretius — although an advocate of the positions that "nothing is ever created by divine power out of nothing" and that "nature resolves everything into its component atoms and never reduces anything to nothing"[22] — opens his poem with an elaborate invocation of Venus: "Endow my verse with everlasting charm," he bids the Mistress of Love, and grant for the afflicted people of the world "untroubled peace."[23] *Dona nobis pacem*, as a later piety would say. Venus remains unreal in Lucretius' atomistic explanation of the world, for his gods while they exist cannot intervene in mundane affairs, but *the image of her* serves metaphorically to remind the non-philosophical of the absolute value both of peace and prosperity, and of the necessity therefore of restraint and reserve in behavior. The Lucretian *Diva* seems to emerge from the concatenation of natural processes, as in the proto-Chaucerian quickening of spring, "when," as Lucretius writes, "in all its force the fertilizing breath of Zephyr is unleashed."[24] Venus gives her emblem to "the vital spirit"[25] that imparts animation to the *membrae* of living bodies and thus resembles the pre-philosophical *anima*, also universally vivifying, as discussed by Cornford; she functions rather like the Absolute Beauty in Plato or the Intelligible Beauty in Plotinus, being a goal and image of aspiration. Opposed to the necessary fiction of the "great goddess" in Lucretius' scheme is the unpleasant empirical condition of incipient empire, "this brutal business of war by sea and land,"[26] which the follower of Epicurus would link with "superstition" and which he would trace back to the Homeric moment when "at Aulis the altar of the virgin goddess was foully stained with the blood of Iphigeneia by the leaders of the Greeks," those "patterns of chivalry."[27]

The Epicurean *ethos* starts with a rejection of any supernatural hypothesis in favor of a severe physics that reduces all explanations to one: the regular behavior of the atomic particles and the vacuum, the only two things that really exist; the same *ethos* sets itself against the *unnatural* disruptions of life attendant on imperial designs, describing these also, however, as matter-bound but in a defectively moral sense. In the account of social evolution in Book V of *De rerum natura*, comparing the rudeness of ancient men to the sophistication of modern men and tallying the respective causes of sickness and death among them, Lucretius avers that then "it was lack of food that brought failing limbs at last to death" while now "it is superfluity that proves too much."[28] Empire tries to make a virtue of *superfluity* in this avaricious or concupiscent meaning of the term. Like Jean-Jacques Rousseau, who likely borrows from him heavily, Lucretius sees the increasing complexity of society and the proliferating specialization of social roles as detrimental to a natural state of being in which men are more or less independent and more or less happy. As humanity reorganizes itself at the village level and then confederates its self-sustaining communities, it makes itself vulnerable to ambitious big-men who install themselves as kings. The *rex* consolidates his office, as Lucretius says, by "parcel[ing] out cattle and lands," a gesture that gives rise to "property," which incites "envy," which unleashes ambition in the form of war, appropriation, and territorial aggrandizement.[29] The general defect is that "greed and blind lust...drive men to overstep the bounds of right."[30]

In their overstepping the boundaries of property and usage monarchs resemble common criminals. Because the *rex*, as pirate, has no right save that of his might *to parcel* the things he appropriates, his gifting of them to sycophantic others must be taken for a misdistribution. It violates the undisturbed naturalness of nature, which, under its own lawfulness, as in the archaic idea of *Moira*, divides its own content and parcels its own determinate things according to the Logos or latent order. The greatest misdistribution of all is thus the imperial state, gained through conquest, seeking to subdue the very world, and expressing itself symbolically in the cult of the god-king. No Roman had yet declared himself such in Lucretius' day, but a slew of Greek tyrants, all in the wake of Alexander of Macedon, already had. What with a succession of war leaders and dictators fighting each other for power, and with the Senate dithering, the poet could see the writing on the wall: hence his admonitory invocation of Agamemnon's foul deed at Aulis, for Agamemnon serves for a symbol of irrational aggression on the largest scale, bloody and violent, such as is characteristic of empire-builders. In public sacrifice, like the gladiatorial games of the imperial centuries, tyrants manipulate superstitious presuppositions of their subjects to cement allegiance, by awe and fear, to themselves and to the state. Epicureanism is, with Judaism and Christianity, one of the earliest articulations not only of anti-imperial but also of anti-sacrificial thinking, although a critique of sacrifice seems also to be incipiently at work in the extant fragments of Heraclitus on the Dionysus-cult in Ephesus. In distinction to the *Logos* as lightning, says Heraclitus, the phallic ceremonies take place in "filth and sewage."[31]

Pater lists the Ephesian as a precursor of Epicurus, an unexpected claim but satisfying once made: *De rerum natura* criticizes Heraclitus' physics, but in its ethics, informed by the notion of perpetual flux, it generally coincides with the doctrine of the *Logos* philosopher. Lucretius must have known that sacrifice, as in a hecatomb, or even as in the *sparagmos* of a human victim as part of the hoarier rites, is, by reenactment, primordially divisional and distributive; but he sees it as falsely so, as violating a pre-established division-and-distribution, and therefore as unjust and offensive. If humanity were, however, to heed the appeal of Epicurus, who appears in Lucretius' poem as a kind of prophet-and-savior, it would need to find a more acceptable way than the state religion (that is, than superstition), of squaring its actions with the natural *right order* of things. Insofar as one rejects a community whose values permit gladiation and sacrifice, both of which are ritualistic, to what model, other than ritual, can one turn for a framework of civics? What comes before sacrifice in Lucretius' anthropology? The answer is, language, the medium of reason and the agency, which, more than sacrifice, binds human beings in moral communion with one another.

Language, for Lucretius, constitutes the pre-imperial order; it also stands prior to any ritual or sacrificial or monarchic order. Language arises from "nature," which is to say that it corresponds to the harmony of just division, prior to social-political distortion. Words work collectively, through corresponding to "a mental image"[32] by which the many prevent any *one person* from *subduing* all others, as Lucretius says; and words are therefore motivationally pacific. The Lucretian speech in this manner interrupts the domination of direct behavioral mimesis; speech is a type of anti-rhetoric. Lucretius says that language, as an institution, emerged in a moment analogous to the one in a modern individual's infantile development when, in response to some "speechless plight," the baby "point[s] with a finger at objects in view."[33] As language stems from existential urgency, so law *(lex)*, the force that countervails arrogant power, stems from language. In their *republican phase,* always a golden age, all people momentarily overcome the "life of violence...enfeebled by feuds"[34] before imperial envy reasserts itself against a general laxness and non-vigilance brought about through material plenitude exceeding sufficiency. Epicurus' discoveries *dispelled,* says Lucretius, "the dread and darkness of the mind";[35] he "proclaimed," like Parmenides, "what can be and what cannot: how the power of each thing is limited, and its boundary-stone sticks buried deep."[36]

Language, as discourse and theory, is mind; and mind, so intimately implicated in *limit* and *boundary,* is *Moira.* Being *Moira,* mind remains necessarily linked to matter, for matter, as food, as bauble, as territory, as the object of desire and the nub of all contention, while entirely indifferent to mind is yet the medium through which one mind coordinates itself with another, whether for good or ill. Ideally, as perhaps it once befell, nature herself rewards the well-tempered mentality by the pleasure of her intrinsic qualities, as when the laudable ancients, not yet tainted by superstition and sacrifice, could, "to melodies that took shape far from the busy highway...recline in company on soft grass" amidst "light-hearted jollity" and "boisterous laughter."[37] For real delectation, a simple fare has always sufficed. Pleasure presumes a community in which basic judgments about limits of behavior are shared. One potentiality in the earliest materialistic doctrines — even in that of Thales and certainly in those of Heraclitus on the one hand and the atomists on the other — is connoisseurship, with its justification of life through the appreciation of refined beauty and moderated pleasure. If the Logos were order, for example, and order were the latent structure of matter, then matter would be beautiful, under the principle of measure. The contemplation of phenomena would be, for the trained observer, already a kind of connoisseurship. But how, in a sophisticated society replete with distractions, might one recreate the republican blitheness of the golden age — how would one go about "fining oneself down," in Pater's figure? Technical progress makes this a difficult project to complete, for it is sadly a fact that, "the discovery of something new and better blunts and vitiates our enjoyment of the old."[38]

II

"The discovery of something new and better," to cite the Lucretian formula, or rather the problem of "the new and the better," overlaps, in the realm of estheticism, with Pater's challenge of "the perpetual weaving and unweaving of ourselves." Few Englishmen, in the Victorian Age, thought of these matters as closely as did Pater; that writer's *Plato and Platonism* posits Ionian materialism as the primary source of Athenian Fifth-Century metaphysics, as we have seen. In his intellectual life, Marius, the Second-Century A.D. protagonist of Pater's *recherché* hybrid of historical novel with autobiography *Marius the Epicurean* (1885), recapitulates the moral and scientific development that begins with Thales and culminates in the innovating Christian piety of the so-called Little Peace of the Church under Antoninus Pius (86–161). In early manhood, while resident in an official capacity in Rome, Marius adheres to "Cyrenaicism," a school of materialism whose author, oddly, studied under Plato; but Marius, his later detached mood notwithstanding, always remembers from his rural childhood an intense attunement to the physical qualities of place and of ritual, as manifested in the moral framework of what he calls "The Religion of Numa." The old ways embodied by the rustic and truly *pagan* cults stand in contrast to the emergent fashions of the "new religions [that] had arisen with bewildering complexity around…the earlier and simpler patriarchal religion"; in the urban centers of the imperial world, the old religion is "dying." The genuine paganism adds up to: "a religion of usages and sentiment rather than of facts and belief, and attached to very definite things and places — the oak of immemorial age, the rock on the heath fashioned by weather as if by some dim human art, the shadowy grove of ilex, passing into which one exclaimed involuntarily, in consecrated phrase, Deity is in this place! *Numen inest!*"[39] Functioning just as effectively without its verb, the phrase has about it the minimalist character of a primordial ostensive — an unadorned pointing to something suddenly attractive to a common interest and arresting to collective behavior.

The name Numa communicates with the Latin noun *numen,* "holy presence," and the Greek verb νεμειν, "to distribute justly." The nominal stem of νεμειν is νομος or "law." Livy (59 B.C.–A.D. 17), in his history, credits Numa with consolidating the incipient Republic under "law and religious observance," whereas hitherto it had existed in the style of its founder Romulus "under force of arms."[40] Livy says that Numa was, for example, "the first to divide the year into twelve lunar months"; he was the one who "appointed priestesses for the service of Vesta" and "the twelve Salii, or Leaping Priests, for the service of Mars"; and he was the one who established the office of Pontifex in order to "teach the proper forms" of ritual behavior and give instruction concerning "which portents manifested by lightning or other visible signs were to be recognized and acted upon."[41] According to Livy, indeed, "many...rites owe their inception to Numa," who conducted himself always during his reign as "the jealous guardian of peace more than of power."[42] Livy, who might have subscribed to Epicureanism, as the Roman upper classes of his time tended to do, takes it for granted that the legend of Numa's regular supernatural communion with the goddess Egeria in a sacred grove was a story made up by the successor of Romulus especially to convince the unruly *plebs* that his conventicles, some quite strict in a moral sense, had divine sanction. Presiding over the apportionment of liberties and interdictions and fostering in his people a "deeply imbued...sense of their religious duties,"[43] Numa appears as *Moira* incarnate.

In *Marius,* Pater reminds his readers that Marcus Aurelius, that later sage and king, espoused Tacitus' maxim, *"Principes instar deorum esse"* or "Princes are as gods," and sought an ancient pedigree for his "doctrine of the sanctity of kings."[44] This is because, Pater says, Aurelius took seriously "the old legend of his descent from Numa, from Numa who had talked with the gods."[45] In his *Meditations,* of which Pater makes Marius the editor and from which he inserts translations into his own text, Aurelius speaks in Stoic terms of a universe "of infinite matter" and of the ephemeral quality of the individual's existence: "nature...will transform whatsoever thou now seest."[46] The mutability of existence, imposing on everything that currently *is* the certain penalty of its dissolution, constitutes a perpetual crisis against which the conscientious subject must assert his sense of "the divine breath...everywhere"[47] so as to achieve an "orderly disposing of all things"[48] within the human purview. Intelligence can grasp that *all is flux* because the *Logos,* in which intelligence participates, remains in place and gives a perspective for the understanding of phenomena under the light of fixed concepts. In this *orderly disposing,* mind again becomes identical with *Moira,* whose impulse gives coherence to the project of Numa at the beginning of the polity over which, late in its day, Aurelius has come, perhaps reluctantly, to rule. Unlike Numa, however, Aurelius has little opportunity to devote himself to works of peace. The German tribes grow restless on the Rhine marches, plagues ravage Italy, and the designated heir to the throne, returning from the East, suddenly and unexpectedly dies.

Persistent "public anxiety" signifies itself by a recursion, in vulgar forms, to a religious fervor long dormant in the capitol, which Marius classifies, using the Epicurean term, as "superstition."[49] The premature death of Lucius Verus, Caesar to Aurelius' Augustus, and especially the funeral rites that ostentatiously commemorate him precipitate orgiastic street demonstrations and bring to mind for Marius the saying of Lucius Apuleius that it sometimes appears "as if the presence of the gods did not do men good, but disordered and weakened them."[50] A celebrated courtesan rides through the thoroughfare in ruddy countenance "still fresh from the bath of blood" that accompanied her Mithraic baptism; meanwhile, finding insufficient solace in a round of animal offerings, some excited people express an appetite for "human sacrifice after the ancient pattern."[51] Such grossness belongs to a civilization, under Aurelius, cumbered by "heaviness and vulgarity," lacking "fineness in temper, yet with a material well being abundant enough."[52] Such crass behavior signifies for Marius devolution from desire to appetite.

Pater understands in his way what Eric Gans makes explicit in *Originary Thinking* (1993), that "religion is in reality the first human science, practicing through myths of origin a primitive form of originary analysis."[53] In offering the model of Numa and its associated ancient piety, Pater seems to be making good on a deficiency in the strict scientism of the materialist tradition, whether that be the Cyrenaicism of the Second Century, the Marxism or Darwinism of the Nineteenth, or the Sociobiology of the Twentieth. While, as Gans writes, "religion provides a discovery procedure that is of limited [epistemological] effectiveness"; and while "the speculations of the pre-Socratics had already eclipsed" mythic thinking in this regard in the moment of their expression: while these things are so, it yet remains entirely unobvious whether pure science, as such, or *mere empiricism,* can tell curiosity more about ethics or anthropology than can religious discourse.[54] Like his equally skeptical Francophone counterpart Joris-Karl Huysmans, Pater gravitates to religious and mystical styles of appreciation; his fondness for Milesian speculation, ascribed to Marius, indicates the proclivity. Thales, the aboriginal Milesian, would anticipate the

Epicureans, who, like Pater's Marius, while starting to dispense with the gods nevertheless prudently hesitate and, *sous rature,* put them back.

A god is a hypothesis, a necessary one, even discounting his divinity or supernatural status. Even Lucretius, who otherwise hovers close to atheism, says that the *images* of the gods, which primitive men saw "in sleep," produce a behavioral effect. His prefatory Ode to Venus at the beginning of his poem seeks a similar effect. The beauty of those dream-figures struck the ancestors as "lordly," because they comported themselves autonomously, and to them they therefore attributed "tremendous strength."[55] Men who transgressed "the compact of social peace" suffered a "secret misgiving" that the gods had witnessed their mischief;[56] they felt "haunted by fear of eternal punishment after death."[57] While this was "not piety,"[58] it nevertheless checked the worst human impulses in most circumstances. Lucretius rejects religion but he thinks that religion makes sense as a type of cryptogram to be decoded by meditation. Religion paradoxically stays ahead of science as a mode of cultural introspection; the deepest introspection would be impossible without religion as its occasion.

As Gans puts it, "religious intuition, by affirming in the absence of empirical proof the historical priority of the ethical," emphasizes the irreducible distinction between the natural and the cultural: so that "the productivity of religious thought in the anthropological domain will end only when human science has come to understand at least as well as religion has done the ethical difference between the natural and the human."[59] A sense of just this special province of the religious mentality explains why, for someone like Pater, Ionian discourse exercises so powerful an attraction: embarking on science, Milesian thought approaches the rigor of science without yet being science; it stubbornly retains its orientation to morality and custom, which it examines severely, in a manner prognosticative of the style of later actual physical science, but it refuses any reduction thereto. While remaining attached in a non-dogmatic way to his Cyrenaicism, "anxious to try the lastingness of his Epicurean rose-garden,"[60] Marius worries about "the isolating narrowness" of a materialism distorted into a "fanatical" parody of itself.[61] In particular, he begins to worry that "in their unfriendly, repellent attitude towards the Greek religion, and the old Greek morality," the Cyrenaics "had been but faulty economists."[62] Pater devotes a three-chapter sequence to weighing the achievements and the sacrifices (as Marius puts it to himself) of materialist philosophy, including Cyrenaicism. The terms *economy* and *measure,* which circulate through these monologues, resonate not only with the *Moira*-concept, but also with the generative anthropological idea all consciousness derives ultimately from a certain injunction or limitation inherent in the character and function of the sign. "To accept alienation from

the object of one's desire," Gans writes, "constitutes "the defining moment of
self-consciousness."[63] Cyrenaicism might abet appetite rather than cultivate
desire and it might therefore disserve intelligence. Marius' contemplation of the
value of the materialist view also impinges on his literary program of essayistic
"euphuism" and his judgments about politics.

Before he critiques Cyrenaicism, of course, Marius must first arrive at it.
Marius' philosophical awakening occurs during his years of scholarly training
in Pisa and turns on the death of his school friend Flavian. "For most people,"
writes Pater on behalf of his protagonist, "the actual spectacle of death brings out
into greater reality, at least for the imagination, whatever confidence they may
entertain of the soul's survival in another life."[64] Marius, in a style instinctively
Epicurean, intuits only a mortal limitation in the friend's fate: "nothing less than
the soul's extinction."[65] Should one count this a curse or a boon? In Lucretius'
De rerum natura, the most emotional passages are those where the poet would
convince his addressee, a certain Memmius, that nothing of conscious existence
survives the body's demise, so that it would be in lasting deeds and works *only*
that a man might outlive his apportioned three-score years and ten. Epicurus
imprinted himself on posterity by just this method. "The vital vigor of his
mind prevailed," says Lucretius of Epicurus (that "Man of Greece"), when he
sallied intellectually against "the constraining locks of nature's doors" and "the
flaming ramparts of the world."[66] One does not physically overcome cosmic-
physical limits, but rather mind, in understanding cosmic structure, achieves
liberation from the shackles of its own prior ignorance. As Gans suggests, while
consciousness begins in an aborted gesture of appropriation from which it infers
a sacred force and later the immortal gods, critical or philosophical consciousness
begins with the thesis that "immortality is not a substance but a representational
category."[67] Marius, reacting to his friend's death, "might have fallen a prey to
the enervating mysticism, then in wait for ardent souls in many a melodramatic
revival of old religion or theosophy"; but a strong "hatred," as Pater writes, "of
what was theatrical" drives him instead to the conclusion that it is at last "in
vigorous intelligence" that "divinity" will most likely "be found...resident."[68]
This insight itself strikes Marius for its "poetic beauty in...clearness of thought."[69]
Pater labels Marius' attitude as "natural Epicureanism," and he yokes it with an
"instinctively suspicious" interpretation of all consolatory discourse that would
design to "alleviate his resentment at nature's wrong."[70]

On the basis of his own transparent resentment, then, Marius becomes, as
Pater writes, "something of a materialist," a materialist even "with...the temper
of a devotee."[71] Marius' remark implies that, as the subject can never overcome
his resentment, he must transform it so that it bolsters his awareness. Resentment

signifies Marius' active involvement in existence. Absence of resentment would, by contrast, amount to animal complacency. Being dominated unconsciously by resentment would, on the other hand, assign the subject to the vulgarity of unmediated passion through endlessly mediated desire. That latter outcome Marius would avoid above all others. Resolved to train to the highest possible rigor "his own untroubled, unassisted intelligence," Marius seeks in books for further clarification about the problem of "personal essence."[72] Marius' musings will entail a "retracing in his mental pilgrimage the historic order of human thought."[73] From Lucretius and Epicurus, Marius moves archeologically, so to speak, "to the writer who was in a certain sense the teacher of both, Heraclitus of Ionia."[74]

Marius perceives Heraclitus to have begun his exploration of soul and cosmos with the "subtle paradox" that while naïve thinking "attributes to the phenomena a durability which does not really belong to them," wisdom, in detecting behind "the processes of nature" the ever-changing "fire of life," comes into communion, as it were *beyond itself* or transcendentally, with its own steady principle of "strenuous self-consciousness in all we think and do."[75] The individual, the *one,* opposes himself to the many, distinguishing himself by the criterion of knowledge. At the core of the *Logos*-philosophy, as Marius interprets it, lies the proposition:

> That continual change, to be discovered by the attentive understanding where common opinion found fixed objects, was but the indicator of a subtler but all-pervading motion — the sleepless, ever sustained, inexhaustible energy of the divine reason itself, proceeding always by its own rhythmical logic, and lending to all mind and matter, in turn, what life they had. In this "perpetual flux" of things and of souls, there was, as Heraclitus conceived, a continuance, if not of their material or spiritual elements, yet of orderly intelligible relationships, like the harmony of musical notes, wrought out in and through the series of their mutations — ordinances of the divine reason, maintained throughout the changes of the phenomenal world; and this harmony in their mutation and opposition, was, after all, a principle of sanity, of reality, there.[76]

Committed now to "an inward...world of vivid personal apprehension,"[77] Marius finds in the Heraclitean dispensation a stepping-stone to Aristippus (435–356 BC), "whose weighty traditional utterances...served in turn to give their effective outline to the contemplations" of the young thinker and who founded the School of Cyrene.[78] A strict materialism gives rise both to a primarily esthetic attitude towards life and to a pronouncedly subjective, if not egoistic, orientation. Matter impinges on mind as sensation; mind makes out of sensations the appearances, arresting the flux of natural process in concepts. Measuring concepts against the flux, mind then doubts their adequacy; the flux is real, but its fixation in concepts is an illusion. Mind works its way out of this impasse by finding in the flux itself an *order* and so intuiting beyond or beneath ever-changing nature an *ordering principle, the Logos,* analogous to itself.

In his musings on Heraclitus, Marius goes so far as to equate the *Logos* with the dictum of Protagoras, not vulgarly that the ego determines reality, but rather in the more resigned sense that the "sensible apprehension of the individual was the only standard of what is or is not."[79] The subjective mind is, as it were, collaborating with the transcendental mind in settling the convenient, if ontologically false, forms by which the living person negotiates the world. Yet this proto-Kantianism entails an aporia because in leaving the subject at last with only his subjectivity as a guide, supposing that was what he had done, Heraclitus might inadvertently have given a brief for "the despair of knowledge."[80] Aristippus, unworried about whether the senses deceive or not, rescues the subject from the threat of epistemological nihilism and actually formulates a *modus vivendi* or *ethos,* "a subtly practical worldly-wisdom,"[81] that well comports with Heraclitean seriousness. "The difference between [Aristippus] and those obscure earlier thinkers," writes Pater, "is almost like that between an ancient thinker generally, and a modern man."[82]

In Pater's historical analogy, mystics and prophets belong to the ancient ritual order as the expert, the administrator, and the cosmopolitan belong to the modern secular order. Modern epigone-thinkers recast "the abstract thoughts of the master" as "terms, first of all, of *sentiment.*"[83] One supposes that a relation obtains between *sentiment* and *ressentiment.* Marius has held it against the world that it struck Flavian with plague and killed him; he has also lost his father and mother, while still in his childhood and adolescence. The mystic withdraws from the world and from "the many," *as might Marius,* whereas the modern man determines to live in the world, but live in it not *like* the many, brutishly and unconsciously — rather, with awareness, "a kind of irony,"[84] and as much refinement as possible. The modern mentality most resents its always pending assimilation to the mass. It would stand out, alone. Cyrenaicism gives the *Logos*-vision "its sentimental or ethical, that is to say its modern," form.[85]

One notes, however, that the words and phrases that Marius uses in his summary of Heraclitus — *rhythmic logic, ordinances, lending* — find synonyms in the words and phrases that he uses in his summary of Cyrenaicism: *tact, grace, delicacy, adornment, beautification,* and *self-respect.*[86] Both vocabularies develop the fundamental *Moira*-idea of measure and apportionment that Cornford detects as the moral background to all physics and metaphysics; both vocabularies also reflect the motifs of injunction and limitation implicit, according to generative anthropology, in the sign. In accounting for the religious impressions that filled his childhood, Marius remembers in particular the adoration that his devout family paid to "Vatican, who causes the infant to utter his first cry," and to "Fabulinus, who prompts his first word."[87] These souvenirs correspond with another, that of honoring the dead with their regular *due portion* in the calendar of ceremonies. These ideas, and the ritual protocols that they inform, deserve the appellation of the *sentimental,* but also that of the *esthetic;* Marius grasps them from a later perspective and hauls them into a new context. He can do this because the new is a transformation of the old. "The sacred," as Gans argues, "crucial to the survival of the community, appears to include the esthetic."[88] The category of the esthetic emerges, in originary analysis, from "the resentment of the...participant toward the central object" because this focus of attention "is now not merely wanted," as an attractant of appetite would be, but "is desired" while yet resisting any possession.[89] It follows that "beauty is originally operative in [a] collective context, repeated in ritual, from which secular artworks will later emerge."[90]

Beauty pervades the *Gestalt* of the sacred-originary scene, as the *numen* of orderliness and propriety, and as the *Moira* of sufficiency. Marius' steady progress in awareness recapitulates the movement of which Gans writes. When the subject learns to contemplate pleasure in the pure *form* of his own renunciation, he "chooses what gives esthetic," rather than what gives grossly appetitive, "pleasure."[91] Rather, he chooses pleasure over satisfaction. It is "through the sign" that "we replace, or supplement, our originary alienation from the center" of consciousness and culture as ritually constituted.[92] Marius particularly prizes in the thought of Aristippus the central theme of the μονοχρονος ἡδονή,[93] which one might translate as the "sense-charged *now.*" Marius espouses a "new aesthetic culture...realizable as a new form of the contemplative life, founding its claim on the intrinsic 'blessedness' of 'vision' — the vision of perfect men and things."[94] If estheticism were the connoisseurship of proper disposition, if it were the *sentiment* of apportionment raised to the highest degree, it would nevertheless embroil itself in a potential contradiction. Estheticism runs the risk always, "as [does] the religious sentiment," of becoming "antinomian, when, in its effort towards the order of experiences it prefers, it is confronted with traditional and popular morality" and finds that it must trespass "beyond the limits of the actual moral order."[95] In light of skepticism about appearances, the Cyrenaic tends to become an esthetician of everything, including those compartments of life, like religion and civic governance, which are conspicuously *other* than esthetic in their pragmatic orientation, or rather *prior* to the esthetic.

Determined to reconcile himself with the sensible and therefore with the actual, Marius simultaneously devotes himself to an idealism of perfect forms whose non-correspondence with actual forms must perpetually irritate him, as in Rome, amidst the sumptuousness of imperial existence, it does. Marius will feel reasserting itself his childhood compassion for the victims of ritual, both animal and human, and for all sumptuary indulgences. With the Emperor Marcus himself, Marius will begin to yearn beyond the actual, the pragmatic Rome, for "that *New Rome*" or *"City on high,"* by which both mean "more than the whole commonwealth of Rome, in any idealization of it, however sublime."[96] Such an ideal republic, Marius thinks, is "incorporate somehow with the actual city" and is indeed "implicate in that reasonable constitution of nature, by devout contemplation of which it is possible for man to associate himself to the consciousness of God."[97] The words of Cornford apply nicely to Marius' oscillation between delectation in the flux of sensory experience — his cult of private sentiment — and his Neoplatonic yearning: mysticism, Cornford writes, is not a "logical deduction" from anything, but rather "a series of efforts to translate a certain view of life, of God, into terms of a physical system."[98]

III

In *Marius the Epicurean,* Pater weaves together strands of fiction and nonfiction, inventing characters, as in the case of his protagonist, and borrowing others from history. Marius meets two writers of the Second Century whose work has influenced him in an endearing and informative way. He read *The Golden Ass* of Lucius Apuleius (125–180) at school and meets the author at an aristocratic dinner party in a posh suburb of Rome; he also knows and cherishes the work of Lucian of Samosata (115–200), the satirist and skeptic, who often betrays in his bristly dialogues a strong sympathy for Epicureanism — and Lucian, too, Marius meets in Rome, when the author-philosopher makes a visit to the precincts of the Imperial Capitol. Pater inserts a chapter from *The Golden Ass* into his own text; the chapter concerning Lucian ("A Conversation not Imaginary") reads much like one of Lucian's comic sketches, on which Pater models his wickedly incisive dialectic, wherein the Syrian-Greek master makes mincemeat of a young intellectual *poseur.*

Yet there is another ancient writer, of the century before Lucius and Lucian, whose work bears strongly on Pater's analysis of the role of beauty in culture and the relation of esthetic awareness to modernity — Gaius Petronius Arbiter (died 65), the Master of Ceremonies at Nero's court, Epicurean, and the hand that wrote the *Moira*-obsessed picaresque novel called *Satyricon*. Of particular relevance to the present discussion is the novel's most notorious section, "Dinner with Trimalchio." The idea of *Moira* assumes in *Satyricon* the figure of the god Priapus, a Greek cultic import who became central to Latin paganism beginning in the early centuries of the Republic. Priapus, a fertility-god always pictured in a state of ithyphallic potency, governs property, property-lines, and the sanctity generally of cultivated land. As there is a "Garden of Epicurus," so also is there a "Garden of Priapus," a nostalgic icon precisely of what Pater calls "The Religion of Numa." Priapus, by origin an agricultural deity, presides again over *measure* both as moderation in behavior and as fairness in commercial transactions. A famous Roman mural depicts Priapus weighing his own distended organ in the scales, surrounded by the fruits of a market garden, ready for barter or sale. In the scheme of *Satyricon*, Priapus functions emblematically, as does Venus in *De rerum natura*. Petronius' point-of-view character in the first-person narrative of *Satyricon*, Encolpius, has trespassed, in his bohemian peregrinations, on the Rites of Priapus, which have become, in the decadent milieu that the novel describes, mostly a sex-cult for jaded women. A priestess of the cult convinces Encolpius that he has incurred the wrath of the patron-deity, which ire, an allusion to the anger of Poseidon against Odysseus, takes the form of sexual fiasco. Because the name Encolpius implies a sensual or hedonistic focus on the genitalia, a fixation that the story bears out, the aptness of the punishment is guaranteed.

As a materialist, Petronius would have doubted the existence of any gods. A preserved fragment of his verse says, "Fear invented the gods,"[99] a tenet of Epicurean reason. Yet Petronius would have acknowledged the efficacy of belief, if only as an excuse for this or that guilty behavior. The same verses affirm that "every guilty wish, every venial instinct, invents its own gods in greedy competition."[100] His theological skepticism aside, Petronius would nevertheless have endorsed the advisability of *measure*. "Dinner with Trimalchio," a parody of Plato's *Symposium*, ruthlessly mocks the immodesty, the material *pleonexia*, of Neronian society. Exemplifying the rule of excess in complicated ways is the billionaire ex-slave, whose Greekified Syriac name means "Thrice Blessed," who throws a dinner-party to impress his friends. Trimalchio makes sure to invite Encolpius and two of his fellow rhetoricians so as to enliven the conversation around the table. Petronius' *eiron*-picaroons have fallen outside the law, outpacing nemesis by a few footsteps only in every episode, but all have competent training in oratory, as well as in literature, logic, and the fine arts. Encolpius makes especially keen esthetic judgments, but the others are hardly less acute. They mainly scheme to get all they can of "a free dinner,"[101] but they also look forward to observing the goings-on with a cocked eye. How rich is the wealthy freedman? Informants tell Encolpius that Trimalchio "doesn't himself know how much he's got, he's so loaded" and that "he's got estates it'd take a kite to fly over — he's worth millions of millions."[102]

The themes of economic *superbia* and extravagant measuring punctuate frequently the garrulous guests' descriptions of their sumptuary host; they also structure the author's descriptions of the feast. Trimalchio "has a clock in the dining-room and a trumpeter all dressed up to tell him how long he's got to live."[103] During the many courses, a bookkeeper sits in the dining hall "going over the accounts."[104] During one course, a foreman reads Trimalchio's daily gazette aloud — "Wheat threshed and stored: 500,000 pecks" and "deposits to the strong-room (no further investments possible): 10,000,000 sesterces."[105] Murals in Trimalchio's house tell the story of his rise from rags to riches; in one scene the god Mercury bestows wealth on the one-time chattel, now a free man. Trimalchio and his guests prattle a good deal about Fate. As Cornford reminds us, the idea of fate informs the idea of *Moira;* just as the Latin *fatum* or *fortuna* translates it. The pictures stake a claim to the justness and naturalness of Trimalchio's great good fortune, but like all propaganda, it makes one suspect a heavy-handed cover-up; the rhetoric, so to speak, is itself exaggerated.

Readers of *Satyricon* tend to remember most vividly the grand suite of dishes that make up the meal. These culinary prodigies suggest, inversely by their material abundance and presentational elaboration, the spiritual poverty and mindlessness of the essentially banal occasion: "The dishes of the first course included an ass of Corinthian bronze with two panniers, white olives on one side and black on the other…There were…dormice sprinkled with honey and poppy seed [and] steaming hot sausages too…with damsons and pomegranate seeds underneath."[106] Waiters remove the lid of an enormous salver, "revealing… plump fowls, sows' udders, and a hare with wings fixed to his middle to look like Pegasus."[107] Encolpius and the others also remark "four little figures of Marsyas with little skin bottles, which let a peppery fish-sauce go running over some fish, which seemed to be swimming in a little channel."[108] More waiters bring out a roast of whole calf, "on a two-hundred pound plate," following which comes a server made up to look like Ajax, "slashing at the calf with a drawn sword like a madman…rhythmically cutting and slicing," whereupon "he collected the pieces on the point and shared them among the guests."[109] The Ajax-allusion, from *Iliad,* points to crisis — hence the "madness." The pervasive crisis in "Dinner with Trimalchio" is the universal crisis of empire, of the transgression of every traditional boundary.

In a discussion of rare vintages, Trimalchio himself tells Agamemnon that he never *buys* wine, but rather that he grows it on his enormous estates, some of which, "as yet I haven't seen."[110] Casually Trimalchio says to Agamemnon, "What I'd like to do now is add Sicily to my little bit of land, so that when I want to sail to Africa, I [can] sail there without leaving my property."[111] The progress of Trimalchio's business-empire parallels that of Rome's political empire, for Rome incorporated Sicily by defeating a confederation of Greek cities in the culminating phase of the First Punic War.

Marsyas and Ajax belong to the category of sacrificial figures *par excellence,* a characteristic that joins them to an important topic of the dinner conversation: gladiatorial spectacle. Lucretius, as one remembers, includes a brief against gladiation in *De rerum natura;* a famous letter by Petronius' Stoic contemporary Seneca also denounces gladiation. In *Satyricon,* a certain Ganymedes complains that nowadays "nobody believes in heaven…nobody fasts, nobody gives a damn about the Almighty."[112] A vulgar Epicurean might say, so much the better. But that is not how Petronius means it. A certain Echion, seeming to agree with Ganymedes, nevertheless chides his interlocutor for his dourness; the wealth of the present, Echion argues, more than compensates for its dearth of faith. In context of Petronius' social analysis, Echion's statement signifies that the community has traded its deepest basis, each individual's deeply internalized sense of behavioral limits, for the appetitive repletion of bread and circuses. Echion launches into an eager description of how spectacular, for example, the gladiatorial games have become. In the immediate offing looms "a three-day show that's the best ever — not just a hack troupe of gladiators but freedmen for the most part," for which the wealthy sponsor, Titus, has spent "four hundred thousand."[113] These games will feature lavish feasts on the order of the one, Trimalchio's, at which the speaker currently sits.

Petronius inserts his key comment on the *déclassé* character of the proceedings when the time for dessert has arrived. Encolpius recounts how:

> The panels [in the ceiling] opened up and suddenly an enormous hoop came down, with gold crowns and alabaster jars of toilet cream hanging from it. While we were being told to accept these as presents, I looked at the table…Already there was a tray of cakes in position, the center of which was occupied by a Priapus made of pastry, holding the usual things in his very adequate lap — all kinds of apples and grapes.[114]

No other author has deployed a literal *Deus ex machina* with such perfectly motivated aplomb. The little pastry-image of the god with the "very adequate lap" reminds readers, just as it reminds Encolpius, that measure has gone missing, not merely from Trimalchio's hyperbolic *coena,* but also from the domains of private and civic life. Thus *Satyricon* features a market-episode in which the bazaar turns out to be dominated by thieves; receivers of fraudulent goods fear taking their case to court because of the corruption of the magistrates. Thus Petronius' novel begins with Encolpius haranguing Agamemnon about the wretchedness of contemporary political speech, unduly influenced by the excessive figural language of the Asian School. Thus a character named Eumolpus laments the decline of poetry, painting, and the arts, all of which suffer the disfigurement of stylistic exaggeration.

The sacrality, in the primitive sense, of the dinner, signified by the mythological references to famous victim-provocateurs such as Marsyas and Ajax, reminds us that the model of any festal repletion, as of all, is *a* or rather *the* scene on which consciousness first appears and asserts itself as an emotionally surcharged commitment to just apportionment short of full gustatory satisfaction.[115] The crisis that urgently calls forth the primordial sign also urgently calls forth the *Moira*-idea of equitable division, no doubt of an appetitive object, perhaps even of a human victim. When Encolpius gets lost on the way out of Trimalchio's house, he refers to it as "this modern labyrinth,"[116] a reference to the lair of the monster of King Minos of Crete, to whom the Athenians sent an annual allotment of virgins until Theseus slew the beast and liberated his homeland from Minos' rule. Trimalchio might be an avaricious smooth operator, but he is not a devouring monster in the homicidal sense. Nero, for whom Trimalchio partly stands, was however just such a ravenous beast. He killed off many — Seneca and at last Petronius himself among the notables; he also spent the imperial exchequer into bankruptcy, among other transgressions. Petronius' imagery makes sense against the Neronian-Imperial background and reflects the fundamental *Moira*-like configuration of morality, as the novelist conceives it from his Epicurean perspective. One of Gans' insights is helpful here, for it deals with the origin of equal shares:

> The division of the central object among the members of the group is the origin of the real economy, of the system of material exchange. Whether or not physical acts of exchange take place among the participants, the latter must accept their portions as equivalent. The equivalence of portions extends the equivalence of signs into the real, appetitive world, and in so doing transforms it. The establishment of formal equivalence between real objects, as opposed to signs, inaugurates the category of value.[117]

The emergence of signification not only gives human beings newly to themselves *as* human beings; it also gives to them the world, grasped as interpenetrated by the *ethos* or indeed by the *Moira*, or principle of justice, of the common scenic situation. The participants leave the scene satisfied with less, in a purely material sense, than each desires. The satisfaction in renunciation itself must suffice them all. At the center of the world lies the sacred object, both attractive and repellant, as is the seductive apple in the garden that Priapus oversees. The luster of the cynosure radiates, however, into all things illuminated by the scene; all objects, no matter how distantly or indirectly assimilated to the sacred center, fall subject to the restrictive protocols of appropriation and exchange. In this manner any random chit or fetish can acquire "value" because consciousness endows everything with the same taboo that froze all attempts at appropriation of the central morsel during the originary crisis.

Because, originally, the participants *renounce* the central object so as to thematize their incipient moral equality on the scene, the culture that this gesture inaugurates, which provides the basis of all subsequent culture, necessarily conforms to one of bold injunctions. Lucretius doubts the gods and thinks that everything is *nothing but matter;* yet he holds it an offense that princes should take more than what is customarily theirs, or anyone's, by building up empires. Trimalchio likewise offends, even while he regales his friends with tasty dishes, by aggrandizing his own condition in an imperial fashion; he offends good taste in the sense of *decorum*. In gladiation, public spectacle, no doubt always sacrificial, takes too many victims in too blatant a way. For their part in the general malaise the bad rhetoricians condemned by Encolpius, in abusing metaphor and ornament, might be said to take more words than are properly theirs; and the painters and sculptors garishly waste material for ostentatious effects. Trimalchio, like the self-deifying emperors, even abuses religion. When boys in priestly vestments set out the household gods, these bear the names of "Cobbler," "Luck" and "Lucre."[118] Compounding the offense, a fourth statue, in gold, represents Trimalchio himself, whose precious image guests affect to pet and kiss. Encolpius feels disgust because the adulation endows a mere mortal with more status than any individual deserves. One remembers the remark that no one believes in the Almighty nowadays, but here the sycophantic mob flatters the big man as though he were the Almighty. Encolpius' reaction constitutes an ethical critique rendered, however, from an *esthetic* perspective; it qualifies as a judgment in terms of good taste on the *ethics* of distorted economy.

The question is how does this esthetic critique of ethics become itself ethical once again? For in being purely esthetic it runs the risk of lapsing back

into the selfsame antinomian unnaturalness that it would condemn. The New
Cyrenaicism of Marius in Pater's novel addresses the identical problem of
grossness in the forms of concentrated affluence and conspicuous consumption,
again from the esthetic perspective; when it reaches its limit, Marius begins to
test again the waters of religion, in the form first of Neoplatonism, for which
Apuleius provides his model, and then of Christianity. At the time when his
interest in materialism dawns, during his studies in the academy at Pisa, he
resolves to make himself a writer and espouses his friend Flavian's notion
of "Euphuism." For Flavian, Euphuism will mean a new and more effective
rhetoric than the old, taking its strength from "the secrets of utterance, of
expression itself," whereby the wielder of the instrument might "restore words
to their primitive power" and gain the political influence of, say, "the young
Caesar."[119] Flavian's hopes arise from naked ambition; in anthropological terms,
they betoken the resentment of the sacred-monarchical center intrinsic to all
imperial settings. For Marius, however, Euphuism suggests less a Caesarean
campaign than an agenda of cultural correction stemming from personal
spiritual refinement. The "Tale of Cupid and Psyche" in Apuleius' *Golden Ass*
strikes Marius as already euphuistic and aids him in conceiving "the ideal [of]
a type of beauty entirely flawless and clean"; rooted also in Praxiteles' canons
of human proportion, this ideal renders the materiality of a beautiful object
immaterial, so that one can, as once did Thales, glimpse "soul or spirit in
things."[120] In correspondence with Marius' "ritual interest," the cultivation of
such verbal perfection will represent "a kind of sacred service to the mother-
tongue."[121]

As Euphuism and Cyrenaicism travel well together, Marius for a long while
sustains them in a synthesis. Marius begins to question the propriety of the
Cyrenaic viewpoint when, at Rome in service to the emperor, he accompanies
Aurelius to the arena. The return to Rome of the heir-apparent Lucius Verus
from Ephesus calls for extravagant public shows in honor of the prince's
initiation in the mysteries of Ephesian Artemis. As that goddess figures in myth
as patroness of the hunt, "there would be real wild and domestic creatures,
all of rare species; and a real slaughter."[122] Witnessing the theater of blood,
Marius remembers that, "the spectacle...was, after all, a religious occasion,"
its "grim acts of blood-shedding" possessing, as he thinks, "a kind of sacrificial
character."[123] When the animal-massacre gives way to gladiatorial combat — to
the death — Marius thinks to himself that, these "bloody contests" also have,
"under the form of popular amusement, the efficacy of...sacrifice."[124] Aurelius
personally disapproves of the show, but permits it to happen in his presence. In
anticipation of a later chapter, Pater adds that Marius "remembered well" the

emperor's complacency "when, a few years later, certain things came to pass in Gaul, under his full authority."[125] Pater refers to a murderous persecution of Christians in Lyons, which Aurelius encouraged.

Where Flavian, by this time many years deceased, had yearned for the power of the imperial center, wanting it jealously for himself, Marius, by contrast, now senses "a permanent point of difference between the emperor and himself."[126] The phrase "legal crimes" appears in the text, as Marius ponders the violent proceedings. The opposite of "a type of beauty entirely flawless and clean," the gladiatorial killings betoken to him the "deadness and stupidity" of the age: "Surely evil was a real thing, and the wise man wanting in the sense of it, where, not to have been, by instinctive election, on the right side, was to have failed of life."[127] Against the offensiveness of "The Deity of Slaughter,"[128] as Marius thinks of Ephesian Artemis, he begins to formulate a reaction to the Cyrenaicism that he has hitherto entertained too uncritically. Aristippus, like his contemporary Epicurus, regarded traditional piety cavalierly. "A religion, which had grown through and through a man's life, with so much natural strength [and] had meant so much for so many generations...might have had its uses, even for a philosophic skeptic."[129] Having jettisoned the pantheon, with its "whole round of...poetic worship," Cyrenaicism satisfied itself with "the merely aesthetic."[130] The decision has practical consequences that trigger a moral response. Marius notes that, on the basis of *nothing but the esthetic,* Aristippus declared "friendship and patriotism [to be] things [which] one could do without."[131] Aristippus so consistently urged those who could no longer enjoy pleasure to leave life — and his followers so frequently took his advice — that the philosopher acquired the name *"Deaths-advocate,"* until at last the civic authorities in Cyrene banned him from lecturing.[132] Marius experiences the *Moira*-intuition of "a companionable spirit at work in all things, of which he had become aware in his readings — in Plato and others," and even in Aurelius; he ponders "that reasonable Ideal to which the Old Testament gave the name of *Creator,* which for the philosophers of Greece is the *Eternal Reason,* and in the New Testament the *Father of Men.*"[133] Not only Plato, but Heraclitus too, stands behind Marius' shifting mood; the *Logos*-doctrine has emerged in a new, as one might say, sentimental context. In his correspondence, Pater remarks that readers had interpreted *Marius* as being more Epicurean than he intended it. It would be a mistake, however, to interpret that "less Epicurean" as implying a correlative "more Christian." The novel is not a work of Victorian mawkishness, on the order, say, of *Ben Hur* or *The Sign of the Cross,* but rather something quite different. Importantly, while drifting from Cyrenaicism and attracted to Christianity, Marius never converts to the new faith.

IV

In mid-January 1962, road-builders working to widen a highway between Thessalonica and Kavala uncovered a cluster of four Macedonian graves containing material from the late Fourth Century BC. The list of items includes several *objets-d'art* whose iconography links them to the local Orphic Mysteries, some humble and practical things such as nails and gardening shovels, and what is still the oldest Greek papyrus known. Called the Derveni Papyrus, after the locale of its discovery, the manuscript consists in its writer's corrective commentary on an Orphic Theogony, which he interprets, against the contemporaneous exegesis of the ignorant many, by sophisticated physical allegoresis. Gábor Betegh, the most thorough scholar of the Derveni Papyrus, argues that the Derveni-author adheres to the cosmo-theology of Anaxagoras, another Ionian monist, religious reformer, and physical speculator, to whom intellectual historians credit the elevation of the term *nous* or "mind" to a philosophical register. Consistent with the manuscript's context, the Derveni-author appears to have adhered to the eschatological ethos of the Orphic Mysteries, in which he likely served as a sacred worker or initiator of some kind.

Betegh stresses, however, the reformist character of the personally unidentifiable writer; this is Orphism of a radically henotheistic, if not quite monotheistic, type strongly under the influence of the Ionian style of epistemological critique. The concept of *Moira* plays an important role in the Derveni-author's metaphysics, where it merges with the concept of *nous*, which itself merges with the concept of *aer* (air) as a primal element, which merges again with the image of Zeus as supreme deity. Air, being invisible, is a different type of primal substance from *earth* or *fire;* it is the least substantial substance. Word *(Logos)* and breath *(pneuma)* maintain a relation. Students of Ionian speculation will detect a Heraclitean parallelism, for in the Ephesian's doctrine *fire, Logos,* and *Zeus* form a single multi-layered semantic unit.

The Derveni-author, interpreting his Orphic poem, identifies the mystic notion of *breath,* as a form of air and as the medium of life, with the ethical notion of *Moira:*

> For Orpheus called wisdom Moira. This seemed to him to be the most suitable out of the names that all men have given. For before Zeus received his name Moira was the wisdom of the god always and through everything. But since Zeus received this name, they think that he was born, even though he existed even before, but was not [then] named.

And when they say that the Moira spun they say that the wisdom of Zeus ordains how the things that are and the things that come to be and the things that are going to be must come to be and cease.[134]

Cornford, in his study *From Religion to Philosophy,* notes that the *Moira*-idea corresponds to a "first representation," which becomes necessary at a moment when a new factor, which he never specifies, disturbs "the collective life" that "pervades the group as a whole" and involves "sympathetic cooperation" with "no image or idea or conception."[135] This type of "sympathy" resembles the instinctive conformism of the animal herd; it establishes only the cohesion of a herd, excluding subjectivity or individualization. The "first representation," on the other hand, arises in "the dawning of a distinction between myself and the [pre-existing] social consciousness,"[136] in which the subject (Cornford's *"myself"*) senses social compulsion or moral obligation as an agency apart from itself, infusing and commanding the whole of existence, to which everyone else likewise must defer. Gans' originary analysis supplies the motive of Cornford's "first representation" in a way that Cornford himself, despite the audacity in his analysis, cannot; originary analysis also specifies the character of the "first representation," or *sign,* in a way that Cornford's argument, otherwise rich and meritorious, cannot. At the originary "moment of crisis," Gans writes, "the strength of the appetitive drive" overthrows "the dominance hierarchy" of the incipiently human group: "hence, in violation of the dominance hierarchy, all hands reach out for the object; but at the same time each is deferred from appropriating it by the sight of all others reaching in the same direction."[137] The focus of this scene "appears to possess a repellent, sacred force that prevents its occupation by the members of the group [and] that converts the gesture of appropriation into a gesture of designation, that is, into an ostensive sign."[138] Thus the sign functions as a "conflict-deferring mechanism."[139]

The Gansian sign mediates the emergence of *self*-consciousness: "The birth of the self within the communal context defines it *against* this context."[140] Gans argues, however, that:

Originary resentment does not focus on the other peripheral humans, but on the center that refuses itself to desire. The center appears to be the only independent actor on the scene; it is the locus of the divinity, which provides the model for human personhood. This model is first realized as the human self emerges in the rivalry of resentment.[141]

This configuration grants the participant liberty in the form of "freedom to obey the categorical imperative that admits of no alternative" in conjunction with freedom "to conceive [his] own unfreedom to act on [his] desire."[142] It is a case, for the first time, of volition in respect to a moral choice. One should remember Marius' dedication to "The Religion of Numa" and to "Euphuism" when Gans adds that, "the primordial cultural institutions are those that reproduce the moments of the scene of the origin of language"; and when he states that, "art, like ritual, is a form of reproduction of the originary," which opposes "the human context of desire" to "the animal context of mere appetite."[143] Concerning "desire," the scene necessarily concerns beauty: for one may define desire as the satisfactory contemplation from afar of the alluring nucleus that one may not or indeed cannot possess. Insofar as all on the scene conform to the liberty of conceiving a universal imperative, the dispensation of the sign also endows on each member of the community the prototypes of the fraternity and equality so much celebrated in post-Christian and neo-pagan societies. Marius maintains solidarity with a virtual community of rare souls who recognize ironically the scenic dependency of their own detachment.

In one of his long sentences appreciable for its lapidary rhetoric, or for its materiality even, Pater writes of Marius' refinement: "Some transforming spirit was at work [in him] to harmonize contrasts, to deepen expression — a spirit which, in its dealings with the elements of ancient life, was guided by a wonderful tact of selection, exclusion, juxtaposition, begetting thereby a unique effect of freshness, a grave yet wholesome beauty, because the world of sense, the whole outward world was understood to set forth the veritable unction and royalty of a certain priesthood and kingship of the soul within, among the prerogatives of which was a delightful sense of freedom."[144] From just this "freedom," balanced between an *"ascêsis"* that came in the century before and returned in the century after Marius, stems the medieval gentility of such phenomena as "Saint Francis, the voice of Dante, the hand of Giotto."[145] Freedom is beautiful and its beauty, argues Pater, is generative; freedom, the last word of the pronouncement, names the "transforming spirit" of the same flowing sentence's first clause.

Marius' intellectual itinerary begins in naïve religiosity, finds its first maturity in the prevailing Epicureanism of Second Century sophistication, qualifies its maturity by a return to pre-Socratic discourse, and culminates — for Marius dies young — in a skepticism about skepticism that resembles faith. Marius is a late participant in a continuum of thinking that begins with Ionian religious criticism of the species that one sees, in Pater's novel, in the fragments of Heraclitus, and which one can also sample in the Derveni Papyrus. For its part, the text of the Papyrus reflects the "originarity" of consciousness, as Gans would say, in its quotation of the Orphic conflict-Theogony, by which a single divine figure emerges to govern the cosmos under the *Moira*-rule of harmony through just shares; it clearly represents godhead as the model of personhood, in its soteriological invocation of Orpheus as the prophet of deity who reveals to the initiate his genuine personhood and redeems him from ignorance and superstition. Betegh draws from the Derveni-author's exegesis a trio of analogies that structure the physical allegoresis: Zeus, the godhead, is to Moira, his practical function, as mind is to wisdom, and as air is to the breath. "Moira," writes Betegh, "is the active, executive, practical aspect of the god."[146] Betegh notes that, in the Derveni-author's interpretation, "Orpheus is not de-theologized...but, on the contrary, it is through physical allegory that we can appropriate the true theological teaching of Orpheus."[147] The many (in the text, *"other men"*) know the name *Moira* but they misinterpret it as crude predestination: "In common usage [they] say that Moira spun for them."[148] Trimalchio's dinner guests in Satyricon show an obsessive interest in this vulgar version of fate. By contrast, "Orpheus called wisdom Moira," for "this seemed to him to be the most suitable out of all the names that all men have given"; this is because, "Moira was the wisdom of the god always and through everything."[149]

The mystery cults makes use of pagan nomenclature and assimilate rituals whose pedigrees reach back to the Neolithic, but already in the Fourth Century BC they exhibit features of spiritual novelty and real intellectual development, communicating with philosophical and physical speculation, as in the case of the Derveni Papyrus. One sees them separating themselves from the uncritical *mimesis* of traditional religious practice and assuming an interest in thematic anthropology. Many of his commentators call Heraclitus, for example, a Dionysiac. From Pythagorean and Empedoclean doctrine, a pronounced anti-sacrificial impulse enters the continuum. Cornford supposes that Socrates was a Pythagorean. The great conversation with Diotima in Plato's *Symposium* has about it the atmosphere of a mystic initiation. The mysticism of the *Symposium* by no means excludes the materialism, the geometric atomism, of the *Timaeus*. Mysticism — with its concentration on the inward characteristics, such as *nous* and *sophrosyne,* that make people human — goes together with the physical speculation that aims at distinguishing the material substrate of existence from everything else.

In Democritus, for example, one finds a discussion of language that stresses its conventionality, its status as *Nomos,* thereby distinguishing it absolutely from all natural phenomena. An interest in language appears in the literary tradition of Orphism too, as the Derveni Papyrus demonstrates. Pater was aware of this. Early in his career, he wrote an essay on Dionysus, the Olympian god with whom tradition almost invariably links Orpheus. In "A Study of Dionysus" (1876), Pater notes: "Obscure as are those followers of the mystical Orpheus, we yet certainly see them, moving, and playing their part, in the later ages of Greek religion. Old friends with new faces…They seem to have been not without the charm of a real and inward religious beauty, with their neologies, their new readings of old legends, their sense of mystical and second meanings, as they refined upon themes grown too familiar, and linked, in a sophisticated age, the new to the old."[150]

In the world of matter, argues Lucretius in his Epicurean style, all events arise from the lawful behavior of the atoms; it is a tenet of Epicurean cosmology that atomic behavior is universally consistent. Yet in arguing for this thesis, Lucretius runs the risk of establishing, by a conviction, precisely the determinism, which, ethically speaking, he wishes to disestablish. Lucretius is thinking of the determinism of false but effective belief, or superstition: fear of the (non-existent) gods. But the physical-mechanical determination of a cosmos absolutely confined to materiality makes for an even bleaker human picture than the one in which superstition permanently triumphs. Epicurus had solved the problem of physical determinism by introducing into his doctrine the thesis of the swerve. Lucretius says, "When the atoms are traveling straight down through empty space by their own weight, at quite indeterminate times and places they swerve ever so little from their course, just so much that you can call it a change of direction."[151]

A vast secondary literature encumbers the *clinamen*, including commentaries by Karl Marx and Jacques Derrida. Suffice it to say that the swerve readmits to the universe the openness of volition and thereby rescues consciousness from the insignificance of unadulterated process. For Lucretius, there are purely natural processes and there are the humanly natural processes of unconscious behavior. "I daresay that the invention of…costume provoked such envy that its first wearer met his death in ambush and the costume itself was so daubed with blood and torn to shreds by rival claimants that it could not be used by anyone."[152] Lucretius draws a line directly from petty envy to "this discontent that has driven life steadily onward, out on to the high seas, and has stirred up from the depths the surging tumultuous tides of war."[153] Only thematic knowledge of himself extracts the individual from the perdition of *mimesis*.

For both Marius and his author, Pater, the individual who has found his way beyond the ritual organization of the community necessarily oscillates between an ethical and an esthetic comprehension of life. Marius' appreciation of Christianity hovers, in this way, between the ethical and the esthetic. During his visit to the House of Cecilia, a Christian of the patrician class, Marius experiences an almost mystic ecstasy under the stimulus of an unseen chorus of worshippers singing the chant, "Hail, Heavenly Light!" Pater writes: "It was like the evening itself made audible, its hopes and fears, with the stars shining in the midst of it...That visionary scene was the close, the fitting close of the afternoon's experiences."[154] The tableau not only constitutes a "scene," as Pater calls it; but it corresponds equally to what Gans calls "the Gospel idea of a centerless moral community, presided over by a God who has renounced any further intervention in human affairs."[155] The non-locatable singing replaces, in Marius' view of religiosity, a haunting childhood memory of a grinning Medusa that had belonged to his grandfather.

Marius need not experience formal conversion to Gospel religiosity in order to participate in the new faith as "the source of the Western liberation from the sacred and ultimately from Christianity itself."[156] The Medusa-mask stands for the sacred concept of *nemesis,* a type of closed or ritual causality — *Fate,* in the sense of inescapable predestination. Pater knew nothing about the Derveni Papyrus, of course, but the moment of Marius' emancipation from the ancient sacred reflects the Derveni-author's conviction that he has discovered a new understanding of the "spinning," in the distaff-sense, of *Moira,* as she lets out the thread of life. Ionian naturalism, atomism, Orphism, Platonism — all belong to the continuum of critical reaction to inherited religion. Christianity absorbs that critical reaction and then bequeaths it to the medieval European civilization that eventually succeeds Rome. *Marius the Epicurean,* informed by Winckelmann and Hegel and probably Nietzsche, manifests belatedly the critical mentality inaugurated by Thales and his epigones.

In describing the reception-esthetic that informs his discussion of the Renaissance revival of classical forms, Pater uses the term *weaving;* in contemplating masterpieces in the mode of rigorous connoisseurship, the esthetically attuned subject perpetually *weaves and unweaves himself,* as Pater puts it. The metaphor suggests that for the distinctly modern subject the esthetic encounter has trumped all other formative experiences. Pater sees the work of art — which always has a material basis, for even singing is vibration in air — as a node of order in a chaos of sensory impressions: "Our physical life is a perpetual motion"; and "experience seems to bury us under a flood of external objects, pressing upon us with sharp and importunate reality."[157] Like the Heraclitean *Logos,* the work of art, whether it is a painting by Botticelli or a statue by Michelangelo or a poem by Joachim Du Bellay, frees us from "facile orthodoxy"[158] such that our "nature" is "modified by its presence."[159] Like the Venus of Lucretius, vividly represented by Botticelli, the work of art pacifies anxiety. The subject is thus delivered beyond mere nature into "a spirit," as Pater writes, "of general elevation."[160] Where Cornford defines mysticism as "a series of efforts to translate a certain view of life, of God, into terms of a physical system," Pater defines esthetics as the effort of the connoisseur systematically to translate the rule of proportion in a wrought object with a material basis into its spiritual implication; the intellect of the connoisseur passes through the material medium to communicate with the genius of the artist-creator.

The sacred is collective; the esthetic is a dialogue of two individuals. The pre-Socratic obsession with differentiating the one from the many — the one who knows from the many who do not know — prefigures the rarefied esthetic awareness of the creator and the connoisseur, as Pater himself understands. It concerns a *fining down:* the modern, esthetic version of the ancient *Moira,* a faith in proportion whereby the individual graduates from dependence on the actual or ritual community to independence in the virtual community of his imagination. In the stubborn *apartness* of the character of Marius and in the esthetic elitism of *The Renaissance,* Pater defines the individual scene that replaces the collective scene as Western civilization moves from its Christian into its post-Christian phase. I grant the last word not to Pater but to Gans: "Art, like ritual, serves to defer conflict, but it operates on the community one member at a time."[161]

Notes

1. Walter Pater, edited by Donald L. Hill. *The Renaissance: Studies in Poetry and Art.* Los Angeles and Berkeley: University of California Press, 1980. 188.

2. Walter Pater. *Marius the Epicurean.* New York: Penguin, 1985. 184.

3 . From Aristotle, *Metaphysics.* In Robin Waterfield, *The First Philosophers: The Presocratics and the Sophists.* New York: Oxford University Press, 2000. 12.

4. 13.

5. Translated by Marianne Cowan. Washington DC: Regnery, 1962. 42.

6. 43.

7. Translated by Brooks Haxton. Heraclitus, *Fragments.* New York: Penguin, 2001. 15.

8. 47.

9. 79.

10. From Simplicius, *Commentary on Aristotle's "On the Heavens."* Waterfield. 185.

11. Walter Pater. *Plato and Platonism.* London: Macmillan and Company, 1910: "And the Darwinian theory – that 'species,' the identifying forms of animal and vegetable life, immutable though they seem now, as of old in the Garden of Eden, are fashioned by slow development, while perhaps millions of years go by: well! Every month is adding to its evidence." (20) But "it was in Plato's day," that "the Heraclitean flux... seemed to have laid hold on man, on the social and moral world, dissolving and disintegrating opinion, first principles, faith, established amorphism, so to call it, there also." (21)

12. From Hippolytus, *Refutation of All Heresies.* Waterfield. 185.

13. From John of Stobi. Waterfield. 190.

14. From John of Stobi. Waterfield. 191.

15. F. M. Cornford. *From Religion to Philosophy: A Study in the Origins of Western Speculation.* Princeton, New Jersey: Princeton University Press, 1991. 14.

16. 15.

17. 80.

18. 123.

19. 159.

20. 19.

21. 49.

22. Lucretius (Titus Lucretius Carus), translated by R. E. Latham. *On the Nature of the Universe.* New York: Penguin, 1994. 13 & 15.

23. 10 & 11.

24. 10.

25. 75.

26. 13.

27. 14.

28. 154.

29. 157.

30. 68.

31. Heraclitus, 91.

32. Lucretius, 155.

33. 155.

34. 158.

35. 13.

36. 12.

37. 164.

38. 65.

39. Pater, *Marius.* 37.

40. Livy (Titus Livius), translated by A. de Sélincourt. *The Early History of Rome.* New York: Penguin, 2002. 52.

41. 54.

42. 55.

43. 54.

44. Pater, 143.

45. 143.

46. 149.

47. 151.

48. 200.

49. 197.

50. 197.

51. 197 & 198.

52. 117.

53. Eric L. Gans. *Originary Thinking: Elements of Generative Anthropology.* Stanford, California: Stanford University Press, 1993. 13.

54. 13.

55. 158.

56. 158.

57. 12.

58. 159.

59. 14.

60. Pater, 181.

61. 181.

62. 185.

63. Gans, 19.

64. Pater, 105.

65. 105.

66. *De rerum natura,* 12 – 13.

67. Gans, 22.

68. Pater, 105.

69. 105.

70. 106.
71. 106.
72. 106.
73. 110.
74. 107.
75. 107.
76. 107.
77. 110.
78. 110.
79. 109.
80. 109.
81. 111.
82. 111.
83. 111.
84. 110.
85. 111.
86. 112.
87. 40.
88. Gans, 22.
89. 118.
90. 119.
91. 118.
92. 118.
93. Pater, 121.
94. 118.
95. 119.
96. 193.
97. 193.
98. Cornford, 159.
99. Titus Petronius Arbiter, translated by J. P. Sullivan. *Satyricon* (with Seneca, *Apocolocyntosis*). New York: Penguin, 1986. 169.
100. 169.
101. 51.
102. 57 & 58.
103. 51.
104. 53.
105. 70.
106. 54.
107. 57.
108. 57.
109. 75.
110. 67.
111. 67.

112. 63.
113. 64.
114. 75.
115. A *feast,* in other words, is an occasion defined by the license to eat and drink more than one normally does, but still not as much as one ideally wants; the principle of *limitation* remains in effect.
116. 86.
117. Gans, 52.
118. Petronius, 76.
119. Pater, 88 & 89.
120. 87.
121. 89.
122. 167.
123. 167.
124. 169.
125. 169.
126. 169.
127. 171.
128. 168.
129. 185.
130. 185.
131. 186.
132. 186.
133. 210 & 211.
134. Gábor Betegh. *The Derveni Papyrus: Cosmology, Theology and Interpretation.* Cambridge: Cambridge University Press, 2005. 200.
135. Cornford, 78.
136. 78.
137. Gans, 8.
138. 9.
139. 9.
140. 18.
141. 18.
142. 56.
143. 120.
144. Pater, 239.
145. 239.
146. Betegh, 202.
147. 205.
148. 39.
149. 39.
150. Walter Pater, *Greek Studies: A Series of Essays.* London: MacMillan and Company, Ltd, 1910. 50.

151. Lucretius, 43.
152. 165.
153. 165.
154. Pater, 233.
155. Gans, 60.
156. 60.
157. Pater, *The Renaissance,* 187.
158. 189.
159. XX.
160. XXIV.
161. Gans, 143.

Intensity and Ambiguity in Romantic Poetics

Matthew Schneider

That for which we find words is something already dead in our hearts.
There is always a kind of contempt in the act of speaking.
                    Friedrich Nietzsche, *Twilight of the Idols* (1889)

The nineteenth century was an age of literary volubility. But the poets and
novelists who flooded romantic-era market society with billions of words did
so in spite of deep misgivings about the capability of language to capture and
communicate the scope and complexity of their inner thoughts and feelings
— misgivings memorably expressed near the century's end in Nietzsche's bleak
aphorism from *Twilight of the Idols*. Nietzsche's sentiment presents a curious
paradox — the heartfelt conviction, expressed in words, that words can't express
heartfelt convictions. But however paradoxical this negative faith was, it would
be difficult to overestimate how widely embraced it was during the nineteenth
century. To the romantic, even the most beautiful words are clumsy, mediated,
ill-suited vehicles for the sublime feelings that stir them: as Matthew Arnold put
it in "The Buried Life," "long we try in vain to speak and act / Our hidden self,
and what we say and do / Is eloquent, is well — but 'tis not true!" (156)

Arnold's frustration with the obstacles that words throw in the way of what
ought to be the simple task of making our hearts plain to ourselves and one
another is typical of romantics. Because the romantic seeks emotional transport
from literature, this frustration is not entirely unwelcome. But the truth of the
heart has its claims, too, and the exasperation with one's inability to express that
truth cannot be swallowed forever. Linguistic ambiguity pulls in opposite directions: by increasing frustration, it heightens the romantic's level of emotional intensity; but by clouding self-apprehension and rendering honest communication
nearly impossible, it precludes deep communion between the self and others.
In other words, the romantic's heightened emphasis on individuality and what
René Girard has called the "parthenogenesis of the imagination," coupled with
the age's millennial and utopian hopes for a new world in which *alle menschen
werden Brüder*, puts the romantic on the horns of a dilemma. The originary
hypothesis — and the romantic's own brand of rudimentary originary thinking
— offer a way out of this dilemma, which entails pulling back in the originary

event from the moment of representational contemplation of the central object to an earlier moment, a moment closer in time to the crucial abortive gesture of appropriation that can be said to have inaugurated representation itself.

Romantic poetics hovers around the abortive gesture of appropriation. By pointing to an object, and thereby making signification visual rather than aural, the gesture minimizes ambiguity, but occurs at the moment in the originary event of highest emotional intensity. Throughout the nineteenth century, the moment of the abortive gesture of appropriation recurs whenever romantics pressed themselves to depict the timeless human truths with which they — by personal inclination and historical circumstance — were especially preoccupied with discovering. Early on, William Wordsworth employed a radically simplified poetic diction and a rhetorical style that can only be described as *ostensive* in order to depict what he called "the primary laws of our nature" (791). In mid century, Charles Dickens depicted his archetypal scene of ethical transformation as a confrontation between loquacity and an implacable, outstretched hand. And at the end of the century, the ostensive, the gesture, and the all-important transition from nature to culture on the originary scene come together in the landscape that plays so important a role in Thomas Hardy's masterpiece *Tess of the D'Urbervilles*.

The central contention of the originary hypothesis is that human consciousness had a punctual origin, and that the paradoxical nature of symbolic representation — the distinguishing characteristic of humanity as a species — is a product of the fundamentally bifurcated structure of the originary scene. The abortive gesture of appropriation creates the center and the periphery, the two loci of the scene, and establishes the centrifugal and centripetal forces that operate between them. As Eric Gans has written, over time — and especially after the "big man" appropriates the redistributive function of the sacred center of the hierarchical society — the resentment of those on the periphery for the center becomes the *engine* of cultural evolution: civilizations evolve new ways to integrate resentment into the social order.[1] From the age of Greek and Roman antiquity until the end of the eighteenth century, the cultural and artistic means through which those integrations were accomplished were relatively stable, and were known collectively as classicism and neoclassicism.

But romanticism broke radically and irretrievably from these venerable forms. "The society that generates romanticism has dissolved its links with the traditional past," Gans writes in *Originary Thinking* (165), and, as a result, the "romantic replaces the esthetic primacy of the public scene with the private" (164). In the romantic era, "the scenic center is no longer public but personal" (167), Gans continues, and as the romantic is called upon to provide his "own model of the scene's constitution" (170), extrapolates his struggles to understand and be understood by others into an anthropological narrative, with ambiguity and intensity as its structuring polarities. In *Poetics*, Aristotle said that the purpose of tragedy was to evoke and then effect the proper purgation of the tragic emotions of pity and fear. We might go Aristotle one better and say that the purpose of literature in the romantic era is to evoke and then balance the originary dilemma of intensity and ambiguity by reviving — rhetorically, imagistically, or thematically — the abortive gesture of appropriation.

I. Ostensive Poetics in Wordsworth

Perhaps no other single figure had as great an influence on the theory and practice of all English-language poets who came after him as William Wordsworth (1770–1850). This influence stemmed both from his verses themselves, which combined simple diction and conventional stanzaic forms with psychological inwardness, and also from Wordsworth's critical pronouncements about poetry, particularly in the series of prefaces he wrote for the three editions of *Lyrical Ballads* published between 1798 and 1802. In these prefaces, which were widely reprinted and excerpted separately from Wordsworth's poems throughout the nineteenth century, Wordsworth made the case for common-language poetry, arguing not only that "there neither is, nor can be any *essential* difference between the language of prose and metrical composition" (793), but that verses written in anything other than "a selection of language really spoken by men" (793) cannot achieve poetry's aim, which is to reveal "the essential passions of the heart" (791). Within a few generations, Wordsworth's ideas had overturned once and for all the neo-classical canons of taste that had dominated English poetry since Saxon times.

But how does the Wordsworthian common-language poetic project work? How, exactly, does it evoke the originary dilemma of intensity and ambiguity? Though Wordsworth has as good a claim on literary originality as anyone, his achievement — and the English romantic literary revolution it inaugurated — did have some important precursors in the second half of the eighteenth century. The first of these was the "graveyard school" of late eighteenth-century English poets, especially Thomas Gray (1716–1761), whose "Elegy Written in a Country Churchyard" (1751) was passionately loved, memorized, and imitated by all poetically-inclined youngsters of Wordsworth's generation. The other major stylistic influence on Wordsworth's common-language poetic project came from the late eighteenth-century ballad craze, which began with the publication in 1760 of Bishop Thomas Percy's *Reliques of Ancient English Poetry* and James

Macpherson's *The Poems of Ossian*.[2] From Gray's Elegy Wordsworth took the slightly melancholy, verbally unassuming, but philosophically serious persona of many of his speakers, as well as the contemplative setting to which his poems repeatedly return: a thoughtful self, alone and confronted with some vague monument of death. From the balladeers Wordsworth took the authorizing simple rhythms of folk expression, and, more important, the ways in which ballads omit, elide, or forget many of the details of the stories they were presumably originally composed to preserve. Clearly, this aspect of ballads fascinated Wordsworth, for this was what gave them their ambiguity and — because emotional depth was hinted at, rather than revealed — their intensity as well.

The best Wordsworth lyrics are often described as *haunting*, because the poet managed to combine in them the philosophical seriousness of Gray's Elegy with the narrative indeterminacy and consequent emotional intensity of folk balladry, as in "She dwelt among the untrodden ways," one of the justly admired "Lucy" poems Wordsworth wrote between 1798 and 1800:

> She dwelt among the untrodden ways
>   Beside the springs of Dove,
> A Maid whom there were none to praise
>   And very few to love:
>
> A violet by a mossy stone
>   Half hidden from the eye!
> — Fair as a star, when only one
>   Is shining in the sky.
>
> She lived unknown, and few could know
>   When Lucy ceased to be;
> But she is in her grave, and, oh,
>   The difference to me! (112)

Notwithstanding the soothing ballad meter and the simple diction, the poem is a puzzle, and its mysteries deepen the closer one looks at and interrogates these verses. Who is Lucy? What put her in her grave? Who is mourning her? Why does the mourner use such a flat, non-committal phrase to describe his grief ("and, oh, / The difference to me!")? What does the middle stanza have to do with the first and third stanzas? If Wordsworth's purpose was simply to generate ambiguity for his readers, he appears to have succeeded. Much of this ambiguity is grammatical: placing the pronouns before the nouns to which they presumably refer in lines 1 and 3 and 9 and 10 — while not technically incorrect — isn't entirely clear, and allows for the possibility that the Maid, the "she" in line 9, Lucy, and the "she" in line 11 are not all the same person. Most of the poem's ambiguity, though, is a product of its narrative incompleteness. The poem suggests several story possibilities: why was the maid unknown? why did she die? what difference does it make to the speaker? All of these stories, however, could only be reconstructed through extrapolation, inference, and speculation. And even if these stories were complete, that wouldn't bring us any closer to recognizing what's standing in the center of the poem, between the beginning and ending stanzas. Though a colon appears between the end of stanza 1 and the beginning of stanza 2, implying that stanza 2 will introduce an image that will further clarify either the who the maid was or why there were so few to love her, stanza 2 presents no such clarification; in fact, this stanza appears to veer off in an entirely different direction, and relates nothing about the maid at all! As in the first and third stanzas, Wordsworth omits conjunctive words and phrases that would otherwise provide the reader with a better sense of pronoun reference and which nouns are modified by which phrases. Is it the violet or the mossy stone that's "half hidden from the eye?" And does the violet correspond to the star, and the stone to the sky, or is the stone like the star, and the violet like the sky?

Obviously, it would be beside the point to try to answer these questions, as beside the point as it has been for the many critics (including Wordsworth's one-time collaborator Coleridge) who have tried to identify Lucy. Taken at face value, each stanza constitutes an encapsulated unit — indeed, a vague encapsulated unit, the first and third stanzas of which begin with the least specific type of word there is: the pronoun. Those stanzas then proceed from these unspecific openings to only slightly greater degrees of specificity: in the first, the initial pronoun "she" evokes an unloved maid; but we're not told why she's unloved; in the third stanza, we are told that that same unloved maid (we presume) is in her grave, and that this makes some sort of a "difference" to the speaker, a frustratingly vague conclusion to which to come, particularly after having experienced the non-conclusiveness of the first two stanzas. In other words, all three stanzas of "She dwelt," either singly or taken together, do not tell a story; rather, the stanzas are arrayed, as it were, side by side, and each gestures toward something, designates something, but does not go much beyond designating it, in much the same way that the most primary form of language, the ostensive, merely designates the renounced object on the originary scene.

If one stanza can lay claim to possessing more linguistic sophistication than the others, it's the middle one, by virtue of its simile. But the real focus of that stanza — and what must have been, moreover, the imaginative germ of the poem itself — is the visually striking image with which that stanza begins: "the violet by the mossy stone," so much more vivid and intensely present than the insipid pronouns that begin the first and third stanzas. The tripartite structure of this poem — parentheses of relative ambiguity encompassing a vivid and well-defined focal point — mirrors both the hypothetical physical configuration and the individual psychic experience of the originary event. For the proto-hominids on the originary scene, the gesture at the moment it is aborted is suddenly transformed from a reflex movement into something altogether unknown — and the unknown is, by definition, ambiguous. Moreover, the accidental object of that gesture's designation will acquire an unprecedented intensity from the new kind of attention that's fixed upon it — an attention that will, in time, evolve into the capacity for forming metaphoric figures like the one that so distinguishes this stanza from the two that surround it.

It is not accidental, though, that a mossy stone stands at the center of this poem. The evocation of a simple funerary monument in the middle of "She dwelt" links this poem to Gray's "Elegy Written in a Country Church-Yard," and thus presents an opportunity to specify exactly how Wordsworth differed from his late neo-classical precursor. Gray's Elegy cautions his readers against disdaining the poor lying buried in the churchyard; remember, Gray warns, "the Paths of Glory lead but to the Grave." Gray's meditations on death as the great equalizer end with a three-stanza epitaph, "Grav'd on the Stone beneath yon aged Thorn":

Here rests his Head upon the Lap of Earth,
A Youth to Fortune and to Fame unknown;
Fair Science frowned not on his humble Birth,
And Melancholy mark'd him for her own.

Large was his Bounty, and his Soul sincere;
Heav'n did a recompense as largely send:
He gave to mis'ry all he had, a Tear,
He gain'd from Heaven ('twas all he wish'd) a Friend.

No farther seek his Merits to disclose,
Or draw his Frailties from their dread Abode,
(There they alike in trembling Hope repose,)
The Bosom of his Father and his God (945).

The epitaph that concludes Gray's Elegy, like "She dwelt," is composed of three quatrains, and both remark on the unknown status of their subject; but there the resemblances end. The melancholy youth of Gray's epitaph rests with God; but we're offered no such assurance about Lucy. Gray's youth had a sincere soul and a large bounty; but no corresponding information about Lucy's soul is provided. Instead, Wordsworth offers only a series of ambiguous nouns and object complements about Lucy's life and death, grouped around an intense, vividly visual depiction of what her grave looks like. For Gray, the point of situating the poetic sensibility in the contemplative space of the country churchyard was to elevate the ostensives of that place — the "short and simple annals of the poor" and "uncouth rhymes" inscribed on the monuments "by the unlettered Muse" (945) — into declaratives, philosophical conclusions valid for emperor and swain. Wordsworth worked in exactly the opposite direction. He re-primitivized poetry both rhetorically — by simplifying, even obscuring poetic grammar and diction — and anthropologically, by returning poetry to its ostensive beginnings. In "She dwelt," the arresting image of the mossy stone is a primeval grave marker, a tombstone before the practice of engraving tombstones with epitaphs had begun. Or it's a tombstone whose engraving, laboriously inscribed in the freshness of grief and meant to last forever, has been rendered indistinct and unreadable by the passage of time, leaving only a tantalizingly ambiguous mystery behind. In either case, what really arrests the imagination of the poet is not the meaning or import of the inscription, as it was for Gray, but the process through which the desire to make inscriptions at all might first have come about.

II. Dickens: The Hand and the Truth

The romantic sensibility valued truth above all else, and, by definition, nothing could be truer than the originary event. Not only did the originary event inaugurate the process by which the conceptual categories of truth and falsehood could be established, but on the originary scene, signification occurred visually — there was therefore no opportunity for aural misapprehension or deception through the misleading use of homonyms. When language is only ostensive, there are no poetic beauties, no flights of fancy, no pleasing metaphoric figures; but there are also no ironies, sarcasms, verbal deceits, or semantic traps. If the first word was the truest word, and the truest word was a gesture, what better way to speak the truth, than to re-employ the human hand in its ancient silent service?

By way of illustration, consider Charles Dickens, though at first glance he seems an unlikely champion of truthfulness. Even in his own time Dickens wasn't thought of as a particularly naturalistic novelist: much of his contemporary appeal stemmed from his prowess as a broad-spectrum caricaturist of

English society and his comic mastery of class dialects. And almost all of his
novels — even the later, more "psychological" works — prominently feature
elements of the fantastic: in *Great Expectations,* there's the demonic Miss Hav-
isham, and *Bleak House* includes an instance of spontaneous human combus-
tion, the actuality of which Dickens vigorously defended first in an exchange
of letters with a fellow novelist, and then in a preface for a later edition of the
novel.[3] But despite his reputation as a fantasist, and despite frequent criticisms
that his characters behaved unrealistically, Dickens always thought of himself
as answering in his works to high, if ultimately self-generated and self-tested,
standards of truthfulness. Upon the publication of his second novel, *Oliver Twist*
(1838), critics expressed doubts that the good-hearted prostitute Nancy would
stay with the brute Bill Sikes. For the Gadshill edition of Dickens collected
works published in 1867-68, Dickens wrote a new preface for *Oliver Twist,* in
which he defended Nancy — and himself — against the charge that her character was unconvincingly drawn:

> It is useless to discuss whether the conduct and character of the girl
> seems natural or unnatural, probable or improbable, right or wrong. IT
> IS TRUE. Every man who has watched these melancholy shades of life,
> must know it to be so. From the first introduction of that poor wretch,
> to her laying of her blood-stained head upon the robber's breast, there is
> not a word exaggerated or over-wrought. It is emphatically God's truth,
> for it is the truth He leaves in such depraved and miserable breasts; the
> hope yet lingering there; the last fair drop of water at the bottom of the
> weed-choked well. It involves the best and worst shades of our nature;
> much of its ugliest hues, and something of its most beautiful; it is a
> contradiction, an anomaly, an apparent impossibility; but it is a truth. I
> am glad to have had it doubted, for in that circumstance I should find a
> sufficient assurance (if I wanted any) that it needed to be told (xiv-xv).

If truth is of paramount importance in characters like Nancy, who are meant
to awaken a complacent Victorian citizenry to the need for economic and political reform, then truth is even more imperative in scenes of individual moral
transformation, such as that which stands at the center of Dickens's best-known
and most influential story — indeed, one of the most widely-known stories to
come out of the English-language tradition — *A Christmas Carol* (1853).

My readers will scarcely need reminding that the moral reprobate Scrooge
is visited by three spirits in the course of his reformation. In typical Victorian
fashion, the first two — the ghosts of Christmas Past and Christmas Present,
are, like Scrooge, garrulous, and engage their charge in extensive conversation

and commentary about the scenes they enable him to witness. The third spirit, the Ghost of Christmas Yet To Come, however, speaks not a single word, and communicates with Scrooge solely through nods and gestures. (The Ghost of Christmas Yet To Come appears to Scrooge "shrouded in a deep black garment, which concealed its head, its face, its form, and left nothing of it visible save one outstretched hand" (50).) Everywhere the Ghost of Christmas Yet To Come leads Scrooge, it indicates the direction he is to follow by gesturing with one outstretched hand, and each scene to which this spirit transports him has a focal point, to which it points with a "steady hand" or "unmoved finger" (57). The object of these gestures is invariably something — either the corpse itself or an associated personal effect of the deceased — that will reveal the identity of a dead man whose passing arouses little grief, and is at times openly celebrated, throughout the city. By arguing, pleading, and attempting to cajole the implacable spirit, Scrooge delays, for a time, the revelation the man's identity, who he fears is himself. His final stalling tactic, however, backfires. After demanding that he be shown some "tenderness connected with a death" (58), Scrooge witnesses the heart-rending grief of his clerk, Bob Cratchit, after the death of Tiny Tim, and this breaks his will to resist; he then submits to the final stage of his moral re-education, which returns him to that familiar Wordsworthian locus, the graveside:

> A churchyard. Here, then, the wretched man whose name he had now to learn, lay underneath the ground. It was a worthy place. Walled in by houses; overrun by grass and weeds, the growth of vegetation's death, not life; choked up with too much burying; fat with repleted appetite. A worthy place!
> The Spirit stood among the graves, and pointed down to One. He advanced towards it trembling. The Phantom was exactly as it had been, but he dreaded that he saw new meaning in its solemn shape.
> "Before I draw nearer to that stone to which you point," said Scrooge, "answer me one question. Are these the shadows of the things that Will be, or are they shadows of things that May be, only?"
> Still the Ghost pointed downward to the grave by which it stood.
> "Men's courses will foreshadow certain ends, to which, if persevered in, they must lead," said Scrooge. "But if the courses be departed from, the ends will change. Say it is thus with what you show me."
> The Spirit was immovable as ever.
> Scrooge crept towards it, trembling as he went; and following the finger, read upon the stone of the neglected grave his own name, EBENEZER SCROOGE (61-2).

At first glance, this graveside scene appears opposed in practically every respect to Wordsworth's: where the mood of the poet's was serene and contemplative, this is hectoring and overwrought; where Lucy's grave marker was so embraced by nature that it was hard to be certain whether it was really her burial site, Scrooge's graveyard is a weed-choked well of death, "walled in by houses." But despite these differences, the scenic architecture of these two encounters between life and death is pretty much the same. The Ghost and Scrooge comprise the peripheral participants on a representational scene, with the gravestone toward which the Ghost points as its center. Scrooge's attention is drawn to the center by the Ghost's gesture; but, again, the gesture, for all the directedness of its reference, is still *ambiguous* in meaning. This is revealed by the fact that Scrooge's questions effectively *defer* the awful finality of the spirit's accusatory finger. Despite his name, the hooded and cloaked Ghost of Christmas Yet To Come is a specter of the originary scene: he is big, silent, threatening, and communicates, as we have seen, wordlessly, through gestures and body movements alone. He exudes a great deal of what might be called originary power. For Dickens, the authenticity of this kind of animalistic menace represents a species of truthfulness, and therefore emerges as attractive for that reason; but Dickens also knows that gestural ambiguity offers little possibility for ethical development. Moral improvement requires the more evolved linguistic form of the declarative, which is what Scrooge employs when he flings his desperate questions at the mute spirit just before he reads his name on the tombstone.

But the name on the tombstone is no revelation. Surely before he was visited by the three spirits, Scrooge knew he would someday die; but that knowledge was insufficient to effect a moral transformation. What terrifies Scrooge is not the inevitability of his death, but the possibility that *he* is the man whose death stirred so little feeling. "Am I that man who lay upon the bed?" Scrooge cries to the Ghost after reading his name on the tombstone. "The finger pointed from the grave to him, and back again" (62). But this information, revealed by gesture on the originary scene, is meaningful only within the narrative context of the previous scenes that the Ghost has gestured toward in the course of this stage of Scrooge's re-education. And these scenes do not just show the brutal finality of Scrooge's death. Rather, they illustrate that after death Scrooge will be *unmourned*. After the Ghost of Christmas Yet To Come whisks Scrooge away from his bedroom, their first stop is Change, where they listen in on the conversation of a "little knot of business men":

> Observing that the hand was pointed to them, Scrooge advanced
> to listen to their talk.

"No," said a great fat man with a monstrous chin," I don't know much about it, either way. I only know he's dead."

"When did he die?" inquired another.

"Last night, I believe."

"Why, what was the matter with him?" asked a third, taking a vast quantity of snuff out of a very large snuff-box. "I thought he'd never die."

"God knows," said the first, with a yawn.

"What has he done with his money?" asked a red-faced gentleman with a pendulous excrescence on the end of his nose, that shook like the gills of a turkey-cock.

"I haven't heard," said the man with the large chin, yawning again. "Left it to his company, perhaps. He hasn't left it to me. That's all I know."

This pleasantry was received with a general laugh.

"It's likely to be a very cheap funeral," said the same speaker; "for upon my life I don't know of anybody to go to it. Suppose we make up a party and volunteer?"

"I don't mind going if a lunch is provided," observed the gentleman with the excrescence on his nose. "But I must be fed, if I make one" (53–54).

For Scrooge (and for his creator Dickens), this is the cruelest fate imaginable: to be jeered at posthumously by hideous monsters of the mercantile class. Unlike Lucy, who lived unknown, but whose death made a difference, Scrooge will die unknown, and his death will make no difference, no matter how indelibly and clearly his name is engraved on his tombstone. Or at least that's one provisional outcome. For all the grim steadiness of purpose with which the ghost indicates Scrooge's tombstone, the gesture is still only an ostensive, and as such cannot begin to answer the complex philosophical questions about destiny and free will that Scrooge puts to the spirit. Those questions can only be answered after language has developed the capacity for the declarative sentence — that is, after it has evolved to the point at which it can free itself from gestures toward concrete objects and become self-referential and conceptual. For all the intensity and air of originary truthfulness that the outstretched hand of truth can seem to bring to the scene of moral revelation, it proves, in the end, a maladroit instrument in practice for effective ethical transformation. As if in illustration of this, Dickens ends the episode of the Ghost of Christmas Yet To Come with Scrooge's declarative triumph over the Ghost's ostensive intractability:

"Spirit!" he cried, tight clutching at its robe, "hear me. I am not the man I was. I will not be the man I must have been but for this intercourse. Why show me this, if I am past all hope?"

For the first time the hand appeared to shake.

"Good Spirit," he pursued, as down upon the ground he fell before it: "Your nature intercedes for me, and pities me. Assure me that I yet may change these shadows you have shown me, by an altered life."

The kind hand trembled.

"I will honour Christmas in my heart, and try to keep it all the year. I will live in the Past, the Present, and the Future. The Spirits of all Three shall strive within me. I will not shut out the lessons that they teach. Oh, tell me I may sponge away the writing on this stone!"

In his agony, he caught the spectral hand. It sought to free itself, but he was strong in his entreaty, and detained it. The Spirit, stronger yet, repulsed him.

Holding up his hands in a last prayer to have his fate aye reversed, he saw an alteration in the Phantom's hood and dress. It shrunk, collapsed, and dwindled down into a bedpost (62).

In both the novel and in his literary afterlife, Scrooge does succeed in expunging the writing from the gravestone, largely by overwriting his name ubiquitously on the institution of Christmas throughout the western world. Scrooge's victory also reveals an important difference between Dickens's attitude toward the originary scene and that of both Wordsworth and Hardy, to which I will return at greater length in the conclusion.

III. Nature and Culture in the Romantic Landscape

What makes an old graveyard *romantic*? Do moldering monuments, tangled thickets of overgrown evergreen foliage, and mossy stones in a setting of lawn and wildflowers *necessarily* stir intense emotions and deep thoughts, or are these just stock responses to what are, after all, a set of literary conventions that came out of late eighteenth-century Gothicism? Why, in other words, are romantics drawn to graveyards at all? Is this a pose they learned from the *Sorrows of Young Werther*, or do these locales possess some greater revelatory significance, not just for the individual, for the broader category of the human?

The attraction of the graveyard — especially the country churchyards so favored by nineteenth-century romantics — lies in the fact that the existence of funereal monuments affords the romantic an opportunity to reflect on humankind's transition from nature to culture. Burial grounds are clearly an essential, even defining, human institution, as old as or perhaps even older than ritualized religion itself. As an open and accessible space permanently set aside for the interment of the remains of the dead, the graveyard serves as a sort of domesticated ritual center for the community. Though sanctified, its precincts are not as sacred and therefore entailed with strictures and prohibitions as those of a church, and therefore may predate built temples. But the aspect of the country churchyard that brings anthropological speculations most forcefully to mind for the romantic is the ubiquitous phenomenon of the tombstone from which time and the elements have effaced the inscription identifying the inhabitant of the grave.

The blank tombstone of the country churchyard is an ancient text that has been accidentally erased, leaving an entrancing mystery behind, and inviting speculation not just about how the erased text might have read, but also about textuality's possible origins in ancient funerary rites and the presumably primordial human practice of burying the dead. To the romantic, in other words, the country churchyard is a minor paleo-anthropological site, with its blank monuments playing the role of little Stonehenges, prompting the romantic to ask, "Who built you? And for what purpose? And what does it mean about humanity — sociologically and psychologically — that people would take the time and effort to try to eternalize these representations by carving them into stone? Furthermore, what does it reveal about humanity that the ambiguity of these mysterious relics is so deeply moving to me, arouses such intense feeling?" In another Lucy poem, "Three years she grew," Wordsworth wrote of the power of "mute insensate things" (113). Perhaps the "mossy stone half hidden from the eye" of "She dwelt" was one of these blank, half-blank, buried, or broken tombstones. Or maybe it had all or part of the name "Lucy" carved on it, but nothing else — no dates, no epitaph, no inspirational mottos or snippets of scripture. In either case, to the romantic imagination, the stone becomes more than a place marker or even a monument dedicated to preserving the memory of an individual. To the degree to which its particular inscription is *indistinct* or *ambiguous*, the blank tombstone becomes an occasion for anthropological speculation on the broader phenomenon of inscription itself, or *representation*, especially the *origin of representation* within the context of death. And since the capacity for representation is humanity's defining characteristic, then that monument, even with its inscription effaced, can symbolize the transition from nature to culture, for in simply having been raised by human hands for some representational purpose, it proves that those who raised it had made the leap from the animal — who has no language — to the human, who does. Like the mysterious circles and avenues of standing stones, earthworks, cairns, tumuli,

and prehistoric burial vaults scattered around Wordsworth's and Dickens's beloved British countryside, the everyday enigma of the blank tombstone invites
the romantic to think across vast reaches of time and history, to hypothesize
about origins, transitions, and essential characteristics.

All the romantics, to varying extents, pondered these enigmas; but the writer
for whom they recurred most frequently was the late nineteenth-century novelist
Thomas Hardy. Like Wordsworth, Hardy wrote about the landscape he knew
best: southwestern England, where he lived all his life — and where, it happens,
may be found the densest concentration of prehistoric sites and ancient ruins in
the British Isles. These romantic settings play a large role in all Hardy's works;
but are especially prominent in his next-to-last novel, *Tess of the D'Urbervilles*
(1891). At first glance, this would seem to be the case because Tess's tragic saga
has romantic overtones in the conventional sense of that term: it is a story of
love gone wrong, the tale of a "pure woman faithfully presented" (as Hardy's
subtitle puts it) whose happiness — and later, life — are sacrificed to the op-
pressive standards of Victorian sexual mores. It seems only fitting that a sad
story ending with the death of the heroine should feature (as Tess's does) ruined
medieval abbeys, empty stone sepulchers in abandoned churchyards, ransacked
tombs inscribed in Fraktur Latin script, and, at the climax, the grandest romantic ruin of them all, Stonehenge, where Tess, awaiting capture by the police after
having murdered Alec D'Urberville, stretches herself out on an "oblong slab"
(318) which her husband tells her was once an altar used by heathens to offer
sacrifices to the sun.

But there's a humbler monument in *Tess* that — despite its lacking the size
and grandeur of Stonehenge — figures more prominently in the plot, and ties
the novel to the originary dilemma of ambiguity and intensity. The monument, which, like Stonehenge, actually exists,[4] is called Cross-in-Hand, and
appears for the first time when Tess passes it on her way to Angel's parents'
cottage in chapter 44. Hardy minutely describes the route Tess takes in this
episode, though none of the place names he uses are real, except that of the
monument:

> Keeping the vale on her right, she steered steadily westward; passing
> above the Hintocks, crossing at right angles the high road from Shera-
> ton-Abbas to Casterbridge, and skirting Dogbury Hill and High Stoy,
> with the dell between them called the Devil's Kitchen. Still following
> the elevated way, she reached Cross-in-Hand, where the stone pillar
> stands desolate and silent, to mark the site of a miracle, or murder, or
> both (239).

Tess passes the monument again on her return journey, this time in the company of Alec D'Urberville, whom she has met unexpectedly; and this time Hardy fills in more of the background of this roadside curiosity:

> At length the road touched the spot called "Cross-in-Hand." Of all spots on the bleached and desolate upland this was the most forlorn. It was so far removed from the charm which is sought in landscape by artists and view-lovers as to reach a new kind of beauty, a negative beauty of tragic tone. The place took its name from a stone pillar which stood there, a strange rude monolith, from a stratum unknown in any local quarry, on which was roughly carved a human hand. Differing accounts were given of its history and purport. Some authorities stated that a devotional cross had once formed the complete erection thereon, of which the present relic was but the stump; others that the stone as it stood was entire, and that it had been fixed there to mark a boundary or place of meeting. Anyhow, whatever the origin of the relic, there was and is something sinister, or solemn, according to mood, in the scene amid which it stands; something tending to impress the most phlegmatic passer-by (250).

Like a blank tombstone or a broken funereal monument, Cross-in-Hand is all that remains of the record of some significant event. It may mark the site, as Hardy puts it laconically in the first passage, of a "miracle, or murder, or both." And when is a murder a miracle? When, in René Girard's version of the originary event, the murder of the first victim "miraculously" ends the mimetic crisis of the community, restores peace, and establishes, in the body of the victim, the category of the sacred and the "transcendental signifier" upon which religion, myth, and ritual, and the forms of secular culture are subsequently based.[5] Hardy was a prescient anticipator of Girard's theory of hominization. But it doesn't take too much imagination to link standing stones and ring monuments with sacrificial ritual: the circular configuration of the sites already suggests the all-against-one set-up of an immolatory rite, and burnt human bones had been excavated at prehistoric monuments since the sixteenth century.[6] Hardy also offers the alternate possibility that Cross-in-Hand may be insignificant — that it's nothing more than a disused fencepost or place marker, around which ghoulish legends have grown up.

The likelihood of the monument's ultimate insignificance, though, is undercut by Hardy's conclusion that despite its origin, Cross-in-Hand makes the spot it occupies ambiguously impressive: it's solemn or sinister, depending on the mood of the observer. No doubt this effect may be attributed to the feature that gives the pillar part of its name: the hand that's "roughly carved" into it. That detail brings together Dickens's hand of truth and Wordsworth's ambiguous ostensive poetics: the crude upright stone, carried to its present spot from else-where ("a strange rude monolith, from a stratum unknown in any local quarry") stands silent as the grave, withholding its story; and blazoned on its surface, with the power of a reproach, the familiar shape of the human hand, implicating the passer-by in whatever crime or glory that monument commemorates. And, again, like the effaced tombstones and magnificent Neolithic standing-stone monuments it evokes, Cross-in-Hand puts passers-by necessarily in mind of the transition from nature to culture. As relatively crude and unfinished, and fur-nished with only a pictorial, rather than a written representation, Cross-in-Hand casts us mentally back in time, to the days before letters, when representation was fresh and immediate. The pillar may be, therefore, a kind of time capsule from the originary event, and by analyzing it we may be able to infer from its shape and features the pristine characteristics of humanity as it made the leap from the state of nature to culture.

Though one of many such time-capsule monuments that appear in roman-tic literature, Cross-in-Hand is a particularly powerful symbol of the transition from nature to culture because the hand carved on the pillar evokes the aborted gesture of appropriation. But why does this monument, and not some other, play so central a role in *Tess of the D'Urbervilles?* During the course of the novel, other monuments appear — at one point, in an obvious instance of foreshadowing, Tess's sleepwalking husband even deposits her in a stone sarcophagus. Why isn't an empty coffin the reigning symbol of the novel? Why Cross-in-Hand?

Cross-in-Hand plays the central symbolic role in this novel because Hardy's overarching theme in *Tess* is nature and culture, particularly transitions or stages in cultural evolution. He shows this by patterning Tess's life as a one-woman march through the history of human economic activity. At the beginning of the story, Tess is a gatherer: she is taking beehives to market when she accidentally kills the family horse, and her first job she takes to try to restore this loss is tending Mrs. D'Urberville's fowls. From there she moves to agriculture, work-ing briefly as a corn-reaper before beginning her pastoral stage as a milkmaid at Crick's dairy, where she meets Angel. After their split Tess returns to corn-reaping, which, since her first stint in the fields, has begun to be taken over by mechanization. From gathering to rudimentary agriculture to the pastoral to mechanized farming — and then Tess walks past Cross-in-Hand and finally ends her days at the heathen temple of Stonehenge. From the standpoint of pa-leoanthropology, Tess's life takes a circular course: from the beginning, through the various stages of primordial cultural development, and then back to the beginning. As an individual, Tess may throb with what her creator called "the ache of modernism" (99); but her fate, and the pains Hardy takes to make the path of her life's course intersect with Cross-in-Hand show that he wants her to be emblematic of the human species, which — no matter how far on this globe it travels — remains tethered by unbreakable bonds to its origins. If in our journeys here and there we are inclined to forget this fact, we need only look around, for the landscape is replete with monuments like Stonehenge and Cross-in-Hand that possess the power to remind us of our common origin in a mysterious, but ultimately conceivable, and somehow strangely familiar event.

IV. Conclusion

The eras of esthetic history may be differentiated by the moments of the originary scene around which they orient themselves. Classicism and neo-classicism, which evolve from primordial sacred rites, hearken back to the sparagmos moment of the originary event, in which the central object is ritually divided among the peripheral participants. Romanticism, as I have suggested, draws back to an earlier moment of the scene, to the moment of the aborted gesture of appropriation, the very instant when appetite transforms into desire, when body posture becomes semiotics — when, in short, nature becomes culture. As the examples from Wordsworth, Dickens, and Hardy illustrate, this shift in focus, rather than diminishing literature's referential possibilities, opened up new realms of experience — inward, personal experience, as well as primitive and prehistoric experience — that could be incorporated into the greater project of human self-understanding.

But a danger lurks in the romantic tendency to isolate, and mentally draw out, the exquisite intensity of the aborted gesture of appropriation. It's all too easy to be carried away by the delicious indeterminacy and emotional transport of that moment of the originary event to a Nietzschean dismissal of the need for words at all: "That for which we find words is something already dead in our hearts." What carried romantics away in this direction was the promise of individual inviolability that originary intensity and ambiguity seemed to hold. If my thoughts are incommunicable and perhaps even inaccessible to me, then my autonomy is virtually absolute — there can never be any danger of anyone else imitating, and therefore appropriating, my inner being. In an age that placed as high a value on individuality and originality as the romantic era did, such guarantees of autonomy carry an obvious reward. But one pays a high price to attain this radical individuality. As Wordsworth and Hardy particularly demonstrate, greater intensity means greater ambiguity, so seeking intensity means running the risk of being forgotten, as Lucy is "unknown" in both life and death, and the original significance of Cross-in-Hand is lost amid a welter of competing legends, mysteries, and speculations. Or, to put it another way, there is always a trade off between intensity and ambiguity. On the one hand, intensity is delectable — as in John Keats's "Ode on a Grecian Urn," where a "bold lover" stands poised for eternity at the moment of sweetest anticipation:

> never, never canst thou kiss,
> Though winning near the goal — yet, do not grieve;
> She cannot fade, though thou hast not thy bliss,
> For ever wilt thou love, and she be fair!

But intensity's necessary concomitant, ambiguity, also appears on Keats's urn, though with the opposite emotional coloring:

> Who are these coming to the sacrifice?
> To what green altar, O mysterious priest,
> Lead'st thou that heifer lowing at the skies,
> And all her silken flanks with garlands drest?
> What little town by river or sea shore
> Or mountain-built with peaceful citadel,
> Is emptied of this folk, this pious morn?
> And, little town, thy streets for evermore
> Will silent be; and not a soul to tell
> Why thou art desolate, can e'er return (282–283).

Keats offers a revealing alternate take on intensity and ambiguity, especially as these twinned concepts appear in Wordsworth and Hardy. Like Lucy's mossy stone, Cross-in-Hand, and Stonehenge, the town on the Grecian urn presents a poetically intriguing mystery — what town is this? Why is it empty? And, again, because the urn is ancient, its ambiguity takes on anthropological overtones. But Keats emphasizes a dimension of this scene that Wordsworth and Hardy gloss over: the little town will for evermore be silent, and therefore desolate, because the urn is ostensive, and therefore *cannot tell its story*. The ostensive nature of ambiguous objects confers distinct advantages on romantics like Wordsworth and Hardy, who seize on ambiguity's having emptied history and narrative from monuments and ostensive objects in order to make those objects into receptacles for their own being. If the real story of Lucy's stone is lost, what's standing in the way of that object symbolizing the poet's own feelings of confusion, loss, or desolation? John Ruskin called the tendency of poets to see their feelings reflected in objects and natural processes going on outside of them "the pathetic fallacy."[7] From the standpoint of the originary hypothesis, though, we might call this tendency of writers to locate their thoughts and feelings in inanimate objects the *originary romance*. The key feature of the originary romance is its postulation that the most authentic self is *wordless* — that is, the truest self is that which was just about to, but did not yet, utter the first word. (This is what makes the originary romance a *romance* — it imagines that a fully formed linguistic consciousness was present in the participants in the originary event before the emission of the first linguistic sign.) The originary romance comes in optimistic and pessimistic versions. Its positive face is the Wordsworthian child-man/priest of nature, to whom, as he put it in *The Prelude*, "the earth / And common face of Nature spake to me / Rememberable things" (132). Its negative manifestation is the Matthew Arnold-Hardy-Nietzsche tragic loneliness, in which words are inevitably emptied of reliable links to their original referents, and everyone is condemned to live a buried life.

Whether one returns to the "mute insensate things" of Wordsworth's nature or the bleak impenetrability that Arnold, Hardy, and Nietzsche see lurking beneath all language and thought, there is no exit from the originary romance, unless we follow the loquacious Victorian Charles Dickens, whose walk through the originary scene leads to a conclusion that anticipates one of the central insights of generative anthropology: the advantage that declarative volubility possesses as a means of ethical and cultural development over the romance of ostensive intensity and ambiguity. Confronted with the Ghost's insistent gesture, Scrooge keeps talking, refuses to give in to that gesture's ostensive closure, clasps the "spectral hand" in his struggle to try to "sponge away the writing on this stone." Scrooge's victory over the Ghost is neither easy nor assured, because even for a mid-Victorian sensibility like Dickens's, the originary romance exerts a powerful attraction. It holds the potential for the over-the-top self-pitying histrionics that has made Ebenezer Scrooge a prized "actor's role" in stage and film adaptations of *A Christmas Carol* for over a century and a half. But the price of forgetfulness that Scrooge — and, presumably, Dickens, identifying with his character — must pay for the histrionic intensity is just too high, so Scrooge keeps pleading, and in so doing talks himself into something approaching an originary understanding of how language operates. "I will honour Christmas in my heart, and try to keep it all the year," declares Scrooge. "I will live in the Past, the Present, and the Future. The Spirits of all Three shall strive within me. I will not shut out the lessons that they teach." In other words, instead of mutely remaining in the ostensive present, tied in an intense wordless trance to the object before him, Scrooge will employ the cognitive suppleness of the declarative linguistic form, which allows the language user to transcend the here and now, to apply the lessons of the past to the present and to project from the present into the future. By definition, such projections are not possible within the gesturally-circumscribed world of the ostensive. With the advent of the declarative sentence, however, moral reflection does become possible, because only through the declarative can one speak meaningfully about things that are not physically present. The declarative first arises out of the negation of an imperative: when someone asks for a hammer, for instance, and no hammer is available, the interlocutee offers a subject-predicate sentence ("hammer is not") instead.[8] Simple sentences establish the pattern for increasingly complex noun phrases, eventually leading to the development of concepts; but the underlying pattern of substituting signs for absent things remains. Confronted with a mute monument, Scrooge responds with what Wordsworth's and Hardy's monuments do not provide: a story — that is, "the Past, the Present, and the Future."

In the end, Scrooge's unwillingness to rest content in the hope that some poet might come along, someday, to ponder the meaning of his neglected monument reveals a split in how romanticism valued the aborted gesture of appropriation in the originary scene. For Wordsworth and Hardy, the originary event was about muteness and regression to the threshold of nature and culture. It was an opportunity to exercise the imagination, to experience some of the most intense feelings of which humans are capable, and to hypothesize about the origins of signification. The scene of origin was all these things for Dickens, too — but unlike his more poetic counterparts, Dickens saw that the price paid for originary intensity was ethical stasis; and as a self-styled liberal and public intellectual, committed to putting his art toward the improvement of society, Dickens found he could ill afford to indulge his taste for the originary romance. As Eric Gans has observed, in the romantic era the sacred center was relocated inside of the individual, giving ethics and morality the unprecedentedly subjective cast they retain to this day. But even within the framework of that era-defining internalization of the sacred center, the differing values placed by Wordsworth, Hardy, and Dickens on the aborted gesture of appropriation demonstrate that romanticism encompassed widely divergent understandings of the scene on which that sacred center was constituted. Primitivist romantics like Hardy and Wordsworth contend with progressive or cosmopolitan romantics like Dickens. All three, however, are united in their quest to anchor their visions of humanity in an ancient scene in which something significant was designated by an unforgettable gesture.

Notes

1. See *The Origin of Language* 286-298, *The End of Culture* 150-158, 227-247, and *Science and Faith* 32-47.

2. Percy's *Reliques* were mostly bona fide rural ballads, though silently corrected and occasionally amended by him; the poems of Ossian, though purported to have been translated by Macpherson from third-century Celtic manuscripts, were later revealed as having been composed by Macpherson. See my "Wordsworthian Song-catching in America," *Anthropoetics* 11, 2

<www.anthropoetics.ucla.edu/ap1102/words05.htm.>

3. See Peter Denman, "Krook's Death and Dickens's Authorities," *The Dickensian* 82:3, 130-141.

4. Dave Sands' Thomas Hardy web site posts photos of Cross-in-Hand, as well as the text of Hardy's poem "The Lost Pyx," which recounts a medieval legend of the monument's origin. For a photograph, go to

<www.thomashardy.co.uk/images/Cross_in_hand.jpg.>

5. This brief summary of Girard's theory of appropriative mimesis, the origin of language, and the process of hominization is largely drawn from *Violence and the Sacred* (Johns Hopkins UP, 1977), chapters 2, 4, and 11 and *Things Hidden Since the Foundation of the World* (Stanford UP, 1987), book I, chapters 1-4.

6. See my "'Wrung by sweet enforcement': Druid Stones and the Problem of Sacrifice in British Romanticism," *Anthropoetics* 2, 2

<www.anthropoetics.ucla.edu/ap0202/keats.htm.>

7. See "Of the Pathetic Fallacy," reprinted in *Critical Theory Since Plato*, ed. Hazard Adams (San Diego: Harcourt, 1971), 616-623.

8. See *The Origin of Language*, 107-125 and 169-175.

Works Cited

Arnold, Matthew. *The Poems of Matthew Arnold, 1849-1864.* Oxford: Oxford UP, 1909.

Dickens, Charles. *A Christmas Carol.* New York: Dover, 1991.

———. *Oliver Twist.* New York: Book-of-the-Month-Club, 1997.

Gans, Eric. *The End of Culture.* Berkeley: U of California Press, 1985

———. *Originary Thinking.* Stanford: Stanford UP, 1993.

———. *The Origin of Language.* Berkeley: U of California Press, 1981.

———. *Science and Faith: The Anthropology of Revelation.* Savage, MD: Rowman and Littlefield: 1990.

Gray, Thomas, "Elegy Written in a Country Church-Yard," in *Eighteenth-Century English Literature.* Ed. Geoffrey Tillotson, Paul Fussell, and Marshall Waingrow. New York: Harcourt, 1969.

Hardy, Thomas. *Tess of the D'Urbervilles.* New York: Dover, 2001.

Keats, John, "Ode on a Grecian Urn," in *Complete Poems.* Ed. Jack Stillinger. Cambridge, Mass.: Harvard UP, 1982.

Wordsworth, William. *Poetical Works.* Boston: Houghton-Mifflin, 1982.

What is the Human?
Eric Gans and the Structure of the Hypothesis

Chris Fleming and John O'Carroll

Language is the house of Being. In its home man dwells.
— Martin Heidegger (217)

No-one really *knows* anything about the origin of language.
— Anthony Kenny (91)

Generative Anthropology, the Humanities, and the Human

If Heidegger was correct in his identification of language as the "house of Being" — and few have contested it — then how are we to reconcile this with Anthony Kenny's claim — that we know nothing of its origin?[1] Despite the analytic tension, the pairing of these claims is not atypical. Indeed, in some instances, the emphasis on the centrality of language to human being is *combined* with the assertion that not only do we know nothing of language's origin, but also, such knowledge is, in principle, unattainable. Jacques Lacan, for instance, told us that "the unconscious is structured like a language" (220), even as he also assured us that speculation on the origin of language was "absolutely impossible" (5). Regardless of the force of such proscriptions — and we have good reasons to doubt them (cf. Fleming 71–2) — Lacan's caution concerns a domain of inquiry which offers no shortage of cautionary tales.[2] In some ways, little appears to have changed since the Linguistic Society of Paris published an edict in 1866 banning the topic from discussion at their meetings. It is difficult to know, therefore, if thinkers like Eric Gans who injudiciously wade into these fraught theoretical waters are to be commended for their bravery or chastised for their naïveté. So unaccustomed are we to the kind of thinking typified by his work on language and culture that we need to do more than reach preemptory assessments of its merit — we need, first, to look at what kind of theoretical activity his "generative anthropology" actually *is*.

First things first: let us look at the name, generative anthropology. It is *anthropology* because it concerns, above all, human being. But why a *generative* anthropology? The word "generative" implies both the question of generation (processes and orders of generation) and of genesis (the origin of things). In this respect, we say, Gans deploys an approach that uses the resources of the present to generate hypotheses about the origin of ethics, language, and ultimately of the human as such. He does this by surveying the present and generating an *a posteriori* reconstruction of its origin. Unlike Foucault's version of the "history of the present," Gans' work is not empirically historical in the straightforward sense of the term, seeking instead to work analytically with as small an empirical footprint as possible.

It is our contention — and the contention, no doubt, of other thinkers in this volume — that his work offers profound new insights into what it means to be a humanities scholar, especially in how it furthers the horizons of what such scholarship can legitimately claim as its terrain. In this chapter, we explore aspects of the single most important innovation Gans has developed: the constitution of a new form of hypothetical inquiry in the humanities, affording for the first time, a variety of knowledge that goes beyond traditional notions of critique and interpretation.

GA: A Brief Orientation to a Mode of Thought

It has certainly been a remarkable journey from his earliest works on literature, through his *Origin of Language* (1981), *End of Culture* (1985), *Originary Thinking* (1993), and *Signs of Paradox* (1997). Early in the first of the above works, Gans wrote, *"Humanity is the species for which the central problem of survival is posed by the relations within the species itself rather than those with the external world.* Humanity is the species that is its own chief problem" (Gans 1993:2). To humanities scholars, such a claim appears stark and uncompromising. Surely, they might protest, we are faced with far greater dangers. What, after all, could be supplied as evidence for such a claim? And if it were upheld, would it be so in a way that fitted humanities-type studies, rather than some other discipline (say statistics or meteorology)? Put simply, the humanities scholar can ask, with some reason in the first instance, what does such a claim say about us as *humans*?

The last of the above questions supplies a route to understanding: all round us is the evidence to support Gans' claim. Humanity alone, with its elaborate laws and taboos, its signs and languages, its self-awareness of its self-awareness, is not just unique for these things, but their very existence is evidence of what culture does, what language, by its deferral of conflict, actively and actually maintains. The evidence is, as we shall see, abundant, but it is not evidence of the usual historico-empirical kind. It is, on the contrary, enmeshed in the work of a powerful variety of hypothesizing. This work leads Gans to argue that the humanities can and should entail reflection on the human condition, and that indeed, the very act of reflection is *itself* a definable part of what it means to be human.

Part of the challenge of Gans's work lies in the fact it is often extremely abstract. Very few other authors demand that the reader follow him from the poetics of the French novel to the intricacies of set-theoretic paradoxes and speech-act theory. The material is difficult, no doubt, but Gans shows little interest in stylistic pyrotechnics or neo-baroque affectation; if anything, his writing is almost forensic in its dissections and its propositional advances emphatically parsimonious. So part of the difficulty in coming to terms with his work relates to the intellectual demands he places on his reader in terms of the matter of fact statement of his argument. The reader wonders: Is it philosophy? (Well, yes, but it tries to think conceptuality itself by situating it in the context of a hypothetical event.) Is it physical anthropology? (Not quite; it operates in ways cognizant of this discipline, but sees its analytical brief as lying elsewhere.) A new type of science, perhaps? (Maybe, but the empiricism is slight and the appeal to explanatory economy is equally ethically as epistemologically predicated.) Then it's cultural anthropology? (To a certain extent, but it isn't simply content to allow structuality itself to be thought as a metaphysical absolute.) Well then, it must be poetry. (At least, that is clear: no.)

So, what is it then? Let us make a few orienting remarks. First, his form of the hypothesis is striking for the fact that it is concrete. Second, it is based on evidence around us today. The Gansian hypothesis is ventured as a form of heuristic speculation. If this seems to fly in the face of usual intellectual practice, his hypothesizing leads gradually to definitional clarity. In this way, he develops hypotheses of origin based on signal aspects (ethics, language, aesthetics etc.) of the human that are observable today. Third, like Girard, Gans argues a mimetic view of the world which has an always potentially appropriative quality. This inflects his argument concerning the foundation of the human (in the deferral of violence by the rise of the sign) as well as in his ideas about exchange and modernity. Fourth (unlike Girard who has no originary scene since his theory is predicated on a mechanism), for Gans, the origin of language, and the human, has an *event character*.

So when — to return to the lines we cited earlier — Gans says that humanity is the species that "is its own chief problem," he does so in a sense that is quasi-definitional. That is, at stake in the observation are two distinct senses, the first and obvious one being biological survival. That is what appears to most people when reading the claim. But surely there is another sense too: it is existential /

intellectual perplexity and *ennui*. In both respects, the greatest danger to our existence is intra-specific conflict or problems attendant upon human sociality. Even so-called "environmental" problems are largely human-generated; and even here, "the human" doesn't threaten "nature" (which is able to go on without human horizons). We have no desire to deride the force of objects; presumably, an ethical relation to others will not avert the probable heat-death of the universe; such a heat-death would be as much about meaning as it is about molecules. It raises questions regarding human finitude and (perhaps) the "meaning" of human existence.

The Gansian inquiry into the human calls attention both to the character of the hypothesis and the mode of hypothesizing itself. In fact, as we explore the hypothesis further, we find the method and the findings inseparable. We have so far been commenting on the hypothesis as if it were a single and simple entity. But the Gansian hypothesis is not monumental in character, and is describable in parts, and this is precisely how we mean to conduct our analysis of Gans' work in this chapter. The parts we have identified fall into two groups, one of which concerns the content of what is postulated, the other concerns how the hypotheses are developed. We do not elaborate all of them the same way (the last two are, for instance, explored in more detail than the others), but we list them and then make systematic observations on all of them so that our analysis afterwards can proceed from the clearest possible basis.

In an earlier essay on this aspect of Gans' work published in *Anthropoetics*, we offered a detailed sketch of the appurtenances of Gans' work with other approaches — the work of Girard of course, but also of Levi-Strauss in anthropology, the critique of this by Jacques Derrida, the work of Edmund Husserl on the transcendental reduction in phenomenology (Fleming & O'Carroll 2002/2003). We do not intend to duplicate that inquiry. Neither can we analyze the relationship between Gans' ideas and the works of René Girard. In brief, we would argue that Girard's crucial insight into the operations of mimesis and sacrifice in all human societies *allowed* Gans to develop his ideas beyond the field of literary culture in the direction of a general anthropology that is broadly compatible with, but distinct from, Girard's fundamental anthropology.[3] Instead of writing about the relationship of Gans's work to other writers, we wish to place the Gansian hypothesis itself in the broader context of thought about varieties of hypothesis, to situate it as precisely as we can so as to better understand its value. In saying this, we find that his variety of *a posteriori* reasoning demands a new place in the humanities, and indeed in terms of thought about hypotheses themselves.

A Synopsis of the Gansian Hypothesis

In our view, the hypothesis, as deployed by Gans, can be described by a number of its aspects. These fall into two related groups. The first group treats the nature of the world to be explained (1–4). It is logically prior to the second group, which concerns the formal properties of the hypothesis (5–10).

1)   The human world is, and was at the point of its origin, actively and appropriatively mimetic.

2)   The origin is characterized by an event structure. The human must have come into being as event; human self-consciousness (of consciousness) cannot emerge other than in an event.

3)   If the world came into human being as an event of origin, then it was also scenic, in that there must have been at least two appropriative players, and by implication a third pluralizing circle of onlookers, *somewhere.*

4)   Because language and the human arose in this way, and because origins of all formations arise in this way, they are tellable (knowledge has, in this sense at least, a narrative structure).

5)   Given all four of the above, we can work *a posteriori* from evidence derived from the nature of the human today to tell us about the origin of the human horizon.

6)   The hypothesis will have a number of levels of originariness, all derived as above. This explains the paradox that some levels are more originary than others, with the founding of language and the human the most originary of all.

7)   The hypothesis is concrete and positive (without being positivistic).

8)   The hypothesis is provisional.

9)   The hypothesis should take a form of minimal expression. That is, a) it entails a communicational ethics akin to Ockam's Razor in which the most parsimonious explanation is the best and b) it should leave the smallest empirical footprint possible, to support the claim of the rise of the human

10)   The hypothesis should be minimal in another sense too: it should work by treating *aporiae* not on their own terms, but by finding the minimal common ground to both.

We trace these aspects of the hypothesis in a way that reflects the decisive contribution of Gans' approach. We do this, first by elaborating the hypotheses themselves. After this, we look at four fields: 1) looking at the power of minimality; 2) looking at how Gans supplants the traditional TV-white-lab-coat explanations of the origin of language that have taken hold in the 150 year absence of the humanities from the field of inquiry; 3) how the Gansian hypothesis can be considered in the history of hypothesizing since the time of Bayes' Theorem;

4) how the work promises to reinvigorate studies in the humanities by looking at his treatment of language itself.

Mimesis and Narration: the First Group

We begin with the first group of aspects of the hypothesis. We have outlined these separately, and will to an extent respect our conceptual map, but we regard this group of aspects as interlinkable in useful ways too. The first group of aspects of the hypothesis reveals Gans' ingenuity in his handling of the issue of human genesis. They remind us of the potential profundity of the humanities, especially in its derivation and analysis of deep intuitions about the origins of humanity, language, and culture. Even on their own terms, they stand as valuable and distinguishable co-hypotheses, able to be assessed and used in the analysis of culture. Not least of their strength lies in the way the ground for conceiving them has been developed (here we invoke the second six, which allows the first to exist cogently as after-the-fact observations on the origin): the first four are *observable today, and speak to culture today.* Let us begin with them, in a logical order.

1. The hypothesis of the origin of the human concerns the mimetic nature of human behaviour. This is a Girardian claim. For Girard, mimesis is active, not just a matter of representation. In the *Origin of Language*, Gans offers one of the few really important critiques of Girard, after a careful summary of the philosophical basis of his argument, phrased in philosophical terms (11–13) contends that Girard has not paid enough attention to the fact that the corpse of the murdered scapegoat is *already significant* (19–20). Of a moment of human crisis, he writes in *Originary Thinking,*

> the strength of the appetitive drive has been increased by appetitive mimesis, the propensity to imitate one's fellows in their choice of an object of appropriation, to such a point that the ["natural" or "animal"] dominance hierarchy can no longer counteract the symmetry of the situation. Mimesis is the fundamental means of learning at every level of the animal kingdom…. Mimesis is the basis of higher intelligence. (8)

For Gans, as for Girard, mimesis is essential to any understanding of the point of origin.

2. As soon, as talk of a point of origin, however, we are hypothesizing an *event*. This origin is "empirically" necessary (1993: 4), and there *are* things we can say about it. Arguing from the evidence about us of the human in everyday purposiveness, Gans remarks at one point that the rival quasi-hypothesis, the

"always already" so dominant since the time of Heidegger, to the extent that it proposes a view at all would have it that an origin somehow did not occur because of paradoxes inherent to action, language and representation. But for Gans, this work actually *helps to identify* what he calls the "founding paradox" of the original scene of representation itself (1997: 7–8). We might put it like this: Gans is not an enemy of paradox *per se*; on the contrary, they often reveal deeper originary dimensions. In this case, Gans sees the origin of representation in terms of the deferral of violence. The repeated discovery (especially by Jacques Derrida) of deferral as an ineliminable aspect of representation (*différance*, and aspects of deconstruction too) far from undoing Gans' version of origins, actually provides evidential support for it. In this respect, the scholarship of Girard is also foundational. Gans puts it like this:

> We owe to René Girard the insight that only the construction of what I shall here call a "transcendental hypothesis" can provide a meaningful ontology — which is at the same time a meaningful epistemology — for the social sciences.... The social or human sciences have the peculiarity of dealing with material that is of the same representational form as the discourse of the sciences themselves. (1981: 4)

Of course, Girard *never put it this way himself.* What is essentially Gansian in this is the process and protocol of formulation of the (up until this point) Girardian project of anthropological inquiry. So the first feature is that the content of the hypothesis concerns the origin of representation, an origin seen as part and parcel of the human itself.

3. Representation is scenic. This aspect arises from the three previous aspects and can be derived from them: the scene is to be construed, if the event itself happens as part of something in which there are players, and it will be retold. The example of mimetic appropriative desire is often given:

> We may conceive the originary event as follows: a circle of protohumans, possibly after a successful hunt, surround an appetitively attractive object, for example, the body of a large animal.... But at the moment of crisis, the strength of the appetitive drive has been increased by appetitive mimesis, the propensity to imitate one's fellows in their choice of an object of appropriation...in violation of the dominance hierarchy, all hands reach out for the object, but at the same time, each is deterred from appropriating it by the sight of all the others reaching in the same direction.... The centre of the circle appears to possess a

repellent, sacred force that prevents its occupation by the members of the group, that converts appropriation into a gesture of designation, that is, into an ostensive sign. (Gans 1993: 7–9)

In this passage, part of which we cited earlier, Gans *recreates* the essential scene on which the originary event is staged.

4. Because the hypothesis postulates the event-character of the origin of representation, it summons a *narrative* form (1993: 10). This is not narrative in quite the sense proposed by Lyotard (1977) — the notion that science is reduced to mere story — but rather, the eventness of the origin means it has to be re-narrated, since that is how events have traditionally been construed (and represented). (It is not a meta-narrative in Lyotard's sense primarily because it is only tangentially meta-theoretical. Lyotard's "meta" signifies a level of explanation not merely the "size" of a story (theoretical or otherwise): a meta-narrative is necessarily a metadiscourse which concerns itself primarily with a first-level discourse — usually theoretical — and not "the world." Like Girard's fundamental anthropology, Gans's originary anthropology is certainly a *mega*narrative, minimally expressed, but it is not primarily metanarrative, as it theorizes theory only in the context of its theorization of representation and the evolution of linguistic forms.)

The Second (Formal Properties) Group of Aspects of the Hypothesis

The aspects of the hypothesis that we have looked at so far could not function as formal knowledge were it not for some justification of the possibility of working with a shared horizon of the human. The most important support for this overt claim lies in the idea that we can deploy *a posteriori* reasoning in this field. We now turn to the formal features of the hypothesis, starting with this, the most important of the six, concerning this kind of evidence.

5. The hypothesis is not to be arrived at in the usual "prior" way characteristic of those sciences which can both repeat and retest. On the contrary, the hypothesis is construed *a posteriori*. In some of its derivative forms, the narrative structures of particular cultures can be an aid to analysis. But for the founding hypothesis, the *a posteriori* reasoning has an almost apodictic quality: first, of course, does the hypothesis accord with what we see today, and what we can structurally determine about what it is to be human, but then and above all, *what is the chain of events which we can reconstruct with reasonable certainty that must have happened* for us to become us, human.

6. The sixth aspect emerges from the fifth. It concerns the fact that there is a distinction between the originary hypothesis in the case of the human and other hypotheses in the sciences. The originary hypothesis concerns representation in general, and language in particular, but its own resources are also of this kind. The apparent paradox leads Gans to remark repeatedly that (to take one such moment) "its verification can never become an established fact, but only a heuristic probability" (1981: 6). Paradoxically, some of the less originary hypotheses, as for instance are to be found in the discussions of the history of Western civilization in *The Origin of Language*, have stronger empirical support, precisely because corroborating accounts *do* exist of moments of origin. As we will see later, these "secondary hypotheses" are important in their own right.

7. The hypothesis is concrete and positive. That is to say, it is a substantive claim. It is also a first order claim, by which we mean (for instance) that it does not just concern theory (although it does concern that too).

8. The hypothesis is provisional and as we have argued elsewhere, vulnerable. This is precisely because it makes a particular concrete claim about an actual issue (7), but it does so as a heuristic (1981: 6; 1997: 6). Because it addresses itself to a specifiable problem or set of problems, it is also to be distinguished in a formal sense from a hermeneutic (which *could* be a purely theoretical reading of any natural or human situation). Occurring within the field it projects — originary analysis — it allows dialogue to occur. This approach makes of the entire field a collaborative prospect. The hypothesis can be modified in light of subsequent findings, can be regularized with other fields, and is a work in progress. (The hypothesis is also only "his" in the nominal sense; it possesses an objective thought content that can be taken up by others for modification, extension, qualification, or critique.) We note briefly that the merits of this approach far outweigh its prevailing alternative in cultural studies: this is the notion that because something cannot be said with certainty that somehow *nothing* at all can or should (for it often has a moral aspect) be said.

9. The hypothesis can be formed in a number of ways, but in its forms of statement it shall be parsimonious. Parsimony, in Gans' eyes, has its own merit. It involves stating only that which is essential. This is closely linked to its minimality (10).

10. The hypothesis is not just parsimonious (9), but also, it is minimal. This means it will search for the common ground of apparently opposed positions. We can usefully relate this to the work of Jacques Derrida (see below).

Minimality

We now wish to elaborate further on some of what we have detailed. Anyone who wishes to make sense of Gans' work needs to deal with the issues of minimality (aspect 9) and parsimoniousness (10), which although conceivable separately, make best sense treated together. On the one hand, then, the hypothesis will entail a communicative ethics of parsimonious expression. On the other, it will seek to minimize differences between positions in order to understand what is essential to them. These two orders of minimality are linked, but we can usefully make sense of them by establishing philosophical provenance for both.

From the very outset of philosophical inquiry, we can point to the value ascribed to felicitous and parsimonious expression of philosophical ideas. For Plato, to be sure, such expression had to do with the fact that he was trying to describe an ideal world of perfect, mystically Pythagorean, forms. But Aristotle, in his practice, was also minimal (witness his *Logic*), and by the time this tradition had been absorbed into Western thought, we find from the tradition of William of Ockham onwards, a value ascribed to miminal expression of philosophical positions. Is there anything to justify this?

Gans certainly thinks so. He argues it in philosophical terms, and we will look at that in a moment. But it has an obvious communicational dimension too. For instance, Gans recognizes, but minimizes the gap between positions that entail belief and those that don't. That is he bridges "religious" and "secular" positions. It is not just a matter of seeing them as nonpertinent to the discussion. For instance, to the question does God invent the human (religion) or did the human invent God (secular) he will see only common ground in the question, not a diametrically opposed view of reality. Indeed, to Gans it is not more — or less (as we will see soon) — of a question than whether he "invented" or "discovered" the origin of language.

Gans seems to see parsimony and minimality as having intrinsic philosophical value (for instance, 1993: 2; 1997: 6). In *Signs of Paradox*, he sees the fact that it has a small empirical footprint as providing the maximum space for a dialogue about the genesis of the human: all we need to agree on is that there *was*, indeed, an origin (6). It establishes, indeed, for any field the possibility of "universal" dialogue (6). This gives the clue as to why, for instance, he criticizes Freud's *Totem and Taboo* not for being wrong or implausible, but for displaying "naturalism...incompatible with minimalist rigor" (1997: 18). Psychology claims to describe all humanity, but because it mixes naturalistic detail into its grounding, it slides into particularity and ethno-specificity.

Gans' attack on psychoanalysis mirrors an earlier attack on the discipline for precisely the same reason. Edmund Husserl saw it as a highly derivative field, precisely because it had not done the work of clarifying and distilling its claims. In fact, both Husserl and Derrida have written critiques of psychology, though from different points of view (Derrida was more interested in the attempt by Freud to "legate" and control the field). And the links between the reduction in Husserl and Derrida's language of the "most irreducible" are obvious, though not well known. Deconstruction, it is true, does at times turn the methods of Husserlian reduction onto phenomenology itself, but this seems to have blinded commentators to the fact that of all the approaches and methods Derrida analysed, only the Husserlian reduction is discernible everywhere in his work. Gans has never himself commented on this aspect of minimality, although Girard has noted its importance in his work when he wrote of his ambition for a "transcendental anthropology" that he meant this word in the Husserlian sense (15).

Derrida is cited by Gans, often in apparent frustration, as he — very correctly — points out that a project in the vein of his *Of Grammatology* does not require the abandonment of inquiry into the origin of the human, but a restatement of the status of such inquiry. Derrida's approach to deconstruction also highlights what both he and Gans gained from Husserl: an ability and a value in finding in apparently opposed positions, a profounder shared ground. In Derrida, deconstruction at this point tends towards a pragmatics: find the shared ground, reverse the field, and displace the hierarchy of subordination (*Positions* 1981, *Margins of Philosophy*). But the approach holds validity in other forms too: the very act of revelation of a shared ground takes us to a more originary position. The working practice of Derrida and Husserl, are in this respect, almost identical. Girard and Gans, in identifying the power of such an approach, have in their very different ways, established an entire field of inquiry. And as for those who think that all inquiry into origins is proscribed, Gans remarks of them that "When they have deconstructed the categories of human thought down to their founding paradox, they think they have found our thinking's fatal weakness, when in fact they have arrived at the source of its strength" (1997: 7–8).

At this point, we come very close to what characterizes Gans' work alone. For Gans, it seems that minimality has a "truth" of its own. Less is, indeed, more for Gans, and in a number of ways. In one this regard, communicative efficacy has an ethical value of its own, in furnishing the conditions of a universal dialogue for the grounding of the human. It provides also an economy of expression arising from superior expression of the ground and nature of the human. But above and beyond all, it leads to a special kind of accuracy of statement. Now one might imagine that in saying this that Gans risks an enlarged empirical requirement: a date, for instance for the origin of the world. But generative anthropology is not like that; it straddles science and the humanities, but does so in a way that minimizes the risk of empirical falsification. Let us look at this footprint.

First, the minimal kernel is, as Gans says of the origin of language, is that there *was* one (1997: 6). This is a *historical* precept. Gans postulates a first event in order to understand human culture — the species that lives in events, in memories, in history, in signs, and so on. Second, in some ways, generative anthropology offers a minimal definition of the human, a *structural* characterization. In this regard, one cannot "show" (empirically at least) that it isn't "like this." Instead, what is at stake is an attempt to capture ethical and cultural values — and if the inquiry does not take account of these, it is not in this regard at least, even examining the human. Finally — perhaps most obviously given that we discuss minimality — generative anthropology defends itself by seeking not to postulate things that are not necessary. In other words, those things not seen as basic are simply omitted from the originary scene. And — traveling the other way — because the phenomenon we seek to describe is the human, this is unitary in nature, and as a result everything that is essential to that phenomenon must be there.

To be sure, it is hard for Gans — or for us — to give a meta-level justification for his approach or for minimality because generative anthropology itself seeks to explain the emergence of thought (and later indeed, of philosophy). In this respect, generative anthropology might employ philosophical modes of argument, but it is also empirical in that the human is precisely the site where these things (like philosophy) are to be found. We might, at risk of being simplistic put it like this — logic is in a sense independent of human beings, but the animal which would invent logic is what requires understanding and analysis.

Situating the Hypothesis

We now wish to sketch something we think a very important area of research. That is, we now seek to *situate* the Gansian hypothesis in relation to other models of argument and hypothesizing. While there are many ways of characterizing the hypothesis in general — and the way we hypothesize on the human in particular — we wish to characterize Gans' work by schematically examining varieties of hypothesis in two groups. On the one hand, there is a longstanding tradition that hypotheses can be assigned reasonably accurate weights, on the basis of probability — whether in terms of hypothesis-preference in the work of Thomas Bayes or in terms of the covering law model proposed by Carl Hempel;

on the other, there is the quite discontinuous (but in our view ultimately prefer-able) tradition that devises a more socially grounded modeling of hypotheses (ranging from the critiques of Thomas Kuhn to the work of Imre Lakatos).

Bayes proceeds by assigning probabilities to the hypotheses themselves. These probablilities are based on evidential support for them. His model is called a "theorem" because it promises the logical formulation consisting of the hypotheses to be compared, the evidence being weighed, and the belief pattern of the investigator: all this gives rise to an answer about the probability of the hypothesis being correct.

In the same tradition, but seeking to address the issue of complexity in the scene of the event itself, Hempel's process of subsuming comparable pat-terns gives rise to the coving law model. This works by subsuming events in groups under a covering law that explains them all in terms of a set of initial conditions. In Hempel's work, we see the reach for an adequate description of broader conditions which correlate (rather than necessarily causing) events (cf. Von Wright 27–28). Equally, one would expect, as in the physical sciences, that true hypotheses of this kind should have predictive explanatory capacity, rather than merely interpretative understanding. Yet even in some domains of the sci-ences themselves, few would seek to require this test of the hypotheses generated (in the case of theoretical mathematicisations of space for instance, a hypothesis can be interesting just because of internal consistence and non-refutation by physical evidence). Gans himself rules out the possibility of demonstration of this kind (1993: viii).

So how does Gans sustain the claim that the things he proposes are indeed hypotheses? At the very outset, he offers a pattern of reasoning that looks like this:

> The hypothesis as such must remain in transcendental relation with the body of the theory, because its verification can never become an estab-lished fact, but only a heuristic probability. Its role is that of a transcen-dental signified to which the representations studied are made to refer through more or less complex sets of mediations. The theory can then be shown to itself refer back to the hypothetical origin, to constitute, in other words, merely the latest and presumably the most truthful of the representations that fall under its purview. (1981: 6)

This means that there is a kind of "testing" — not in terms of verification, but rather one in terms of probabilism (as in the first group of course), *and heuristics*. A to-and-from movement akin to a hermeneutic circle seems to be implied — the hypothesis is part of the explanatory structure, but so too is the evidence adduced from it.

This might look closer to the work of Thomas Kuhn. In a certain sense this is true, but Kuhn's work has more critical than explanatory usefulness — that is, Kuhn is only a path to another stronger variety of hypothesizing that takes account not just of the internal logic of research programs, but also, of the historical horizons of the research itself. To Kuhn, though, we can concede this insight: all knowledges, including scientific knowledges, have an ineliminable historical dimension. In his *Structure of Scientific Revolutions* (1962), he advanced the now-common thesis that there are no theory-independent "facts"; more significantly, Kuhn suggested that normative claims that take the shape of putative prerequisites for rational scientific work and change — like empirical fruitfulness and/or predictive power, internal coherence, elegance or minimality, conceptual generative capacity, and so on — are neither *necessary* nor *necessarily sufficient* to predict previously successful theories (and so, by implication, furnish criteria which would be able to direct current selection among rival scientific theories) (*RP* 92–116, esp. 99–100). But if we take his most tenable definitions of the paradigm seriously, Kuhn's account of the hypothesis is — despite his denials in afterwords and subsequent accounts — a variety of relativism. In our view, though, the problem lies less with the prospects for the hypothesis than with the way Kuhn frames his analysis. In other words, the force of his highly elastic notion of the paradigm lay less in it being an acceptable alternative to Bayes' theorem or Hempel's covering law, than in pointing out the problems and limits to these models of the hypothesis and of explanation in general.

If we consider Gans' work as a case in point, we can legitimately ask what, if anything, Kuhn's notion of the paradigm could tell us about it. This is especially true in the "social" sense of orthodoxy implied for what counts as knowledge. After all, in Kuhn's terms, Gans lies outside the mainstream of humanities' preoccupations and theories, where talk of origins of this kind is anathema. It is not that we could not adapt Kuhn's ideas, rather, it is that his model does not capture adequately the complexity of the very social world he sought to invoke in his own criticisms of the alternative models of knowledge.

In this respect, the work of Lakatos is highly suggestive. Lakatos was able to see that the critiques offered, first (more tentatively) by Popper, and then more decisively by Kuhn, had hit their intended targets and forced on the philosophical community the soundness of many of their shared conclusions. But how successful, Lakatos wondered, had Popper's and Kuhn's *reconstructive* efforts been? Lakatos takes as his task a serious reflection on a host of epistemological *aporiae* which emerged in epistemology subsequent to the fall from favor the philosophies of positivism and noeopositivism. From Karl Popper's "critical philosophy" to Thomas Kuhn's work on "paradigms" and "scientific revolutions", chinks in the armor of everything from Carnap and the Vienna Circle's [*Wienerkreis*] criterion of meaningfulness to Hempel's hypothetico-deductive account of scientific change began to appear more like gaping holes. Lakatos was in no doubt that the critical salvos of both Popper and Kuhn has been probative against the so-called "justificationists" (*RP* 94–5).†

In response to this situation, Lakatos offered a "solution" that, at first sight, seems untidy, but which when examined closely affords a reasonably accurate map of the process of knowledge itself. According to Lakatos, a research program can be broken up into two main components:

1. A research program has a *hard core* — that part of the program that furnishes an overall ontology. That is, at its broadest, the core theory specifies the (putative) nature or character of the entities under investigation (*RP* 133–4).

2. A research program has — around the core — a series of *auxiliary hypotheses*. Lakatos described these as constituting something approaching a "protective belt" — a series of lower-level theories which are both seen to support and specify the core theory. Such auxiliary hypotheses may, for instance, include theories of observation or instrumentation (*RP* 134–8).

A research program, in this sense, can be seen as (being sustained by a) history of inquiry *itself* constituted by a series of theories whose core remains relatively constant while the protective belt of auxiliary hypotheses are intermittently either: (a) extended in response to corroborative data or (b) reformulated or replaced in lieu of incongruous data. For instance, at the level of the "protective belt," explanations are amenable to multiplication in response to seemingly anomalous observations.

Now as we noted, such explanatory multiplications may *seem* to show a weakness in a research program, this may not necessarily be the case. Indeed, Lakatos argues that part of the ingenuity of (so-called) "great scientists" has often shown itself *precisely* in such explanatory maneuvers — not merely to re-interpret experimental results in light of theoretical improvisation, but to challenge experimental outcomes *themselves* and even have them reversed. One means by which this might be achieved may be by refiguring the theory such that the anomaly can be subsumed under a law; the putative anomaly here becomes not an exception, but a *consequence* of the theory.

---

†For Lakatos, "justificationist" was a category that included both logical positivists / empiricists like Moritz Schlick and Otto Neurath, as well as "classical rationalists" like Kant. For a characteristic statement of Popper's against foundationalism, see his *Logic* (111).

Given what we have said, it should be clear that Lakatos is arguing that the project of attempting to supply necessary and sufficient conditions for the practice of "rational inquiry" lies vanquished; yet he does not see this conclusion as somehow sufficient in itself. Indeed, such a conclusion would suffice only if one were to impute to science an ahistorical aura — to think of it in terms of simple (and singular) "theories" or "conjectures," each amenable to instant assessment. "One can understand very little of the growth of science," Lakatos suggests, "when our paradigm of a chunk of scientific knowledge is an isolated theory... standing aloof, without being embedded in a major research programme" (*RP* 175). Well in advance of later thought which admits the mutual imbrication of epistemology and axiology — the ineliminably normative element of rational activity — Lakatos does not himself give up on normativity itself, merely some of its more dubious formulations. Additionally, one of Lakatos's signal contributions to the debate is that he effectively dispenses with a temporal notion of science — common to philosophies as seemingly disparate as Carnap's, Hempel's, Popper's, and Kuhn's — as constituted by of a series of *successive* theoretical matrices or problematics. Rather, he argues, the theatre of scientific reason is better characterized as being populated by *contemporaneous, competing* research programs.

This is when we get to the heart of Lakatos' insights into the way a research program (such as generative anthropology for instance) should be evaluated. This is his distinction between *progressive* and *degenerating* research programs (*RP* 116–38). According to Lakatos, the latter is such that its core is rescued from critical demolition by the *ad hoc* piling on of a seeming surfeit of theoretical entities — what Lakatos occasionally refers to as bare "face-saving" devices, "empty prevarications," or semantic "tricks" (*RP* 117). To simplify Lakatos's account somewhat, a progressive research program, on the other hand, is characterized by the following three features:

1) Each novel incarnation of the theory — core and auxiliaries — preserves the content of its predecessor.

2) Each novel incarnation of the theory possesses excess empirical content over its precursor — it is able to predict novel facts.

3) At least some of these (predictions) are corroborated.

When (1) and (2) are met, a theory is said to be *theoretically* progressive; when (1), (2), *and* (3) are fulfilled, a theory is then said to be both theoretically progressive *and* empirically progressive (*RP* 116).

How does Gans' hypothesizing fit into this schema? Working backwards, we see that his is a progressive rather than degenerating program. This evident not by some rule of succession or time, but rather, because of what his theory is able to explain. Put bluntly, his work *does* preserve the content of preceding theories (as we saw in the case of poststructuralism, for instance, but also, more importantly, of Girard's work on mimesis and sacrifice). Crucially, it does this in a way adequate to the original theories, and yet also on its own terms (self-corroboration and the probably best explanation). Gans' approach to the human can be assessed not against an empirically irretrievable past, but against what we are continually learning about the human *today*.

But more important there is a strange symmetry between Gans' work and that of Lakatos itself—and it has relevance to both. We have noted in *both* the self-referential and historical coherence of the two pieces of work. In the case of Lakatos, we might put it like this: the theory *itself fits very well with his own account of scientific research programs*. This at least confounds the criticism that most twentieth-century philosophy of science has not been self-referentially coherent, but it is also indicative of the possibility that in working for itself, it goes far beyond what many other model-makers have managed to do (notably Kuhn — for how can he, *on his own terms*, claim to be "right" rather than merely, say, "popular" as behooves a paradigm itself? Then, if this applies to his own model, how can his model be applied to *anything* else?). Gans' work too has an internal consistency that is impressive: a posteriori reasoning allows him to throw out the always-open question: you offer a better explanation, *or this one stands*.

Gans' work on consistency, clarity, and positive statement of the hypothesis all justify seeing the work in terms of the broad theatre of hypothesizing. These are the formal features we detailed earlier in the chapter. But as we have been seeing, the actual programme of research that is implied in the first five aspects of the Gansian hypothesis is progressive rather than regressive in nature. Were we to ask, therefore, whether it would be possible to draw a diagram of Gans' work using Lakatos, our answer would be affirmative. It would look a little like this: Gans' work gives form to a wider tradition that includes Girard and Girardian scholarship concerning at least the following precepts: the hard core notions are (to use Lakatos' terms) a) the idea that humanity should be explored as *Homo imitans*; b) the function of culture is to avert mimetic conflict and c) there *was* an origin to the human. The last feature is not argued by Girard, but is, in our view, an implicit feature of most of his work, especially his work on founding myths.

The value of this work lies in two areas: on the one hand, it is likely that the actual content of the hypothesis is correct, in which case the work is a decisive contribution to studies of the origin of human culture, and of language. On the other hand, even if the hypotheses needed to be modified, it might be that Gans has modeled an entirely new way for the humanities to do its work. The claim

THE ORIGINARY HYPOTHESIS

for the latter is even stronger than the former. But there are a range of possible objections. We wish to consider a few of these.

Objectors in White-Coats

We have argued that Gans has made a contribution to the question of the origin of language that is rare in the humanities, but not unusual in the field of the sciences. In seeking to venture back into terrain that the humanities has long vacated, one could be forgiven for wondering about the value of the contribution. Let us, briefly, outline how Gans' work looks in relation to extant versions of the origin of language as proposed by dominant models in the sciences.

To start with, like Girard, Gans posits an origin not because of some *a priori* commitment to a punctual origin of the human, but because such a retroductive postulate makes sense of the present more adequately than thinking of an (metaphysically restrictive) "originless" humanity, humanity as an divinely instantiated "immaculate conception," or merely the epiphenomenal smoke produced by random variation and natural selection.

This takes us into the terrain of what might best be called physical anthropology. In this field, Steven Pinker's *The Language Instinct* is a well known landmark. Pinker's book is well-written and his analyses of the necessary bio-physical architecture that humans require for language acquisition is both meticulously catalogued and deftly synthesized. But empirical fastidiousness is a poor substitute for conceptual acuity, and it is precisely in his analyses revolving around the title of his book that the weave of Pinker's begins to unravel. In an attempted riposte of Noam Chomsky's theory of LAD (the so-called "language acquisition device" of universal grammar) Pinker's will to exaggerate the differences between himself and psycholinguistics perhaps forces him to advance a claim both unwarranted by empirical study and evidentially unsupported by his preceding arguments: "Language is not a cultural artifact that we learn the way we learn to tell time or how the federal government works. Instead, it is a distinct piece of the biological makeup of our brains." Language "develops in the child spontaneously, without conscious effort or formal instruction." Despite the psychologistic bias of cognitive science and psychology, Pinker admits that here "prefer[s] the admittedly quaint term "instinct." It conveys," he tells us "the idea that people know how to talk in more or less the same sense that spiders know how to spin webs" (Pinker 18).

There is much that could be questioned in Pinker's claims. Most obviously, the claim that language is a "distinct piece of the biological makeup of our brains" requires no scientific training to judge: language is not a "piece" of anything, least of all a weigh-able slice of our central nervous system. This is an instance of what A.N. Whitehead called "misplaced concreteness." Surely, we may choose to weigh up Pinker's claims, but the metaphor of critical examination should not lead us to believe that we'll need to purchase a scale to equip us for the task. Language may require a certain physical architecture — it may supervene on a finely calibrated electro-chemical operations of the occipital lobe, the angular gyrus, and the visual cortex — but holding up a cross-section of Wernicke's area and proclaiming it "language" fails to convince. But the more important claim is the second one — that language is an "instinct." Pinker refines this claim by furnishing an analogy: that "people know how to talk in more or less the same sense that spiders know how to spin webs."

We contend, in this regard (with Gans), that once again, "less is more." The term "instinct" has a complex history in behavioural science, but its meanings are only relatively flexible. Usually the term points to a supposed "internal" control mechanism which regulates complex behavior, operative even without "external" inputs like imitation or instruction. At its most ectoplasmic, the term may refer to any functionally integrated behavioural system — which would render it vacuous to the extent that it would appear to fit any human behaviour indifferently. Pinker's choice of term here is, at least, brave; current ethology has, for the most part, asserted the invalidity of the concept as applied to human behavioural control systems, both at the developmental level and at the level of mature behaviour (Hinde, *Ethology*). But we can make a very simple point: human language acquisition is precisely *not* instinctually isomorphic to arachnoid home-making for the simple reason that no baby-spider ever requires mumma-spider to show her the "tricks of the trade." But human speech requires — in addition to neural architecture — a speaker's familiarization and integration into a speech community. No doubt, he recognizes this at some level (Pinker 292), but his Darwinian religiosity forces him to generate a further aporia that we can state as a question: If language is an "instinct" begotten by a fortuitous reshuffling of DNA (or what Pinker, at one point, calls "new-fangled circuitry" (365), who might have the poor genetic mutant confided in? In his legitimate desire to refute the notion of homo sapiens as tabula rasa, Pinker has produced the impossible: an orator without other language-users.)[4]

Hypothetical Objectors

There are a number of objections one can — and should — raise when looking at Gans' work on the origin of the human, and of culture. These fall into two groups. The first is that one should not hypothesize about such things. The second is that some of the actual contentions are wrong, or mis-stated, or mis-construed.

Let us be clear about what we seek to establish concerning the right of the humanities hypothesis: all we seek to show is that it deserves consideration. Many scholars believe the only paths to knowledge are those we now have. Broadly, for them (even if they would never write it this way), there is the mathematical or logical proof, circular, but of potential application; there is empiricism in the narrow sense of testable and repeatable knowledge; and then there is herme-neutics, the field of humanities, in which knowledge can only be a matter of discourse and argument. We have no objections to any of these practices—but neither do we see any reason to limit modes of knowing simply on the basis that this is all we do nowadays. The Gansian hypothesis, is as we have seen by look-ing at Lakatos, able to be posited, and explored.

Let us consider some of the hypotheses from the point of view of alterna-tives. There are two in particular that need examining: these are the co-foun-dational aspects that on the one hand, there was indeed an origin, and on the other, that this origin was characterized by mimetic impulses. Let us contend — for illustrative purposes — to the contrary that there was no origin, and then separately from that, let us contend that even if there was an origin, it was oth-erwise than Gans or Girard claim.

1.   *There was no origin.* Stated like this, we see problems straight away. If there was no origin, then two further choices impose themselves on us. We could argue that we have always somehow been already here. Or — second — we could propose a gradualist hypothesis, that is to say, that gradually the human shaded into being out of the non or proto-human. The first hypothesis is patently unacceptable, entailing an eschatology at complete odds with every-thing from the fossil record to common sense. Needless to say, it is the appar-ent default position of the contemporary humanities, but no one else. In this regard, it is an interesting case in which there is convergence between religious and non-religious positions: almost all agree that there was an origin. About the first counter-hypothesis, we need say nothing at all — it is ridiculous. The human has not been here forever be it as a species or as culture-in-general; there *was* a time when there was no human horizon. The second counter-hypothesis is more difficult. It corresponds to one version of evolutionary biology: genetic mutation, followed by more adaptation, followed by more mutation, followed by more adaptation etc. Squawks become signs, shrieks of pleasure become words. Implicit, but inessential to the model is the idea that somehow language is itself somehow advantageous to propagation of a species. Rather more essential — but rarely explored — is *when, why, and how* a squawk would become a sign. This

is Gans' aperture of critique, which begins by him seeking first of all to clarify *what it is* to be human. This allows him to postulate the originary thesis in very clear terms

Because the origin of language must be justified, not merely posited, the minimal act of humanity is best described not as "human using language" but as a prehuman creature *becoming* human by using language in a situations where this use is inevitable — that is, one to which the creature can adapt only by means of the acquisition of language. (1993: 2)

What Gans offers — and the competing commonsense model certainly does not offer — is an explanation of what the human is, what language is, and under which circumstances — using current evidence — it came about.

2. *The origin happened but it was not primarily mimetic.* Now this is the kind of hypothesis that engages squarely with generative anthropology — in its own terrain, and on its own terms. It retains the structure of hypothesizing, as well as key tenets (the eventness of the origin, the narrative nature of knowing, *a posteriori* reasoning). But it offers instead another kind of origin.

a. *Preservation.* Territorial borderlines between two proto-human groups maintained at first by a kind of instinct-grunt, at a point of crisis, suddenly undergo an explosion of signage which becomes in routinization something like Erving Goffman's "facework."

b. *Grief.* A scene of death in which — unlike Girard's murder — the situation is one in which a shared bewilderment arises at the demise of a protector — giving rise to something like grief held in common, again crossing the line from the dog loyal to its owner howling outside the door into something else, into *signing*.

c. *Love.* Parent-offspring communication passes from instinct to something closer, as sharing develops more than a pecking order, but a language.

About all these — and other — hypotheses, Gans has simply replied, let's see the *argument*. But before we consider this, let us first see what adoption of a counter-position suggests: at the very least it involves accepting the validity of this sort of inquiry, of building within it a scholarly discourse that proposes and challenges views about the origin of the human itself, and that does so with the view that that is such a thing as the human that can and should be studied in this way. In this respect, we should note that despite both Gans and Girard proposing mimetic theories of human origin, these differ profoundly in orientation. Gans, who sees mimesis as appropriative in the first instance, posits the origin as happening around something — or someone — held in common as an appetitively desirable object. As both hands reach out to appropriate, violence is deferred by the emergence of the sign. Girard, on the other hand, posits the origin as occurring around the corpse of a victim, which as sign comes to stand to everyone for what will thereafter be a feature of human society — the scapegoat.

The power of the mimetic hypothesis as against its rivals is that it is one of the most powerful and demonstratively constant tendencies in human culture *today*. Self-preservation, grief and love are also observable today (and that is how we generated the hypotheses — *a posteriori*, like Gans). Arguably, the second pair are already derivative of something else (an animal, arguably, cannot feel either unless it is already human). For those who see an almost Hobbesian pessimism about human nature pervading both Gans' and Girard's versions of human genesis, we would remind them that imitation is not cause for despair — but rather, an insight into how and why we know, and if our form of its is unique, yet there is a unity in all higher order lifeforms's modes of learning and skill-acquisition.

Coda on Language

If, as we have argued, Gans' approach is even *potentially* foundational of a renewal of inquiry into the human in the way Gans has imagined, then many of the orthodox protocols of the last fifty years in the humanities can simply be set aside as the equivalent of a debate on how many ghosts could fit into a medium-sized helium balloon. In place of such closed and defensive horizons, we have argued for the value of generative anthropology as a field in which the human can be studied in terms of the genesis of particular cultural formations, as well as of the human *itself.*

Gans' originary hypothesis is looking increasingly tenable not just as support for other fields of humanities research, but also, as a new way of making sense of the question concerning the origin of language itself. Perhaps the most powerful evidence of the relevance of this sort of inquiry lies in precisely this field. Many today see it as a variety of inquiry that is best conducted by biologists and archaeologists. Yet it has long preoccupied the best analysts of the human condition. From the time of Herodotus, there have been attempts to recreate the originary scene of language, to see if children can spontaneously acquire language. Despite the failure of all such attempts, almost no-one dares to conclude that no human could ever have learned language without some sort of originary event to trigger it. Not only is there no seeming point to talking if no-one comprehends such talk, there is likely no possibility of talking if no-one comprehends, as there is no-one to affirm or contest one's usage.

But if so, who spoke first — and why? Few have put the matter better than Lucretius during the first century BC:

> To suppose that someone on some particular occasion allotted names to objects, and that by this means men learnt their first words, is stark madness. Why should we suppose that one man had this power of indicating everything by vocal utterances and emitting the various sounds of speech when others could not do it? Besides, if others had not used such utterances among themselves, from what source was the mental image of its use implanted in him? Whence did this one man derive the power in the first instance of seeing with his mind what he wanted to do? One man could not subdue a greater number and induce them by force to learn his names for things. (Lucretius, *On the Nature of the Universe* 155)

Lucretius is not attacking a straw-man here, then or now. Yet the Epicureans' own solution to the problem generated its own conundrums. They argued that speech began as natural sounds and gestures, and that cultural specificity and historical circumstance engendered all the different languages. One obvious criticism here is that the specificity of human language is that the links between sign and referent are arbitrary, that much language possesses no clear referent, and that some of those that do, don't actually exist. Another obvious criticism is that for all the power of natural noises as an explanation, there is no reason given for its actual development beyond that of the other animals.

Gans and Girard, in their different ways, suggest another way forward from either of these two alternatives: to Lucretius' question, they reply, yes, something *did* happen — and we can, on the evidence before us about human behaviour today, generate strong hypotheses about what *sort of thing* it was. To the idea that speech evolved out of natural sounds, they point to the fact that the very human horizon comes into being only with speech. Gans himself explicitly addresses the modern equivalent of the gradualist position. This is the notion that the human is "always already" constituted (see especially *Signs of Paradox* 5–8). We cannot, it is true, go back to check. But neither in that circumstance, is it incumbent on Gans to "prove" the other position "wrong": on the contrary, it is sufficient to offer the most plausible explanation. In this respect, the *a posteriori* approach he brings to this aspect of the problem is extremely powerful and suggestive.

Moreover, the work on mimesis supports *both* kinds of work: be it on contemporary culture, or be it work on the origin of the human horizon in general. By augmenting and making use of Girard's work in this area, Gans has laid the basis for a new kind of inquiry in the humanities as a whole. This is true in the substantive claims he makes about the human we see a new set of possibilities for the humanities as a field of the widest scope. It is also true in the specific forms of thinking in which he engages: an attempt to think the human and its origin within the disciplinary matrix of the humanities actually lends renewed promise to many of those individual fields of pursuit. For all these reasons we believe the Gansian theoretical endeavor *is* foundational — or *should* be. The humanities "zero degree" *does* involve reflection on the human. Above all, it is Gans who has so repeatedly shown us that the very act of reflection is *itself* a definable part of what it is to be human — and that is part of what could make the humanities a field that justifies its name.

Notes

1. Another notable thinker here is Ernst Cassirer and his notion of the human as the "symbolic animal." Recent, more scientifically oriented, corroborations of this notion can be found in the work of thinkers such as Merlin Donald, Terrence Deacon, and Steven Mithen.

2. For another, see David McNally, *Bodies of Meaning: Studies on Language, Labour, and Liberation* (Albany: State University of New York Press, 2001), esp. pp. 85–105. A good discussion of this text — from a thinker sensitive to generative anthropology — can be found in Amir Khan, "Cultural Studies and Anthropology." *Anthropoetics* 12.1 (Spring/Summer 2006) <http://www.anthropoetics.ucla.edu/ap1201/khan>

3. We can make this comment too: where with Girard, there is an indeterminacy of discipline (he is perhaps best seen as an anthropologist of Judaeo-Christian society who brings a number of "scientific" characteristics, such as sustained observation practices to bear on his materials), with Gans there is an actual framing work concerning the humanities, and the place of his work in relation to it.

4. To be fair to Pinker, Darwin himself had no real answer to the same question; although the latter hedges his bets somewhat (calling language a "half-art, half-instinct"), his solution to its origin is largely isomorphic to Pinker's solution and the aporia it generates identical (*The Descent of Man* 463. Cf. 463–72). Slightly different but equally question-begging accounts have bridged *The Descent of Man* and *The Language Instinct*. Examples would have to include nineteenth-century biologist Ernst Haeckel (299, 360–4) and twentieth-century physical anthropologist Elliot Smith (152). Where Haeckel sees language as an outgrowth of, first, bipedalism, and then the "perfection" of the larynx (Haeckel 299. Cf. 293–300 & 360–4), Smith begins his "explanation" at the other end, concentrating on encephalization (the development of the brain) (Smith 152).

References

Amico, Robert P. *The Problem of the Criterion* (Lanham, Md.: Rowman & Little-field, 1993).

Cassirer, Ernst. *An Essay on Man: An Introduction to a Philosophy of Human Culture* (New Haven & London: Yale University Press, 1944).

Chisholm, Roderick. *The Problem of the Criterion* (Milwaukee, Wisconsin: Marquette UP, 1973).

Darwin, Charles. *The Origin of Species* and *The Descent of Man*. New York: Modern Library, 1948.

Deacon, Terrence. *The Symbolic Species: The Co-Evolution of Language and the Human Brain* (London: Penguin, 1997).

Donald, Merlin. *Origins of the Modern Mind* (Cambridge, Mass.: Harvard University Press, 1991).

Fleming, Chris. *René Girard: Violence and Mimesis*. Cambridge: Polity, 2004.

Fleming, Chris, and John O'Carroll. "Notes on Generative Anthropology: Towards an Ethics of the Hypothesis." *Anthropoetics* 8, no. 2 (Fall 2002/Winter 2003) <http://www.anthropoetics.ucla.edu/ap0802/fleming.htm>

Glidden, David K. "Parrots, Pyrrhonists and Native Speakers." In Stephen Everson (ed.) *Language* (Cambridge: Cambridge University Press, 1994). 129–48.

Haeckel, Ernst. *The History of Creation* (New York: Appleton, 1868).

Hanson, Norwood, R. *Patterns of Discovery* (Cambridge: Cambridge UP, 1958).

Heidegger, Martin. "Letter on Humanism." Trans. Frank A. Capuzzi & J. Glenn Gray, in *Martin Heidegger, Basic Writings*, 2nd rev. edn., ed. David Farrell Krell, Routledge, London: 1993 pp. 217–65).

Herodotus, *The History of Herodotus* (written 440 BCE). Trans. George Rawlinson <http://classics.mit.edu/Herodotus/history.2.ii.html> Accessed 20/4/06

Hinde, Robert A. *Ethology: Its Nature and Relations with other Sciences* (Glasgow: Fontana, 1982).

Kenny, A.J.P. "The Origin of Language." In A.J.P. Kenny, H.C. Lounguet-Higgins, J.R. Lucas and C.H. Waddington, *The Development of Mind* (Edinburgh: Edinburgh University Press, 1973). 91–107.

Khan, Amir. "Cultural Studies and Anthropology." *Anthropoetics* 12.1 (Spring/Summer 2006) <http://www.anthropoetics.ucla.edu/ap1201/khan>

Kirwan, Christopher. "Augustine on the Nature of Speech." In Stephen Everson (ed.) *Language* (Cambridge: Cambridge University Press, 1994). 188–211.

Lacan, Jacques. *The Seminar. Book II. The Ego is Freud's Theory and in the Technique of Psychoanalysis, 1954–55.* Trans. Sylvana Tomaselli, notes by John Forrester. New York: Norton, 1988.

———. *The Seminar. Book XI. The Four Fundamental Concepts of Psychoanalysis, 1964.* Trans. Alan Sheridan. London: Hogarth, 1977.

Lakatos, Imre. "Falsification and the Methodology of Scientific Research Programmes." In Imre Lakatos & Alan Musgrave (eds.) *Criticism and the Growth of Knowledge.* Proceedings of the International Colloquium in the Philosophy of Science, London, 1965, volume 4 (Cambridge: Cambridge University Press, 1970). 91–196.

———. "Introduction: Science and Pseudoscience." In J. Worrall and G. Currie (eds.) *Imre Lakatos: Philosophical Papers, Volume 1* (Cambridge: Cambridge UP, 1978)

Lipton, Peter. *Inference to Best Explanation.*

Lucretius. *On the Nature of the Universe.* Trans. R.E. Latham and revised and introduced by John Godwin (London: Penguin, 1994).

McNally, David. *Bodies of Meaning: Studies on Language, Labour, and Liberation* (Albany: State University of New York Press, 2001).

Mithen, Steven. *The Prehistory of the Mind: A Search for the Origins of Art, Religion, and Science* (London: Thames and Hudson, 1996).

Pinker, Steven. *The Language Instinct: The New Science of Language and the Mind* (New York: Harper Collins, 1994).

Popper, Karl. *The Logic of Scientific Discovery.* Routledge & Kegan Paul, 1963.

Quine, W.V. *From a Logical Point of View* (Harvard UP, 1953).

Accusations of "Playing God" and the Anthropological Idea of God

Andrew Bartlett

The Phrase "Playing God" as a Language Phenomenon Worthy of Investigation

1. We live in an age of genetic engineering. Most of us have heard about some of the wonders worked by molecular biology (or the horrors concocted): cloned frogs, cloned sheep, sheep-goat chimeras; glow-in-the-dark mice infused with jellyfish genes, a mouse with a human ear growing out of its back; human children saved from terrible hereditary diseases, human embryos aborted in reaction to what is now called "genetic counseling." The third edition of a college textbook on "issues" in genetic engineering distinguishes helpfully between somatic gene therapy and germ-lime therapy. Somatic gene therapy is "considered ethical by most scientists" and "seeks to alter the genetic constitution of cells of a particular sick individual, inserting a 'good gene' for one that is faulty" (Nossal and Coppel 201). The effects of this less ethically fraught form of human genetic engineering (HGE) are, "for good or for harm...confined to the individual being treated." Somatic gene therapy has been carried out, is being carried out now. Germ-line therapy, the more ambitious futuristic projection of HGE, aims "to repair a gene defect at the earliest stages of embryonic development." Because any negative side-effects are perpetuated into the next generation, indeed, because most such side-effects can not be predicted with any confidence, the college textbook informs its readers that "most scientists oppose germ-line therapy... [although] this near-absolute opposition is softening somewhat" (Nossal and Coppel 201). On the whole, while dozing complacency about the risks of HGE is unjustified, alarmed panic at its current effects is unnecessary. The most successful genetic engineers still stand distant from the place where they will be able to produce anything meriting the label "designer baby." Major technological obstacles (not to mention political and legal roadblocks) stand in the way of making the dream — or nightmare — of the first human clone deliberately grown from the transferred nucleus of an adult donor's cell into a reality. As a recent *Time* cover story accurately reports,

politicizing and posturing aside, fantasizing hype over HGE is disproportionate
to realistic hope in it (Gibbs).

2. Nevertheless, people worry, and not without reason, about the real impact
genetic engineering will increasingly have on human lives. John H. Evans points
out that as long ago as the late 1970s, "the carriers of at least fifty genetic dis-
orders could be conclusively, not probabilistically, identified through chemical
tests" (93). It may not be an exaggeration for Jean Bethke Elshtain to assert
that, at least in the developed West, with prenatal testing and the vigilance
that it invites now normalized, "the machinery of technology now surrounding
childbirth turns every pregnancy into what was once labeled a 'crisis' pregnancy" (162–63). It is curious to observe that the pleased people who exclaim "It's
genetic!" when their young children show particular behavioral resemblances
to parents or other ancestral kin, and the people who eat food made from genetically modified organisms three times daily without blinking, are often those
who without hesitation protest the hubris of molecular biologists threatening
to cross the line from genetic theory into practice. The philosopher Gordon
Graham encapsulates this odd contradiction between the serene acceptance of
biological determinism as pure science and the shocked distress at it as applied
science: "once the debate turns from genetic explanation, where 'science' rules
supreme, to genetic engineering, where 'ethical' issues are thought to arise, the
image of Frankenstein overshadows that of Einstein, and even the secular world
of ideas tends to reach for concepts that by its own assumptions are outmoded"
(144). Among such "outmoded" concepts Gordon Graham is correct to count
the idea of God, as in the expression "playing God." The unforgettable Victor
Frankenstein of Mary Shelley's novel is the most popular figure of the modern
scientist playing God. As Jon Turney has demonstrated, the potent Frankenstein
allusion has frequently stuck as a thorn in the side of those scientists open to
accusations that they are "playing God" when all they wish, they protest, is to
continue their research.

3. My primary thesis in this study is that "the anthropological idea of God"
constructed by Eric Gans over the last quarter century, one of the most original
elements in his heuristic of originary thinking, provides a compelling way to interpret some of the puzzles presented by real-world deployments of the accusation
that genetic engineers (among others) are "playing God." It is always possible,
of course, to expel the phrase "playing God" from the realm of things worth in-
quiring about. One can do so by teasing religious believers and facetiously opin-
ing that playing God is "a constant temptation...inevitable...a heady prospect"

for everybody anyway, as does the human cloning advocate John Harris (26), or by cracking jokes about a cartoon Yahweh as "Celestial Cloner" as does that fearless veteran foe of biological determinism, Richard Lewontin (156–57). Impatient atheistic or materialist contempt for religion, however, is not originary thinking. Eric Gans refrains from describing himself as a "religious person." Nonetheless, anyone familiar with his work will not be surprised that Gans has seen fit to declare: "Perhaps the *deepest motivation* for Generative Anthropology is the need to raise the level of our discourse about the existence of God" ("Does God") [emphasis added]. In his own musings about human genetic engineering (not one of his thematic preoccupations), Gans briefly considers "the necessity of restraining a constructive rather than a destructive technology" ("GA Futurism"). He conjectures that "the necessity of renouncing our ability to 'play God' would reinforce not simply religious faith but a deeper understanding of the anthropological function of this faith than that common among either believers or nonbelievers" ("GA Futurism"). Religious faith has an anthropological function which we *all* need to understand, regardless of our beliefs.

4. An assumption of this study is that the phrase "playing God" opens a way into such needed understanding of the anthropological function of religious faith, in that it is an expression used by both believers and nonbelievers, a little like the prayers said in foxholes by soldiers both faithful and atheistic (see Gans, "Unique"). As Diane B. Paul observes, "Indeed, it seems that many who condemn the notion of playing God are not theists" (138). Gordon Graham likewise notes that playing God is "an idea regularly invoked by those who otherwise have no use for theological language" (145). The self-contradictory aspect of the nonbeliever's attachment is most revealing when the nonbeliever has been trained in logical positivism: "For many secularists it is not just that something that might have existed does not; rather, they think that the very idea of God is meaningless. But in that case any anxiety about playing God must be meaningless also" (Graham 145). Graham is ironically hinting at his own anxiety about the meaninglessness of the anxiety in a nonbeliever's implied statement of belief. But his fear of the meaningless is unfounded. In such a context, Gans' anthropological idea of God helps. Fear of "playing God" can be meaningful regardless of God's "existence," indeed, regardless of our nonbelief. Graham is writing as if God *must* either exist or not exist on the model of the declarative sentence before accusations of playing God can possess significance. Not so, Gans would reply; the "must" is a premature imperative based on a premature demand for declarative verification that robs the anthropological idea of "God" of its very reason for being (see "The Two Varieties of Truth" in *Signs of Paradox* 51–63). To submit

the anthropological idea of God to such a metaphysical testing according to the law of non-contradiction is already to fail to understand that which you are testing, to fail to grasp the origin of human language in ostensive rather than declarative signifying.

5. Asking "Does God exist?" is not the first question to ask when one is responding to a believer or a nonbeliever's often "rhetorical" use of the expression "playing God." Instead, in such cases of offhand appeal to "God," we are wiser to ask about the way we got to be able to use such expressions as "playing God" or to ask such questions as "Does God exist?" in the first place. How did humans become creatures who could even have a language that can name someone or something like "God"? No animal language has ever led to animal religion. None of the songs of the humpback whale are being sung to a whale-being in whose image the humpbacks believe they were made. Lucy the champion of chimpanzee sign language never graduated to shamanistic independence. As Gans puts it, "Animals possess communication systems, 'languages' if you will, but no one has yet claimed to find a prehuman form of religious belief. God, however unnecessary, is at any rate a purely human preoccupation" (*Originary* 37).

6. When we ask about the origin of human language itself, one answer is the originary hypothesis. Gans proposes that the first human use of language was the communally reinforced use of an ostensive sign, the abortive gesture of appropriation of a central object, an abortive gesture which deferred conflict in a moment of intense mimetic competition for a central object of appetite. A group of protohuman "animals" became human by virtue of their signifying the object, even if only momentarily, before appropriating it. (No supernatural deity on the model of "creationist" belief or Intelligent Design is necessary for this event to have occurred, so even John Harris and Richard Lewontin can join our discussion without embarrassment.) This abortive gesture of appropriation, in its creation of the difference between sacred center and human periphery, is a sign that creates the sacred center of attention which we now think of under the name of "God." To be anxious about "playing God" on this model is, paradoxically, to be anxious about being human: being human in such a way that not only will this center-periphery structure be preserved but also human-destroying conflict (whether over nuclear bombs or human cloning) will be deferred, and the originary human difference created by the naming-of-God at the beginnings of symbolic language be respected.

7. But we get ahead of ourselves. For now, it is enough to establish our assumption that the phrase "playing God" is worth investigating. We agree with Leon Kass, chair of President George W. Bush's Council on Bioethics, that "properly analyzed and understood, the concerns expressed in phrases such as 'playing God' or 'dehumanization' are expressions of wisdom" (quoted in Evans 114). We agree with the philosopher of ethical individualism Ronald Dworkin that, even though it may seem "deeply unclear what the injunction really means," it can still be said that the injunction against playing God "appeals to…a detached rather than a derivative value" (473). In his terminological system, Dworkin posits that detached as opposed to derivative values are "intrinsic to objects or events in some way" rather than "parasitic on [deriving from] the interests of particular people" (428). He intuits that the idea of "God" has an independent ostensive force, dependent on *all* humans universally rather than some in particular. We would add, in the context of originary thinking, that the "detached value" in question is "intrinsic" to the preservation of the human and to the commemoration or the hypothesizing of a model of the event of human origin. For Gans, God and humanity are coeval. We ought not to play God if "playing God" means denying the uniqueness of the event of human origin. The human can be created only "once": the otherness of the being named by the originary sign can never be re-created, re-done, re-made; the unique originary event cannot be made to re-occur as such.

8. In what follows, I will build on these notions in two stages of investigation. The first stage of investigation seeks to offer an exposition of Gans' anthropological idea of God. It collects and connects formulations from over two decades of Gans' writing to offer the reader an introductory account of the theme in his work. The second stage presents an analysis of selected literature that has discussed the "playing God" idea, mostly writing by philosophers and theologians; it emphasizes the seemingly intractable conflict between those who initiate and those who suffer accusations that somebody is "playing God." The second stage of analysis is organized not by way of a chronological series of names, titles, and texts summarized, but rather by way of exploring four interpretations of the phrase, ordered from least to most evocative. In the second stage, the quotation-heavy explicit exposition of Gans' work gives way to an analysis implicitly putting to work his "anthropological idea of God." We will find ample opportunity in the second-stage analysis to confirm the validity of Gans' longstanding contention that the human as such is best theorized as an "ethical" category (rather than biological, sociobiological, theological) — best theorized as such in keeping with generative anthropology's definition of culture as *the deferral of*

violence through representation. The deferral *is* the ethical project. Everywhere, we shall see, the accusation that the hubristic scientist is playing God leads directly to questions less about God and more about what the "human" is or does. The leading is consistently so direct and so quick, almost like a short circuit or snapped elastic, that Gans' hypothesis concerning the coeval emergence of God and humanity is covertly implied without being overtly proposed.

9. It must be acknowledged that my attitude to the "playing God" literature has been influenced by John H. Evans' magisterial sociological analysis, *Playing God? Human Genetic Engineering and the Rationalization of the Public Bioethical Debate* (2003). Evans' work situates ethical debates about "playing God" in the context of real historical American negotiation between scientists, theologians, medical practitioners, philosophers, and politicians from the 1960s through the mid-1990s. In the 1982 President's Commission report on human genetic engineering (a commission initiated by Carter and completed under Reagan), Evans demonstrates, "bioethics" itself gained ascendancy and established itself as an independent field. But in bioethics, anthropological questions as much as theological questions were rendered peripheral: "...the profession of bioethics was defined by distancing its form of argumentation from both theology and analytic philosophy. More precisely, bioethics distanced itself from the *substantively rational form of argumentation of theology*, but retained the formally rational type of argumentation of analytic philosophy, while *rejecting philosophy's interest in abstract, speculative, and impractical questions*" (160) [emphasis added]. Instead, "principlism," an ethical discourse limited to considerations exclusively of the four ethical ends of beneficence, nonmaleficence (safety), justice, and autonomy, triumphed. Principlism, Evans is determined to demonstrate, "could not easily be used to make ethical arguments *against* HGE" (136). Substantive rationality lost, in short, to formal rationality; correspondingly, a regulatory body along the lines of the Securities and Exchange Commission was never created and instead Presidential Advisory Commissions — themselves given to using formal rationality rather than substantive rationality — were the political-institutional means created to deal with the public debate around human genetic engineering. Those who wrote the 1982 President's Commission explicitly dismissed the figure "playing God" as irrational scare-mongering or "vague" speculating not to be allowed in the utilitarian, consequentialist discourse of bioethics. In the last decade (Evans's exhaustive empirical work ends in 1995), an uneasy awareness has grown up that "autonomy," one of the only four ends sanctioned by principlism, is insidiously elbowing out the other three ends and weakening even further the public HGE debate. Since current bioethics seems in need of

mediating ways to speak of substantive matters such as "the human" and "God" without degenerating into an obstinate knockout competition between coercively fideistic positions (whether of the atheist-Promethean or the restrictive-theological variety), there seems to be a place where Gans' anthropological idea of God may help.

10. Our thesis throughout will be that the prohibition again "playing God" alludes to anthropological truths accessible and meaningful to believers and nonbelievers alike, while originary thinking ultimately provides the best model for a discourse of God that opens up those truths as common ground to be shared during debates about the hopes and fears raised by human genetic engineering.

An Exposition of Gans' "Anthropological Idea of God"

The Originary Ostensive Sign and the Identity of Linguistic Verticality with the Transcendental

11. Several behavioral features and unique aspects of the human have served philosophical anthropology in its quest for the evolutionary origin of the human — bipedalism, meat-eating, tool making, cultural learning, rational thought. As do many contemporary thinkers, Gans privileges human language — the use of symbolic reference (as distinct from iconic or indexical reference) — as the quintessential feature "defining" the human (Dupre 5, 68–69; Proctor 248; Shannon 279; Tattersall). But Gans goes farther: he insists on "the identity of human origin and human language" ("Rhetoric"). A coherent philosophical anthropology must, Gans insists, offer a hypothetical model of the origin of human language in evolutionary history. And the model of the origin of language must be anthropological: "no research program based on biological categories can explain human language.... The idea of God makes explicit the mystery implicit in language" ("Does God").

12. Gans makes two preliminary moves before he quite gets to God. One is to posit that for millennia, the first humans' language consisted of the use of the ostensive sign: "Human language does not begin with the declarative sentence, but with the ostensive. To go beyond the declarative of propositional thought to the ostensive reference that ultimately founds it is the gesture of originary thinking" (SP 51). The originary ostensive is unique in that it was alone: hu-

man language in the beginning had neither imperatives and interrogatives nor
sentences, declarative language. We can grasp it by considering the ostensive as
we know it: that curious form of linguistic practice that designates something
already present. As Gans explains, "An ostensive utterance points to what is
already present, as in 'Fire!' or 'Man overboard!' These are typical ostensives
in that they are used in moments of crisis; we do not cry 'Fire!' every time we
strike a match. One may even say that the use of an ostensive *constitutes* crisis"
("Unique" 54). And what crisis founds the human in the originary event, according to generative anthropology?

13.   We are asked to imagine a circle of hominoids that already have a "hard-
wired" capacity for mutual imitation and for inter-generational learning at the
animal level. At a moment of heightened mimetic competition propelled by appetitive reinforcement — a moment of "crisis" — these protohumans reach for
one object (most simply imagined as a food object). The crisis is one where
appetite and imitation intensify the potential conflict over the central object
(perhaps a hunted, slain animal ready for consumption). At the origin of the human, merely animal dominance systems, which would instinctually determine
one animal's appropriation of the object (and subsequent dispersion of its re-
mainders into "leftovers" for others) and would thus dissolve the crisis, are here
suspended. They are suspended by an event which makes all the difference. This
event is the creatures' abortion of their gestures of appropriation at this moment
of crisis. The first humans imitate each other's abortive gesture of appropriation
of the central object. This abortive gesture of appropriation itself constitutes the
originary ostensive, the originary symbolic reference. When this happens, the
first properly human use of language also happens. The crisis of competition
for the object is deferred, and the ostensive sign-users differentiate themselves
from the object of appetite. The originary ostensive does something never done
before in terrestrial history. It generates a new form of communally-determined
attention. The (new) humans *defer* their "violent" appetites for possession of the
object and they *differ* — as a "community" now, created by their common use of
this minimal ostensive symbol — they *differ* from the signified central object at
the center of the scene. (I emphasis *defer* and *differ* to hint at Gans' re-visioning
of Derridean *différance* on an anthropological plane.) So the first move (before
we get to "God") is to return again and again to this scene of sign-users on the
(human) periphery aborting their appropriative gestures for the object in the
(sacred) center, to see in a scenic ostensive symbolic reference and its center-
periphery structure the event-origin of the human being as such. (For richer,
extended accounts by Gans, see *Science and Faith* 1–17 or *Originary Thinking*
1–28, among many others).

14. The other preliminary move Gans makes is to posit "the ultimate identity of linguistic verticality with the transcendental in general" ("Unique" 52). The abortive gesture of appropriation creates a new center of attention: the first humans are thinking for the first time not of the appetitive object alone but of their mutually reinforced ostensive sign that makes that object significant; they are thinking of and with the sign that signifies, and that by virtue of its signifying, creates a moment of peace in the crisis of appetitive competition. Only signifying converts animal appetite into human desire. Even here in the originary scene, millennia before conceptual or rational discourse in the form of sentences in declarative language, here with ostensive reference only (see "Ostensive Culture," *End* 105—112), we have the birth of the transcendental.

> Language...is a source of sacralization.... To represent by means of a sign is to cut off from worldly action. The supernatural quality of what is designated by the sign does not arise from the formal reality of the sign's existence in a different world from that of things; it is rather this formal difference that arises from the human community's "absolute" need of putting the desired object beyond the reach of its potentially contentious members. ("Body")

Accordingly, under the originary hypothesis, language is neither secondary nor epiphenomenal to the event of human origin. Our common ancestry with the first participants in this scenic event determines our "species" definition, anthropologically, not biologically, as the community of human language users: "Biological speciation does not take place as an event; it requires [only] a unique population, not a unique community" (*Science 6*). We ceased to be only animals when our pre-human, already heightened mimetic capacity both generated the "absolute" need to overcome crisis in appetitive animal competition and opened the possibility for the minimal originary use of human language in the ostensive sign that deferred "violence."

15. We must grasp that the sign defers violence if we are to grasp its moral and ethical power, its sacred strength: "the designation of the central object cannot be reduced to a release of aggressive tension. The moment in which the logos is with God and is God is not a moment of animal aggression but of human deferral of aggression..." ("In the Beginning"). We might be tempted (especially the theists among us) to suspect or reject this idea of a moment in which an animal "need" in terrestrial evolutionary history seems alone to generate human difference and its unique dignity, to suspect it as "naturalistic" account of the

origin of sacralization, which it is. But inasmuch as the attribute "naturalistic" risks reducing the anthropological to the biological, we do better to insist on the scientific (hypothetical) independence of the "anthropological." Biology can not explain the origin of the human sign, because the sign can not be reduced to an entity functioning only within a biological category without ceasing to be a human sign. Our species identity can not be primarily that of a biological species, even though "species" itself is a biological category: this paradox is one of those anthropological truths scandalous to science which religion has always found easy to take up (*Science 1; Signs 51–52*). On Gans' hypothetical originary scene, the ostensive sign may seem to come from "outside" the anthropological domain but that seeming itself is a result of our need for the sign: the human use of the sign *is* the origin of the moral and the ethical.

> Although we obligatorily situate the transcendent prior to the ethical or human realm, the *ultima ratio* of our gesture is itself ethical. We may call this "the paradox of transcendence": the temporal need to maintain order among human beings generates the eternal verticality of the sacred sign. ("Unique" 53)

This identity of linguistic verticality with the transcendental is a prerequisite to our understanding Gans' anthropological idea of God. When appreciated in its originary incarnation on the scene of human origin, the human linguistic sign becomes the "model for all transcendental entities...which [do] not 'exist' in the spatio-temporal world" ("Body"). Clearly, words disappear from languages, falling out of use altogether, and human languages (tragically) die, just as some cultures die. But the point, Gans suggests, is that words possess "a different relation to temporality than things, one that is the basis for our concept of immortality. Gods too may be considered mortal in the sense that when their believers are gone, they are no longer 'real' gods, but this form of 'death' is not directly comparable to the decay of the flesh" ("Body"). When the ostensive sign on the originary event cuts off from worldly action the central object, only then does that object become "significant"; that originary "significance" is also the origin of the sacred and the transcendent: "the transcendent is a hypostasis of the world of representation; the common source of both the Ideas [of Plato] and the Word [of the Gospels] is the timeless sign existing in its own domain above the temporal world to which it refers" ("Unique" 60). Especially in the post-enlightenment era, after Kant, Gans proposes, "there is no longer any useful way to distinguish religion from metaphysics, the transcendence of God from the verticality of the Idea" (*Signs* 125). Gans' anthropological idea of God, to summarize our account so far, presupposes, first, an inextricable ethical link between human language and the deferral of violent conflict; second, an intense intimacy between linguistic verticality and our intuitive senses of the transcendental (the "immortal," "eternal," "divine," or "supernatural"). The form taken by human culture is that of the deferral of violence through representation (primordially, ostensive reference), in keeping with the fact that humanity is *"the species for which the central problem of survival is posed by the relations within the species itself rather than those with the external world"* (*Originary* 2).

The Co-emergence of God and the Human

16. In the originary event, then, the previously merely appetitive object is transfigured by the nascent community's use of the ostensive sign, transfigured into an object of desire and resentment. We "desire" it by becoming aware, only via the sign, that others want it as we do: the object becomes more desirable the more it seems inaccessible and inviolable as a result of our awareness of others' using the same sign that points it out (as not to be appropriated, "out of reach"). Simultaneously, we "resent" it by attributing to the signified thing itself (rather than to our fellow humans on the periphery) the strange power that prevents us from appropriating it. We assign to the central object the power of repulsion that is, in fact or in "reality," the power not of the "natural" physical object itself (as that which arouses appetite alone), but of the communal power of the mutual incompatibility of the desires of the humans reaching for it, holding back from taking it, and so signifying it. Now the nonbeliever might be tempted to see in this (mistaken) attribution of agential force to the desired, sacred central object the primordial religious delusion — which it was and is. The object was in reality only a material object, nothing "really" meriting the ascription of sacred power, the nonbeliever might stand up to point out. And this objection holds true, except that the impatient "only" in "only a material object" betrays the fact that the nonbeliever is partly missing the point.

17. The point is that we could not have become human in the first place without sacralizing the central object that we would only later become capable of desacralizing. Humanity needed the sign, the sacred, "religion" in this minimal sense, in order to become human. It was not a matter, however, of one clever hominoid insinuating this need to the others, originary shamanistic deception if you like. On the originary scene, the nonbeliever must be reminded, we are not calmly debating whether the central object of appetite is or is not sacred.

The originary ostensive sign designates the center-as-significant; it does not assert its significance [on the model of declarative predication]. The all-or-nothing nature of the first sign reflects the fact that, in the originary event, the individual experiences the divinity in a collective context. The central object is the focus of all desires; its substantiality is *not a matter of belief, but of terrible reality, of life or death.* (*Originary* 43) [emphasis added]

On the originary scene, the sacralization of the object is not only at one with its designation via the first ostensive sign but also at one with the deferral of extremely intense mimetic conflict, "violence," that threatens to destroy the group. The urgency of ostensive signifying has nothing to do with "making claims" about the being of God as material or immaterial. The sign prohibits our appropriation and consumption of the object; we each hold back from taking it alone to ourselves; we feel equally resentful of the center and equally alienated from it, equally influenced by each other's desire for it — there is the "real" basis of the moral equality at the origin of the human. In this holding back, and in the signifying of this holding back, we create the center-periphery scenic structure of human representation.

18.   We take the next step toward filling out the anthropological idea of God when we grasp that the naming of the being understood to be figured in or revealed by the central object is the naming of "God"; but that the object itself is not experienced as the being, not experienced as "God," but as only its revelation. We must differentiate between the object itself (slain hunted animal, desired physical thing) and the unforgettable quality of the center-as-such, the locus which that object occupies. The central object itself may be "sacred" without itself alone deserving to be named "God." The being named "God" subsists only *after the physical object has been destroyed,* distributed, consumed in the meal at the originary event's conclusion. The sign defers violence, but that is not say it abolishes violence. Our hunger will never be satisfied with a picture of a steak, to borrow from Gans. An extended account of the conclusion of the originary event in sparagmatic violence and the interval between the event itself and its (first) ritual re-enactment is beyond the scope of this study (see *Originary* 50–61). But for our purposes, differentiating between the "temporary attention" the first human would have given to the object itself and the "permanently subsisting center of attention" (*Originary* 38) given to the center-as-such of the scene is a necessary step. The anthropological idea of God does not separate the being of God from the human activity of remembering by means of the sign. Gans writes: "the indepen-

dence of the permanent center-as-such from its temporary material occupant…is the source of the idea of God, as opposed to the undifferentiated concept of the sacred" (*Originary* 53); "The sacred is something quite different from God, who must be thought of as a being, even as a person" (*Originary* 31). God appears in the material object on the originary scene; the humans take the object as a *revelation of* divine being; but the revelation of the being is not the being itself:

> For the idea of God is the idea of what subsists in the physical being's absence, and this supratemporal subsistence of the scenic center with respect to the temporal being that fills it is a direct consequence of the originary experience of representation. The sign can…designate [only] what occupies the center of the scene, and the being of this center, the center-as-being, is what we call God. (*Originary* 38)

We recall that the physical object is an appetitive object; the sign converts mere animal appetite into mutually mediated human desire. But we can understand that the participants in the originary event would not and did not suspend their desires in an ascetic eternal frustration, an originary fasting. They eat what they have signified. "God" comes into "existence" after the eaten object has been destroyed, as the being whose centrality is thought to have generated the decrease in mimetic tension conferred by the use of the sign: "Thus the first word is the name-of-God that both designates the object of desire and at the same time does not merely signify this mortal object but [signifies also] a sacred Being that will subsist after the object has been destroyed…the animal that the word designated is no more, but *the word and its peace-bringing power remains,* and God, or the sacred, is what it [the word] means" ("Body") [emphasis added]. This subsistence of divine being at the center occurs even despite the "violence" or aggressive consumption of the eating that destroys the material occupant of the center-as-such: this communally mediated sign creates a communally sanctioned memory of the scene. "But the revolt against God must end in failure," Gans insists in *Signs of Paradox*; "The participants in the sparagmos, in seeking to destroy the center itself, attain only its material occupant; their [destructive] intent is frustrated by the persistence of the sign and the significant memory that guarantees it" (149). So another step for us, at this juncture, is to foreground Gans' rather understated inclusion of "significant memory" as the human condition of divine being, the divine inspiration for human being.

19. If it is impossible for human language and culture ever to establish a derivation for themselves other than the scenic structure of an originary event — as

Gans hypothesizes — then it is equally impossible for the idea of the being of God ever to be utterly abolished. We may not always "believe in" God, but, paradoxically, we will never cease trying to forget the idea of God. Gans' challenge to what he will call "revolutionary atheism" consists in a hypothesis that relocates God to the "merely" human realm, while nevertheless making the idea of God as necessary to our understanding of the evolutionary emergence of the "human" as an explanation of the origin of human language is necessary to it. The understanding of the human is itself a moral project, but an impossible one if attempted in a context where the total forgetting of God is vainly pursued or artificially forced. We will quote Gans at some length in one of his more stirring paradoxical passages.

> We retain the idea of God without necessarily believing in it because of the indispensable persistence of the communal ground of the scene [of representation] independently of the individual members of the community. The nonbeliever may be spared the undignified examination of what one "really" believes. Once the idea of God exists, it can not be forgotten; and once it has been forgotten even for an instant, human culture is already engaged in the process of secularization of which the contemporary atheist is the final product. Our hypothesis attempts to convince the [atheist] only that because the idea of God, to which anyone is free to deny belief, is coeval with the origin of humanity, the process of this forgetting can never be concluded. Even if someday not one believer remains, the atheist will remain someone who rejects belief in God, not someone for whom the very concept is empty. (*Originary* 42–43)

A consequence of the formulations in this passage that Gans tends to understate (as an anthropologist, not a theologian) is that the "being of God" in this minimal sense will continue to be "present" whenever human linguistic communication is occurring. Any two humans openly communicating with each other (rather than, for example, attacking or killing each other in wordless hate) are realizing the presence of the sacred being whom their distant ancestors named at the origin of the human species itself. A less dramatic way of saying this is to suggest that the scenicity of human culture implies the center-as-such of significant attention: "Any use of language implies the latent or virtual presence of the communal scene between any two members of the community, the equivalent of a nonthematic faith that…they are not merely making certain gestures and obtaining certain results, but that they are employing the same set of significations. What guarantees this [nonthematic] faith is nothing other than what we have described as the imaginary idea of God" (*Originary* 43).

20. Such formulations will give pause to the religious believer accustomed to richly anthropomorphic images of God. This idea of God may, nevertheless, offer to the open-minded a way to minimize the difference, hence the need-less conflict, between belief and nonbelief. The originary hypothesis invites us to entertain the possibility that all humans *as humans* share a common derivation from a scenic event in which we named our Other as the divine being "God." Clearly, modernity has deleted much figural content from this being: "the progressive liberation of social exchange from the prescriptions of ritual makes the being of this center ever less figural and more virtual" (*Originary* 44). But the indispensable scenicity of human culture with its "central locus" persists, and as long as it does, some realization of "God" as this being, both minimal and necessary, will persist: "The primary necessity is that the central locus, whether or not hypostatized as a being by the individuals involved, be realized between them in the act of communication. God in this minimal sense is thus present in the mutual presence of any two members of the community. God's being is that of this presence itself" (*Originary* 44). God will never leave the scene of human culture, abandon it, disappear from it entirely, because human culture will always be scenic in the sense that human language will always have been explicable only as having emerged not from declarative sentences but from scenic ostensive reference. To expel God from the scene of culture, which we are (yes) free to do, is to *forget* the *moral and ethical configuration* of that originary event, in which we were all equally human, equally resentful of and desirous of the sacred center; but such a forgetting, were it to occur, would mean conceiving of the origin of human language on a model which does not make our *moral and ethical being* the origin of our humanity. It is possible for scientists playing God to indulge in such forgetting, or to force themselves into such forgetting. Our argument is, therefore, that the prohibition against "playing God" — for believers or nonbelievers alike able to entertain the originary hypothesis — expresses a fear, our well-founded human fear, of such a forgetting. It is a forgetting to be human.

21. The nonbeliever may be pleased to notice that this anthropological idea of God is not the idea of any particular ethnic or geographical deity, but the idea rather of an unfigurable central being: "God is the central locus of the scene of representation conceived as a being. This being does not reveal itself as such; it is revealed only in the figure of whatever occupies this locus in the originary scene. God and the human are born simultaneously from this scene; this is the immediate consequence of the hypothesis" (*Originary* 40). Gans aims to minimize the difference between believer and nonbeliever, theist and atheist, by inviting

us to take up common ground in recognizing the event of human-with-God difference and mutuality as our shared ancestry. We are invited to "refuse to assign ontological priority to the human or God by refusing to assign chronological priority" (*Originary* 35). The impatient revolutionary atheist can see in ideas of "God" only the contemptible invention of cynical priestcraft, the invention of some humans over against others; for the nonbeliever, the true dignity of the human is corrupted by the utterly unnecessary imposition of religious delusion. Let us grant "science" its proper authority and reject "religion" and proceed. On the other side, the hesitant believer can see in ideas of "God" only names of an agency exterior to all humans, cosmologically existing in self-sufficient detachment prior to the evolutionary emergence of the human species, indeed, prior to the existence of matter, the universe, anything; for the devout believer, the true dignity of the Creator is demeaned if we posit His or Her dependence on human agency.

22. We would emphasize that Gans' anthropological idea of God challenges *both* believers and nonbelievers: it is "the hypothesis that God and the human came into existence simultaneously: that the referent of the first human thought, the first human word, possessed for the first humans the essential attributes of the entity that we now call God and was historically continuous with it" (OT 35). To take up Gans' challenge regarding the "essential attributes," let us return to the abortive gesture of appropriation, the first ostensive reference. There, the central being was experienced as "omnipotent" in its being equally resented by all and equally desirable to all. It was experienced as "omniscient" by appearing to possess in itself that mysterious repellent force of prohibition (which, we noted, was in reality conferred by the incompatibility of the desires of the participants on the periphery). It was felt to be "omnibenevolent" in deferring, however briefly, the mimetic conflict in the scene, conferring on the first human sign-users a decrease in critical tension thanks to the (minimally) peace-making effects of the sign itself. Inasmuch as the event hypothesized "really" happened in human history, we may suggest that "God really" existed at the birth of the human and will never cease to have existed as the creator of the human. At the same time, however, the originary hypothesis "does not require us to believe in God because it does not presuppose the anteriority of the sacred to the human" ("Does God"). By "believe in God" here, Gans refers to belief in a God antecedent to humanity. The skeptical nonbeliever applauds this. But before the skeptic climbs too eagerly into the elevated seat from which he might condescend to theistic naiveté, we remind him that neither is Gans defending the anteriority of the human to the sacred. The anthropological idea of God presupposes that for his own existence as a nonbelieving human the nonbeliever will always be indebted

to the totally human naming of "God" at the origin of humanity. Atheistic intuition, as opposed to atheistic belief, is human before it is atheistic; the human as symbol-using creature came into being only in company with the sacred being of the center-as-such on the scene of originary representation.

Neither Anti-scientific Theology nor Anti-religious Philosophy

23. Generative anthropology's formulation of the anthropological idea of God may fail to satisfy either doctrinaire theists or doctrinaire atheists. It does require of everybody, doctrinaire or not, a new, never facile approach to "God." Theological interpreters of culture may resist Gans' consistent preference for positions from which there is "no need to appeal to supernatural agencies" (*Originary* 35). Gans himself has expressed dismay at the persistence of "childishly anthropomorphic" descriptions of God: "If we attribute to God a human psychology from the outset, we will never understand the emergence in the world of either God or humanity" ("Talking"). His challenge to orthodoxy may take on a daunting aspect which satisfies neither those enamored of the apocalyptic judge nor those attached to the unconditionally compassionate: "Not only the big daddy God of old-time religion, but [also] the 'feminine spirit' God of [Marcus] Borg cannot help but be radically transformed by a way of thinking that makes God's revelations to man the bearers of not merely religious but anthropological truths" ("Marcus"). Gans distances his work from that of "theological interpreters" of the story of the serpent's temptation and the disobedience of Adam and Eve in Genesis; the theologians, he suggests, "a priori cannot understand the text [in anthropological terms] because they maintain *as given* the absolute difference of the sacred" (*End* 317, note 5) [emphasis added]. Gans readily concedes that the being who "subsists" on the originary scene of representation is "not yet the deity of any conceivable religion. What the believer believes…is necessarily more than this formal definition. Even a minimal description of belief requires a thematization of God as a substance other than the mere subsistence of a locus" (*Originary* 41). This is to appreciate in advance that those of us accustomed to think of God as a "supernatural" entity or a Person cosmologically independent of the human, may resist this "idea of God" as one too emptily abstract.

24. And yet in his Chronicle "God is Love," arguably the most emotively charged condensation of his thinking about God, a series of reflections that delicately moves between figures of God as either substantive Person or human process (and between this division itself and a synthesis of its opposites), Gans makes with a certain wistfulness this suggestion: "unless we replace the

traditional substantive notion of God as supernatural entity with the insight that what stands behind the significance of the central object is not a substance at all but an *interaction*," we will never quite grasp the notion of God-is-love: "The Being that defers our violence through representation is no more than our act of deferral itself" ("God is"). Believers resolutely attached to a "supernatural" God may be dissatisfied by this seeming reduction. But is the humanization of divine presence in fact a reduction, or (paradoxically) a necessary relocation of God to the place where the divine matters most because it is where it must reveal itself — our midst? God exists "for us" on this anthropological model. Further, if we wish to be free moral agents, the deferral of resentment that we call love must be, indeed, "*our* act of deferral"; that is to say, if it were an act coerced, pre-determined, engineered by an exterior Agency, then it would no longer be "our" act and God would already begin to be alienated from us.

25. Although the anthropological idea of God presents thus a challenge to fideistic theology, we hasten to add that it likewise implies a rejection of anti-religious philosophy. The scenicity of Gans' model of culture implies an ineradicable respect for the moral intuitions latent in the religious, ritual origins of human being. In the intellectual lineage of Emile Durkheim and René Girard, Gans privileges the sacred as a fundamental component of the human, observing dryly that "it is necessary to remind the vast majority of social scientists that human language could not have emerged without the sacred" ("In the Beginning"). Gans assumes that the question of God's existence is no less a meaningful question than that of the origin of language: "If we declared the question of God's existence meaningless, as the logical positivists thought they could do, all religious questions would be expelled from rational discourse. On the contrary, it is the very importance of religious questions that makes the usual terms in which they are debated so frustrating" ("Does God"). Those "usual terms" are often dogmatically philosophical, in their presupposing that the declarative sentence is the fundamental model of human thought and in their refusing to consider even the hypothetical possibility of communally mediated ostensive reference as the origin of human language in a scenic, punctual event.

26. Gans does not confess any faith in a deified secular "Reason" that would take upon itself the task of expelling the memory of religious experience from human history as little more than an accretion of superstitious error. Even when faced with the distressing "sectarian excesses" of religious fundamentalisms that sanction terrorist assassination, Gans rejects the secular deity of revolutionary enlightenment: "…it is an Enlightenment fantasy to think that 'fanaticism' can

be eliminated and Reason enthroned. The human is the realm of reason, but also that of paradox which makes reason inadequate"; "... if 'we' all got together to eliminate fanaticism and initiate the rule of reason, things would quickly get much worse" ("'God Told'"). The presence of the problem of God makes trouble for conceptual thought: "But whether the place of God be filled by Being (Heidegger) or left ostentatiously vacant (Derrida), its central locus in the metaphysical edifice is something that philosophy can neither explain nor eliminate" (*Originary* 33). Indeed, the atheism that Enlightenment rationalism bequeaths us is paradoxical at its core: "Revolutionary atheism is an inverted religious fundamentalism that makes use of our verticality to tell us that the vertical does not exist" ("Unique" 54, note 3). Gans is no less suspicious of revolutionary atheism that he is wary of religious fanaticism.

27. The enlightenment fantasy of Reason deified often manifests itself in a neglect of the *communal* origins of human language, Gans notes. We will never find an explanation of the sacred "within the limits of individual experience" ("Talking"). Nor can we maintain the validity of the Cartesian cogito as a fundamental model for anthropological inquiry: we ought to "reject the Enlightenment misreading of the cogito ... the self as an autonomous entity whose dependency on human interaction is merely incidental. Even the Lacanian 'return' to a language-constituted self takes place within the biological ambit of Freudianism, from which [ambit] the human collectivity is altogether absent" ("Rhetoric"). The originary scene in which human language emerged was a collective scene. We observed above that the traditional theist might find the anthropological idea of God too abstract; ironically, Gans for his part finds metaphysical philosophy a disappointment in that its concepts must fail to inspire worship. The experience of the sacred is an experience irreducible to belief in a concept in the same way that the use of ostensive symbolic reference can not be reduced to a mere deformation of (or primitive attempt at) the declarative sentence. It is the originary experience of the act of naming the sacred central object of desire and resentment, not any philosophical predication, which best illustrates the fundamental humanness of the thought of "God": "We could not conceive the existence of God, even in order to deny it, without basing our conception on an experience of the sacred, an experience of which the name-of-God is the crystallization. In contrast, the construction of a concept of God that needs no name is the task of metaphysics" (*Signs* 202, note 2). But this task of metaphysics, with its austere refusal to take up the scenic ostensive as the originary form of human language, will prove itself vain and hopeless: "The god who would be satisfied by the Platonic definition of piety is one no longer capable of being

worshipped" (*Signs* 83); "When revelation is no longer a living truth, religious reflection becomes metaphysics and God [becomes] a construction like Aristotle's 'unmoved mover' rather than an object of worship" ("Thinking"). The God that needs no name is not a god worthy of worship; such a god dies, religion sacrificed to philosophy. So the anthropological idea of God is still an idea of a God of the ostensive truth of faith, as prior to (*not* opposed to) the declarative truth of reason. It is the idea of a God worshipped, worthy of being worshipped, a sacred central mystery who must be named as a Person. If we hypothesize that only ostensive language and culture (not the language of the declarative sentence of philosophy) make possible the origin of the human, then there will always ever remain an essential component of the human that can be grasped only by way of religious categories.

28. As a consequence, the ostensive faith our earliest human ancestors had in such being(s) as we now name "God" is not to be thought of as mere delusion-prone "gullibility"; rather, that faith made the sign itself come into being, made language and representation possible in the first place: "…all Enlightenment thinking about religion begs the question of separating ontology from pragmatics, truth from usefulness. If 'we' are gullible enough to accept the rhetorical appeal to God, must there not be something inherent in the use of language that makes us gullible in this way?" ("Rhetoric"). What is that "something inherent in the use of language"? It is something which becomes visible only when we entertain the originary hypothesis. Language did not emerge with hominoids sitting about dreaming up supreme beings and ascribing to them qualities that would render them deserving of worship. In the originary event, our "gullibility" had a pragmatic function: it deferred violence. This valuation of the truth of religious faith does not entail that we must all vainly attempt to side-step the scientific revolution and "believe in God" in order to behave ourselves or to find a purpose to life, as if secular modern market society were founded on a mistake. Originary thinking is not just another try at the moral interpretation of religion, which the atheist Kai Nielsen (for example) tirelessly pursues and corners into untenability in *Ethics without God*. It does require us to conceive of the *human* use of language as uniquely human (different, for example, from all animal communication systems), as the deferral of violence through representation; it requires thinking of culture as irreducibly scenic, configured as a structure of sacred center and human periphery in the linguistic event; that configuration entails a respectful commemoration, however minimal, for the humanly necessary "God" present in it. Generative anthropology requires that respect (which, granted, is not "worship") as part of the require-

ment for an explanation of the origin of human language, an origin for which philosophers such as Nielsen bother not to propose any explanatory model, even as they happily use human language itself to such chastely disenchanting, relentlessly demystifying effect.

29.   In subscribing neither to a metaphysics that seeks to expel all thinking about God in the name of "reason," nor to a fideistic theology that seeks to isolate God as a being existing external to humanity's needs, generative anthropology instead returns consistently to its own mediate heuristic: "The real language of God is anthropological; we can come no closer to absolute being than to formulate anthropological models of its origin" (*Signs* 104). Originary thinking situates itself on "the ultimate crux of secularization" where the task is "that of constructing a model that explains without recourse to sacrality the originary emergence of the verticality of representation from within the horizontal world of animal appetite" ("Unique" 54). In this sense, Gans is most definitely a "secular" thinker, not a theologian speaking for a "faith community" as the current phrase has it. But it does not follow that the anthropological idea of God offers no direction worth taking to the contemporary believer interested in a dialogue with the authority of "science." Even as we struggle (if we struggle) to find ways in language of describing God as a being whose presence we sense, we do well to return to thinking about language itself: "But the point is not to seek the 'thing itself' beyond the phenomenon, but to explain the origin of the language without which there would be no phenomenon, pure or otherwise" (*Originary* 41). At times, it may be untimely to demand a content-specific description of "God." What Gans says of the word "tree" may equally be said of the word "God," without impiety: "To the extent that the word 'tree' exists, it does so not in my brain but in the collectivity of English speakers.... Changes of meaning in one mind do not instantly propagate themselves to other minds.... But the point of language [or the name-of-God] is not to arrive at absolute transparency but to defer violence; the originary sign designates not a rigorous concept but the sacred source of this deferral" ("Body"). This priority of deferral of violence through representation (or the priority of Love, the deferral of resentment) over conceptual rigor alone, helps explain the fondness Gans expresses for what he calls the "rhetoric of God," as distinct even from the idea of God and belief in God.

30.   The "rhetoric of God" includes all noncompetitive emotive uses of the name of God in times of crisis, as a being to whom the needy human, atheist or believer, appeals: "In times of crisis, God is present, not in some ineffable sense, but as

the interlocutor of last resort. God is whoever is named by the name we call out in our panic" ("Unique" 51–52). The standard response to such panic-provoked acts of calling on God is censorious disapproval. To call on God only when desperate is considered insincere, inconsistent, hypocritically expedient; it is a failure of skeptical asceticism or a breach of atheistic rigor, or an unjust appropriation of that which properly belongs only to the "true" religious believer; it is blameworthy. Only the "untrue" believers limit their appeals to God to times of panic; the true believer is expected to pray frequently, even when all is calm. And it is only the *lapsed* atheist who slips into the rhetoric of God, so the scolders insist, believers and nonbelievers: the rigorous atheist's conscience scolds him internally, the believer jealous of God's name (no prodigal son) seconds the disapproval from outside.

31. Gans, however, positions himself in a new place to suggest that the rhetoric of God, the recourse to such acts of calling on God links all of us to a certain good common humanity. It is not a matter of cravenly collapsing into a psychological weakness when times get tough. It is rather the intuitive owning of a shared origin in a long-distant event, in the first properly human linguistic act. We are members of the symbol-using species. To call on God, the creator or maker of the universe, is to recall that act in which humanity was born in company with its inaccessible Other, the first referent. By sacralizing the object, by transfiguring horizontal animal appetite into vertical human desire, by generating our awareness of the Other being on the scene of ostensive representation, we began to become ourselves.

32. The God invoked by the expression "playing God" is, we may now begin to see, an example of such rhetoric. Although this well-known phrase lacks the prestige value conferred by rarity, it possesses the merit of wide circulation and universal availability. The phrase "playing God" may be used in an accusation of spiritual misconduct. It may form part of an exclamation of shock and horror. It may be included in a cool-tempered observation that a certain form of human action is representing the inappropriate usurpation of tasks believed to be the prerogatives only of (an anthropomorphic) God. We are prepared now to apply generative anthropology to an analysis of this phrase, a phrase both worn down by familiarity and oddly opaque to conceptualization. "Playing God" is a phrase that has the sly ability to lead us, believers and nonbelievers, unaware toward a readiness to consider the originary scenic event.

An Analysis of the Literature about "Playing God"

"Playing God" as Interfering with Sacred Nature

33. A first form of the "playing God" accusation may be translated as a warning against "interfering with nature," where the domain of "nature" includes a (genetically) fixed, substantive human nature that we should leave untouched. As many commentators have noticed, however, a moment's reflection reveals that such uses of the phrase point too many accusatory fingers at too many possible violators; they presuppose a notion of "playing God" far too broad to be incisive. The "playing God" warning, says Ronald Dworkin, "can't mean that it is always wrong for human beings to attempt to resist natural catastrophes or to improve the hand that nature has dealt them. People do that — always have done that — all the time" (443). The 1982 President's Commission testified: "But in one sense *all* human activity that produces changes that would otherwise not have occurred interferes with nature. Medical activities as routine as the prescription of eyeglasses for myopia or as dramatic as the repair or replacement of a damaged heart are in this sense 'unnatural'" (55). We may include here the lighthearted syllogism of British philosopher Simon Blackburn: "If 'interfering with nature' is... 'playing God' and therefore wrong, then we...play God as well when we put up an umbrella, interfering with the natural tendency of rain to wet our heads" (57). Kurt Bayertz points out that "It did not take reproductive technology for the human being to start playing God. It has been said that human beings play God each time they spray pesticides or carry out surgery..." (176). Jeremy Rifkin, whose 1977 book *Who Should Play God?* may be the popular work that first "thrust" the expression "before the public" (Peters 186–87), whose flamboyant protests against genetic engineering have earned him an activist's notoriety, has always "called for the 'resacralization of nature,' which he considers 'the great mission of the coming age'" (Paul 138). It is not surprising that environmentalist avatar Rachel Carson is on record claiming that "the [human] 'genome is a sacred possession'" (quoted in Paul 136) deserving of protection from alteration. Mark Sagoff correctly connects the attacks of green politics on an allegedly amoral industrial-scientific establishment and this too-wide casting of the "playing God" net: "Calls to protect the human genome from manipulation...have much in common with arguments environmentalists and others present to protect what is 'wild' from human intervention, particularly from genetic engineering. The underlying idea may be that nature is sacred...divine" (74). The common tendency linking all these uses of the accusation is that in their haste to sacralize the "natural" or nature, they rush past the obligation

theologians insert to place God first as the Creator of nature; and, for originary thinking, the obligation to place first the event in which God and the human emerged together. This hasty rushing past revelation and linguistic representation corresponds to an overzealous arresting of the scientific usurpers of God's central position as Referee of natural processes.

34. Those scientists and doctors who invented vaccinations and anesthesia, those who first performed heart transplants, those who first assisted infertile couples with artificial insemination, those who first succeeded with in-vitro fertilization — each group of scientific promoters was forced into heated debate in the public sphere and subjected to accusations of "playing God" (see, for example, Dworkin 444; Verhey 63; Sagoff 79-80). Who now remembers the name of the first test-tube baby, born in 1978, whose artificial creation ignited a gigantic public outcry? (Louise Brown.) But few of us now consider children procreated with the help of IVF technology or artificial insemination to be "unnatural" or undesirable. One generation's "unnatural" is the next generation's "normal." This does not mean we must resign ourselves to indifference, as if all ethical prohibitions regulating science were nothing but vain sandcastles built on beaches washed flat by the tides of the most recent moral fashion. The lesson of such examples is rather that we ought to relocate the targets of the "playing God" accusation from actions that interfere with "natural" processes to actions that interfere with "cultural" systems. On the originary scene, there is no access to the "object" itself that is not mediated by the sign and its use in the human community.

35. Simon Blackburn sensibly advises such a redirection of attention, asking us to take our attention away from interferences with "nature" and to direct it toward the context of our (cultural) anxiety: "The charge of playing God has no *independent* force. That is, people only raise it when the interference in question upsets them. If we have already determined that some natural process must be allowed to run unchecked...we might use the words as a way of crystallizing our worry" (Blackburn 58). Blackburn is suggesting here that, given cultural universality, the "playing God" accusation refers not to nature "out there" but to moral disequilibrium "inside" the human community. We must concede that the "upset" that animates the "charge" and the "worry" that gets "crystallized" have to do first with rules governing human conduct, second with laws governing nature: it is first human violence that is being deferred by culture, not natural wonder that is being tamed or named. In the language of originary thinking, we would say that the central object gets sacralized only as an object of

communally mediated ("cultural") desire, not as an object of (merely "natural" animal) appetite. One way to sharpen this observation is to remind ourselves that the anxieties about interference with nature are expressed in the uniquely human form of a language that includes reference to such *extra*-natural beings as God. The most "unnatural" aspect of the human behavior that arises in the context of allegations of scientific "interference" with nature may in many cases (certainly not all), be "God talk" itself, the invocation of the very "God" whom we hope will give force to our allegations against the hubristic scientist. This recalls our observation above that we are the only animals in nature who have a language that includes "God."

36. It helps to narrow the accusation, then, to spell things out such that "playing God" refers to this: *exercising scientific knowledge and technological skill in such a way that a significant segment of the human community to which the scientist belongs resentfully disapproves of the exercise as a violation of the sacred laws of nature.* By adding the requirement of community resentment, we make explicit not only the fact that the scientist has no doubt taken the central position of divine authority and so we resent him or her as we resented the sacred center in the originary event, but also the fact that "God" and "nature" are always elements in a cultural system, accessible to us only as revelations or representations. If in a given case the person under question is not interfering with communally sanctioned morality, then that person — whether scientist or client of a scientist — can relax a little. It makes sense now in such a context that, for the most part, those with faith in science will be free to wear eyeglasses, to spread lawn fertilizer, to make appointments with the fertility specialist or the surgeon without feeling vulnerable to accusations of "playing God." As Gans has said, "he is guilty of hubris who inspires resentment in his fellows"; where there is no resentment, there is no playing God.

37. The cosmological model lurking behind this naïve, overbroad use of the phrase is the dead material universe of a withdrawn or a watchmaker God, supervising more or less passively that mechanical version of "nature" first made famous by the law-governed universe of Isaac Newton at the dawn of the scientific revolution. "God" stands outside this nature, having set it in motion and let it be, "intervening" occasionally to reassert a miraculously revealed authority by means of this eruption of a violent volcano or that holy healing of a leper (see Szerszynski, esp. 152–53). If we conceive of the natural world as a machine whose workings can be submitted to a description in predictable, mathematical laws, only then does "playing God" as "interfering with nature" seem to make sense.

Two noticeable ironies, however, follow from this awkward binding together of God and a sacred Nature.

38. The 1982 President's Commission, its avowed purpose to *calm* public anxiety about human genetic engineers playing God, wryly pointed out one of those ironies.

> In another sense, human activity cannot interfere with nature — in the second sense of contravening it — since all human activities, including gene splicing, proceed according to the scientific laws that describe natural processes. Ironically, to believe that "playing God" in this sense is even possible, would itself be hubris according to some religious thought, which maintains that only God can interfere with the descriptive laws of nature (that is, perform miracles). (55)

In other words, according to the "some religious thought" here seized upon, if only God can perform miracles outside the laws of nature, anything the human scientist does must be non-miraculous, acceptably "within" the laws of nature. Here the moral impropriety belongs not to the genetic engineer in the Frankenstein mould, but rather to the very defender of God who by accusing the scientist has implied (unintentionally, to be sure) that God's natural laws are not in fact natural laws but only ethical laws: has implied that scientists *can* in fact perform miracles, but only *ought not* to perform them. (Thus our contention that the accusation "playing God" is better understood as the charge of "interfering with [ethical] culture.") The scientific usurper can not be accused of playing God without God's being accused of having given up some of that miracle-working power which must be God's alone.

39. A second irony, not unrelated to the first above, comes not from the clever scientific skeptics in the debate but from the theological party on the floor. Here, the theologians argue that the scientific usurper should not be accused of playing God because, paradoxically, the "laws of nature" are rules that God has made to be broken — at least some of the time. To treat the supposedly untouchable law-governed realm of "nature" as itself a sacred Being, rather than separating God from nature and treating God alone as the sacred Being, is to slip into the error of worshipping the creation instead of the creator. In 1989, Hessel Bouma and his colleagues at the Calvin Center for Christian Scholarship formulated the error in this way, as Ted Peters reports,

"God is the creator. Therefore, nothing that God made is god, and all that God made is good."

....

This implies [Peters comments] we should be careful when accusing scientists of "playing God." We must avoid idolatrous expectations of technology, to be sure; "but [Bouma writes] to presume that human technological intervention violates God's rule is to worship Mother Nature, not the creator. Natural processes are not sacrosanct." (Peters 14)

Our next section concerning notions of "beneficent co-creativity" will spell out fully the problems with this move. For now, we note only that the "laws of nature" which God has set in place ("God's rule") may inoffensively be violated because they are not sacred, not "sacrosanct." Hessel Bouma and his colleagues have pointed out the hole in the dyke that will flood all of "Nature" with human intervention and subject the territory previously reserved exclusively for divine intervention to an openness to human coverage. Whereas the President's Commission was arguing that it would be impossible for God's "laws" of nature to be broken, here Bouma and colleagues are arguing that it would be impertinent to expect those laws not to be sometimes broken ("violated"). God is not jealously possessive or protective of the laws of Nature.

40. The first irony exposes the problem of a metaphysical rigidity created by infusing all the elements of "Nature" with the quality of the sacred: "playing God" is impossible under such an infusion because all human actions possible in nature — including the making of human clones or designer babies — are permissible because possible. The second irony exposes the problem of a theological vacuity created by detaching the quality of sacred inviolability from *some* (it might as well be *all*) of the elements governed by God-ordained natural laws. God's rules seem less like rules when God does not care if they are violated ("Natural processes are not sacrosanct").

41. For our purposes, the shared crux is that in either case, God becomes irrelevant to the *moral or ethical* concerns of those beleaguered humans desiring to mark off this or that bit of "nature" as "sacred." This irrelevance obtains in the first case by God's failure to prohibit any possible human "interference with nature" whatsoever; in the second case, it follows from God's being indifferent to his own "natural laws" to such an extent that the free-thinking scientist may put God's jealousy to the test on a case-by-case experimental basis.

42. The anthropological idea of God takes the linguistic sign as conceived on the originary scene as its model for all transcendent entities. It helps us avoid the anthropomorphic conundrum of a supernatural Being who sometimes commands that we keep our hands off "nature" and at other times demands that we intervene in "nature." We recall Gans' hint about the risks involved in ascribing a human psychology to God from the outset. In this "interfering with nature" version, the "playing God" accusation invokes a supernatural Being who seems at one moment jealously possessive of every speck of sacrosanct matter and at the next moment serenely detached from the whole fizzling cosmos. Some rather unwieldy ideas lurk behind the sacred-nature notion. By contrast, the anthropological idea of God subordinates cosmology to anthropology: "One can no longer take seriously the nineteenth-century science of religion that wanted to derive the concept of God from our awe of the cosmos. The reality is just the opposite: *having sufficiently deferred human violence by means of the concept of God, we become interested in the relatively dangerous cosmos on the model of extremely dangerous humanity*" (SP 25) [emphasis added].

43. We should notice that this truth toward which Gans nudges us is a very difficult — perhaps even painful — truth to confront in our world, where environmentalist dogma, the most extreme proponents of which oscillate between damning the omnipotence and preaching the secondariness of the human as opposed to the "natural," are so deeply entrenched in both the intelligentsia and popular opinion. For originary thinking, the God-is-to-Nature-as-creator-is-to-creation analogy does not grant sufficient priority to the very human beings who (alone in nature and creation) form the symbol-using communities capable of making such analogies in the first place. The playing God accusation at this level has no helpful anthropological reference. If "natural law" does not have explicit cultural, that is to say, ethical consequences, then it does not have any intimate bearing on the ties binding humanity to God and humans to each other. But if natural law lacks such consequences, then why not call it cultural law or religious law? God must exist "for" humans, for the human community, in the first place, before God can reveal the divine self in "nature" and before humans can begin to use symbolic language to figure out natural processes as such: "for believers and nonbeliever alike, God is accessible only through the signs by means of which he persuades us of his presence" (Gans, "Rhetoric"). The knowledge will follow the interest: "we become interested in the relatively dangerous cosmos [only] on the model of extremely dangerous humanity" (*Signs* 25). Such is the direction of generative anthropology.

"Playing God" as Beneficent Co-creativity

44. Some postmodern theologians ready to compromise with the undeniable authority of science (as demonstrated by its instrumental reliability) attempt to remove the sting from the accusation of "playing God" by adding a "while" clause to our standing definition, such that it will now read: *exercising scientific knowledge and technological skill in such a way that a significant portion of the human community to which the scientist belongs resentfully disapproves of the exercise as a violation of the sacred laws of nature, while others cautiously approve of the exercise as a god-like intervention intended to improve a natural course of events.* These theologians either reject the idea that "playing God" forms a meaningful and legitimate prohibition, or encourage "playing God" — surprisingly converting the prohibition into a blessed commandment — under the restrictions implied by *cautiously approve* and *improve a natural course.* Theologians have done as much as scientists themselves to defend those accused of playing God against an overzealous red-light prohibition against improving upon nature. Ted Peters, Allen Verhey, Ruth Page, Bart Hansen and Paul Schotsmans, among others, speak for the doctrine of "*creation continua,* continuous creation" (Peters 14). Allen Verhey rejects the theology of the "God of the Gaps." The "God of the Gaps" exercises his forbidding authority only on certain areas of human life, those "where human beings have been ignorant or powerless" (64) — the very areas that attract the scientific desire for knowledge and power. Verhey affirms instead the idea that "the God of creation and Scripture made *and sustains* the order we observe and rely upon" (64) [emphasis added]. The "sustaining" includes God's commissioning and caring for those exercises of scientific power directed by God's good will. The rejected perspective that creates a "confusion of God with natural process" is one that "nurtures irresponsibility," says Verhey, because it prohibits human agency from intervening when good can be done. It is good to heal the sick and to alleviate the suffering caused by "natural" illnesses and disasters. For Christians, Jesus' unquestionable determination as a healer legitimates a form of divine "interference with nature" on a quasi-medical model. Ted Peters' formulation resembles that of Verhey: "The creative act whereby God brought the world into existence *ab nihilo,* at the beginning, is complemented with God's continued exercise of creative power through the course of natural *and human* history" (14) [emphasis added]. We have abandoned the mechanical universe supervised by the withdrawn watchmaker, and abandoned the universe occasionally interfered with by the capriciously intervening God of unpredictable miracles. This universe, in which God and humanity are more dynamically interactive, at least allows technologically aggressive people a legitimate

role as cultural producers and — more importantly — contains a definite space in which scientific workers will *not* be accused of playing God. The scientist as divinely-sanctioned miracle worker has found a home. Those with faith in science were above released from the blanket condemnation of "interfering with nature" so as to be permitted to consume certain benefits of scientific practice; here, the theologians who add the "while" clause rightly make space for them to produce such legitimate benefits.

45. The protection against the accusations is necessarily limited, however. What will qualify as an "improvement" on the "natural course" of events? The theological model of divine and human co-creativity enrolls a number of familiar metaphors designed to mark out strict boundaries for God-approved human interference with nature. For example, the Hebrew "made in the image of God" attribute is translated as "made to be creative" in the sense of "sharing in the transforming work of God's ongoing creation" (Peters 15). Ruth Page reports that Douglas John Hall, one of the principal elaborators of this theology, has gone so far as to convert "image" into a verb so as to denote the good, God-like form of human co-creativity that alone merits the application of the scriptural descriptor "in his image" to a human agent. Douglas John Hall promotes the argument that "only when humans are actively *imaging* God in what they do to any part of creation is the term ["in his image"] applicable" (Page 75). This seems a rather Draconian coinage that would leave many people outside. The familiar metaphor of "stewardship" is a second theme in the discourse: "the more positive conception of scientists playing God...such that they become at least stewards of creation is the more hopeful line to pursue" (Page 79); "the task before us is to be good stewards of the advance of genetic science and technology such that it contributes to human welfare without creating new injustice" (Peters 2). Scientific freedom is contained by the tacit supervision of the laboratory's absentee owner, the cosmological landlord who will someday return for an ethical accounting. The scientists' awareness of divine ownership of the world bars them from indulging in "a mood of elimination of God and domination over nature" (an attitude usefully dubbed "Promethean freedom" by Ted Peters), commanding instead "co-operation with God and nature" (Peters 26). The continuous co-creation model insists on the sacred difference between relative human freedom and creative power (submissive to limits, vigilant against causing offense) and the absolutely free and powerful creativity of God. The scientist may act in the way God would act in the scientist's place; the scientist is not, however, ever invited to think he or she can substitute for God (see Elshtain 156; Peters 15; Hansen and Schotsmans 44–46).

46. This softened translation of the playing God accusation aims to disconnect from its source the community resentment of scientific and medical practice whenever such practice can be described as God-like in its imitation of the divine attribute of omnibenevolence. The scientist must be permitted to proceed and be judged humane rather than hubristic inasmuch as the scientific work in question obeys the biomedical principle of beneficence, a translation of scriptural "neighbour love" into secular parlance. Ted Peters says it this way: "Beneficence is not playing God in the sense of substituting the human for the divine. Yet, it is living in a godly way. It is the exercise of moral freedom" (Peters 25). We have no quarrel with this legitimation of desirable and morally worthy scientific activity; but we do have a quarrel with the misappropriation of the phrase "playing God" to describe such activity. The phrase needs to be kept as an ethical marker, its warning character inviolate. Therefore, when some commentators go so far as to suggest that playing God as such is a good thing, that the phrase can be emptied of its pejorative connotations and we should encourage each other to "play God" with God's approval, we part ways with them and their particular version of the co-creative legitimation of science.

47. It is now, ironically, the secular nonbelievers who use the accusatory phrase occasionally who might wish to rescue "playing God" from this believer-promoted angelic interpretation, this de-fanging of the expression. One objection to the decriminalizing direction is its strangely oblivious bypassing of the long traditions of discourse about *imitation Dei* (see Buber, Marmorstein) and about the imitation of Christ. For when we contrast the two expressions "imitation of God" and "playing God," we ought to sense the sarcastic edge of the latter, with its thoroughly postmodern irony. Can we imagine ordinary religious believers in the nineteenth century using with approval this expression, oblivious to its flippant edge? "Playing God" contains an implied wry awareness of the scandal that Auschwitz and Hiroshima definitively revealed: excessive human violence on the model of the Apocalyptic Destroyer is now both easy of access and terrible, but too easy to be thought truly terrible. It is as if our guilt at having definitively played God (dropping the bomb on the originary victims of the nuclear age, experimenting without right on the victims of the camps) has made us all equally blase about playing God (in fact), but also equally ready to accuse each other of playing God. The "God" being played is almost always one of prejudicial, inscrutable, unfair or cruel judgment. It implies loss of (genuine) faith in a ("really existing") benevolent God.

48. The expression has ineradicably negative connotations, no? One of them is the sarcastic overtone of *childish* playing, as when children play King of the Castle, or play doctor, soldier, spaceman. The ominous shading we should notice is that the role of "God" seems radically inappropriate for the child, by definition an uninitiated creature not yet prepared for command and control. Indeed, the most mature human being imaginable will stay unable to appropriate the uniqueness of God — an implication certainly in keeping with Gans' anthropological idea of God as the *originary* center-as-such of human attention. A second is the overtone of *game-playing* itself, detached from the childish or child-like attribution, as in playing charades or cards or Monopoly. Presumably the object of this game would be to "play God" better than one's amused competitors. But at the risk of playing the killjoy, we take the position of the secular skeptic who likes the phrase sharp and nasty and who suggests that thinking of God as a "game" to be "played" (the profound dignity of *homo ludens* notwithstanding) is to betray a certain desensitization to the God-human difference, a desensitization a little surprising when it is most displayed by theologians. The "playing" of such a game would carry an element of mockery. One does not need to believe that a supernatural God "really" exists to understand the inescapability of that mocking. "I am the winner" in the context of Monopoly or crazy eights can be spoken straight; "I am the winner, like God" can only be spoken ironically. It must insinuate an irreverent competition with God.

49. A third uncomfortable connotation inherent in the phrase is the *theatrical* metaphor, as would be suggested by an actor "playing" a role according to a script or a designated part in an improvisatory performance. Surely, however, the absolute otherworldliness of God makes the theatrical-script metaphor a catachresis from the outset in that the actor assigned the part of God must feel a certain absurd inability to ever quite fit the role. (We speak here of the unfigurable God of the Mosaic revelation, not the incarnate Christ, who obviously can be and has been dramatically "imitated," in performances ranging from those of medieval mystery plays to that in the cinematic *Jesus of Montreal*). A script for performance presupposes a formally circumscribed scene. "God," however, is by definition not subject to figuration on a scene, as is understood even by our (merely) anthropological distinction between the revelatory central *object* and the a-figural being of the central locus, the center-as-such. Writing a script to play God in the theater or on the street would require the absurd opening set description *the universe — enter God*. It would lead inexorably to the comic book figures of white-bearded old men leaning on staffs, figures of which the clumsy anthropomorphism embarrasses people who take the idea

of God seriously. When people use the phrase, they are arguing that a "playing" which would be harmless if merely fictional is *not* actually fictional: the implied dramatic metaphor is a scandal in its self-canceling falsehood. We use the phrase when we feel the "playing" is becoming dangerously factual and real (not formally circumscribed in a fiction). In fact, as we shall see in our closing section, it is the violation of the "dramatic" scene of the originary event itself that the phrase rhetorically invokes and ostensively signifies.

50. "Playing God" therefore must be heard as carrying a note of the sarcastic, a hint of the sassily irreverent, a relishing of the logically impossible; if we hear the note, we respond with understandable discomfort or fear. The human who says "I am playing God" in all seriousness without a tremor of discomfort has forgotten something of his humanity for the time being, forgotten how close he or she is to saying "I am God." The dignified traditions of the *imitatio Dei* or *imitatio Christi* never cut themselves adrift from the paradoxical quality of the sacred injunction: to imitate God is to imitate the *inimitable*. Such humble imitation is at once morally necessary to begin and perfectly impossible to complete. The created cannot imitate the creator to such an extent that created *replaces* creator; or, in the language of generative anthropology, the human community can never quite do without the otherness of the sacred being named by the sign in the event of human origin. "Playing God" intuitively points toward reason for the fear of a human praxis which assumes that no such event has ever occurred, which assumes there is no *real* human-divine difference, despite centuries of cultural wisdom, preserved by religion, teaching otherwise.

51. The call to the paradoxical imitation of the inimitable is the call against which the beneficent co-creator discourse must fall into indecision. For it should be clear that the "beneficence" of the moral figure of the healer, once attached to the scientific projector engaged in genetic therapy, does not provide a substantive criterion for resolving ethical dilemmas, in somewhat the same way that "compassion" alone cannot be the basis of an ethical system (Gans, "Marcus"). Unfortunately, the political question of *who decides what is good* or what qualifies as an improvement remains. God lets his rain fall on pro-life and pro-choice, anti-cloning voices and pro-cloning voices alike. The will to beneficence is empty unless informed by the wisdom to know what the most beneficent aspect is, and such wisdom eludes the best and brightest among us, as we see next.

"Playing God" as Pretending to Impossible Wisdom

52. Our third interpretation of "playing God," slightly revised, looks like this:
the accused scientist is charged with *exercising scientific knowledge and technological skill in such a way that a significant portion of the community to which the
scientist belongs resentfully disapproves of the exercise as a violation of the sacred laws
of nature, while an equally significant portion cautiously approves of the exercise as
a benevolent intervention to improve upon a "natural" course of events.* The cau-
tious aspect of those people who approve and the resentful aspect of those who
disapprove converge, however, as one front, in a shared conviction. The conviction is that the scientist in question possesses neither the concrete pragmatic
certainty of prediction nor the moral authority — neither the requisite factual
certainty nor the evaluative wisdom — to justifiably proceed in the projected
exercise without some hesitation and consultation. Those who "approve" do so
with reservations, that is, with latent resentment. The resentment that the scientist continues to inspire from his position of centrality remains sufficiently
pervasive to make the accusation of playing God "stick." This sticking is only a
social fact; the project may or may not prove ethically justifiable in the long run.
The divine attribute of omniscience, necessarily missing in the human scientist,
finds expression here by virtue of its ironic absence.

53. The 1982 President's Commission frames this version of the accusation
thus: "the warning not to play God is closely related to the Socratic injunction 'know thyself': in this case, acknowledge the limits of understanding rather
than assuming that people can foresee all the consequences of their actions"
(58–59). Ted Peters elaborates on this particular layer of significance in the
phrase: "'playing God' means we confuse the knowledge we do have with the
wisdom to decide how to use it. Frequently lacking this wisdom we falsely assume we possess, scientific knowledge leads to unforeseen consequences such as
the destruction of the ecosphere" (Peters 12). The frequent appearance of this
dichotomy of inferior, merely scientific knowledge as opposed to superior, invaluable moral wisdom is noticed also by Allen Verhey, who writes that "knowledge
of that which transcends 'use' has no place in [Francis] Bacon's theory" (63);
and by Ruth Page, who summarizes it thus: "only God has the wisdom to order
creation, and the intervention of scientists arrogates to themselves the preroga-
tive and is thus hubris" (77). Nonbelievers may be more comfortable with the
secular vocabulary in Diane B. Paul's description of this deployment of "playing
God" as constituting "a protest against the readiness of *some* people, who are
necessarily fallible, to make decisions with potentially irreversible consequences

for us *all*" (138) [emphasis added]. Kurt Bayertz locates the "insufficient wisdom" theme in a specifically moral (rather than theological) sphere of reflection; he notes that the idea of playing God "may be understood in a moral sense for referring to the fundamental limitations of human knowledge…. Interventions in human reproduction…presume a knowledge both vast and reliable" (175). Those interventions include all human reproductive technology, which may or may not include genetic engineering. Bayertz puts the question, for example, "How serious must an embryo's prenatally diagnosed disease be…in order to justify an abortion? In the light of such life and death decisions…the 'playing God' accusation…[is] fuelled by fears that the human being can not cope with the moral burden of such decisions" (182). In all these cases, the assumption of a *consequentialist* ethics contributes to the sense of danger: the epistemological lack (inability to calculate consequences) engenders the ethical overload (frequency of painful dilemmas). Doing the right thing is one thing, knowing the right thing to do quite another. We are "playing God" when we pretend to know the consequences, what it is right to do, in cases where we know not.

54. Let us limit our accusations of playing God under this interpretation only to those made in the context of individual cases of medical decision-making. We include, just for now, only the "negative" eugenics of somatic gene cell therapy, not the more disturbing reaches of genetic "enhancement" (designer babies) or reproductive cloning. We include here only cases, for example, where a disease may be cured as a result of genetic surgery or, less happily, an embryo rejected as potential fetus as a result of decisions made in response to genetic screening (the decision to save the possible baby from, for example, an excruciatingly painful and inevitably brief life). Such puzzling decisions as the latter, decisions about purely "potential" people, constitute the special domain of *genethics* as distinct from bioethics, according to David Heyd. Even under our decision to limit the types of cases we include at this stage, the deep existential pathos of the moral burdensomeness in situational ethics frequently gets invoked. The position of playing God ceases to be an enviable one.

55. A refreshing diversion from the earnestness of the burden-bearing may be enjoyed in Leroy Augenstein's *Come, Let Us Play God* (1969), the earliest monograph that I have been able to locate that has our key phrase in its title. A surgeon and a public lecturer of some repute in his day, Augenstein in this compact volume zestfully catalogues a stunning variety of ethical dilemmas related to organ transplants, population control, euthanasia, the allocation of kidney machines, the education of deprived inner-city youth as cultural brainwashing, the

abortion of fetuses that may carry birth defects or terrible hereditary diseases, and the like. Augenstein concludes his book with a list of questions for discussion groups ready to ponder such problems. Most curiously, with a dated 1960s enthusiasm, Augenstein is far less troubled to take sides than delighted to prove simply that sides must be taken, that we must "play God" in making difficult decisions. Faced with the dilemmas he describes, we are indeed forced to make painful choices: there will always be terrible risks, somebody will always be left suffering or vulnerable. The "God" whom Leroy Augenstein invokes (his sincere Christian faith notwithstanding) is One who possesses the Mind of an ethical philosopher so powerful as never to be met in debate by mere mortals.

56. "Playing God" at this level means pretending to an impossible moral wisdom, in circumstances such that the pretending generates immediately an oddly *involuntary* moral responsibility. Once we have it, we do not want it. After God the omnipresent pantheistic Bouncer guarding the doorways to the sacred nightclub of Nature from human gatecrashers, after God the Benevolent Inventor who intervenes in history to do good for and through human beings, we come to God the Supernatural Bioethicist, calculating costs and benefits, weighing risks, commensurating "values." "Playing God" under our first interpretation meant deciding to interfere with a natural course of events when one should not; "playing God" now means deciding *not* to interfere with a natural course of events when one should (or should at least consider doing so). Having opened the door to the occasional, exceptional co-creative project, we learn that we have invited across the threshold a mob of innumerable considerations about co-creative obligations, so many that all the rooms of our spiritual house are packed to the ceilings with difficult cases begging that we "play God" and adjudicate. Even the wisdom of Solomon would soon be worn down to nothing here. The figure of a heavenly indifference (irresponsibility) begins to regain its attractiveness.

57. Ted Peters inserts this paradoxical "involuntary freedom" into the continuous co-creation model: "we are condemned to be creative. We cannot avoid it....We cannot be human without being technological, and technology changes things for good or ill" (15). Mark Sagoff observes with deliberate irony: "The nice thing about the nature we inherit — even if it is full of defects such as the propensity for disease — is that it was no one's responsibility" (90). Undeterred by the risks of Promethean freedom, Ronald Dworkin warns us that "a decision to turn away from what science may provide is itself a choice we might have made differently" (448). Kurt Bayertz presents the problem most pithily: "even reaching no decision is a decision, the results of which we are responsible for; whether we like it

or not, there is no way back to the idyll of irresponsibility" (186). The legitimate co-creationist model of submissively imitating a benevolent God has shifted into a model of reluctant human replacement of an absent God who is no longer appearing to provide sufficiently detailed ethical instructions. The human community awakes to discover, as Allen Verhey describes it, "we are responsible not so much to God as instead of God"; and, as Verhey astutely observes, the "shift puts an enormous (and messianic) burden on genetics" (65–66). The force of the accusation under this interpretation depends on the notion of an absent moral wisdom to which we must aspire even as we must confess it is beyond us. Whatever ethical choice we make, the resentment of a significant portion of the human community is guaranteed. The accused scientist is no longer the other we fear but the one we fear being forced to become ourselves.

58. When submitted to originary analysis, this level of significance in the prohibition against "playing God" intuitively marks the passage from the moral to the ethical: from the "universal" moral equality in the originary *event* to the partial, necessarily linear cultural narratives that follow with human history — that result from the *ritual repetitions* of the originary event and the various competing systems of signification produced by differing religious communities. The anthropological idea of God does not provide any "prescriptive ethic" ("Unique" 64) to negotiate such disputes for us and thereby absolve us of individual responsibility. Gans does provide reasons for granting Judaism and Christianity among religions a special status as sources of anthropological truth that, not accidentally, lead humanity toward the cultural productivity of modernity — which includes the creative freedom that finds expression in "science" — and the market model of society (see *Science and Faith*). (This is to set aside as beyond the scope of this study the equally essential cultural productivity of the esthetic, the Classical form of which we owe to ancient Greek culture.) Generative anthropology, as Gans has openly conceded, is neither a political programme nor an ethical system. The scenic structure of culture and the foundational power of the originary ostensive, however, do imply two "ethical meta-principles" which offer some guidance. Gans enumerates these two basic principles as follows.

> 1. The reciprocal exchange of signs is the fundamental ("moral") model of human interaction. This model justifies our intuition that "we are all created equal."
> 2. The fundamental operation of the social order is the deferral of conflict through the generation of significant differences (*différance*). ("Unique" 64)

There are certain implications that follow from these meta-principles as applied
to our third interpretation of the "playing God" accusation. One is the advisability of a deliberate reluctance to accuse others of playing God when, as we
have seen, we are all *equally deprived* of the equalizing central power of the
divine Being present on the originary scene. Notice that this warning against
overuse is not simple agreement with the co-creativity model, which we have
rejected as an unattractive compromise, but instead an endorsement of a certain
asceticism with respect to the deployment of the phrase. It is a weapon, and like
any weapon, should be used only when very clearly crisis-like circumstances
justify its being taken up: "originary thinking evaluates [an action] by its capacity to expand the exchange of representations and, negatively, by the capacity to
arouse resentment, the sentiment of non-reciprocity that forecloses reciprocal
exchange" ("Originary and Provisional"). Our well-worn term *accusation* assumes the resentment in the phrase which would tend to exacerbate rather than
defer conflict; if we wish the differences generated by the phrase to be *significant*
differences, therefore, we should use it only when the scientist (or other powerful
person in a socially central position) is taking up an *exceptionally* "violent" attitude as the usurper of what can only finally ever be the authority of the human
community. It is that special exceptionality, that unusual circumstance in which
the phrase as accusation finds its concrete and legitimate moral applicability,
which we will describe in our closing fourth interpretation.

"Playing God" as Attempting to Double the Origin of Humankind

59. We limited the scope of our attention just above to the case-by-case situational ethics in which utilitarian calculation of consequences could operate.
However, a substantive rationality will wish to consider ethical ends other than
the quartet of beneficence, nonmaleficence, justice and autonomy to which the
"principlism" of standard bioethics limits itself. Substantive rationality is willing to entertain debate about ends such as *the preservation of the human* or *fidelity
to God* and thus open the door to a "thick" debate in which the ends considered
might not be easily commensurable. Such a debate would lead to the species
question, itself necessarily a moral question, as Felipe Fernandez-Armesto makes
abundantly clear in his polemical survey of hypotheses about the definitive features of the "human."

60. Human genetic engineering threatens the composition of the human at the
level of the biological species. Recall that "germ-line therapy" makes changes to

the reproductive cells of the organism, such that the disease removed or the "enhancement" added (bigger muscles, blonder hair, greater longevity, specialized neurological equipment) is passed on to all offspring of the person who receives the therapy. Consider that gene splicing may someday add to the human gene pool genetic material from another species, initiating evolution by deliberate genomic re-design. As Kurt Bayertz puts it, "With technological control over its reproduction, the human being makes human nature a 'piece of Nature,' and itself master above it all" (173). In the words of Ted Peters, the "gene myth" announces that "the human capacity for influencing the future becomes the capacity for influencing what would be human in the future" (19); or, as Gordon Graham observes, "playing God" to most people expresses fears about "the context of humanity itself as a species, and in particular the fashioning of our own nature...of setting about the alteration of humanity itself" (150). Imagining the "consequences" of decisions in genetic screening, reproductive technology, and human genetic engineering only on a case-by-case basis distorts the real scope of the debate: such arbitrary self-limiting is one of the founding strategies of bioethics. We would argue that it is not irresponsible to imagine farther and wider and to consider what the accumulated total effect of numberless isolated decisions might be. When we do so imagine, a curious fear for the one human species itself may understandably arise. Our assumption of the general predictability of this fear sets aside, we confess, the exception of post-human boosterism. Enthusiasts of the post-human welcome unblinkingly all possible android and cyborg and genetically engineered futures, endorsing a program nourished by a hunger to do away with the human species as we know it, which is felt to be contemptibly defective anyway (see Winner's essay).

61. What is it, exactly, about HGE that creates the "moral novelty" (Graham 120) or the "meta-responsibility" (Bayertz 189) that demands of us not only thinking with an inventory of established values but also the "creation of new" moral values altogether (Bayertz 192)? Ronald Dworkin spells out with an extended series of oppositions the upset that registers our intuition of a moral seismic shift, the upset that accompanies imaginings of future implementations of human genetic engineering. The passage, though lengthy, has a thoroughness and clarity unusual in the literature.

> For that [overall] structure [of our moral and ethical experience] depends, crucially, on a fundamental distinction between what we are responsible for doing or deciding, individually and collectively, and what is given to us, as *a background against which we act or decide, but*

which we are powerless to change. For the Greeks, this was a distinction between themselves and their fate or destiny, which was in the hands or the laps of the gods. For people, even today, who are religious in a conventional way, it is a distinction between how God designed the world, including our natural condition in it, and the scope of the free will he also created. More sophisticated people use the language of science to the same effect: for them, the fundamental distinction falls between what nature, including evolution, has created, by way of particles and energy and genes, and what we do in that world and with those genes. For everyone, the distinction, however they describe it, draws a line between *who and what we are, for which a divine will or no one but blind process is responsible*, and what we do with that inheritance, for which we are indeed, separately or together, responsible. (444) [emphasis added]

The psychological basis for this distinction, Dworkin correctly notes, is the deep-rooted belief that "what God or nature provides" — that which is simply given as a moral background for our action, fated to each of us as our genetic inheritance or our luck in the genetic lottery, that for which we ourselves are *not* morally responsible — is "defined physically, in terms of what is in 'the genes' or...'the blood'" (445). Dworkin goes on to emphasize that many of our moral values become *obsolete* once the given is no longer certainly a given, but possibly the result simply of some other person's decision, just another human's decision. The fear of "playing God" is not a fear of science alone, or technology alone, or some "natural" catastrophe caused by these. The fearsome aspect of the biological tinkering and genetic engineering derives from the endangering and delegitimation of the belief that we are, individually and collectively, *not responsible* for our "natural" or "bodily" or "species" inheritance. We fear "playing God" because we believe that neither we nor the accused can be made or should be made to bear such "responsibility." For generative anthropology, this belief is mistaken; we have no choice but to be responsible. But the mistake is there only in the sense that the quest for an extra-human guarantee (a biological, physiological, cosmological, theological guarantee) of reciprocal exchange is hopeless; the responsibility for the human is human, in that "human" can not mean anything other than membership in a linguistic community as configured by the originary scene where "the reciprocal exchange of signs is the fundamental model of human interaction" (recall Gans' ethical meta-principle cited above). Meanwhile, generative anthropology would suggest that the genetic engineer playing God is producing in any case the scandalous exposure, ironically, of the *non-biological* foundation of the human. Again, "natural law" impinges on us only as "cultural rule," finally; even though to say this is not to say that everything is permissible, but only to say that an originary *anthropology*, not a biology, must be the hypothetical foundation of our morality and our ethics. It is our common humanity, dependent as we have seen on a minimal re-membering of God, that we must agree to hold sacred. It is ironic that the feared usurper scientists, if acting in the belief that they were altering only the "biology" or "genetics" of the human creature and keeping their neutral hands off the moral question, would have their position all wrong. Almost all of the impact of their technological power in such instances would be moral before being technological.

62. We need a new translation of the "playing God" accusation that takes into account this new territory of the shifted chance-choice boundary. The scientific projector accused in this context is best described as *exercising scientific knowledge and technological skill in such a way that a majority of the human community to which the scientist belongs deeply doubts the pragmatic viability and moral wisdom of the exercise, whereas the scientist (and any minority in the community supporting him) neither feels nor expresses such doubts.* In such a case, the scientist and his party in their utter lack of doubt are *usurping the originary power which ought to belong only to God (the Being of the inaccessible center-as-such).* This formulation decisively alters the content of the interpretation. The scientist now explicitly occupies the central position; technologically empowered, yes, but democratically challenged and vulnerable to resentment as any big-man, priest, king, politician or central mortal authority is vulnerable. Whereas the non-interference and co-creationist translations kept the scientist in a passive role as silent target of the accusation, the new configuration presupposes an imperative for dialogue between the scientist "playing God" and the community. The "doubt" signals only the difficulty of the meta-responsibility or moral novelty resulting from the power of HGE to invoke the species question. Decisive is the binary structure of the presence as opposed to absence of doubt: the scientist ought to feel some doubt, but feels none. The *ought* is dictated solely by the community as mimetic model, in that the obligation is not determined by a supernatural, "natural" or extra-cultural truth exterior to this scene. There is no advance guarantee the accusers are "right" and the scientist "wrong." We have no access to an objective test for the justifiability of the structuring doubt itself. We are appealing not to "nature" alone, not to brute majority rule, not to the escape valve of "community standards," but rather to the anthropological model of a dialogue between center and periphery; a dialogue between the *merely human representative of* the divine and the human community. There ought to occur an exchange between the scientist in his central role as the one who *can* try something and the members

of the community who wonder whether it *should* be done. It ought to occur because the scientist is only human although he occupies the position belonging to (or that once belonged to) "God."

63. Notice the difference between this scene, an historical one, and the scene of the originary event as such. We have insisted that the scientist engage in center-periphery dialogue; God, however, in the originary event, did no more than reveal the divine Being in the central object of desire and resentment. In the originary event, there is an absolute and unrepeatable divine-human symmetry: God does not exchange signs with us; rather, we exchange the signs that name God. In that sense, as we have already noticed, it is a consequence of the originary hypothesis that the "real" historical dialogue will turn out, following the progress of ethical and technological revelations, to have been really "only" an interaction between the humans on the periphery. Nevertheless, we would emphasize that in our revised interpretation of "playing God," the scientist accused of doing it may not logically, morally or (to be pushily commonsensical) even chronologically, ever hope to *replace* or *substitute for* that originary divine Being. It is God's originary "silence" or powerful passivity on the originary scene that can *not* be usurped by the scientist. Occupying that central position is not the same as appropriating the central "being" of the "God" named at the origin. And so the human, scientist or not, is required to remember the *peripherality* of his or her originary position; to forget it is to forget both his or her own humanity and to forget the anthropological idea of God.

64. Generative anthropology, in proposing for the human sciences this *scenic* model of culture as a fundamental heuristic, reveals that the wisdom contained in the playing God accusation "rings true" for numberless people because those people, believers or not, are capable of grasping the paradox of the divine as the inimitable Other of human imitation, at once an inaccessible being who may seem morally indifferent to us and the anthropologically concrete, invaluable foundation of our moral equality: "The relation of man to the sacred is the pure difference between the sign and its referent.... Whatever man does, he will be identical with God and yet never be him" *(End of Culture* 192). It is that *moral indifference* in the seeming historical passivity of God, the paradoxical inversion of all the "positive" attributes of the agential God, which it must be disastrous for any human person to imitate. Our anthropological model recommends only a dynamic openness; it does not provide a program for ethical progress, nor does it foreground visions, whether the vision be one of a utopian final state toward which to direct our technological projects or one of an apocalyptic finale

in the anticipation of which we are called to cultivate a sacred dread. But the originary hypothesis does posit a minimal basis for the sense of a sacred inviolability that the expression "playing God" invokes. The scientist — just as any "person in power" — must respect that inviolability. All that is required for the scientist to cease "playing God" is his or her opening up to a minimal but sufficient *doubt* about the morality of his project. We might say, with a certain exasperating irony, that the scientist must participate in the "situational ethics" of community debate because our scenic model of culture is a minimal universal "situation" — and *the being of God must never have been totally forgotten as an originary participant* in the situation we always have. All that is required is that one human not seriously pretend to be "above" or "outside" the debate, as only God may be.

65. It is no accident that the significantly democratic abstractions "majority" and "minority" have made an appearance in our discourse in this last interpretation of our phrase. These abstractions function as signifiers of ethical debate converting itself into political struggle. They open a way for us to confront one anthropological truth we would notice being implied by the wise popularity of the rule against "playing God." This truth is the fact that minorities are particularly vulnerable to expulsion and disfiguration when the *majority of the human community to which the scientist belongs,* characterized as accusatory in our definition above, *ceases* to feel any doubt and closes off dialogue, instead "siding" with the central scientist and scientific project. The verdict of history has lessons for us here. The archival evidence for the dehumanizing and disfiguring effects of the eugenics movements in the first half of the twentieth century is surely an ethical touchstone few may ignore without moral discomfort. This is to recall the results of both the forcible sterilization programs aimed at species "improvement" and carried out by Anglo-American racialist eugenicists (see Howard and Rifkin), and those of the extermination-directed "purifying" eugenics of National Socialism. There is no escaping the linear connection between eugenics and human genetic engineering, regardless of the infinite reassurances proponents of the latter have to offer. (See John Evans for molecular biology's strategic withdrawal of explicitly species-oriented eugenics in the late 1960s and the re-emergence of species-oriented eugenics under the much more pleasing label of "genetic enhancement" in the 1990s). We recall the second meta-ethical principle Gans explicitly provided, that *the generation of significant differences* should be valued as a *fundamental operation of the social order.* Scientists who defend attempts to reduce the diversity of the human species, erasing significant differences in the name of some superior uniformity of kind, may legitimately

be questioned as to what they think about "playing God" in our anthropological sense. Keeping those historical revelations of the vulnerability of minorities in mind should give us courage to own our doubts, if we have them, about projects falling under the HGE umbrella that seek to promote a drastic genetic uniformity that violates the right to consent of those who would be subjected to it, whether the subjection would be the result of programmatic state-sponsored utopianism or the result of "free" unregulated market forces at work. Without going to the draconian lengths of the "precautionary principle" (Harris 13–16), we can grasp the value of a prohibition against playing God, believers in God or not, when the god-like behavior seeks to cancel, erase and expunge human difference rather than asking it to "be fruitful and multiply." We might go so far as to suggest that the well-known technological imperative — *"If something can be done, then it should be done"* (Howard and Rifkin 90) — lacks not only moral content but anthropological content: a prohibition against prohibition must be dehumanizing, because human language itself emerged as a prohibition against all-for-oneself appropriation of the central object.

66. Anxiety over the technological imperative inspires one particularly compelling preventive formulation in the "playing God" literature. One way of trying to protect people from majority-sanctioned projects that seek to expunge human differences through eugenics is to respect the principle of what Gordon Graham calls the appeal to "the essentially first-person perspective on the worthiness of a human life" (182). Graham summarizes this principle: "There is a profound error in any assumption of moral superiority on the part of the physically and intellectually superior because...an essentially first-person judgment — 'This life is not worth living' — cannot be made in the third person" (152). Graham continues: "those who choose to play God (by genetically engineering certain outcomes over others) are assuming that they are in a position to decide, in this case [decide] in advance, that some lives are more worth living than others. And no one is actually in this position" (152). Nobody is "actually in [the] position" of perfect *moral* authority, Graham means; but such positions do get taken, such decisions do get made by virtue of real-world juridical authority all the time nevertheless (as Leroy Augenstein correctly predicted they would). Our point is not to propose a blanket condemnation of such decision-makers as those who are "playing God." It is rather to require the concessions that the "assuming" of a "position to decide" has a hubristic quality and that, if unaccompanied by doubts and dialogue on the model of the reciprocal exchange of signs on the originary scene, such assuming necessarily tends toward dehumanization. Ronald Dworkin's second of two principles governing his system of "ethical

individualism" is an expanded version of this principle of first-person authority over the worthwhileness of a life. Dworkin writes: "one person — the person whose life it is — has a special responsibility for each life, and…in virtue of that special responsibility, he or she has the right to make the fundamental decisions that define, for him [or her], what a successful life would be" (449). Inasmuch as a "successful" life must be considered by the first person living it a "worthwhile" life in the first place (prior to his or her taking up responsibility and making decisions to shape it), Dworkin merely repeats Graham's formulation; but he maximizes it when he adds all the individual freedoms of taking responsibility, making decisions, defining the details of the life. In both accounts, we would point out, moral indifference constitutes indifference to the validity of the "first-person positions" of other humans: in originary terms, such "playing God" obliterates the equality established on the originary scene of linguistic exchange. The first person who has not been consulted, whose right to consent has been erased, is the silenced victim of the human usurper who has disowned his or her originary peripherality and has taken to "playing God" in the sense of imitating the *inimitable* central Being of the originary scene.

67. We would emphasize that our originary analysis is not denying the possibility that the accused scientist may well be "objectively" correct and proved "right" at a later moment of verification of his hypothesis, justified in his strictly scientific predictions. The centering and making vulnerable of the scientist is not designed to invite the scapegoating of courageous innovators, nor do we claim that such exceptional moral indifference is shown by any but a minority (albeit a terribly dangerous minority) of people in the real world who refuse dialogue in pseudo-divine madness or would-be-Godly wrath. But all the same, another of our points is that when we submit the "playing God" accusation to originary analysis, we find an anthropological legitimation for what most of us already intuitively share as a tendency to reject the myth of any value-neutral "science" that would entitle its practitioners to an absolute moral freedom, meaning a freedom from any responsibility to the wider (partly non-scientific, partly religious) community. Obligation may presuppose capacity, but capacity alone never creates obligation. The scientist, as scientist, can tell us only that something *can*, but not whether it *should* be done. To believe otherwise is to be held in thrall by the technological imperative. The technological imperative lacks ethical content: it paradoxically implies the prohibition of prohibition itself. But the originary scene provides a non-fideistic account of the anthropological source of the moral intuition that legitimately resents such a lack of content.

68. The originary hypothesis therefore provides another ground for protecting people from dehumanizing majority-sanctioned projects that seek to expunge human difference: it grounds our insisting with renewed vigor on the impossibility of absolute scientific detachment from the human scene of culture, both in the context of moral philosophy and in the context of evolutionary theory. Timothy K. Casey laments the fact that "the myth of a value-neutral science has continued to assert itself…science and engineering are still looked at as standing above the fray, concerned with matters far from the messiness of human affairs and the contingencies of particularity, paradox, and anomaly" (54). David Heyd roundly concludes: "We cannot imagine a completely 'selfless' Archimedean point for [resolving ethical dilemmas] which will still be *human* in any relevant sense. We human beings can only partly take on a godly standpoint…. We can never fully extricate ourselves from the human standpoint and thus can never achieve a fully impersonal view of the universe" (15). Both writers are expressing in mostly non-theological language the impossibility of "playing God"; the prohibitions are, notably, pragmatic in import, advising against the attempt of that which would prove impossible anyway. For originary analysis, the necessity of the subordination of "science" to "culture" follows from the claim that culture is the deferral of violence through representation; science must belong to *moral* culture if it wishes to be *human* science. We intend the *double entendre*: "human," given the originary hypothesis, includes the implication of a moral configuration of equal exchange; the hypothesis presents the originary scene as one in which the participants are both open to difference through ritual repetition and the cultural productivity of historical change, and yet never-separated from the unity conferred by a common origin in a single founding event. To be accused of "playing God" means in this context to be accused of aspiring to just such a position of impossibly supreme detachment.

69. A final elaboration of this theme arises in response to the concluding sentences in Gordon Graham's essay, "'Playing God' without God"; it bears a particular relevance to our investigation since Graham has intuitively remarked the ethical cost of *evolutionary gradualism*. It is the gradualist model of human origins that Darwinism authorizes which has come to dominate philosophical biology and evolutionary anthropology. Gans' originary hypothesis is unorthodox and unusual in its proposing a *punctualist* model of human origins, in its proposing a *scenic event* as the heuristic model for our minimal species difference from our hominoid ancestors. Gans has varied its name to the *evenemential hypothesis* more than once, to stress the punctuality of the scenic event. According to the originary hypothesis, the origin of the human coincides with the origin of *moral*

differentiation: the human community on the periphery discovers itself despite itself in the production of the first ostensive symbol that designates the central object. In naming the being that occupies the center-as-such — that which we later understand under the sign "God" — the first humans defer the mimetic violence internal to the group and differentiate all members of the group equally from that being which is named "God." Having refreshed our memory of this description, we are now ready to reflect on Gordon Graham's sensitive and accurate observations.

> ...the idea of "playing God' without God [i.e. without *belief in* God], though it amounts to more than [Jonathan] Glover, [John] Harris, and [Ted] Peters allow, is severely limited in the moral constraints it can put upon technology.
>   Why does that matter? It matters because even the most convinced Darwinian who greets the demise of religion with enthusiasm wants, it seems, to retain an ethical perspective that transcends and can stand in judgment on the human.
>
>   ....
>
> But... Darwinism *cannot* "temper the self-centered way in which we assess our place and actions in this world" [Frederick Crews' phrase]. To ask it to do so is to seek far more than Darwinism can supply. In the end... in so far as the fear of Frankenstein will not go away, the secular mind that utterly rejects religion must rest content with a fractured view of science. (184–85)

We would suggest that Graham is forced to believe the idea of "playing God" is "severely limited" in its power to prohibit dehumanizing technology because he knows nothing about Gans' anthropological idea of God, an idea which, we suspect, he would be happy to learn about. Eric Gans' mind is a "secular mind" but not one which "utterly rejects religion." His originary hypothesis, with its scenic model of culture, offers a way of understanding the human-ness of both the desire to take up and the resentment of the impossibility of taking up "an ethical perspective that transcends... the human." Meanwhile, generative anthropology's model of the *punctual* origin of culture offers something which neither "Darwinism" nor "the Darwinian who greets the demise of religion with enthusiasm" can offer. Originary thinking locates the origin of language, religion, desire, resentment, the sacred, the esthetic, "God" and "ethical transcendence" all in the one event of the originary sign as the abortive gesture of appropriation that defers violence and sacralizes the central being revealed by the desired object; it thereby offers a view of science that is *not* "fractured" in that it proposes a model of human science that refuses to subordinate anthropology to biology, biotechnology, or genetics. No human science is possible without such a refusal of self-subordination.

70. The anthropological truth expressed by the prohibition against playing God the creator may now be read as the idea that the human community is "created once by God" in the strictly anthropological sense that the name of "God" names the sacred "Other" of the human, that which the human simply can neither be, nor be without; and therefore, that which the human ought not to try to be if the human wishes to remain human. Humanity can not do without this "God" (Other) — both resenting its otherness and desiring in vain to appropriate its otherness, both depending on its absolute difference from the human for "definition" and carrying away from that absolute difference the freedom despite unity that makes humans "one" in their not being, and their not being able to be, God. As the Other who seems to create human difference by inviting the sign-signifying-the-significant at the origin of humanity, the Being named "God" can not be re-placed by any one human: it is impossible, and so immoral, to "play God." This truth is one with the fact that the scene of origin, as a *unique event*, can neither happen again nor be made to happen again by somebody wishing to "play God," wishing to re-make the human species according to the most disastrously underthought fantasies of the Promethean usurper (Frankenstein, Dr. Moreau, Rossum of Rossum's Universal Robots). The origin of humankind can not be doubled. Such a doubling ought not to be tried.

By Way of Conclusion

71. We imagine a scientist who wishes to "play God," which means the scientist deliberately cultivates a moral indifference to community doubts and to dialogue inclusive of "different" minorities. We imagine a scientist who wishes to "play God" by rejecting outright the possibility of the punctuality and scenicity of human origin, which rejection has turned out surprisingly to entail an indifference to the categorical integrity of the anthropological. Such a scientist has condemned himself to a "fractured view of science" (Graham) because his gradualist Darwinism licenses him to despise — or at least ignore with conscience undistracted — the scenicity of the origin of humankind, a scenicity which human religions have always commemorated in myth and ritual, and which generative anthropology now attempts to formulate only as an anthropological (scientific) model. His gradualist Darwinism licenses him to pretend to a *science*

of the human that is not in fact an anthropology, a coherent (generative) philosophical anthropology, but rather an evolutionary psychology, or sociobiology, or biology, or — worse — a chemistry, a physics of the human. Or the "scientist" may be doing cultural studies, patiently laboring in the infinitely rich textual archives of the *humanities* but never deigning to dare a definition of "human" or to propose any anthropological models of the origin of human language at all, because such questions do not happen to be in fashion. Why should anybody worry about others playing God or playing God oneself?

72. Our answer is that one ceases to be human when one plays God. On the originary scene, the immaterial "God" is the central Being whose power and centrality we all equally desire and equally resent, the One in the sacred center-as-such whose being we each imagine appropriating all to ourselves but whose appropriation we mutually forbid one another. The first use of properly human language, "human" here understanding the goodness of moral equality, is the naming of God: "The inalienably reciprocal structure of linguistic communication lies at the core of our humanity; it is a model of good that precedes any possible model of evil" (Gans, *Signs* 150). We all hold back from trying to "be" God, to have God, and by holding back, we guarantee his "existence." It is to the being of God we therefore owe both our moral equality and our species difference: our species difference *is* our moral equality as mediated by the reciprocal exchange of signs that names "God" at the origin: "...God is significant difference itself. The love of God is not the worship of his superiority, but the willingness to accept [God's] difference...as a source of mutuality" (Gans, "God is Love"). It is to our moral equality that we owe our membership in the human community — we do *not* owe our membership in humankind to some gift from sacred Nature, or to the lease of a supernatural Landlord, or to a random accident that resulted in a genome, or to the emergence of the suddenly human from some undefined point in an infinitely divisible gradual process. Always in danger of becoming strange to one another, we might as well not tire of reminding each other that we finally owe our membership in humankind to each other. The prohibition against "playing God" is a particularly potent reminder of this debt. "Playing God" is pretending to be superhuman, inhuman, non-human, other-than-human, when we have always already had our other in God. The prohibition against "playing God" seeks to preserve the scenic model of originary moral equality as against those who would deny the existence of the One difference from which the beautiful multiplicity of all other human differences must have originated. It is the minimal but making-all difference between the sacred other being named "God" and human being that is at stake.

Works Cited

Augenstein, Leroy. *Come, Let Us Play God.* New York: Harper and Row, 1969.

Baillie, Harold W. and Timothy K. Casey, eds. *Is Human Nature Obsolete? Genetics, Bioengineering, and the Future of the Human Condition.* Basic Bioethics [series.] Ed. Glen McGee and Arthur Caplan. Cambridge, Mass.: MIT Press, 2005.

Bayertz, Kurt. "Playing God." *Genethics: Technological Intervention in Human Reproduction as a Philosophical Problem.* 1987. Trans. Sarah L. Kirkby. Cambridge: U P, 1994. 174–87.

Blackburn, Simon. *Being Good: A Short Introduction to Ethics.* Oxford: U P, 2001.

Buber, Martin. "Imitatio Dei." In *Mamre: Essays in Religion.* Trans. Greta Hort. Westport, Conn.: Greenwood Press, 1970.

Casey, Timothy K. "Nature, Technology, and the Emergence of Cybernetic Humanity." In Baillie and Casey (2005), 35–65.

Deane-Drummond, Celia, ed. *Brave New World? Theology, Ethics, and the Human Genome.* London and New York: T and T Clark, 2003.

Dworkin, Ronald. "Playing God: Genes, Clones, and Luck." *Sovereign Virtue: The Theory and Practice of Equality.* Cambridge, Mass.: Harvard UP, 2000. 427–52.

Dupre, John. *What Evolution Means Today.* Oxford: UP, 2003.

Elshtain, Jean Bethke. "The Body and the Quest for Control." In Baillie and Casey (2005), 155–75.

Evans, John Hyde. *Playing God? Human Genetic Engineering and the Rationalization of the Public Bioethical Debate.* Chicago: U Chicago P, 2002.

Fernandez-Armesto, Felipe. *Humankind: A Brief History.* Oxford: UP, 2004.

Gans, Eric. "Body and Soul." *Chronicles of Love and Resentment* 194. 15 Jan. 2000.

———. *Chronicles of Love and Resentment.* Anthropoetics [homepage]. Available: <http://www.anthropoetics.ucla.edu/views/html>.

———. "Does God Exist?" *Chronicles of Love and Resentment* 190. 4 Dec. 1999.

———. *The End of Culture: Toward a Generative Anthropology.* Berkeley: U California P, 1985.

———. "GA Futurism." *Chronicles of Love and Resentment* 181. 11 Sept. 1999.

———. "God is Love." *Chronicles of Love and Resentment* 119. 6. Dec. 1997.

———. "'God Told Me To...'" *Chronicles of Love and Resentment* 18. 25 Nov. 1995.

———. "In the Beginning was the Word." *Chronicles of Love and Resentment* 154. 14. Nov. 1998.

———. "Marcus Borg's Spiritual God." *Chronicles of Love and Resentment* 118. 22 Nov. 1997.

———. "Originary and Provisional Morality." *Chronicles of Love and Resentment* 259. 27 April 2002.

———. *Originary Thinking: Elements of Generative Anthropology.* Stanford: U P, 1993.

———. *Science and Faith: The Anthropology of Revelation.* Totawa, N.J.: Rowman and Littlefield, 1990.

———. *Signs of Paradox: Irony, Resentment, and Other Mimetic Structures.* Stanford: U P, 1997.

———. "The Rhetoric of God." *Chronicles of Love and Resentment* 138. 30 May 1998.

———. "The Unique Source of Religion and Morality." *Contagion: Journal of Violence, Mimesis and Culture* 3 (1996): 51–65.

———. "Talking about God." *Chronicles of Love and Resentment* 71. 14 Dec. 1996.

———. "Thinking Religion." *Chronicles of Love and Resentment* 138. 27 Feb. 1999.

Gibbs, Nancy. "Stem Cells: The Hope and the Hype." *Time* August 7, 2006: 27–32.

Graham, Gordon. *Genes: A Philosophical Inquiry.* London and New York: Routledge, 2002. 143–85.

Hansen, Bart and Paul Schotsmans. "Stem Cell Research: A Theological Interpretation." *Genetics, Theology, and Ethics: An Interdisciplinary Conversation.* Ed. Lisa Sowle Cahill. New York: Crossroad / Herder and Herder, 2005. 15–52.

Harris, John. *On Cloning.* London and New York: Routledge, 2004.

Heyd, David. "Introduction: Playing God." *Genethics: Moral Issues in the Creation of People.* Berkeley: U California P, 1992. 1–20.

Howard, Ted, and Jeremy Rifkin. *Who Should Play God? The Artificial Creation of Life and What It Means for the Future of the Human Race.* New York: Delacorte Press, 1977.

Lewontin, Richard. "The Confusion Over Cloning." Orig. 1997. *The Human Cloning Debate.* 3rd. ed. Ed. Glen McGee. Berkeley: Berkeley Hills Books, 2002.

Marmorstein, Arthur. "The Imitation of God ("Imitatio Dei") in the Haggadah." *Studies in Jewish Theology: The Arthur Marmorstein Memorial Volume.* Ed. J. M. Rabinowitz and M.S. Lew. Freeport, N.Y.: Books for Libraries Press, [1972].

Nielsen, Kai. *Ethics without God*. Revised edition. Buffalo: Prometheus, 1990.

Nossal, G.J.V. and Ross L. Coppel. "Scientists Playing God." *Reshaping Life: Key Issues in Genetic Engineering*. 3rd. ed. Cambridge: U P, 2002.

Page, Ruth. "The Human Genome Project and the Image of God." In Deane-Drummond (2003), 68–85.

Paul, Diane B. "Genetic Engineering and Eugenics: The Uses of History." In Baillie and Casey (2005), 123–51.

Proctor, Robert N. "Human Recency and Race: Molecular Anthropology, the Re-figured Acheulean, and the Unesco Response to Auschwitz." In Baillie and Casey (2005), 235-69.

Peters, Ted. *Playing God: Genetic Determinism and Human Freedom*. New York: Routledge, 1997.

President's Commission for the Study of Ethical Problems in Medicine and Bio-medical and Behavioral Research. *Splicing Life: A Report on the Social and Ethical Issues of Genetic Engineering with Human Beings*. Washington, D.C., November 1982.

Sagoff, Mark. "Nature and Human Nature." In Baillie and Casey (2005), 67–98.

Shannon, Thomas A. "Human Nature in a Post-Human Genome Project World." In Baillie and Casey (2005), 269–316.

Szerszynski, Bronislaw. "That Deep Surface: The Human Genome Project and the Death of the Human." In Deane-Drummond (2003), 145–63.

Tattersal, Ian. "How We Came to Be Human." *Becoming Human: Evolution and the Rise of Intelligence. Scientific American [Special Edition]* 16/2 (2006): 66–73.

Turney, Jon. *Frankenstein's Footsteps: Science, Genetics, and Popular Culture*. New Haven: Yale U P, 1998.

Verhey, Allen. "Playing God." *Genetic Ethics: Do the Ends Justify the Means?* Ed. John F. Kilner et al. Grand Rapids, Michigan: Eerdmans, 1997. 60–74.

Winner, Langdon. "Resistance is Futile: The Posthuman Condition and its Advo-cates." In Baillie and Casey (2005), 385–411.